ON ALBERTI AND THE ART OF BUILDING

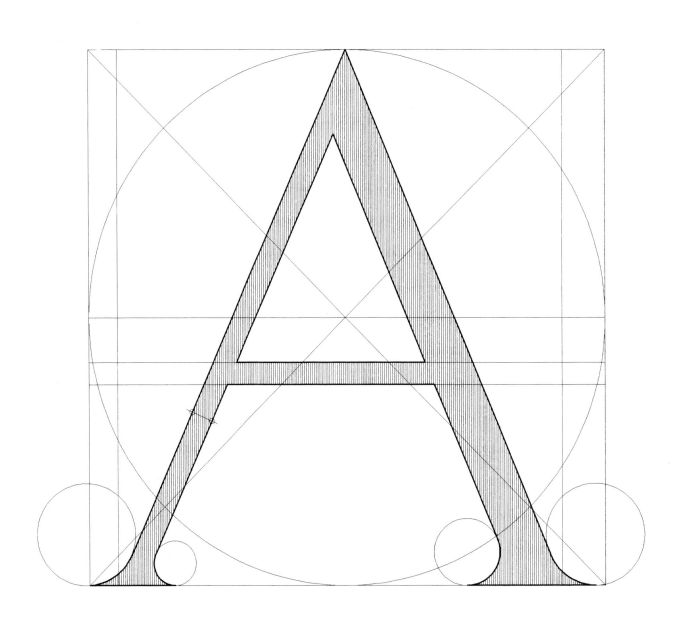

ON
ALBERTI
AND THE
ART OF
BUILDING

ROBERT TAVERNOR

YALE UNIVERSITY PRESS NEW HAVEN AND LONDON

Designed by Gillian Malpass

The lettering on the title page was designed by Alberti
for the frieze of the Rucellai sepulchre in Florence.
The layout here was designed by Gillian Malpass
and manipulated digitally by Robert Tavernor
and by Joe Robson of CASA at the University of Bath.

Printed in Singapore

Library of Congress Cataloging-in-Publication Data

Tavernor, Robert.
On Alberti and the art of building / Robert Tavernor.
p.   cm.
Includes bibliographical references and index.
ISBN 0-300-07615-0 (cloth : alk. paper)
1. Alberti, Leon Battista, 1404–1472 – Criticism and interpretation.
2. Architecture, Renaissance – Italy.
3. Architects and patrons – Italy.
I. Title.
NA1123.A5T38   1998
720′.92 – dc21   98-15258
                                        CIP

A catalogue record for this book is available from
The British Library

Frontispiece: Alberti's design for the letter 'A',
derived from a rubbing of the frieze of the Rucellai sepulchre, Florence,
and digitally reproduced and described geometrically
by the Alberti Group.

Page vi: Detail of frieze running around the base of the exterior
of the Tempio Malatestiano, Rimini,
with its display of Malatesta family emblems (photo/author).

For my family,
and especially Joanna, Faye and James
who have known Alberti all their young lives.

CONTENTS

PREFACE

Leon Battista the Florentine, of the great Alberti clan, was a man of rare brilliance, acute judgement, and extensive learning. [. . .] Surely there was no field of knowledge however remote, no discipline however arcane, that escaped his attention; you might have asked yourself whether he was more an orator or a poet, whether his style was more majestic or graceful. So thorough had been his examination of the remains of antiquity that he was able to grasp every principle of ancient architecture, and renew it by his example. [. . .] He had moreover the highest reputation as both painter and sculptor, and since he achieved a greater mastery in all these different arts than only a few can manage in any single one, it would be more telling, as Sallust said about Carthage, to be silent about him than to say little.[1]

LEON BATTISTA ALBERTI (1404–72) was recognised by his contemporaries as an extraordinary man who, through his writings and his practical example in the arts, influenced the way in which the natural and artificial world was perceived and represented during the Italian Renaissance. This is clear from the enthusiastic endorsement of Alberti by his young friend, the poet and greatest textual scholar of his age, Angelo Poliziano (1454–94), quoted above. Another contemporary, Cristoforo Landino (1424–92), the literary theorist who was appointed to a chair of poetry and rhetoric at Florence University in 1458, considered that 'in prose Battista surpassed the greatest' – praise indeed, to 'surpass' Dante, Petrarch and Boccaccio.[2] Yet, today, Alberti is no longer widely applauded for his prose, and the example of other Italian Renaissance painters, sculptors and architects is better appreciated world-wide.

This is partly because many of Alberti's forty, or so, literary works are available only in specialist publications and are known mostly to scholars, and partly because none of the paintings surviving from his lifetime has been identified unreservedly as his, though there is an innovative and very fine self-portrait plaque (which exists in two versions). His main buildings in Rimini, Florence and Mantua are publicly accessible and are wonderful tactile expressions of his approach to architecture. They were admired by his contemporaries and proved influential for later Renaissance architects, including Donato Bramante, Giulio Romano and, the best known of them all, Andrea Palladio. But they were not all completed as he wished, or were altered subsequently, and to understand the full effect he had intended their fabric has to be interpreted through his writings and the letters and accounts that concern their construction.

Alberti's approach to architecture developed from his supreme knowledge of antiquity – of thought and buildings – which he wrote about in books on science and the visual arts. This literary background set him apart from his immediate predecessors and contemporaries who wished to be recognised as architects, but who were usually master craftsmen – like Giotto and Brunelleschi – who built their reputation on manual dexterity, proven qualities of leadership and occasional ingenuity, and were remarked on less for their intellect. By contrast, Alberti received a first-rate schooling and university education, and acquired a reputation as a man of learning and culture, attributes sometimes thought to be incompatible with the essential practicalities of building. He also practised architecture unconventionally. After university he held positions in the church for the rest of his life, and was probably not paid to produce architectural designs, accepting accommodation and a place of privilege in his patron's court instead. By planning every detail of a project and making precise drawings and models before building work began, he could afford to be absent from the building site and entrust the building of his designs to others. This distance from the day-to-day aspect of building was interpreted by those who practised traditionally as an indication of his lack of commitment – that he was a scholar who only dabbled in architecture. The biographer and architect Giorgio Vasari (1511–74) describes Alberti in both editions of his *Lives of the Most Excellent Italian Architects, Painters and Sculptors . . .* (1550 and 1568) as a kind of dilettante, who had mastered the theoretical but not the practical side of architecture. Vasari's opinion, based on poor information and prejudice, has conspired against Alberti: he knew little of his role as a practising architect outside Florence – in Rimini and Mantua – since the only accurate account of his activities is generally contained in contracts and letters in court archives in those cities. Indeed, these documents have proved to be largely inaccessible until even quite recently. Since the early 1970s, they have been pored over to great effect and presented by historians in specialist journals, and in monographs on individual buildings. Similarly, detailed photogrammetric survey drawings of his buildings are now accessible on the Internet (see below). The book on Alberti's architecture that is most widely available, Franco Borsi's *Leon Battista Alberti: L'opera completa* (1973), translated into English in 1977, has not been updated since its original appearance. My book, therefore, is the first attempt at a digest of more recent thoughts about Alberti's buildings.[3]

Alberti's achievements as an architect were great by the standards of any age (Vasari does not equivocate on this point), and the role he established for the architect in society, and the design procedures he devised, are no less relevant to architects today than they were just over five hundred years ago. His treatise *De re aedificatoria* is the primary source for his ideas about architecture, and their extension into major building projects, for various patrons across Italy, is the main subject of this book. The cultural context and composition of *De re aedificatoria*, especially as it relates to Vitruvius' *De architectura*, will concern me less, since such matters have been discussed in considerable detail by others elsewhere. Nor are Alberti's views about the shape and composition of the complete city explored here. Instead, my principal aim is to show how Alberti translated architectural theory into practice, and established a professional role for the modern architect within the complex process of building; how ultimately he raised the status of architecture to an art – one that sought to be in harmony with the natural world.

This book has been organised to introduce Alberti and his main writings, particularly as they informed his architecture. His writings are constantly being reinterpreted by scholars, with texts and artefacts of uncetain origin being ascribed to him – either directly, or as a product of his influence, and these issues are outlined in the section 'On Alberti'. What then follows, 'On the Art of Building', is concerned with his formulation of architectural ideas, and their translation into designs for buildings. Alberti is one of the few individuals who wrote comprehensively and convincingly about this complete process. He was articulate about what is required of a patron and about the natural and human resources necessary for a building to be considered beautiful as well as useful and appropriate to its purpose. Consequently, the various building projects with which Alberti is known to have been involved are described in some detail – in relation to Alberti's architectural patrons and his builders – and placed in approximate chronological order. Thus, each chapter introduces the project's patron and its location, before threading a way through the many recent interpretations of each building history. From my particular reading of his architectural theory and practice, I conclude with an attempt to summarise his design process.

To hazard a complete picture of Alberti's architectural achievements, rather than remain silent (as Poliziano suggested), has led me to be conjectural on the impact of Alberti's intellect. For this, I hope the more prudent historian will forgive me.

ACKNOWLEDGEMENTS

MY INVOLVEMENT WITH ALBERTI BEGAN in earnest when I undertook post-graduate research in 1980 at St John's College, Cambridge, which led to my Ph.D. thesis, '"Concinnitas" in the Architectural Theory and Practice of Leon Battista Alberti' (University of Cambridge, 1985). Then followed a three-year collaboration with Joseph Rykwert and Neil Leach on a new English translation of *De re aedificatoria*, published as *On the Art of Building in Ten Books* (Cambridge, Mass., and London, 1988). In 1988 I formed the Alberti Group with Joseph Rykwert to organise an international exhibition on Alberti, which was sponsored by Olivetti SpA. Olivetti's involvement meant that my earlier studies could be developed using facilities not usually afforded to students of architectural history. Under the auspices of Olivetti, the Alberti Group commissioned surveys of Alberti's built works, and assembled a team of architecture students (first at Bath, then Edinburgh University) to make visual sense of the survey or's reports. Some of our findings were presented at the exhibition held during the autumn of 1994, at the Palazzo Te, Mantua, using computer animations and large wooden models to reconstruct Alberti's buildings. However, the limiting criteria of time, cost and space, and the expected intolerance of visitors to the presentation of complex arguments, restricted the amount of material we were able to display. Also, the catalogue which accompanied the exhibition (Rykwert and Engel, 1994) represents a broad cross-section of current research on Alberti, not just our own findings, so that some of our conclusions – presented in the various models – were not fully explained. This book may therefore be read as a companion to the catalogue, and complement our translation of Alberti's *De re aedificatoria*. However, I should stress that this book has been written to stand alone, and it represents my own views, for which I take full responsibility.

My thanks for the completion of this book are due to many. To Joseph Rykwert for opening my eyes to Alberti some twenty years ago, and for nurturing my initial enthusiasm. Also, to the members of the Alberti Group, who brought with them over the six years of its existence, a range of expertise and had a creative impact on the Alberti exhibition in 1994 and, subsequently, on the outcome of this book. Jason and Julie Cornish helped shape the direction of the Alberti Group and had a considerable influence on the visual impact of the exhibition; and I am grateful to the following for their individual contributions: Tim Anstey, Chris Bearman, Prue Chiles, Barry Clark, Melissa Doughty, Lucinda Gifford, Ann Griffin, Carl Gulland, Nigel Hetherington, Gary Hunt, Alun Jones, Pey-Ran Niew, Suzanne Thurlow, Sandra Trkulja and David Vila Domini.

Andrew Gilmour, Head of the Department of Architecture, University of Edinburgh, was enormously supportive of the Alberti Group during its three year sojourn north of the border. Alan Day of the Department of Architecture and Civil Engineering at the University of Bath provided insight, caution and wisdom when we confronted the latest that computer technology had to offer our researches. I would also like to thank him as Head of Department for some generous financial support, and my other colleagues at Bath for creating such a convivial environment in which to work.

The Alberti Group photogrammetric drawings were produced by Computer Mapping Services (CMS), Selsey, England, under the direction of Alfred Kenny. The surveys of Alberti's buildings made by his team involved closing streets and overcoming considerable bureaucracy, for which the authority of Olivetti was essential; and certain key personnel at Olivetti have also helped me greatly, especially Mauro Broggi, Alessandro De Maria and Anna Galeazzi. Renzo Zorzi, President of the Centro Internazionale d'Arte e di Cultura di Palazzo Te, Mantua, made possible the wooden models which have been illustrated for the first time in this book, and Felice Ragazzo of Rome saw to their making with wonderful dexterity. Aldo Signoretti, Gian Maria Erbesato and Elena Aiello of Palazzo Te have helped with aspects of this book – in providing access to information, and introducing me to some eminent local historians.

I should like to single out the following scholars for their help over the years, for reading and offering frank criticism of the text, or for providing expert information willingly: Arturo Calzona, Ian Campbell, Carlo Bertelli, Paul Davies, Caroline van Eck, Anne Engel, Livio Volpi Ghirardini, Vaughan Hart, David Hemsoll, Charles Hope, Emily Lane, Neil Leach, Hans-Karl Lücke, Lionel March, Henry A. Millon, John Onians, Giovanni Orlandi, Joseph Rykwert, Richard Schofield, Luke Syson and Mark Wilson Jones.

This book was guided from its inception by Gillian Malpass at Yale University Press with considerable patience and skill, and I am immensely grateful for her constancy. My thanks are also due to Ruth Thackeray and Delia Gaze who have provided this book with an accuracy and consistency it would otherwise have lacked. Any remaining blights are of my own making.

Finally, and most personally, my thanks are due to my wife, Denise. Since 1979, when I was a Scholar in Architecture at the British School at Rome, she has supported me in my determination to understand Alberti, and I owe her an enormous debt – whether or not I have succeeded in that aim.

AUTHOR'S NOTE

THE USUAL ACADEMIC APPARATUS of extensive footnotes and a bibliography have been provided for the reader who wishes to pursue other lines of enquiry more comprehensively than space allows here. I quote extensively in the text from the most recent English translation of Alberti's *De re aedificatoria*; the book, chapter and page numbers of this edition, Alberti (1988), are given in brackets after each quote or citation. In the margins of Alberti (1988) is marked the pages of the *editio princeps*, and scholars will readily find the corresponding passages I have quoted from in the parallel Latin-Italian text of Orlandi (1966).

When describing churches I have used the terms 'north', 'south', 'east' and 'west' in accordance with standard liturgical usage. The east end of the church is always therefore at the main altar end, and the opposite west porch is always the main entrance. For the true relationship of the plan of each church to the geographical, cardinal points readers should refer to the relevant building plan and the north point drawn adjacent to it.

Those who wish to scrutinise the Alberti Group photogrammetric survey drawings (and which are referred to thus in the main text), which were made for the Alberti exhibition held in Mantua in 1994 and very accurately describe the present state of the elevations, internal and external, of most of Alberti's buildings, can do so by visiting the following world-wide web site:http://www.bath.ac.uk/Centres/CASA. The surveys are in AutoCAD format and dimensions can be taken from one point to another on the selected elevation, as the user chooses, to find dimensions in metres or the relevant local measure.

The dimensions of buildings are referred to in metres (m.) for large dimensions, and millimetres (mm) for smaller dimensions, as is usual in the U.K. building industry. Various artefacts referred to in the text and illustrations are dimensioned in centimetres (cm).

Lege Feliciter

ON ALBERTI

1 Leon Battista Alberti, *Self-portrait*. Bronze cast oval plaque, uniface, *c.*1435, 201 × 135 mm. Washington, D.C., National Gallery of Art, Samuel H. Kress Collection, no. 1957.14.125.

I

THE EARLY YEARS

THE ALBERTIS WERE A MAJOR Florentine banking family. Many of them had been in exile since 1393, following a battle for supremacy which their faction lost. Members of the clan were ordered out by the victors: some moved to northern Europe, others remained in Tuscany but outside the city limits. Lorenzo de' Benedetto degli Alberti, who had been exiled in January 1401, settled temporarily in Genoa. Here he met a widow, Bianca Fieschi. They had two sons, Carlo and then Battista (later called Leon Battista), the subject of this book, who was born on 14 February 1404.[1] Bianca died two years after Battista's birth during an outbreak of plague and before marrying Lorenzo. Both sons were therefore left to bear the stigma of illegitimacy in their early years.

Because of the plague in Genoa, Lorenzo sought sanctuary with his sons in Venice, where he ran the family bank with his brother Ricciardo. He returned to Genoa only briefly, in 1408, to marry Margherita di Pietro Benini, a Florentine.[2] After several years in Venice, in 1415 the family moved to Padua, where Battista was a boarder at the finest school in northern Italy, the Gymnasium, named after the ancient Greek model of education on which its methods were based. Here Gasparino Barzizza instructed his pupils through the writings of classical rhetoricians and dramatists, especially Cicero, Quintilian, Terence and Seneca.[3] Many of his students became famous for mastering the ancient texts and projecting their learning in public life, and thus actively promoting ancient values. This was the very essence of humanism, and some of Barzizza's pupils became revered humanist scholars, such as Francesco Barbaro and Francesco Filelfo: Alberti thrived in this environment.[4]

The Gymnasium was both a place of intellectual stimulation and a refuge from many of the distractions of daily life. Still, Barzizza could not offer protection from the recurring threat of plague, or the fear that accompanied it. He revealed in a letter to Lorenzo the anguish suffered by his charge in those early years:

Last night our Battista came to me in tears, for he had learnt from our kinsman Leonardo that the plague had killed off your bailiff in four hours and that you risk catching the illness yourself. You are not acting at all prudently and are driving your children to despair. Think less of your business matters and more of your survival: [. . .] think of your children's peace of mind, not about any possible financial loss.[5]

After the Gymnasium Battista continued his education for seven years at Bologna University, where he pursued his doctoral studies in canon and civil law which set him on course for a career in the church. Tommaso Parentucelli of Sarzana, the future Pope Nicholas V, was a fellow university student and friend, who became famed for his enthusiastic support of Greek and patristic studies during his papacy.[6] Alberti also learnt to value Greek texts and encouraged others to persevere with the language. His friend Lapo da Castiglionchio translated *Sacrifices*, by the second-century Greek satirist Lucian, which he dedicated to Alberti. There he tells Alberti how in Bologna he had started Greek:

because you repeatedly recommended it, and also to take my mind off the troubles oppressing me. There was no greater solace for us, and no one had more influence over me than you. I made progress in those most liberal and complicated studies thanks not only to your friendship and help but to your stimulating example and encouragement.[7]

Alberti needed the support of his friends. Lorenzo Alberti had died in 1421, soon after Battista had started at university, and Ricciardo, who was appointed guardian to the two orphans, swiftly followed him. Relatives proceeded to plunder the vulnerable boys' inheritance, using their illegitimacy as a cover for greed.[8] This proved to be one burden too many for Battista, and with the sad loss of loved ones, financial insecurity and the demands of his own high self-expectations he collapsed into ill-health.

Battista showed no signs of his father's love of commerce, and his studies and friends came first. From study grew an appreciation of the virtues of antiquity, which he expressed for his contemporaries in numerous pamphlets and books. His first literary triumph, the comedy *Philodoxeos* (Greek for 'lover of glory', 1424), written at the age of twenty, was worked in the antique manner after Plautus and Terence as a practical joke, which he succeeded in passing off for a long time as the work of a fictional Latin writer, Lepidus – meaning 'the joker'. He later owned up, and dedicated it to Leonello d'Este, Marquis of Ferrara, though as late as 1588 it was still published as antique Roman.[9] His friend the poet Antonio Beccadelli (1394–1471), better known through his literary name, 'Il Panormita' (from the Latin for his birth place Palermo, 'Panormus') and for being something of a joker himself, wrote of their relationship. A passage in his poem *Hermaphroditus* of 1425 (whose subject-matter – amorous encounters in a brothel – brought him instant fame and notoriety) refers to Battista directly:

> You are pleasant company, very handsome, witty, wholly dedicated to the liberal arts, born of the true blood of the Albertis, incomparable in the nobility of your manners. You are liked for your rare talents, and I like you for your genuine simplicity. You are a true and honest friend. Tell me how you get on with women.[10]

As far as is known, entanglements with women were avoided by Battista, and he stuck to the certainties that study and his faith provided.

In the autumn of 1428, the year Alberti graduated from university, Pope Martin V issued a bull that permitted the exiled Albertis to return home to Florence.[11] Many had not survived their peregrinations, and they were fewer in number, poorer and a spent force in Florentine politics. When Battista first saw the city of his ancestors remains unknown, as he may have followed university with a period as secretary to Cardinal Albergati, Bishop of Bologna.[12] The pope sent Albergati on an embassy through northern Europe to attempt a peace between the warring French and English, and Alberti may have accompanied him. By 1432 the Council of Basle was in session, and the cardinal was papal representative. Even if he were in tow with Albergati, Alberti may have had little involvement as during that year he moved to Rome to take up the appointment as secretary to Bishop Biagio Molin (Biagio da Molina), head of the papal chancery.[13] Molin nominated Alberti to the College of Abbreviators in the Papal Court (*abbreviatori apostolici*), where he remained for the next thirty-two years drafting papal briefs (the primary function of the Abbreviators), though with time too to pursue his own intellectual interests. Further security came on 7 October 1432 when Pope Eugenius IV (who had succeeded Martin V) lifted the ban that

prevented illegitimate sons from receiving holy orders and ecclesiastical benefices.[14] Alberti was later identified in a papal bull which permitted him to receive a prebend, or income, from the church, and he was deemed to hold the priorate of San Martino a Gangalandi at Lastra a Signa (near Florence) 'in commendam'. He was to become a canon of Florence Cathedral (*canonico fiorentino*) and, as such, may have been ordained priest. At the instigation of Pope Nicholas V, from 7 December 1448 he was also appointed rector of the parish of San Lorenzo in Mugello.[15]

His literary expositions continued during this period, and he followed the success of *Philodoxeos*, whose central character Philodoxus was the 'lover of glory', with the *Intercenales* ('Dinner Pieces', 1429), a collection of dialogues and fables, which includes a hero called Philoponius, or 'lover of hard work'.[16] The more sober *De commodis atque litterarum incommodis* ('The Pleasure and Pain of Letters', 1429–30) is a dissertation on the life of an intellectual. For Alberti, the joy of literary studies was in acquiring knowledge, and communicating his learning through writing. It proved to be an all-consuming passion in his search for recognition and fame. He tells how he desired 'with ferocious tenacity everything that was illustrious. There was nothing that with fatigue, anguish and watchfulness I did not try to reach and look for. [. . .] I was really convinced that I had begun the most praiseworthy of all labours'.[17]

At about the same time he wrote a discourse on the nature of love, a mixture of verse and prose. He called this *Amator* (*c.*1429), the Latin original being rendered into Italian by his brother Carlo as *Ephoebia*. In a similar vein he wrote *Ecatonfilea* ('A Hundred Loves', *c.*1429), in which a woman relates the qualities of her perfect man, one who is 'possessed of many virtues [. . .] excelling in music, letters, painting, sculpture, and every good and noble art', and *Deiphira* (*c.*1429–34?), which explores different ways of escaping from failed relationships.[18] His writings often seem to reflect his own sense of self-worth, which he makes readable for others by framing it with satire, even self-deprecation. *Canis* (1441–2) is a panegyric to his pet dog, whose constant loyalty and affection he admired, and on which he projected his own person: it was a mongrel, he a bastard; it had a tenacious memory, mastering Greek, Latin and Tuscan![19]

Similarly, Alberti attempted to make sense of the various painful episodes in his early life through an account of the duties and tribulations of family life. In *Della famiglia* (1433–4) he wrote of the need – perhaps reflecting his own need – to become independent of the tangible greed and weakness of others by looking inward, towards the soul. Consequently, he built his life on the pillars of reason (*ragione*) and virtue (*virtù*), for: 'Whenever a man thinks and acts with reason and virtue, he will be like a mortal god'.[20] Educated reason was his antidote to opinion, and virtue was the route to the personal excellence he sought: virtue, he believed, would shape, direct and condition the actions of men towards performing only good acts, for the benefit of society.[21] In mid-life he declared that 'there is nothing, aside from virtue, to which a man should devote more care, more effort and attention' (I, 8, p. 18; and Glossary, p. 426).

After little over a year in Rome, Alberti was to enjoy a long sojourn in Florence (1434–43). The move of the whole papal curia to Florence came about because the stability Pope Martin V had won in Rome was short-lived, and the papacy changed its character with Eugenius' succession to the Holy See.[22] Martin had concentrated his energies on restoring the territory of the Papal State, and regaining control over Rome, his native city. As a member of the powerful Colonna clan, he favoured nepotism to re-establish the authority of the popes over Rome, and the stability he created there was factional and proved very temporary. This caused his successor considerable problems locally. For Eugenius was a Venetian – an outsider – and a conciliator rather than a fighter. His secular authority was quickly challenged by the Romans, led by the Colonna, who declared their city a republic.[23] Alberti was swept along by these events, and in 1434 retreated with the papacy to Florence, which was to be its temporary home for the next nine years.

With this move Alberti shifted his literary attention towards the visual arts. His interest would have been stimulated by his exposure to the work of leading artists in Florence – Lorenzo Ghiberti, Donatello, Luca della Robbia – and the architect Filippo Brunelleschi, whom he encountered directly in these years.[24]

His account of the techniques by which true perspective is achieved, and the proper composition and content of paintings, is presented in *De pictura* (1435). Subdivided into three 'books', or parts, it was completed within his first year in Florence: more precisely, 'on the day of Friday at 20.45 hours on 26 August 1435'.[25] The Italian (Tuscan) version, *Della pittura*, followed in the first half of 1436 and was dedicated to Brunelleschi[26] – by then the most respected architect in Florence – who had himself made some famous demonstrations on the effects of perspective, using a painted image of the Florentine Baptistery of San Giovanni and a mirror, and of the Palazzo della Signoria.[27] In the dedication of *Della pittura* Alberti marvels at the achievements of the Florentines:

after I came back here to this most beautiful of cities from the long exile in which we Albertis have grown old, I recognised in many, but above all in you, Filippo [Brunelleschi], and in our great friend the sculptor Donatello and in the others, Nencio [Lorenzo Ghiberti], Luca [della Robbia] and Masaccio, a genius for every laudable enterprise in no way inferior to any of the ancients who gained fame in these arts.

The dedication closely followed the completion of Brunelleschi's great dome of Florence Cathedral, which was consecrated by Pope Eugenius IV on the Feast of the Annunciation, 25 March 1436.[28] On this most significant day in the history of Florence (and of Western architecture), the pope had processed to the cathedral from the Dominican convent of Santa Maria Novella on the western edge of the city where he and his court were based. It is reasonable to assume that Alberti would have been among the party of clergy and laymen, which certainly included at least one of his future patrons, Sigismondo Malatesta, Lord of Rimini (see chapter 6 below).[29] The magnificence of the dome of Florence Cathedral was to make a great impression on Alberti. He thought it to be a mighty achievement: was it not

vast enough to cover the entire Tuscan population with its shadow, and done without the aid of beams and elaborate wooden supports? Surely a feat of engineering, if I am not mistaken, that people did not believe possible these days and was probably equally unknown and unimaginable among the ancients.[30]

Brunelleschi was, of course, more than an engineer, and as an architect was an influential exponent of the manner, known as *all'antica*, which developed in reaction to Gothic and the 'modern' German influences on north Italian (Lombardic) architecture. It is reported that Brunelleschi and Donatello had surveyed and measured Roman monuments together so as to perfect their art through a direct knowledge of ancient sculpture and architecture.[31] Roman remains were certainly closely studied by successive generations intent on a similar path. However, while Brunelleschi and Donatello were pioneers, and were designing in a city whose intellectual leaders were swayed by the moral and visual values of ancient republican Rome, there are doubts whether the physical remains of Rome were their primary source: the Florentine Baptistery was in any case thought to be Roman, and its appearance, along with the churches of the Santissimi Apostoli and San Miniato al Monte, bear more obvious comparison

26

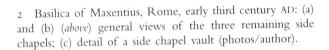

2 Basilica of Maxentius, Rome, early third century AD: (a) and (b) (*above*) general views of the three remaining side chapels; (c) detail of a side chapel vault (photos/author).

with Brunelleschi's designs.[32] Similarly, Donatello had developed his art from his master Ghiberti, possibly assisting him on the first bronze doors made for the Baptistery. Certainly, his sculptures combine the naturalism of this work with the more disciplined architectural ornamentation learnt from antique examples. Notable are the bronze bas-relief he made of the *Feast of Herod* for the Baptistery in Siena (*c.*1425) and his bronze work of two decades later for the altar in the basilica of St Anthony in Padua. His depiction there of the *Life of St Anthony* has a scene framed by an interior view of three large vaulted spaces like the still-standing triple barrel vaults of the Basilica of Maxentius in Rome[33] (fig. 2); these resemble Alberti's design for the interior of Sant'Andrea in Mantua (see chapter 8 below). Perspective was a means to the life-like realism Donatello sought, and Brunelleschi's demonstration as to how the visual 'rays' of this geometrical discipline worked was probably well known to Florentine artists.

Alberti wrote *De pictura* to codify these early Florentine explorations in perspective, and to explain how perspective operates and can be successfully imple-

mented by others.[34] While influenced by the work of Florentine artists, *De pictura* is nevertheless highly original, and Alberti was the first author to write coherently about a theory underlying the art of painting, as opposed to providing a history of painting (explored in antiquity by Pliny the Elder in his *Natural History*), or a practical guide to painting (which had been supplied by Cennino Cennini in *Il libro dell'arte* in the 1390s). Alberti sought something different, as the structure of his treatise suggests: Book I of *De pictura* sets out the mechanics of perspective; Book II, the design (*disegno*) of paintings, as lines and composition (according to a narrative or *historia*); and he concludes in Book III with the education and character of the artist. What he wished to demonstrate in *De pictura* was that nature can be interpreted and represented rationally (using the Laws of Perspective); that the subject-matter and composition of paintings have a cultural and social basis; and that only an artist who is a complete person (through education and good character) can create a painting that will be judged as worthwhile. Clearly, a successful painter will be an exceptional individual, who, with god-like powers, re-creates and interprets Man and Nature for the benefit of his fellow men.

Alberti demonstrates the Laws of Perspective using a male figure, a 'view through a window' and the window itself. He set the height of the man as 3 *braccia* high which is equivalent to 1.75 m.: the *braccio*, or arm length, was a measure commonly used in Italy but varied in length from one city to another; in Florence it was 583.6 mm long.[35] The window, or 'picture plane', he drew as a rectangle, and on its base, the 'ground line', he marked intervals one *braccio* apart. Using the same scale he marked a point at the centre of the frame which is directly opposite the artist's viewpoint (and therefore always at the height of the spectator's eye in the finished painting) and 3 *braccia* up from the ground line: this central point was called the vanishing point by subsequent perspectivalists. Lines connecting the ground line intervals converge on the central point and are called orthogonals (fig. 3). To be able to locate objects within this framework of lines, and which appear to be correctly sized relative to one another, he constructed a side view of the picture plane and drew the ground line at right angles to it (on which the man is standing) and divided this into *braccio*-long units. With the front and side views next to each other he drew lines on the side view connecting the artist's viewpoint to the subdivisions of the ground plane, as visual rays that emanate from the eye of the artist like a pyramid. Where this visual pyramid is cut by the picture plane horizontal lines are drawn. These horizontals are drawn to extend across the orthogonals of the front view: they are called transversals. The orthogonals and transversals create the effect of a chequer board receding in space. This provides the framework for locating figures, objects and buildings accurately in one-point perspective.

To assist in the accurate reproduction of images from life, or from paintings and sculptures, Alberti also invented the *velum*, or veil. This is placed, as the picture plane, between the artist and the subject to be painted, and provided artists with the principal outlines which could be worked up to make a shaded drawing or a painting:

> the veil, which among my friends I call the intersection, and whose usage I was the first to discover [. . . is] loosely woven of fine thread, dyed whatever colour you please, divided by thicker threads into as many parallel square sections as you like, and stretched on a frame. I set this up between the eye and the object to be represented, so that the visual pyramid passes through the loose weave of the veil.[36]

It allows the artist, as Alberti writes, 'to see any object

that is round and in relief, represented on the flat surface of the veil. From all of which we may appreciate by reflection and experience how useful the veil is for painting easily and correctly'.[37]

Alberti wrote *De statua* some time after *De pictura*, presumably between 1443 and 1452.[38] It is a much shorter treatise, and focuses on the precise measurements of the human form and the appropriate composition of sculptures, whatever their scale. Appended to it is a summary of idealised human proportions, the *Tabulae dimensionorum hominis* ('Table of Human Dimensions') (fig. 4). To compile these dimensions he invented a measuring tool, and as bodies are three-dimensional, the measure is made of three different components, a horizon, radius and perpendicular, known collectively as the *finitorium* (fig. 5). The horizon, or disc, is three 'feet' in diameter, divided around its circumference into six degrees, and each degree is subdivided into six minutes. A moveable radius, which rotates from the centre of the horizon (also divided into degrees and minutes), has a plumb-line hanging from its outer tip. This assembly is placed on top of the body to be recorded and the plumb-line lowered to coincide with junctions and other easily discernible parts of the body. These parts are measured vertically against the perpendicular measuring rod called the *exempeda*: mobile squares called *normae* are used to measure physical widths of the body.[39]

In both *De pictura* and *De statua* Alberti was responding to the evidence of ancient texts, then verifying information for himself before presenting a coherent argument in his treatises for his erudite readership. Similarly, ancient knowledge is updated for a modern audience in his *De iure* ('On Law', 1437), a commentary on the relationship between Roman Law then in use (which Alberti had studied at Bologna University) and 'natural' divine Law.[40] In *La prima grammatica della lingua toscana* (dated around 1450 when he was in Rome, but presumably started when he was still in Florence)[41] he proposed reforms to the Tuscan dialect by introducing latinised terms and phrases. In so doing he wrote the first Italian grammar ever written, and *La prima grammatica* is at the root of modern Italian.

The church was also attempting to reform itself at this time. Present in Florence between 1438 and 1439 were leading intellectuals from Greece and Italy, there to establish the Decree of Union: namely the reuniting of the Latin and Greek churches. It had developed from the Council of Basle, called by Pope Eugenius IV in 1431, and the Council at Ferrara in 1437, which was aborted prematurely when radical voices of the lower clergy refused to transfer there to meet the Greek representatives. The Council of Florence, convened in the

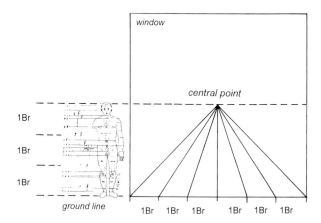

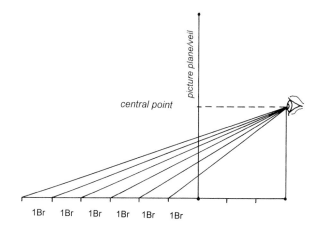

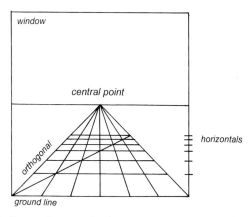

3 Alberti's linear framework for constructions in single point perspective, after *De pictura*, showing three steps: frontal view (*top*); side elevation (*centre*); frontal view (*bottom*) (drawing/author).

following year, was to be the most major event of Eugenius' pontificate.

The assembled intellectuals had a considerable impact locally, engaging with the élite minds of Florence, for example Niccolò Niccoli and Ambrogio Traversari. Traversari, head of the Camaldolese Order in Florence since 1431, was one of the framers of the Decree, and he had developed a keen interest in the early church and contemporary architecture.[42] His commitments were in fact diverse: he was an active translator of the Greek Fathers into Latin, and it is thought he may have contributed to the programme related in bronze bas-relief on the Baptistery doors: it is believed that his intervention was decisive in initiating the construction of Brunelleschi's design for Santa Maria degli Angeli in Florence. Traversari's own passion in architecture was in the 'renaissance of Christian antiquity', and he urged his contemporaries to return to the pristine sanctity of the Early Christian church as the solution to contemporary ecclesiastical and spiritual dilemmas.[43]

Traversari's activities were inspired by Niccolò Niccoli, one of the most influential members of the Florentine humanists, and himself a brilliant scholar and a classicist. Niccoli had a lively interest in the arts, studied 'the laws of architecture', made detailed surveys of antique buildings and was an intimate of Brunelleschi.[44] With his great library and erudition he shared, and in some cases shaped, the interests of not only Traversari but his most powerful ally Cosimo de' Medici, head of the dominant family in Florence. Alberti was presumably thought to be close to this circle, for just after Traversari's death (in 1439) he was asked to write his biography, an invitation he declined.[45] As secretary to Bishop Biagio Molin in Florence, another signatory of the Decree of Union, Alberti would certainly have been close to the main characters involved in the debates and negotiations that ensued there.[46]

During their brief stay in Ferrara the delegates had been the guests of Marquis Niccolò III d'Este, head of its ruling family. Niccolò's authority extended over the eastern half of the Po valley, and he was a determined and passionate ruler. His son, Leonello d'Este, was a gentler, more cultured man, who surrounded himself with highly regarded scholars and artists and to whom Alberti was drawn (fig. 6).[47] He had dedicated his earlier work, the pseudo-antique comedy *Philodoxeos*, to Leonello in 1436. It came with a letter of recommendation from one of the greatest established scholars at that time, Poggio Bracciolini.[48] On the death of Niccolò in 1441, Alberti sent Leonello a copy of *Theogenius* (1441), which is concerned with proper gov-

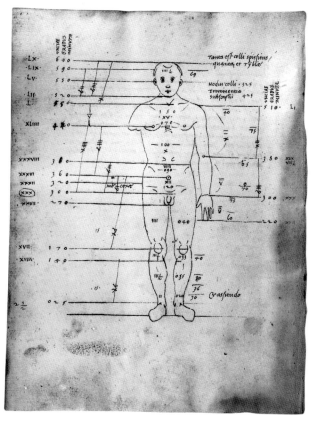

4 Male figure with dimensions overlaid, appended to and demonstrating the *Tabulae dimensionorum hominis*. Oxford, Bodleian Library, MS Canon. Misc. 172, fol. 232*v*.

5 The *finitorium* in Alberti's *De statua* (Fresne, 1651).

not seek great praise, glory, and immortality in this magnanimity of yours? Not with pomp; not with ostentation, nor with crowds of flatterers will you earn real whole-hearted praise, for this can only be won by virtue'.[50]

Alberti's own 'praise, glory and immortality' had been denied him that same year, when he was the victim of what he felt was an unfair judgement in a literary competition for verse in the vernacular, the Certame Coronario, which he had helped to promote. This took place in Florence on 18 October 1441, and was funded by Piero de' Medici. The theme was friendship, but animosity reigned when the competitors fell out with the judges who failed to agree on a winner. Both Leonardo Dati and Alberti considered themselves strong contenders for the silver garland – the *corona*, or crown – which was to have been awarded to the winning contestant.[51] Later that year, Alberti was invited to Ferrara by Leonello to help judge a competition for an equestrian statue to commemorate his father. This time there were joint winners, and the prize was split, between two Florentines, Antonio di Cristoforo and Niccolò di Giovanni Baroncelli. Antonio was to build the marble podium and cast the bronze rider, while Niccolò was to cast the horse. Their combined endeavour was placed opposite Ferrara Cathedral outside the Palazzo del Comune (figs 7 and 8).[52]

Historians have wondered whether Alberti provided more than good judgement and involved himself in the design of the base to Niccolò's statue.[53] This is antique in manner, and looks as though it were made of cannibalised fragments of a more ancient work – that is, pseudo-Latin, like Alberti's *Philodoxeos*. But its combination of arch and cornice supported by columns (one half-round and attached to a wall), a system that Alberti was later to reject,[54] was a heavy interpretation of the Florentine *all'antica* manner, and its composition strongly suggests that it was designed by Antonio di Cristoforo. Similarly, the attribution to Alberti of the design for the campanile of the cathedral (begun in 1451) has nothing of substance to support it.[55]

Alberti is on record as having declared that 'I, who take no small pleasure in painting and sculpture', admired Niccolò di Giovanni Baroncelli's artistry in forming the horse.[56] But, in fact, he expressed more interest in the living majesty of the horse, and he wrote a short book on their nature and behaviour, *De equo animante* (1441), which he dedicated to Leonello in 1442. Such knowledge came from his reading – he cites ancient Greek and Roman authors – and from direct experience: apparently 'He was such a fine horseman that even the proudest, most mettlesome

ernment; it was further relevant to Leonello for its poignant theme of parental loss.[49] Alberti spoke in *Theogenius* of virtuous leaders, and his regard for Leonello is presumably implied when he wrote: 'do you

6 Antonio di Puccio called Pisanello, *Leonello d'Este* (1407–50). Bronze medal, *c.*1443, 68 mm diam. London, British Museum, Department of Coins and Medals, George III Collection, Ferrara, medal 25, obverse.

horses seemed to fear and tremble when he mounted them'.[57]

Although Leonello d'Este was a supporter of Alberti, apart from offering him an adjudicating role in the one competition in Ferrara, he does not appear to have provided him with any further tangible opportunities. Alberti pursued other potential benefactors. The Gonzaga were the ruling family in Mantua, a city further north and west of Ferrara, and Alberti dedicated the Latin original of *De pictura* (1435) to 'Gianfrancesco Illustrious Prince of Mantua', probably between 1438 and 1444.[58] He clearly longed for a position at the Gonzaga court and wrote for his wish to be effected:

> You could know my character and learning, and all my qualities best, if you arranged for me to join you, as I indeed desire. And I shall believe my work has not displeased you, if you decide to enrol me as a devoted member among your servants and to regard me as not one of the least.[59]

Gianfrancesco Gonzaga should have been sympathetic to Alberti's plea. He had invited another prominent product of Barzizza's Gymnasium in Padua,

7 (*above right*) and 8 (*below right*) Antonio di Cristoforo and Niccolò di Giovanni Baroncelli, equestrian statue of Niccolò III d'Este. Bronze horse and rider on a stone column and arch base, *c.*1442. Ferrara, Palazzo del Comune (photo/author).

9 Antonio di Cristoforo and Niccolò di Giovanni Baroncelli, equestrian statue of Niccolò III d'Este. Stone column and arch base compared to Corinthian column variants in *De re aedificatoria*, VII, 9, *c.*1442. Ferrara, Palazzo del Comune (photo-grammetric drawing by CMS/Alberti Group).

Vittorino da Feltre, to establish a school in Mantua in 1423. This too was based on classical foundations and a humanist ethos, and was attended by Gianfrancesco's sons and those of his principal courtiers: Federico da Montefeltro, Lord of Urbino, was also educated there. But Alberti may have been poorly served by Fate as Gianfrancesco died in 1444. None the less Alberti was received warmly by the courts of Mantua and Urbino during his lifetime and they provided him with accommodation – presumably the board and lodging considered appropriate for a courtier.[60] The church, however, was to be his most constant keeper, and allowed him the freedom to pursue his search for knowledge and reason in theory and practice whenever opportunities did present themselves.

Alberti's concern for direct knowledge and objectivity was raised in his earlier complaints to the judges of the Certame Coronario whom he accused of 'whim' and 'mere opinion'. As he put it, without reasoned judgements 'Each man will criticise the writings of others according to his own whim and not according to the subject itself'; instead of reliable verdicts 'there will be mere opinions that contradict the views of others'.[61] This has its parallel in his *Profugiorum ab aerumna* ('Refuge from Mental Anguish', 1441–2), in which the concluding dialogue teaches that only a man of letters can properly judge human affairs 'according to the truth and certitude of reason'.[62]

In fact, the primary message of the *Profugiorum* was the pursuit of inner peace – hence Alberti's title for the Italian version, *Della tranquillità dell'animo* ('Of the Tranquillity of the Soul'). It includes an early discussion by Alberti of the qualities of architecture, and emphasises a delight in colour in buildings through fine materials and ornament: this comes across in an extended description of the surface ornaments of the Temple of Diana at Ephesus. As yet in his writing he does not make a clear distinction between beauty in buildings (as form and structure) and its embellishment through ornament (as something attached and additional) – a key formulation in his later architectural treatise.[63] Nor is there any sense of the significance of proportion as a concept with which to bind the disparate parts of a building together. Dialogue takes place under Brunelleschi's dome of Florence Cathedral, and buildings and their design are regarded by Alberti's main character, Agnolo Pandolfini, as one route to restoring composure: 'I have mentally composed and built some very complex buildings, adding [... cornices and] columns with different and unusual capitals and bases [...]. And with such concoctions as these I would occupy myself until sleep took me'.[64]

II

ROME REVEALED AND RE-PRESENTED

IT WOULD APPEAR THAT Alberti was mostly resident in Rome after the return there of Eugenius IV and the papal court in 1443 (fig. 8). It was a city suffering from much decay and neglect, and it was not until Alberti's university friend became Pope Nicholas V in 1447 that a drastic restructuring of Rome's fabric was begun. Nicholas united disparate factions in Rome, calming clan-rivalry, and he used this base to re-establish political stability. His task was enormous, but he succeeded in laying the foundations of a new infrastructure for the papacy, as well as renovating Rome's physical image. He was well aware of the power of architecture as propaganda, and major building works were in progress in Rome and the Vatican by the early 1450s.

Alberti's short treatises on painting and sculpture represent his determination to establish a basis for sound criticism in the visual arts – his search for 'the truth and certitude of reason' – a self-appointed mission he continued throughout his life in order to provide the well-educated man of virtue with a platform on which to build a better society. His physical survey of Rome in the *Descriptio urbis romae* (c.1444) is integral to this ambition. It was the first accurate record to provide the co-ordinates of Rome's boundary walls, principal monuments, and the course of the river. It represents the first accurate cartographic mapping of the city (fig. 11).[1] Alberti achieved this survey by inventing a measuring disc which had a pointer pinned to its centre. Both were calibrated, and he rotated the pointer to align with buildings in distant view by placing it on a high vantage point, the Campidoglio (perhaps at the summit of the Palazzo Senatorio, to afford a clear view), the approximate physical (and administrative) centre of Rome (fig. 12). The position of the pointer relative to lines on the surface of the disc allowed him to establish the radial co-ordinates of Rome's main churches and the towers on the city walls and to plot these in plan.

The device is a larger version of the measuring disc described by Alberti in *De statua*. Whereas the sculptor's horizon has a diameter of 3 feet and a circumference divided into 6 degrees and 60 minutes, the surveyor's has a diameter of 10 feet and a circumference divided into 48 degrees and 192 minutes. It is not known why the surveyor's horizon was calibrated with these particular numbers, though Alberti appears to have chosen subdivisions that were fitting to the size of the disc and its purpose. He later applied a similar idea of a calibrated disc for a quite different purpose, as a cipher wheel for writing and decoding cryptic messages. It is described in *De componendis cifris* (1465) as composed of a larger wheel with a smaller one inset and sharing the same centre point.[2] An alphabet of twenty letters is placed on the outer disc, and the inner disc of twenty-four letters is moved relative to it. The numbers 1 to 4, expressed as arabic numerals and associated with the outer alphabet, add to the flexibility of this tool.[3] The practicality of certain numbers relative to size does not of course rule out the possibility that Alberti was concerned with symbolic considerations as well: since the diameter of the surveyor's horizon may have been conceived of by Alberti as being in direct proportion to the earth's – 10 feet being one-five-millionth of the earth's diameter according to ancient reckoning.[4]

Alberti had long been fascinated by the relationship between mathematics and geometry. Soon after arriving in Florence he had written mathematical and geometrical pamphlets that described the techniques to be used in painted compositions, and provided some worked-through examples. These appeared in manuscript form as *De punctis et lineis apud pictores* (c.1435) and in translation as *Elementi di pittura* (c.1436) around the time that *De pictura* was being translated into Tuscan for Brunelleschi.[5] During his early years in Rome Alberti wrote on mathematics (*Ludi rerum mathematicarum*, c.1450, which, after Leonello's death, he dedicated to his brother Meliaduso d'Este), and a separate work on geometry is also attributed to him (*De lunularum quadratura*, c.1450).[6] Alberti's mastery of mathematics and geometry and his concern to be able to turn such pure knowledge to practical advantage were recognised in Rome, particularly by Cardinal Prospero Colonna.

10 Maerten van Heemskerck, view of north façade of St John Lateran, Rome, *c*.1532. Kupferstichkabinett, Staatliche Museen zu Berlin – Preussischer Kulturbesitz. Römische Skizzenbücher, inv. no. 79D2, I, fol. 12*r* in original (12*v* in facsimile).

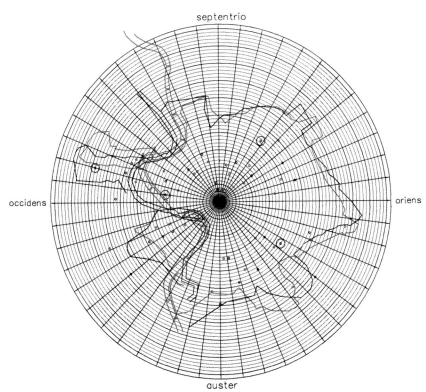

11 After Alberti's *Descriptio urbis romae* (*c*.1444). Computer pen plot: in red, the city walls of Rome, the Vatican, Tiber and its bridges today; in black, according to Alberti's *Descriptio* (Olivetti/Alberti Group).

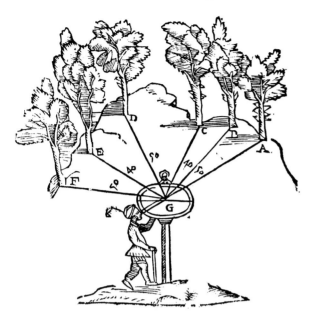

12 Surveying by means of the horizon. From C. Bartoli, *Del modo di misure*, Venice, 1564.

to influence decision-makers and to generate change.[14] His treatise on building, *De re aedificatoria*, arranged in ten books, fits into the latter category. It was to become his most influential work in Latin (fig. 3). It was probably begun around 1440 as a commentary on *De architectura* by the Roman architect Vitruvius, but it developed into a more major and ambitious enterprise which took Alberti at least a decade to complete, and the manuscript was possibly worked on and refined by him right up to his death in 1472.[15]

In writing *De re aedificatoria* Alberti not only made sense of Vitruvius for a modern audience but assimilated the views of other writers since antiquity, particularly of the Early Christian period, for example the *Etymologies* (*c.*623) of Isidore, Archbishop of Seville, written in admiration for Pliny the Elder's *Natural History* (*c.*AD 70), and the mid-ninth-century encyclopaedia *De universo* of Hrabanus Maurus.[16] Alberti incorporated in his *De re aedificatoria* their use of building terminology, including descriptions of the different

Prospero was a powerful patron of several leading humanist scholars in Rome. He helped to establish the reputation of Flavio Biondo, and oversaw two famous archaeological investigations: excavating on his land on the Quirinal Hill to reveal ruins erroneously identified as the palace of Emperor Augustus's cultural minister Maecenas;[7] and the attempted raising in 1446 of two ancient ceremonial barges from the floor of Lake Nemi, close to a Colonna castle in the Alban Hills. Only fragments of the barges could be raised.[8] But enough was gathered about their form for Alberti, who is generally believed to have been involved in the project, to write a treatise on ancient ships, *Navis* (v, 12, p. 136).[9] The entire event is celebrated in Biondo's 'Italia illustrata'.[10] Alberti has also been associated with the renewal of an ancient aqueduct, the Acqua Vergine, and its outlet in Rome in the Piazza di Trevi, near to the Colonna palaces. Work on the outlet is dated 1453 and may have been instigated by Prospero, but there is no hard evidence with which to link either man to this project.[11] It is known, however, that Prospero thought highly of Alberti, referring to him as 'il nostro Leon Battista Alberti, geometra egregio': 'our distinguished geometer'.[12]

Alberti also occupied himself in Rome with writing various dialogues, and stories in either the vernacular or Latin. Lucian was his primary inspiration for *Momus* as well as *Musca* ('The Fly') and *Virtus Dea* ('Divine Virtue').[13] While some of these lighter stories were intended only for the pleasure of his circle of intimates, the more serious treatises were undoubtedly intended

13 Leon Battista Alberti, *De re aedificatoria*. Frontispiece of manuscript, late fifteenth century, 330 × 209 mm. Eton, Eton College Library, MS 128.

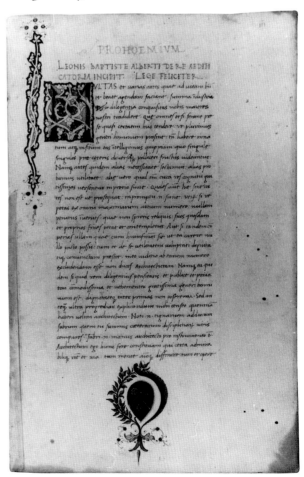

column types, and their chapter headings. However, Alberti wished to identify himself with the theory and practice of the ancient Roman world, and he does not mention Isidore or Hrabanus in his treatise: perhaps because the great medieval encyclopaedists offered theory alone. Nevertheless, their contributions had provided Alberti with an intellectual framework, and the means with which to interpret the opacity of Vitruvius' prose. Alberti explained his frustrations with Vitruvius' text halfway through his own treatise:

> I grieved that so many works of such brilliant writers had been destroyed by the hostility of time and of man, and that almost the sole survivor from this vast shipwreck is Vitruvius, an author of unquestioned experience, though one whose writings have been so corrupted by time that there are many omissions and many shortcomings. What he handed down was in any case not refined, and his speech such that the Latins might think that he wanted to appear a Greek, while the Greeks would think that he babbled Latin. However, his very text is evidence that he wrote neither Latin nor Greek, so that as far as we are concerned he might just as well not have written at all, rather than write something that we cannot understand (VI, 1, p. 154).

As with his treatises on the visual arts, Alberti's *De re aedificatoria* elevates the practicalities of making into an exalted act of creation. The first half of *De re aedificatoria* is concerned with practical considerations when building: the rudiments of design, materials, construction, and public and private buildings. The second deals with the appearance of different types of building and, in the final book, how to remedy building errors. This is reflected in the titles of the ten books: I Lineaments; II Materials; III Construction; IV Public Works; V Works of Individuals; VI Ornament; VII Ornament to Sacred Buildings; VIII Ornament to Public Secular Buildings; IX Ornament to Private Buildings; X Restoration of Buildings.

The first printed edition of the text appeared well after Alberti's death, and was published in Florence on 29 December 1485.[17] It was the first publication on architecture to be turned into a printed book, and thus appeared even in advance of Vitruvius' *De architectura*, printed in 1486. The manuscript version of *De re aedificatoria* had some other works appended to it, including *Navis* ('The Ship'), *Aeraria* ('Economics'), *Historia numeri et linearum* ('Arithmetic and Geometry'), and *Quid conferat architectus/o in negotio* ('The Service that the Architect Provides' or 'What Might Help the Architect in his Work'), but these were left unpublished and are now lost.[18] It is thought that Leonello d'Este

had prompted the writing of *De re aedificatoria* around 1440, and Alberti would probably have dedicated it to him.[19] Following Leonello's death in 1450, however, the work was given to Pope Nicholas V some time between 1452 and 1454, possibly before all ten books were written. This was a time of considerable building activity in Rome which had been prompted by the pope, at great expense.

It was the pilgrimage potential of Rome that Nicholas exploited as a means to fund his ambitious renovation programme for the Vatican and the main monuments of the city. There was also, of course, considerable financial gain to be had from so many visitors to Rome, as Pope Boniface VIII had realised in 1300, when he instituted the first Jubilee: full remission of sins would be granted to penitent Christians, provided they made the pilgrimage to St Peter's and the main Christian churches of Rome.[20] Other Jubilee Years followed, at fairly regular intervals, in 1350, 1375, 1400 and 1423;[21] Nicholas V chose 1450. Pilgrims were required to follow a sacred itinerary, and according to Nicholas's schema, this route was determined less by convenience than by symbolic intent. It began at the basilica of St Peter, progressed outside the city to San Paolo fuori le Mura, back towards the urban centre and Santa Maria Maggiore, and then outwards again to St John Lateran.[22] In Nicholas's urban scheme the Vatican was preferred as the unequivocal spiritual and administrative focus of Rome, and St John Lateran was relegated in status.[23]

There was increasing interest too in Rome's more pagan monuments, and it was Poggio Bracciolini who opened the door to the monumental splendours of Rome for Florentine humanists. He was fascinated by the ancient inscriptions on Rome's monuments and he recorded them in a small sylloge of 1403,[24] and in *De varietate fortunae*, begun after 1431.[25] The monuments were verified and catalogued, and the myths which surrounded their forms were gradually stripped away, like the earth and weeds which covered them. Bracciolini had long been uncovering ancient literature in the Vatican library, and Flavio Biondo applied what would be understood today as a more rigorous archaeological approach to the study of ancient buildings. Biondo completed *Roma instaurata* ('Rome Restored') between 1444 and 1446,[26] as an objective response to the sensational *Mirabilia romae urbis*, which had been a popular guide for tourists in Rome since the twelfth century.[27] Alberti's *Descriptio urbis romae* is thought to have been finished around 1444, and it was a visual complement to Biondo's accurate, written account of the topography of Rome. However, attitudes were slow to change outside the papacy: the

14 Alessandro Strozzi, view of Rome (fifteenth century). Florence, Biblioteca Medicea Laurenziana. MS Laur. Redi 77, CC. VIIv–VIII.

Mirabilia remained popular, and Rome continued to be depicted on maps impressionistically, rather than accurately, well into the latter part of the Quattrocento (fig. 14).[28]

Giovanni Rucellai was one of the many who continued to make extensive use of the *Mirabilia*. He was a Florentine banker of great wealth and influence: he was later to be an important patron for Alberti.[29] During the Jubilee Year of 1450 Giovanni stayed in Rome for four weeks, between 10 February and 8 March. He was persuaded by its accounts of the monuments,[30] and he wrote of one famous ruin, named in the *Mirabilia* as Templum Pacis or the Temple of Peace (but today as the Basilica of Maxentius), with little concern for architectural history: 'The Templum Pacis, which one says was a temple of idols and which, the Romans said, would last until a virgin gave birth, and

it fell in and was ruined on the very night that our saviour Jesus Christ was born'.[31]

What is new about the travel entries in Rucellai's notebook, the *Zibaldone*, is how he edited his notes to reflect the urban hierarchy established in Rome by Nicholas V, in accordance with the categories of buildings that Biondo had made.[32] Rucellai starts with the basilicas and sepulchres (Christian and pagan); then moves to describe ancient Rome, beginning with temples (first the Pantheon – which had been christianised as Santa Maria Rotonda – built by 'a private citizen called Marco Agrippa'), followed by triumphal arches and baths, concluding with the Templum Pacis. Finally, he describes the accommodation of certain cardinals (whose standing he equates with Florentine patricians like himself), whom Biondo had regarded as the 'fathers and spouses' of Rome, the equivalent of

15   Maerten van Heemskerck, *Roman Forum*, *c*.1532. Kupferstichkabinett, Staatliche Museen zu Berlin − Preussischer Kulturbesitz. Römische Skizzenbücher, inv. no. 79D2, 1, fol. *6r*.

ancient senators,[33] and miscellaneous sites and objects, from open spaces to hills and towers (fig. 13). The *Zibaldone* is succinct in its descriptions, and well structured: it is quite unlike the *Mirabilia* with its lively but legendary accounts of the monuments. Whether Alberti had any influence on Rucellai at this time is unknown, though there can be no doubt Alberti was also intent on promoting a sensible, realistic view of Rome, as his *Descriptio urbis romae* indicates.

It is unclear whether Alberti's architectural ideas as they are expressed in *De re aedificatoria* contributed to Nicholas's overall conception of the Vatican, or reflect the policies as they were being implemented: Nicholas's transformation of the Constantinian basilica of St Peter began with a new choir and transept (which was abandoned before it was completed), the fortification of the Vatican walls and extension of the Vatican palace (to enhance the existing accommodation for the convenience and pleasure of his expanding curia); he had also laid plans for a new processional way through an area known as the Borgo, linking St Peter's to the Castel Sant'Angelo.[34] In principle, Alberti shared the belief implicit in the papal scheme that the well-considered

city, through its constituent buildings − which 'drew and kept men together' (Prologue, p. 2) − would enhance the quality of life (IV, 2, p. 95). Alberti describes straight streets lined with porticoes, buildings of equal height, and urban districts of distinctive character, with different craft activities confined to separate streets and districts of the city (IV, 5, pp. 105–7; VII, 1, pp. 189–192; VIII, 6, pp. 261–8). The account by Nicholas's secretary Giannozzo Manetti of the proposed Borgo scheme is similar, and Nicholas went some way towards implementing the strategy he relates: first, by issuing edicts in 1447 to curb the activities of butchers and tanners in residential areas, so that a hierarchy of streets could be formalised in the statues of the 'maestri di strada', dated 1452.[35]

While there is no proof from any contemporary source that Alberti contributed to Nicholas's urban plan, it is significant that he mentions the sorry state of two principal monuments which would be key to its eventual success − Old St Peter's and the Ponte Sant'Angelo, formerly the Bridge of Hadrian. The poor condition of St Peter's is described early in *De re aedificatoria* (I, 10, p. 26), and he later proposes a remedy

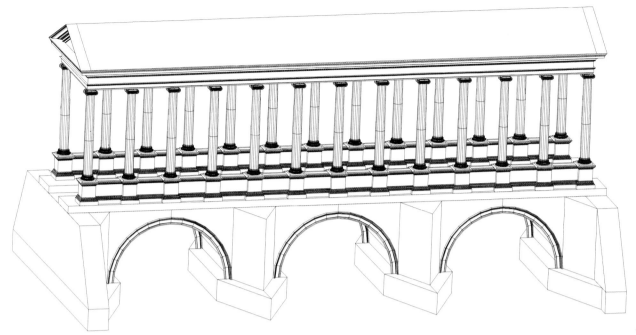

16 Reconstruction of the Bridge of Hadrian, Rome, after a description by Alberti in *De re aedificatoria*, VIII, 6, p. 262. Computer view (Olivetti/Alberti Group).

to straighten a bowing wall, using sailing tackle to provide temporary support to the existing roof beams while straightening the walls and columns beneath (X, 17, pp. 361–2). Alberti may have made a design for the Ponte Sant'Angelo, which linked the 'abitato' of Rome with Castel Sant'Angelo and the Borgo beyond. It had been damaged on 19 December 1450, when a crowd returning from St Peter's panicked in a crush, and its parapets collapsed. Nicholas had the bridge repaired and two chapels erected at its head to commemorate the several hundred fatalities.[36] Vasari states that he owned a drawing by Alberti for Ponte Sant'Angelo (now lost).[37] This was probably Alberti's reconstruction of the original Bridge of Hadrian, which he had described in *De re aedificatoria* (fig. 16):

> Some bridges even have a roof, like that of Hadrian in Rome, the most splendid of all bridges – a memorable work, by heaven: even the sight of what I might call its carcass would fill me with admiration. The beams of its roof were supported by forty-two marble columns; it was covered in bronze, and marvellously decorated (VIII, 6, p. 262).

It is usual for Alberti in *De re aedificatoria* to describe the form, geometry and ornament of individual city buildings and institutions – the temple, basilica, curia, senate house, palace, etc. – but, unlike later urban visionaries, he does not prescribe the ideal city figure with which to contain them.[38] Presumably, this is

because the overall shape of a city is determined by its site and its history, and Alberti was taking a pragmatic line which was justified by his understanding of the changing urban morphology of ancient Rome, its shrinkage during the Middle Ages, and the attempts during his lifetime to reshape it. His advice to his reader in *De re aedificatoria* was therefore sound: that is, follow the ancient example of Plato who, in *The Republic*, argued that the most perfect city in reality could only ever be the closest approximation of an ideal.

> when [Plato was] asked where that magnificent city which he had dreamed up could be found, [he] replied, 'That does not concern us; we are more interested in what type of city should be considered best. Above all others you should prefer that city which most closely resembles this ideal.' We too should project a city by way of example, which the learned may judge commodious in every respect, yet which will none the less conform to the requirements of time and necessity (IV, 2, p. 96).

In his moral and political satire *Momus* (variously dated 1443–54),[39] Alberti confronts the relationship between power, wisdom and creativity – of creation and its mismanagement. Momus is 'The Prince', son of Night or Sleep – a comic and tragic figure.[40] Influenced in its content and style by the dialogues of Lucian and a novel by Apuleius (humorous writers whom Alberti had recommended as an antidote to depression),[41] it was probably written alongside *De re aedificatoria* during the 1440s and early 1450s, and its narrative may relate to the building activities of Nicholas V.

Momus opens with Jupiter's ambitions to create the world, highlighting the miscalculations of his philosopher advisers and certain unpremeditated developments, particularly the delivery by Prometheus of the sacred fire of creation to mankind, which enables mankind to challenge the authority of their creator. Momus is presented by Alberti as a victim of the circumstances that unfurl. A dispute leads him to be banished from heaven to earth, where he lives as a vagabond. In search of approval and reinstatement he plays a mediating role between the opposing forces of heaven and earth, and encourages mankind to build a fabulous theatre with which to appease Jupiter who, by now, is intent on destroying the world so that he can begin it anew. Constructed as a microcosm of the heavens, the theatre contains niches in which the gods are invited to stand and be honoured by men. Jupiter is flattered by the attempt, and impressed by the qualities of the architecture, which leads him to appreciate the creativity of architects on earth, in contrast to the words of philosophers whose advice shaped his own world plan. Momus further forestalls Jupiter's destruction of the world by presenting him with a 'tabella', or book, with which to reorder the world through effective government. Jupiter is persuaded by the text and Momus restored to favour. But his fortune is quickly reversed when, spurred on by envious gods, the philosophers successfully unite against him. Consequently, Jupiter loses interest in the book and deposits it in his vast library, and the intellectual vision of Momus is effectively nullified. Momus suffers a similar fate physically, being cast out, castrated and chained to a rock in the ocean with only his head above water. But mankind retaliates on his behalf: when Jupiter descends to earth with his gods and enters the theatre that they believe was created to honour him, the walls collapse, inflicting great injury. In humiliation, Jupiter returns to the heavens and seeks the sanctuary of his library. There he rediscovers the 'tabella' of Momus, and the political wisdom it contains. Realising his folly, Jupiter promptly releases Momus from his torment and returns him to favour. Eventually, Momus' book was to be his pathway to survival. Through direct experience of creation, and the lessons he learnt about the needs and actions of men, Momus rose above the philosophers whose only contribution had been abstract theorising, removed from reality.

It is tempting to see Momus as an Alberti-like figure, Alberti having been deprived of the wealth of his clan through the circumstances of his birth, but who used his influence to keep his head above water. His 'tabella' might be construed as something like Alberti's *De re aedificatoria*, which describes the nature of building, the process of creation, the role of the patron, the city of the tyrant and good prince, remedies for human error and how to resist through considered building practices the constant threat of natural forces. *Momus* therefore carried a message complementary to Alberti's *De re aedificatoria*: that urban ideals should be tempered by down-to-earth experience, and reasoned advice should be heeded above the untested opinions of 'philosophers'.

It has been suggested that *Momus* presents a devastating image of the papal court under Eugenius IV.[42] But there are also parallels to be drawn between this satirical allegory and the events unfurling in Nicholas V's Vatican, at least, according to the testaments of the Pisan chronicler Matteo Palmieri, and Nicholas's biographer Manetti. Palmieri reported that Alberti presented a version of his architectural treatise to Nicholas at the outset of the pope's building enterprise, and that the pope subsequently abandoned his own plans for reviving the physical fabric of the Vatican:

> The pope, wanting to make the Basilica of the Blessed Peter a greater adornment, laid deep foundations and erected a wall of thirteen *braccia*, but he stopped this great work, which could be compared to that of any of the ancients, by the distinguished advice of Leon Battista, and then an untimely death cut short this enterprise.
>
> Leon Battista Alberti, a scholar endowed with sharp and penetrating intelligence and an excellent education, and well versed in doctrine, presented these learned books on architecture, which he had written, to the pope.[43]

Also, according to Manetti, Nicholas V justified his great building campaign by declaring that magnificent buildings were more effective than the arguments of intellectuals in convincing ordinary people of the natural authority of the church and in confirming their faith.[44] Nicholas's proposals for the Borgo and Vatican may be reconstructed from Manetti's outline description.[45] Principally (and if Manetti's description truly reflects Nicholas's intentions, about which there can be no certainty), it would appear that Nicholas was concerned to formalise the existing public spaces and access routes to St Peter's, to heighten the experience of sacred space on arrival at the basilica, by building on to the existing nave and aisles a new 'tribuna' of transept and choir, surmounted by a dome where they intersect. For the defence of this sacred site, the perimeter walls of Old St Peter's were to be reinforced and were to

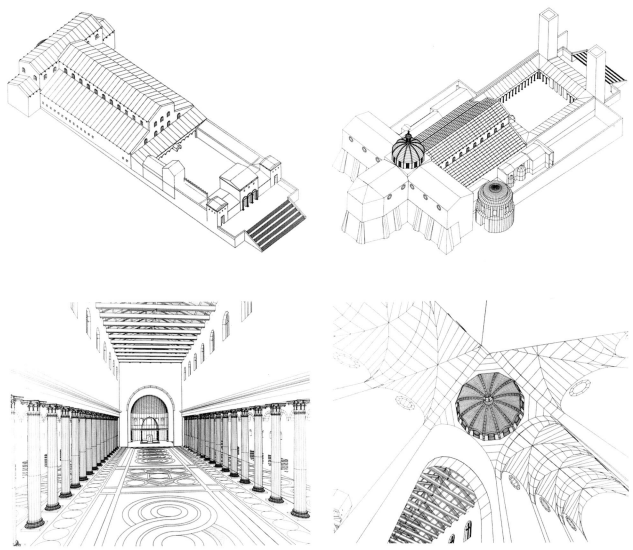

17 After Alfarano (1914), reconstructions of the Constantinian basilica of St Peter. Computer views (Olivetti/ Alberti Group): (a) (*top left*) Constantine's basilica externally; (b) (*bottom left*) Constantine's basilica internally, looking towards the main altar; (c) (*top right*) the new transept and east end according to Manetti's description of Nicholas V's proposals; and (d) view internally, upwards towards the roof beams of the basilica's nave and the proposed groin vaults and dome of the crossing.

become part of a complex of fortifications which would embrace and protect the Borgo and Vatican hill (fig. 17).

Work on the defensive walls as well as on the restoration of Roman monuments was pursued with some energy. From 1450 onwards the Lombard workshop of Beltramo di Martino da Varese was contracted to work on Castel Sant'Angelo, the new tribune and fortifications to St Peter's, as well as restoration work in Rome itself.[46] Beltramo supplied both labour and materials; he had kilns providing bricks for the various sites, and a boat ferrying stone across the Tiber. (His men also served the pope in other ways, providing brute force to foil a republican uprising instigated by Stefano Porcari

and to assist with his capture. Alberti recorded the revolt of 1453 in *De Porcaria coniuratione*, and this included Porcari's oration made several days before the revolt began.[47])

Building progress on the tribune of St Peter's was slow and involved. Venerable antique structures had to be demolished, which included newly discovered tombs below the surface, as well as the apse of Old St Peter's. The foundations had to be dug deep to take the weighty, battered masonry defensive walls of the tribune and the dome they were to carry. When work on the tribune halted in the early 1450s these walls were at least 3 Roman *braccia* above the existing floor of the basilica.[48]

It would have been an extraordinary event in human affairs if, even considering Alberti's very considerable abilities, one man and his book were able to halt a vast and already expensive building programme. Indeed, it probably took something more devastating than a 'tabella' to do this. *Momus* may provide some clues to what happened: when Jupiter visited the theatre on earth built in his honour the structure collapsed, causing injury to the gods and to Jupiter's pride. Similarly, Nicholas suffered a humiliating and injurious disaster when his vision for the Vatican was shattered by the collapse in early September 1454 of the great tower or Torrione. Nicholas's architect Bernardo Rossellino was probably responsible for its faulty design and consequently the death of several men.[49]

In Alberti's satire, Jupiter did not 'rediscover' Momus' architectural 'tabella' until after the disaster. What, then, if the final version of *Momus* was completed after the autumn of 1454, as a reflection on recent events within the Vatican?[50] This would be one way of explaining the impact (according to Palmieri's statement) that *De re aedificatoria* had on Nicholas:[51] Nicholas perhaps turned to Alberti after the collapse of the Torrione, fearing that the work on St Peter's might also fail because of unsound foundations and advice. No matter,

time was not on the side of either man. As Palmieri reflects, the pope died during the spring of 1455, and any ambitions for rebuilding the Vatican went with him.[52]

Nor was Nicholas's immediate successor able to carry Alberti's vision forward. The Borgia pope Calixtus III succeeded Nicholas V aged seventy-eight, and during his three-year reign he addressed more pressing global concerns, namely the imminent threat posed by the Turks, Constantinople having fallen to them in 1453 (during Nicholas's pontificate). Pope Pius II, who succeeded Calixtus in August 1458, had building plans of his own, and while he made some physical changes to the Vatican,[53] he made a more coherent impact after 1459 on his home town Corsignano, near Siena, with buildings and spaces which remain as he left them; on its completion Pius renamed the town Pienza, eponymously (fig. 18). To implement his designs there he used one of the designer-masons that Nicholas V had employed on his abortive Rome project, Bernardo Rossellino.[54] The buildings by Rossellino in Pienza are eclectic and the amalgamation probably followed his patron's whims, the body of the cathedral having been inspired by German Gothic hall churches and the façade by classical Roman examples Pius had seen

18   Pienza. Aerial view of the town detailing Pius II's cathedral and palazzi built around a piazza after 1460. Computer view (Olivetti/Alberti Group).

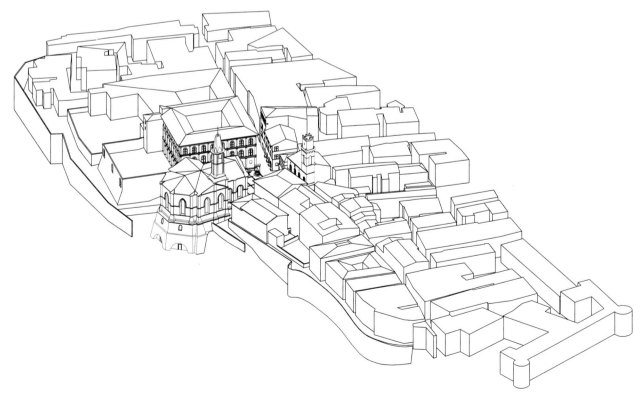

(fig. 75).[55] The Palazzo Comunale (across from the cathedral), incorporates a campanile and Tuscan loggia, and is Trecento in character. The Palazzo Piccolimini, as discussed below, resembles Alberti's design for the exterior of Palazzo Rucellai in Florence (see chapter 7).

The names of Alberti and Rossellino have been linked with building projects in Rome, Florence and Pienza. Rossellino's career is quite well documented, and there is nothing hard and fast with which to prove that they ever collaborated. Rossellino acquired his skills in Florence, where he was well regarded as an excellent sculptor and stonemason, though he was not immune from the occasional blunder during his build-ing career.[56] Giannozzo Manetti thought very highly of Rossellino, crediting him with a far greater involvement in Nicholas's projects than is suggested by the account books of the time – perhaps as a Florentine himself Manetti was being partial. Rather grandly, Manetti compares Nicholas with the biblical Solomon, and Rossellino as the counterpart of Solomon's architect:[57] in practice Nicholas probably conceived of the build-ing projects, while Rossellino designed them and super-vised the builders led by Beltramo di Martino da Varese who executed the works.[58] When creating Pienza, Pius II and Rossellino probably developed a relationship similar to that which Alberti later enjoyed with his various patrons.

19 Reconstruction after Alberti's *De re aedificatoria* of Doric, Ionic and Corinthian columns and entablatures (VII, 7, 8 and 9) (Olivetti/Alberti Group).

III

ARCHITECT AND VISIONARY

THE FIRST KNOWN ARCHITECTURAL PROJECT designed by Alberti was his radical transformation of the exterior of the old church of San Francesco in Rimini into a 'temple', built for Sigismondo Malatesta, the city's ruler. Sigismondo was determined to build on the reputation of Rimini's historic monuments, its ancient Augustan bridge and arch. Perhaps because he was present at the consecration of Florence Cathedral, he sought advice from Brunelleschi for the layout of his castle in Rimini and during the late summer of 1438 Brunelleschi visited the city.[1] However, he entrusted the redesign of San Francesco to Alberti, sometime around 1450 (four years after the death of Brunelleschi), and what became the Tempio Malatestiano was to be the most important building constructed in Rimini since antiquity. Alberti's design for the exterior of the church is composed far more rigorously than the earlier interior work by two sculptors in Sigismondo's employ, Agostino di Duccio and Matteo de' Pasti, who were retained to build Alberti's design (fig. 37).

It was a remarkable first project for Alberti, and the only structure that may have been designed by him before that time was a new apse for San Martino a Gangalandi, at Lastra a Signa (near Florence), the priory church for which he had been granted a benefice in 1432 (fig. 20). The frieze of the apse bears his family's arms, though it could have been designed by him any time between 1432 and the late 1460s, as it is mentioned in his will as still incomplete.[2] It is in any case a tiny work by comparison with the buildings with which he is usually identified. The absence of evidence of his involvement in a major project is one reason why so many unattributed building designs in Rome, and elsewhere, have been credited to him. Of course, he had made 'architectural compositions in the mind', which he referred to in the *Profugiorum ab aerumna*. Still, to have achieved such a mature first building would have required frequent three-dimensional testing of his ideas, perhaps through drawings or even physical models.[3] There is tangential evidence for this since his descriptions of the various Roman building types in Book VIII of *De re aedificatoria* are clearly based on more

than Vitruvius' accounts of ancient buildings. For Vitruvius' descriptions are not always complete, nor were there always surviving remains of the buildings he refers to.[4] It is likely therefore that Alberti reconstructed them, through drawings or models, before describing the buildings in his treatise (fig. 21). Maybe the drawing of the Bridge of Hadrian, which Vasari attributed to Alberti, had also been made for this purpose.[5] It is conceivable then that Alberti also made drawings of St Peter's and the Borgo, either as a pointed counterproposal to the one being followed by Nicholas, or to prove his own worth as an architectural adviser. Perhaps he even considered it worthwhile restoring the existing basilica rather than destroy ancient relics through new building works (as Nicholas was doing), an approach that would have found a sympathetic hearing from some.[6]

If papal support for Alberti as architect was not forthcoming, other patrons certainly sought his advice from the early 1450s onwards: Sigismondo Malatesta of Rimini has been mentioned already; and in Florence Alberti designed a group of buildings for the wealthy banker Giovanni Rucellai – a chapel, a sepulchre and church and palazzo façades. After 1459, Marquis Ludovico Gonzaga (the eldest son of Gianfrancesco) provided Alberti with opportunities to design two churches in Mantua. He also completed for Ludovico the tribune of the church of Santissima Annunziata in Florence (some time after 1453, and definitely by 1470), developing an incomplete design by another architect. His design for a bath building, which was possibly to have been attached to the great palace Federico da Montefeltro was building himself in Urbino, was – as I shall argue later – either only partly completed, or perhaps never begun.

Alberti's role in all these projects, as his broad intellectual commitments suggest, was as a philosopher-architect (like his fictional anti-hero Momus, perhaps), for once he had designed the building he did not supervise its construction full-time. This role was performed by an architect on site: possibly Rossellino and Antonio Manetti in Florence, and Luciano Laurana

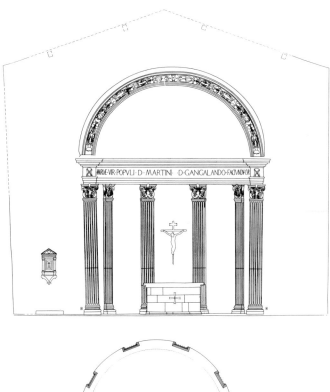

20   Leon Battista Alberti, the apse of San Martino a Gangalandi: (a) (*above left*) view of the apse internally (photo/author); (b) (*left*) detail of capital and frieze (photo/Prue Chiles); (c) (*above*) elevation and plan (drawing Olivetti/Alberti Group); (d) (*below*) view of the apse externally (photo/author).

21 Reconstructions after Alberti's *De re aedificatoria*
(Olivetti/Alberti Group): (a) triumphal arch (VIII, 6); (b)
Alberti's Corinthian and composite (Italic) capitals, Alberti
(1550); (c) watch-tower (VIII, 5) (Olivetti/Alberti Group).

in Urbino; and certainly Matteo de' Pasti in Rimini and
Luca Fancelli in Mantua. The evidence for Alberti's
building projects in Rimini and Mantua suggests that
his patrons and men on site relied heavily on his
advice throughout the various stages of construction; it
also suggests that he was treated as the essential creative
force – the architectural visionary – who could turn a
potentially commonplace building into something
exceptional.

It is unlikely that he was ever commissioned to
produce a design in return for a fee, though he sought
the good favour of men of power, and accepted
payment in kind through board and lodging, alongside
other eminent scholars who were attached to or visited
their courts.[7] Clearly, his long association with the
church provided him with independence and the
means with which to think and write. Not that he was
immune from the vagaries of those in power, and his
final years in particular were marred by the disbanding
of the College of Abbreviators by Pope Paul II on his
accession in 1464: an institution to which Alberti had
belonged for most of his adult life.[8] This papal action
signalled for Alberti the closing of an era in which he
had enjoyed the unconditional support of the church
and had flourished. Paul was concerned primarily to
regain control over the appointment of staff in the papal
chancery, which required breaking the local power base
of the humanists. Some of them fought an intellectual
battle with him over the next four years, forming a
provocative Academy in Rome which propagated an
extreme devotion to pagan ceremonies and the acquiring of names. It is not clear whether Alberti was a
member of this Academy in which Giulio Pomponio
(known as Leto) and Bartolomeo Sacchi (Platina) were
prominent. Paul suppressed the Academy in 1468 on
the grounds of irreligion and republicanism, and Leto
and Platina were imprisoned.[9] Alberti wrote his last
work at this time, De Iciarchia ('The Prince', 1468),
which is concerned with the role of the head of the
household, and derives from Lucian's Dialogue of the
Gods and Dialogues of the Dead.[10]

The enigmatic Hypnerotomachia Poliphili ('Poliphilo's
Dream of Love's Struggle') was also completed in
manuscript form around this time. It is a love story
relayed as the dream of Poliphilo and his search for
Polia, a journey set in a landscape of forests and fantastic monuments. It was written by 1467 (in Treviso
according to the book), but not published for another
thirty-two years.[11] Its author is keen on concealing his
identity and does not declare himself straightforwardly
next to the title, though his name has been deciphered
from the initial letter of each of the thirty-nine chapters of which the book is composed. The acrostic, in

Latin, reads POLIAM FRATER FRANCESCUS COLUMNI A
PERAMAVIT: 'Brother Francesco Colonna loved Polia
immensely'.[12] Of course, this does not necessarily mean
that Francesco Colonna was the author, though this is
a standard interpretation, and it might alternatively be
read as a dedication to Francesco Colonna by the
anonymous author. Even if the name of Francesco
Colonna is taken to be that of the author, however, the
question remains unresolved as there are two candidates
for this name: one was a rather dissolute Dominican
friar, who lived between 1433 and 1527, mainly in
Venice;[13] the other was altogether more respectable,
his uncle being Cardinal Prospero Colonna, Alberti's
supporter in Rome.[14] The latter Francesco Colonna
(1453–1538) would have been aged only twenty-four
when the Hypnerotomachia was supposedly completed,
but he is known to have been regarded as a connois-
seur of classical antiquity even at the age of twenty.[15]
But why should he be referred to as 'Brother Francesco'
in the acrostic (a title more fitting to the Dominican
friar, unless the author was related to Francesco
Colonna),[16] and why should the publisher – the very
famous Aldus Manutius of Venice – have lavished his
own fortune (which he did not recoup) on publishing
a work by an unknown author? Neither Francesco had
produced books before, nor did they do so after.

Because Alberti was a prolific author who did not
always choose to identify himself, and because the two
main subjects of the Hypnerotomachia, love and architecture, are themes that Alberti was fond of writing about,
he has been linked with the book. Indeed, the author is
an expert on ancient architecture and is clearly familiar
with De re aedificatoria: besides Poliphilo's amorous
adventures, there are many lengthy descriptions of
fantasy buildings all'antica in the Hypnerotomachia;
Poliphilo describes edifices unlike any then in existence,
some of them monumental in scale; he is also creative
as an engineer, analysing how water devices work and
artefacts built. The descriptions make sophisticated use
of various languages, Greek, Roman and Tuscan – even
Hebrew.[17] It is perhaps not surprising, therefore, that
painstaking scholarly research suggests that there are
close philological associations between Alberti's writings
and the Hypnerotomachia. It has been proposed by
Emanuela Kretzulesco-Quaranta that either Alberti was
the model for Poliphilo, as he was a friend of the
Colonna family; or, more tentatively, that Alberti was
himself its author,[18] an argument that has been pursued
with considerable vigour by Liane Lefaivre.[19] Lefaivre
even proposes that Alberti designed the numerous illustrations, which were later translated into woodcuts for
the book's first publication in 1499 (fig. 22). The graphic
exposure of male and female genitalia (which is

22 Woodcut. *Hypnerotomachia Poliphili*, Venice, 1545.

commonplace in this book, along with scenes of seduction) was not something Alberti condoned. Describing the appropriate subject-matter of paintings in *De pictura*, he wrote: 'let us always observe decency and modesty. The obscene parts of the body [. . .] should be covered with clothing or leaves or the hand'.[20] In this spirit, a copy of the *Hypnerotomachia* in the Vatican library was appropriately modified.[21] Of course, the erotic illustrations may explain why the author was reluctant to be identified, particularly in the climate of restraint on humanist excess imposed by Pope Paul II. The notion that Alberti was its author is tantalising, but, on the evidence so far, remains unproven, as there are strong arguments for and against.[22]

Certainly, as Alberti had spent much of his adult life in Rome, and was an expert in ancient architecture, he was consulted *in situ* for his knowledge. In early autumn 1471 he guided Lorenzo de' Medici (the dedicatee of his treatise on oratory, *Trivia senatoria*, *c*.1460) around Rome's antiquities. Lorenzo was leading a party of Florentine noblemen – including Bernardo Rucellai, his brother-in-law (and son of Giovanni), who were there to pay their respects to the newly elected Pope Sixtus IV and to explore the ruins with Alberti. Bernardo was inspired enough by what he saw to write *De urbe roma*, a book promoting Rome as an urban ideal; it includes references to *De re aedificatoria* and *Descriptio urbis romae* as well as a reminiscence of a trip with Alberti to the Antonine Baths, where the party read Latin inscriptions together amid the ruins.[23]

Alberti died in Rome the following spring, on (or around) 25 April, just before the foundation stone was laid of his largest and most impressive building, the church of Sant'Andrea in Mantua.[24] His writings and buildings are his monuments and have rightly provided him with the glory he sought throughout his life.

Oh! How sweet is the glory that we gain through our efforts. What worthy efforts are ours, through which we may show to those who are not yet alive, that we lived with other values than those of our times, and we have left something of our mind and name besides a mere funeral stone, inscribed and positioned! As the poet Ennius said: do not cry for me, do not hold funeral rites for me, for I live in the words of learned men.[25]

23 Matteo de' Pasti, obverse of the medal in fig. 25.
Larger than actual size.

IV

SELF-PORTRAITURE AND
ALBERTI'S EYE FOR THE FUTURE

THE KNOWN FACTS OF Alberti's early life come from a miscellany of statements and reports of his own and of those who knew and admired him. Most perplexing of these is the *Vita di Leon Battista Alberti*, otherwise known as the *Vita anonima*, which records the main experiences and achievements of Alberti into his early thirties.[1] Although it does not read like an autobiography, Alberti may have disguised his writing style as he had successfully fooled his readers before, claiming that *Philodoxeos* had been written by the Roman Lepidus. Who else would have laboured over a biography of a promising young man and then left it unsigned? Especially, since – while his treatise on painting is mentioned in it – Alberti had not yet begun the other works for which he would be remembered. Indeed, the evidence of considerable philological and textual scrutiny suggests that Alberti probably was its author. He wrote in a similar vein in his hagiographic *Vita Sancti Potiti* (1433), an account probably prompted by his mentor in Rome, Bishop Biagio Molin (to whom it is dedicated), who had encouraged Alberti to undertake writing a series of saints' lives.[2] He was evidently empathetic to the idea:

> I wanted the early life of Potitus to be the first subject on which I could test my abilities. His youth was marked by a singular perseverance and by a multitude of miracles. Whoever makes the effort to study this youth will find much material for discussion and much application to his own life.[3]

Despite Molin's suggestion, Alberti wrote no other saint's life, but within six years he had written his autobiography.[4] It is an extraordinary example of 'anonymous' self-aggrandisement.

Alberti left other kinds of memorial. According to the *Vita anonima* he would either paint or make wax portraits of his friends, and 'He did his own head and portrait, so that from a painted and modelled likeness he should be more readily known to visitors who had not met him'.[5] One of his closest friends, Cristoforo

Landino, knew of 'excellent works done by him of painting, sculpture, engraving and casting',[6] and Alberti made a fundamental contribution to the development of medal portraiture with a bronze self-portrait plaque (fig. 24). Based on his youthful appearance, it is generally thought that this was made around 1435, a date that suggests that his influence on Antonio Pisano, called Pisanello, who has been credited as the originator of the Renaissance medal, has been underrated. Pisanello was a prolific and gifted exponent of this art, which was inspired by antique coins, but his principal portrait-medals, which include those of the Malatesta and Gonzaga, were created after 1438, and so probably post-date Alberti's self-portrait plaque.[7]

There are, in fact, two self-portraits on bronze oval plaques which depict Alberti when aged about thirty.[8] There is also a later portrait of Alberti on a medal dated around 1450,[9] by Matteo de' Pasti, a sculptor and mason who supervised the transformation of San Francesco at Rimini into the Tempio Malatestiano according to a design by Alberti (fig. 25). It is thought he made the medal to commemorate Alberti's role in the project.[10]

The self-portrait plaque and Matteo's portrait-medal of Alberti bear the same device (known as an *impresa*) – the so-called 'flying eye'; an open eye borne by a pair of feathered wings, accompanied by the Latin motto QUID TUM: this translates as either 'What then!' or 'What next?' (fig. 26). It was a phrase used in oratory by Cicero, in exclamation or for effect, as a pause to reclaim the attention of his listeners.[11] Matteo's version of this device has a laurel wreath enclosing the composition, and the combination of 'flying eye', laurel wreath and motto was also penned – perhaps by Alberti himself – on one manuscript version of *Della famiglia*, dated 1438 (fig. 27).[12] It is therefore assumed, quite reasonably, that this was Alberti's personal device, the precise meaning of which is something of a riddle.

Another version of it appears in his *Anuli* ('Little Rings', 1421–39), where twelve gold rings are described, one depicting a winged eye in a crown. In

24   Leon Battista Alberti, *Self-portrait*. Bronze cast oval plaque, uniface, *c.*1435, 201 × 135mm. Washington, D.C., National Gallery of Art, Samuel H. Kress Collection, no. 1957.14.125.

25   Matteo de' Pasti, *Leon Battista Alberti*. Bronze medal, *c.*1450, 93mm diam. London, Victoria and Albert Museum. Inscription: LEOBAPTISTA ALBERTUS.

26   Matteo de' Pasti, obverse of the medal in fig. 25, with the *impresa* of the 'flying eye', the motto QUID TUM, and the inscription MATTHAEI PASTII VERONENSIS OPUS.

the context of the narrative, the rings link the divine with the mortal – as Jarzombek has expressed it: 'that which is guided by the spirit of God with that which is necessary for proper implementation of God's will on earth'.[13] Alberti later refers to the eye in *De re aedificatoria*, in a chapter on inscriptions: 'The Egyptians employed the following sign language: a god was represented by an eye, Nature by a vulture' (VIII, 4, p. 256). He concludes this passage by citing the advantages of Egyptian emblems over alphabets: 'the method of writing they used could be understood easily by expert men all over the world, to whom alone noble matters should be communicated'.[14] At the corners of the 'flying eye' on the medal and plaque are curvilinear extensions. These have been interpreted as Jupiter's thunderbolts, suggesting that the eye is not only all-seeing but is incisive too.[15] More straightforwardly, when the 'flying eye' is coupled with the motto QUID TUM, it would suggest that everything can be grasped

by the applied intellect, that there is nothing that endeavour cannot accomplish.[16]

Matteo de' Pasti encircles the portrait of Alberti with the formula LEOBAPTISTA ALBERTUS on one version of the medal, LEOBAPTISTA ALBER on another.[17] On the

27 ?Leon Battista Alberti, the flying eye enclosed by a wreath with the inscription QUID TUM. Ink sketch on a manuscript of *Della famiglia* (*c.*1438). Florence, Biblioteca Nazionale Centrale, MS II.IV.38, *c.*119*v*.

the cryptic motto on his self-portrait plaque remains elusive. They may have been adopted by Alberti as a constant reminder of God, the all-seeing eye, while the lion's eye – so it was believed – retained the creature's majesty after its body was dead: a power likened by philosophers and poets to the longevity of the name of a famous and virtuous man after death.[21] Certainly, Alberti believed that man had to earn his place in heaven and that admission among the greats was guaranteed only by displaying excellence on earth. He articulated this in his *Apologi centum* ('One Hundred Justifications', *c.*1437–8), written for a Bolognese friend, Francesco Marescalchi. In his apologia of the Lion, he writes how,

> Burning with desire for a like glory, he set himself the most arduous tasks so as to excel among lions. 'Why drive yourself like this?' asked Envy. 'The

28 Anon., *Leon Battista Alberti*. Pen and ink on paper, 300 × 200 mm. Rome, Biblioteca Nazionale Centrale, 'Vittorio Emanuele', V.E.738, cc. II + 75 + II.

self-portrait plaque Alberti abbreviates this to L.BAP, and places the flying-eye emblem under the chin of his profile, and versions of this device are also used, in miniature, as kinds of punctuation mark to the lettering: with an open eye at either end of the lettering, and what look like spread wings and an eye between the L and BAP. His self-portrait plaques are probably the earliest surviving works to bear the name Leo, though Alberti did not use it in his signature, and he concludes letters with the form 'Baptista de Albertis'.[18] It would appear that he used his acquired name only to mark personal items, like the medals, and it was a nickname, a form of address adopted only by his friends and close associates such as Angelo Poliziano.[19] Since the late nineteenth century, however, it has become customary to use all three names together when referring to him, and the spelling has been regularised in modern Italian to 'Leon Battista Alberti', with only occasional deviations.[20]

The particular significance to Alberti of the combination of Leon (*Leone*, Leo or lion), the personal device of 'flying eye' (with or without the laurel wreath), and place in heaven which the other lion won has already been awarded.'

'It is enough, then,' Leon replied, 'simply to be worthy of it'.[22]

To achieve his goals Alberti combined insight with strength, both physical and intellectual. Thus, according to his *Vita*:

He used to play ball-games and archery, and he ran, wrestled, and danced. Above all, he practised mountaineering, but more to strengthen his body than for relaxation or pleasure. He distinguished himself in military exercises when still a boy, and could jump the height of a man from a standing position; no one could beat him at high-jumping.

As for his mental determination: 'There was nothing too mean or too difficult he did not desire to master. [. . .] He was never idle or lazy, and once he started something he always went through with it'.[23] His personal drive was tempered by a real concern not to displace or upstage others. This is clear from his later architectural treatise, when he spoke of the virtues he expected of an architect, and any man:

I expect no more humanity, good nature, modesty, honesty, than in any other person [. . .] for anyone who lacks these qualities, in my opinion, does not deserve to be called a man. But above all he must avoid any frivolity, obstinacy, ostentation, or presumption, and anything that might lose him goodwill or provoke enmity among his fellow citizens (IX, 10, p. 315).

The accuracy of Alberti's literary self-portrait in the *Vita anonima*, and its emphasis on strength of character, great will and intellect, is similarly reflected in his other writings. He introduced the subject of painted portraiture in *De pictura*:

Painting possesses a truly divine power in that not only does it make the absent present (as they say of friendship), but it also represents the dead to the living many centuries later, so that they are recognised by spectators with pleasure and deep admiration for the artist.[24]

Concerned with the technique and subject-matter of paintings, Alberti stresses the appropriateness of depicting historical themes and subjects in painted compositions, which he called *historiae*.[25] A *historia* may be a scene from literature, legend or history, and he thought the choice of subject, its organisation and its execution the most important consideration of the

artist. His influence was such that this format was to become the highest category of painting for five hundred years. Within *historiae* there should be variety and abundance, and scenes populated with human figures in contrasting attitudes. They should also contain the portraits of eminent men, past and present, for 'the face that is known draws the eyes of all spectators, so great is the power and attraction of something taken from Nature'.[26] Alberti goes on to urge painters to imitate the likeness of others from objects in relief rather than from paintings, 'for from painted objects we train our hand only to make a likeness, whereas from sculptures we learn to represent both likeness and correct incidence of light'.[27]

Self-portraiture was a valid memorial that might bring practical benefits too. According to the *Vita*, Alberti had made such a self-portrait so that 'he should be more readily known to visitors who had not met him'.[28] It was important for future patronage that paintings were favourable interpretations of the likeness of the sitter to reflect well on the painter and the person painted. The Rucellai family owned paintings by Alberti, including a self-portrait. These still existed in the sixteenth century and were seen by Vasari, who states that a grandson of Giovanni Rucellai (for whom Alberti designed several buildings in Florence) owned a 'self-portrait [of Alberti], done with the aid of a mirror, and a panel with large figures in chiaroscuro'.[29] While these are now lost, Alberti's self-portrait plaque is presumably a reasonably accurate likeness. His parents were apparently good-looking: his father was handsome and his mother 'bella', according to one report.[30] Il Panormita referred to Alberti as 'very handsome',[31] and there is a lean virility about the self-portrait plaque which would support this compliment. Alberti had proposed that his portrait be painted by artists indebted to his treatise on painting, and he concluded Book III of *De pictura* with the following suggestion:

This is all I have to say about painting in these books. If it is such as to be of some use and convenience to painters, I would especially ask them as a reward for my labours to paint my portrait in their 'historiae', and thereby proclaim to posterity that I was a student of this art and that they are mindful of and grateful for this favour.[32]

Attention was drawn to this passage in the English translation of *De pictura* published in 1972, and since then several paintings (and a carved stylised building capital) have been identified as portraits of Alberti.[33] As none of these carries his name, and his portrait-medals are the main source for comparison (which reveal only his profile and, because of the medium, lack tone and

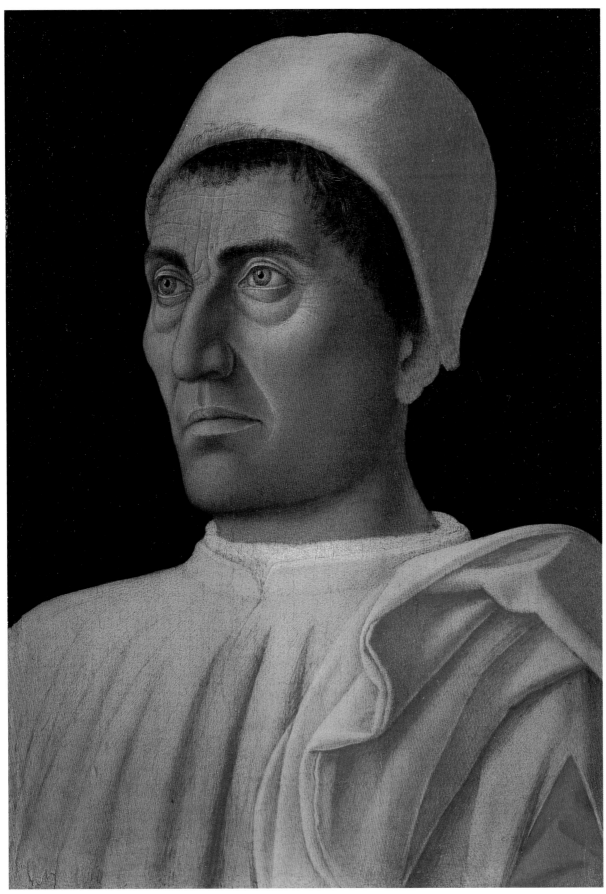

29 Andrea Mantegna, *Portrait of a Man – ?Leon Battista Alberti* (*c.*1470–75). Tempera on wood, 413 × 295 mm; painted surface, 402 × 286 mm. Florence, Galleria degli Uffizi, inv. no. 8540.

colour), there will always be doubts about whom these heads represent.

Only one of these suspected portraits bears Alberti's name directly. In this depiction his body is drawn full-length, in pen and ink, along with his name written as MESS.B.ALBERTS (fig. 28). It has been proposed that this is a self-portrait, but the formality of the title 'Messer' would suggest otherwise: L.BAP was enough for his self-portrait medal.[34] The rather crudely drawn Alberti figure is to be seen wearing a long gown, or cassock, over a sleeved undergarment with (what appears to be) a buttoned, collarless shirt underneath, similar to the garment he is modelled as wearing in the Matteo de' Pasti medal. He may or may not be wearing a skullcap as the lines are ambiguous (though he is clearly holding a book in his left hand, while pointing sideways, for reasons unknown, with the right). The face, in three-quarter view, is not unlike the profile head recorded on the medal by Matteo de' Pasti, though the drawing is too imprecise and stylised (the body and hands are drawn over-long) to be able to offer more than a passing likeness.[35]

Paintings by Masaccio, Paolo Uccello and Francesco del Cossa are among those that may include portraits of Alberti,[36] though, inevitably, there are problems with such attributions.[37] There is also a painting attributed to Andrea Mantegna in the Uffizi, Florence, that exhibits several of the facial characteristics of Alberti's self-portrait plaque (fig. 29); although since 1912 it has been identified as a portrait of Carlo de' Medici, this has been questioned.[38]

There are several superficial reasons for suggesting that Mantegna's painting is a likeness of Alberti: the physical characteristics of the painted head closely resemble those of his self-portrait plaque (as I have suggested in some detail elsewhere[39]). Mantegna was court artist to the Gonzaga in Mantua, and it is conceivable, though there is no proof, that Ludovico Gonzaga ordered this painting from Mantegna to commemorate his association with Alberti, who built two buildings for Ludovico in Mantua, and completed another for him in Florence.[40] If the portrait by Mantegna was painted around 1470, Alberti would have been in his mid-sixties and about to design Sant'Andrea in Mantua and complete the tribune of Santissima Annunziata in Florence. Or perhaps it was painted posthumously, after 1472, for it should be remembered that Mantegna made use of busts and medals in his portraits (as Pisanello had done before him), and his paintings were not necessarily made from life. Were this painting not attributed with some certitude to Mantegna, the curious combination of genius and amateurishness in its execution may be used to suggest the hand of Alberti himself in its making.[41] However, as Alberti's treatise on painting provided the intellectual foundation of Mantegna's art, so Alberti's practice may have exerted an influence over the younger man. Consequently, if this portrait is not by Alberti, it may be a version by Mantegna after one of Alberti's self-portraits, either one of the surviving plaques or a now lost painting. After all, none other than Paul Kristeller at first omitted this portrait from his early and authoritative monograph on Mantegna and, in a subsequent translation, included it only as a copy of a lost work by Mantegna.[42]

While doubts will remain about the identity of this portrait, the persona of the man depicted shines through the uncertainty with some strength. The lean, tanned face and the clear blue eyes, fixed with determination on some distant concern, would certainly constitute a suitable icon for the qualities of manly virtue that Leon Battista Alberti promoted in his writings and called for in the art of portraiture.

ON THE ART OF BUILDING

V

BEAUTY IN ART AND BUILDING

IN SEARCH OF BEAUTY

ALBERTI DEVELOPED SPECIFIC MEASURING devices for painters and sculptors so that they could define figures with precision. By carefully measuring the best examples nature and mankind have wrought, the artist creates – in paintings and sculptures – figures and objects that appear natural, yet may actually improve on nature's accomplishments. The aim is to strive towards perfection: to excel in art is to create something beautiful, and Alberti wrote the treatises *De pictura* and *De statua* to explain how beauty can be achieved. To this end he codified for painters the rules of perspective, and devised the veil; for sculptors he emphasised the need to reveal the precise proportions of the subject, using certain measuring tools.

Alberti also defined key terms to translate the idea of beauty into something tangible: so that it is visible to the artist, and ultimately to those who will judge the beauty of his endeavour. He described three main concepts in *De pictura*: *circumscriptio*, *compositio* and *receptio luminum*. The first of these, *circumscriptio*, concerns the definition of each object through finely delineated outlines; *compositio* relates the parts of the painting to the whole *historia*, while *receptio luminum* concerns the application of tone and hue to the outlines that have been delineated. In *De statua* there are two main terms for the sculptor to master, *dimensio* and *finitio*. As I have mentioned already (p. 7, and fig. 5), to achieve perfect *dimensio* the ideal 'dimensions' of a figure are revealed using the devices of the *exempeda* (to determine lengths between points) and *normae* (widths or breadths); these are translated to the sculpture being made using the *finitorium*: this comprises a horizon with a rotating radius at its centre and a perpendicular, or plumb-line hanging from its outer tip.

The *finitorium* locates parts to the whole in three dimensions, and the different parts of the body relative to the *finitorium* are measured with the *exempeda*. The *exempeda* is a rod made up of six *pedes* ('feet'). Its length is always equivalent to the height of the body being measured.[1] As the *exempeda* is a relative measure it records the relationship between the parts of the body as proportions, making possible a direct comparison of bodies of varying heights; such that one 'foot' (*pes*) is one-sixth of the height being measured. Alberti lists the ideal proportions of the male body for the sculptor to emulate in the *Tabulae dimensionorum hominis*. These led him to his definition for bodily beauty in *De statua*, which he called 'similitude'. Similitude is a harmonious combination of human proportions which characterise a body, and which differentiate it from any other.[2] Only by measuring a body can similitude be revealed and subsequently imitated.

BODILY REPRESENTATIONS IN ART AND ARCHITECTURE

One of the most extraordinary paintings to display the new demand for natural realism through the precision of perspectival composition is the fresco of the *Trinity* in Santa Maria Novella, Florence (fig. 30), painted in 1425–6 by Masaccio,[3] whose authority as an artist Alberti mentioned in *De pictura*.[4] The group of figures comprises Christ on the cross, held by the Father, with the Virgin and St John standing on either side of the cross contained by a painted coffered vault. The painting extends to the frame, which depicts an arch supported on Ionic columns, and flanked by Corinthian fluted pilasters carrying an entablature. The donors are shown kneeling almost on the viewers' side of the picture plane. The architectural elements are convincing in their detail and resemble built compositions by Brunelleschi and his followers. Later, they reappear in Alberti's architectural work, with certain refinements.[5]

Masaccio's representation of Christ resembles the form of Brunelleschi's sculpture in wood of *Christ Crucified* (*c.*1410–15), also in Santa Maria Novella (fig. 31). Both depict Christ naturalistically, and Ragghianti's study of the figure by Brunelleschi reveals its geometrical and dimensional properties as *Homo quadratum*;[6] as such, it is probably derived from Vitruvius' account of the perfect proportions of the

Masaccio, *Trinity*. Fresco, 1425–6. Florence, Santa Maria Novella (photo/Scala).

31 Brunelleschi, *Christ Crucified*. Wood and painted sculpture, early fifteenth century. Florence, Santa Maria Novella (photo/author).

mental to architectural design and practice *all'antica*. These three numbers were regarded as 'perfect' due to the discoveries of ancient philosophers and mathematicians. Vitruvius believed that these same numbers have inherent qualities and characteristics in the context of bodily proportion. Consequently, he emphasised the connection between perfect number, measure, body and architecture: 6 is perfect as it is the sum of its factors (1 + 2 + 3) and because the foot is one-sixth of a man's height; 10 is perfect because of the ten 'digits', five of which make a palm and four palms make a foot, and is the sum of the first four numbers, 1 + 2 + 3 + 4; the numbers 6 and 10 combine to make what Vitruvius considered the 'most perfect' number of all, 16 (it is also the square of the first square: thus 2 × 2 = 4; 4 × 4 = 16). Architects in antiquity used these perfect numbers to structure the measuring standards in the design of buildings, so that perfection in the human body was mirrored in the symmetry of perfect architectural expressions, especially that of the sacred temple.[9]

BODY MEASURES FOR BUILDINGS

That Brunelleschi had apparently been making a link in his *Christ Crucified* between such ancient notions of human perfection and the sacred body of Christ is obviously of some consequence. The link between the perfect body and architecture was explored further by Alberti, who was determined, as ever, to test received wisdom to his own satisfaction. Apart from Vitruvius' writings and Brunelleschi's example, he knew of the traditional concern to comprehend perfect bodily proportions. For example, St Augustine, an early doctor of the church, had observed in his *City of God* that 'there is a harmonious congruence' between the parts of the body, 'a beauty in their quality and correspondence' which 'would be more apparent to us if we were aware of the precise proportions in which the components are combined and fitted together'.[10] In the *Tabulae dimensionum hominis* Alberti recorded for posterity a list of valued numbers in relation to bodily perfection. He found measure to be the key, and to summarise the ideal human proportions in the *Tabulae* he states that he proceeded 'to measure and record in writing, not simply the beauty found in this or that body, but, as far as possible, that perfect beauty distributed by Nature, as it were in fixed proportions, among many bodies'.[11]

ideal man. A square drawn around Brunelleschi's sculpture of Christ has sides of 3 Florentine *braccia* in length, while Vitruvius' ideal man is contained within a square of 6 feet: 3 Florentine *braccia* (1.75 m.) closely approximate to 6 antique *pedes* (1.78 m.), and may have been regarded by Brunelleschi and his contemporaries as equivalent to the ancient measure.[7]

Vitruvius was Alberti's main witness of ancient architectural theory and practice. He had defined the laws of symmetry and proportion in temple architecture through the physical characteristics and qualities of the human body, opening Book III of *De architectura* with a list of numbers that comprise the 'symmetrical proportions' of the ideal body.[8] These he combined with the pure geometry of square and circle to generate the image of geometrical and corporeal unity now inseparable from Leonardo da Vinci's famous drawing of a man with outstretched limbs located within a square and circle. From the square and circle all other shapes can be generated, and embodied in the ideal human figure are the numbers 6, 10 and 16, which are funda-

The measures with which Alberti chose to measure the human body were divided decimally: each 'foot' of his *exempeda* was subdivided into 10 inches and 100 minutes. The decimal system avoided awkward fractions when recording small dimensions, something that Alberti had perhaps borrowed from contemporary astronomers, whose tables were also divided decimally. Also, *De pictura* was written while Alberti was living in Florence, and decimal divisions of the *exempeda* worked well with the Florentine measuring standard, the *braccio da panna*, used by artists and builders. As Alberti suggests in *De pictura*, a man's height equates well with 3 Florentine *braccia*, and each *braccio* subdivides into 20 *soldi*.[12] Consequently, the *exempeda* of 6 feet and 3 *braccia* are equivalent to 60 'inches' and 60 *soldi*, respectively.[13]

Compared with measuring the variety found in human bodies, surveying ancient buildings was perhaps less demanding. What Alberti needed – to be able to 'collate material from sources so varied, heterogeneous, and dispersed' and then later 'arrange in a proper order, to articulate precisely and explain rationally' – was the same standard to survey the buildings of antiquity as had been used to design them (VI, 1, p. 155). They were designed, as Vitruvius had already explained, with measures derived from 'the members of the body [. . .] the finger, palm, foot and cubit'.[14] Alberti knew this, and his descriptions of ancient buildings in *De re aedificatoria*, after Pliny, Varro and others, do without the need to invent any helpful interpretative device, as he had done for his earlier treatises on painting and sculpture. As ancient buildings had been described as related to the idealised dimensions of human form, it was therefore a simple matter of refining a set of bodily measures by comparing them with the physical dimensions of the buildings he had surveyed – a task made easier because the ancients usually employed whole number multiples of the palm, foot, etc., when setting out their buildings.[15] For example, Vitruvius had described his design for the basilica at Fano in some detail, and its dimensions are dominated by the 'perfect' numbers 6 and 10, or their subdivisions, recorded in 'feet'.[16]

Alberti would have encountered some variation in the standards used in antiquity, and there is still no definitive length for the Roman foot or *pes*: its length was established during the seventeenth century as the equivalent of between 292 and 297 mm, the most widely accepted length being 295.7 mm; slightly shorter than the Roman *piede* in use during the fifteenth century in Rome, which was about 298 mm long.[17] At the lower end of this range, at 292 mm, the *pes* is half the length of the Florentine *braccio*; Florentines remarked on this, perhaps to assert their cultural inheritance as a former colony of Rome.[18]

Equating different measures in this way was part of everyday experience at the time. There was a constant need to translate standards to overcome exchange dif-

ferences in weights and measures between Italian city states, and proportion was a commonplace concept in commercial life.[19] Proportional formulae involving the 'mean and two extremes', which went under the names of the 'Merchant's Key', or 'Rule of Three', were taught as part of the basic curriculum of the *scuola dell'abbaco* during the fourteenth and fifteenth centuries.[20] Indeed, it would appear that there existed a relationship between the newer European measures as they had developed from the universal standards of antiquity through proportional increments, and they often related 'naturally' to those of other European cities as well as the ancient foot or cubit.[21] The perceived relationship between the *pes* and half of the Florentine *braccio* is just one example within the 'family' of measures which existed before European metrication.[22] Once Alberti was confident of the approximate size of the *pes*, he could adjust its length according to the monument he was surveying, much as the *exempeda* he described in *De statua* was to be adjusted to the size of the body being examined. In his search for the natural laws that define beauty in architecture, there can be little doubt that Alberti measured Roman ruins with the same zeal that characterises his work on bodily proportion in the *Tabulae dimensionorum hominis*. Consequently, he is insistent in *De re aedificatoria* that he had examined carefully any 'building of the ancients that had attracted praise, wherever it might be', and he 'never stopped exploring, considering, and measuring everything, and comparing the information through line drawings' (VI, 1, p. 155).

ARCHITECTURE AND THE BODY ANALOGY

Using this resource of information about the ancient practice of architecture, the architect was to select what would be appropriate for a new design in a specific situation. This, Alberti believed, requires an uncommon individual, one who is capable of balancing the complex intellectual demands of what is necessary and useful with the desire and ability to strive for physical perfection in a building:

> A great matter is architecture, nor can everyone undertake it. [. . .] The greatest glory in the art of building is to have a good sense of what is appropriate. For to build is a matter of necessity; to build conveniently is the product of both necessity and utility; but to build something praised by the magnificent, yet not rejected by the frugal, is the province only of an artist of experience, wisdom, and thorough deliberation (IX, 10, p. 315).

Alberti placed particular emphasis on the need to define the various main building types, and how they may be formed to be considered beautiful. This is clear from the Prologue of *De re aedificatoria*, in which he first sets out the structure he adopted for the treatise:

> first we observed that the building is a form of body, which like any other consists of lineaments and matter, the one the product of thought, the other of Nature; the one requiring the mind and the power of reason, the other dependent on preparation and selection; but we realised that neither on its own would suffice without the hand of the skilled workman to fashion the material according to lineaments. Since buildings are set to different uses, it proved necessary to inquire whether the same type of lineaments could be used for several; we therefore distinguished the various types of buildings and noted the importance of the connection of their lines and their relationship to each other, as the principal sources of beauty; we began therefore to inquire further into the nature of beauty – of what kind it should be, and what is appropriate in each case. As in all these matters faults are occasionally found, we investigated how to amend and correct them (Prologue, pp. 5–6).

This approach accords with the most usual expectation of a patron: that, on the completion of a long and complex building project, there should be an enclosure that is useful and physically sound. To this end, five of the ten books in Alberti's *De re aedificatoria* are devoted to the construction and structure of the discrete parts of a building: its foundations, floors, walls and roof, and the openings within them, as well as the materials by which building elements are most sensibly constructed. Of the remaining five books, four are concerned with the transformation of these building components into a finished building that conforms to one of the ancient building 'types' of sacred or secular buildings (described in books VII and VIII). Alberti concludes with a book on defects, and he offers his readers remedies and methods of restoration by which the completed but imperfect building may be made whole.

The observation of Nature and ancient wisdom had provided Alberti with the evidence that each building type should have a discernible shape, like a body,[23] and he argued that man-made structures on land should imitate the bodies of animals, such as horses, because the ancients 'found that grace of form could never be separated or divorced from suitability of use' (VI, 3, p. 158), and that ships at sea should follow the lineaments of a fish (V, 12, p. 136).[24] His reasoning was informed by 'The great experts of antiquity [. . . who] have instructed us that a building is very like an animal, and that Nature must be imitated when we delineate it' (IX, 5, p. 301).

Similarly, roofs should be composed of 'bones, muscles, in-fill panelling, skin'(III, 12, p. 79); as for walls, the 'physicians have noticed that nature was so thorough in forming the bodies of animals, that she left no bone separate or disjointed from the rest. Likewise, we should link the bones and bind them fast with muscles and ligaments, so that their frame and structure is complete and rigid' (III, 12, p. 81); 'with every type of vault we should [. . .] bind together the bones and interweave flesh with nerves' (III, 14, p. 86); and, taking 'their example from nature, they [the ancients] never made the bones of the building, meaning the columns, angles, and so on, odd in number – for you will not find a single animal that stands or moves upon an odd number of feet' (IX, 5, p. 303).

According to Alberti, the architect has to consider three main criteria when turning an idea for a building into tangible form: the lineaments (*lineamenta*), materials (*materia*) and construction (*constructio*); these provide the focus of his first three books. Book I, entitled Lineaments, relates to the very nature of architecture: its history; the elements of building; and the three norms which a building should satisfy, of *firmitas*, *utilitas* and *venustas* – structure, use and beauty. Book II, Materials, concerns the translation of the mental design into drawings, sketches, models and plans appropriate to buildings; it also discusses the main building materials and methods of construction and emphasises the need to consider the conditions on site. Book III, Construction, describes the sequence of construction that will be adopted on site: from the foundations to walls, masonry and mortar; from roofs and arches to vaulting; and finally the pavement of the building. Books IV and V then detail the main building types, public and private, under the titles Public Works and Works of Individuals.

The second half of *De re aedificatoria* mainly explores how the design and construction of the different building types will appear once harmonised according to the separate concepts of beauty and ornament. He defined these terms simply and clearly:

> I believe, that beauty is some inherent property, to be found suffused all through the body of that which may be called beautiful; whereas ornament, rather than being inherent, has the character of something attached or additional (VI, 2, p. 156).

A building should be properly composed to be considered beautiful, and it is the role of ornament to enhance its form, and offer it character and presence.

Alberti is quite literal about the distinctions to be made between the lineaments of a building defined by beauty and its later embellishment through ornament:[25] 'The work ought to be constructed naked, and clothed later; let the ornament come last' (IX, 8, p. 312). The delay is – in part – an opportunity to give proper consideration to the ornament required. It is also a safeguard to protect expensively wrought stone and precious materials from accidental damage during the construction process. Certainly, a state of undress is intended to be temporary, especially for public and sacred works, 'since no man would allow them to be naked of ornament' (IX, 8, p. 312). Indeed, Alberti regards ornament as a necessary overlay to any well-defined building, for it has 'the effect of making the displeasing less offensive and the pleasing more delightful' and is 'a form of auxiliary light and complement to beauty' (VI, 2, p. 156). Alberti describes the column as the principal ornament; secondary is the setting for a building and its interiors, and he considered groves of trees, lakes, books and mathematical instruments to be appropriate adornments for a building.[26] The combination of these building elements can be beyond criticism and be considered beautiful only when they appear like a natural body: that is, when – according to what he understood to be Socratic philosophy – there exists a 'reasoned harmony of all the parts within a body, so that nothing may be added, taken away or altered, but for the worse' (VI, 2, p. 156).[27]

Alberti is far more circumspect about how beauty and ornament should be harmonised with one another, largely because he finds it 'extremely difficult', and 'at its most ambiguous and involved' when dealing with buildings (IX, 5, p. 301). Nevertheless, it was not an inquiry he wished to avoid, as harmony is central to the art of building and 'every kind of beauty and ornament consists of it; or to put it more clearly, it springs from every rule of beauty' (IX, 5, p. 301).

Vitruvius had demanded durability, convenience and beauty in a building using the concepts of *firmitas*, *utilitas* and *venustas*, though without describing a clear process for achieving such ends. For example, he describes beauty, or *venustas*, as having been achieved 'when the appearance of the work is pleasing and in good taste, and when its members are in due proportion according to correct principles of symmetry'.[28] In order to carry this out, Alberti believed that a beautiful building must embrace the following definition of beauty: 'Beauty is a form of sympathy and consonance of the parts within a body, according to definite number, outline and position, as dictated by *concinnitas*, the absolute and fundamental rule in nature' (IX, 5, p. 303).[29]

BEAUTY THROUGH *CONCINNITAS*

Alberti coined the Latin term *concinnitas* specifically to explain the means by which a beautiful building can be achieved. While it has proved difficult to translate simply, it was considered by Jacob Burkhardt to be Alberti's 'most expressive term'.[30] Yet, despite its obvious importance, Alberti does not state how the architect is to apply its formula in practice.[31] It stems from the Latin adjective *concinnus*, which is understood to mean 'skilfully put together or joined' and 'beautiful'; and 'pleasing, on account of harmony and proportion'.[32] Cicero had used it to mean a 'harmony of style' in oratory,[33] and there is little doubt that Alberti's adoption of the term *concinnitas* was inspired by Cicero and his approach to rhetoric. For, in contrast to the shortcomings of his contemporary Vitruvius, Cicero was a Latin writer whom Alberti admired greatly, and he found the orator's high moral tone and rhetorical terms particularly useful when dealing with major concepts in architecture in *De re aedificatoria*.[34] The notion that a verbal delivery should be composed like well-formed bodies preceded Cicero and, according to Plato, it was Socrates who had compared the structure of speech to that of a living being 'with a body of its own as it were, and neither headless nor feet-less, with a middle and with members adapted to each other and to the whole'.[35]

Vitruvius does not use the term *concinnitas* in his architectural treatise, but refers instead to the *dispositio* and *symmetria* of a building. Through *dispositio* the architect would achieve a congruity of all the parts of a building, so that measurement and form are interrelated. By *symmetria* Vitruvius meant not only the mirroring of form across an axis (the modern reading of 'symmetry'), but the use of a consistent module throughout the whole design, so that every aspect of the building is governed by complementary ratios. The module is derived from a standard measurement, such as the Roman foot, and is related to the diameter of a column. Each module would be multiplied by certain preferred numbers. Vitruvius believed that temples were to be the most highly valued and consequently most refined building type, and he wrote: 'we can have nothing but respect for those who, in constructing temples of the immortal gods, have so arranged the members of the works that both the separate parts and the whole design may harmonise in their proportions and symmetry'.[36]

It would appear then that Alberti brought the Vitruvian notions of *dispositio* and *symmetria* together, and refined them as *concinnitas*. This has led Alberti scholars to argue that *concinnitas*, *dispositio* and *symmetria* are equivalent terms. Principal among them is Rudolf Wittkower, who concluded that the 'chief characteristic' of *concinnitas* is proportion, the 'classical idea of maintaining a uniform system of proportion throughout all parts of a building',[37] a reading inspired by the parallel Vitruvius had drawn between the temple and the human body, where proportion is described as 'a correspondence among the measures of the members of an entire work, and of the whole to a certain part selected as standard. From this result the principles of symmetry (*symmetria*)'.[38] Wittkower moves on to associate measure, the 'part to be selected as standard', with Alberti's principal ornament, the column.[39] He explains how this postulate worked in practice by illustrating the façade composition of Santa Maria Novella overlaid with squares proportionally related to each other: they were derived from square incrustations on the attic, and the diameter of the columns attached to the lower storey (fig. 32).[40] He later referred to Palladio's façade for San Francesco della Vigna in terms of 'a unit of measurement, the *modulus*' equal to the diameter of the small columns, governed by a 'meaningful relationship of numbers' which, Wittkower concludes, was Palladio's interpretation of Vitruvius' *symmetria*.[41] By association, Wittkower appears to imply that Palladio's practice is a direct extension of Alberti's theory.[42] When discussing Palladio's use of 'motifs of the same species', he argues that Palladio, by the consistent application of these motifs in church architecture, 'achieved congruity of all the parts, *dispositio* in Vitruvius' terminology. Moreover, his structures also obey Vitruvius' all-important postulate of *symmetria*, which is the fixed mathematical ratio of the parts to each other and to the whole'.[43] Subsequent scholars have followed Wittkower's lead when studying the built works by Alberti and other Renaissance architects and, invariably, a column, pier or pilaster width is 'selected as standard' from the building in an attempt to reveal its overall proportions.[44] But there have been problems with this approach, as many different modules have been identified on these buildings, revealing a bewildering variety of proportional systems.[45] Consequently, findings have been disparate, contradictory and, for the most part, inconclusive. The most obvious reasons for this lack of success derive from too heavy a reliance on Vitruvius for an explanation of *concinnitas* (a term he does not use) and too great an emphasis on the proportion of applied ornament as something separate rather than integral with the beautiful body of his designs.

It is therefore necessary to redefine *concinnitas* in the light of Alberti's theory, and before reviewing its application in practice.

REDEFINING *CONCINNITAS*: THROUGH *NUMERUS*, *FINITIO* AND *COLLOCATIO*

It is the task and aim of *concinnitas* to compose parts that are quite separate from each other by their nature, according to some precise rule, so that they correspond to one another in appearance. [. . .] Everything that Nature produces is regulated by the

32   Rudolf Wittkower's geometrical analysis of Alberti's, façade of Santa Maria Novella, Florence (Wittkower (1973), p. 46).

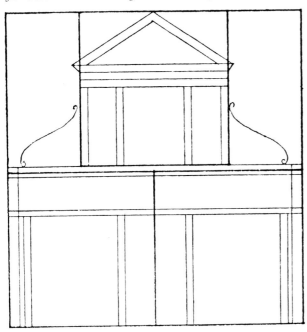
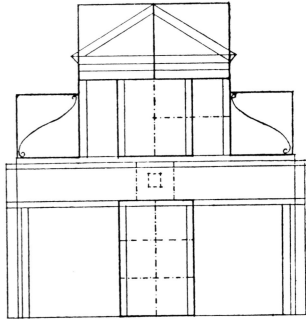

law of *concinnitas*, and her chief concern is that whatever she produces should be absolutely perfect. [. . .] Beauty is a form of sympathy and consonance of the parts within a body, according to definite number, outline and position, as dictated by *concinnitas*, the absolute and fundamental rule in Nature. This is the main object of the art of building, and the source of her dignity, charm, authority, and worth (IX, 5, pp. 302–3).

The three categories of which Alberti states *concinnitas* is composed – *numerus*, *finitio* and *collocatio* – have been interpreted variously.[46] In the edition of *De re aedificatoria* by Rykwert, Leach and Tavernor these three terms are translated as number, outline and position,[47] for the following reasons.

Numerus *as 'number'*

In 1976 George Hersey took issue with the usual reading of this category, which had been influenced by Wittkower's writings:

> With Wittkower the importance of number in Italian Renaissance architecture began to be perceived. But number, for Wittkower, was a question of proportion and proportion only. He ignored dimensions and distributions. He ignored the five orders. And numbers, for Wittkower, were modern numbers; they were abstract quantities and nothing more, as in modern mathematics. Wittkower will say, for example, that an 8:6 proportion is really 4:3.[48]

Conversely, Hersey set out to show that the numbers that humanists used were adopted for their Pythagorean qualities, and they were not 'mere quantities', nor were they abstract. William Westfall went further still, and when describing the perfect number 6 he included geometry and form under the heading of *numerus*:

> Six is especially favoured because like any natural object it consists of nothing but its own parts. Six is the number of sides of the hexagon which, according to the philosophers, is like a circle in that a circle is all angles and the hexagon's side is the radius of a circle. The number six, the hexagon, and the circle are interchangeable; some geometric forms and simple numbers can be used interchangeably in architectural designs just as they are found to be interchangeable in nature.[49]

Westfall is convincing, as number and geometry have been inextricably interwoven with the measured outline of a building since antiquity. For example, quad-rature is explained by Vitruvius as a means by which a plan area can be 'squared' geometrically: the diagonal of any square is equal to the side of a new square double its area, and from this beginning a progression of related squares can grow or diminish.[50] Vitruvius also demonstrated the use of the equilateral triangle in setting out the plan of ancient Greek and Roman theatres by rotation around a fixed point.[51] These design methods, known as *ad quadratum* and *ad triangulum*, undoubtedly underlie the design of the great medieval cathedrals of Europe;[52] as Wittkower stressed: 'nobody in his senses will deny that mediaeval geometrical concepts survived and were still being used in the Quattrocento'.[53] Indeed, studies of Florentine architecture confirm the view that Brunelleschi conflated geometry with arithmetical modulation in his buildings and, later that century, one theorist proclaimed quite dogmatically that 'there is no proportion without number and no form without geometry'.[54]

Finitio *as 'outline' (or 'measured outlines')*

Wittkower defined *finitio* as 'harmonic relations', but Westfall reverted to Leoni's English translation (1726) of *finitio* as 'finishing', since it 'controls number and means proportion in the three dimensional space of the building'.[55] Leoni had taken this definition from Cosimo Bartoli's Italian edition (1550) of *De re aedificatoria*, where *finitio* is translated as 'finimento' (finishing), though Bartoli also translated *finitio* as 'forma'; and Pietro Lauro, in his Italian edition (1546), rendered it as 'figura'.[56] In 1966 Giovanni Orlandi translated *finitio* as 'delimitazione' (delimitation, or boundary).[57] More convincing, however, is the interpretation of *finitio* as 'measure', for which Joan Gadol had found evidence in Alberti's recommendation of the term *finitorium* for sculptors to establish relative position and scale.[58] A *finitor* is literally a measurer of boundaries: thus, in relation to designing a building, *finitio* surely means the measured outlines, or lineaments of walls.

Susan Lang has argued that the 'all-embracing key to the whole building' is the measured ground-plan, *de lineamentis*, since from the *lineamenta* all the proportions of a building can be deduced.[59] She is undoubtedly correct. Study of Alberti's own practice makes it clear that he first designed the plan of a building and presented this to his patron before describing the elevations (see chapter 9 below).

Collocatio *as 'position' (or 'composition')*

This category refers to the arrangement of a building to ensure that every part is in its appropriate position.

While this would be called planning today, a distinction needs to be made between the overriding pragmatism of many modern plans, and the Natural ordering advocated by Alberti, such that man, society and cosmos are in complete harmony.[60] To be able to perform his role as a mediator between God's Natural order and society, the architect needs to receive the correct education in order to become a man of *virtù*, a concept that conditions and directs the action of men,[61] permitting man to be like 'nature itself, complete and well-formed'.[62] Consequently, the success of any building project is dependent on the *virtù* of the architect. As Westfall explained, *concinnitas* is an extension of *collocatio* because 'it brings together the intentions and abilities of the architect and the intentions and achievements of God in creation and of man in society. Through his concern with *concinnitas* the architect enters society'.[63]

An education appropriate to the virtuous architect begins with an appreciation of the classical world through its literature, and, especially, direct experience of the best of ancient buildings. However, unlike Vitruvius, Alberti does not believe that the architect should acquire a vast range of skills, and he emphasises just two 'vital arts' in which he should be proficient, painting and mathematics (IX, 10, p. 317).[64] Alberti thought that a sound knowledge of his *De pictura* would suffice for painting, alongside a 'sufficient knowledge of mathematics for the practical and considered application of angles, numbers, and lines [. . .]. If he combines enthusiasm and diligence with a knowledge of these arts, the architect will achieve favour, wealth, fame for posterity, and glory' (IX, 10, p. 317). His focus, again, is on precision of line and outline, and the correct placement of the parts within the whole using the judgement of mind and eye: and the definition by Christine Smith of *collocatio* as composition is perhaps the best single word with which to translate Alberti's intention here.[65] But as with the inappropriateness of the modern term 'planning' it must be stressed that, by *collocatio*, Alberti means more than a composition of form. For once beauty is set in a societal context it acquires a moralistic patina, and architecture is subject to what has been called 'aesthetic rectitude'.[66]

COMPOSITION

From Alberti's own statements in *De re aedificatoria* it would appear that the architect's first task is to select the building type that is physically suitable to the needs of the patron, its users and the situation in which the

building is to be placed. For this the architect needs to draw upon his knowledge of a vast repertoire of buildings which he has studied and recorded in detail:

> I would have [the architect] take the same approach as one might toward the study of letters, where no one would be satisfied until he had read and examined every author, good and bad, who had written anything on the subject in which he was interested. Likewise, wherever there is a work that has received general approval, he should inspect it with great care, record it in drawing, note its numbers, and construct models and examples of it (IX, 10, p. 315).

The idea that architecture has a language of forms that can be reused and referred to in new designs was commonplace. Builders have always copied buildings they admired (in part or in whole), but Alberti was raising the practice of 'quotation' to an art, by associating designing with oratory.

Once the general form of the building has been decided on, the architect refines – literally harmonises – the parts of the building with the whole. Alberti, like Cicero before him, believed that the tangible harmony of a building is analogous to the harmonious composition of notes within music:[67]

> The very same numbers that cause sounds to have that *concinnitas*, pleasing to the ears, can also fill the eyes and mind with wondrous delight. From musicians therefore who have already examined such numbers thoroughly, or from those objects in which Nature has displayed some evident and noble quality, the whole method of outlining is derived (IX, 5, p. 305).

Architects are expected to use the 'method of outlining', to which he refers, to place the walls, roofs and openings appropriate to the building. This information is translated into drawings and wooden models before the more intricate detail of its intended ornament – columns and mouldings – is described. This process has its parallel in painting, and in *De pictura* Alberti instructs artists to build up their design in three stages, by outlining the object in view, composing its elements and finally rendering its surface.[68] It is the duty of those who build such a harmonious design to translate faithfully such measured outlines into masonry.

The transference of responsibility from designer to builder has seldom worked smoothly, and has led to many a dispute on site before and since Alberti's times. Often this is because the builder fails to understand the architect's total conception for the building, and is inclined to make expedient changes when construction difficulties arise on site (which happens more frequently with work on an existing building). It is incumbent on the architect to communicate his conception as clearly as possible, to give clear instructions, directly and simply, so that each skilled worker can perform his role effectively.

Alberti's concern for correct proportioning of every part of a building is evident in *De re aedificatoria* where he describes a proportional procedure to explain the numbers behind the evolution of the main column types. At first, he says, columns were 6 and 10 units high (the Vitruvian 'perfect' numbers), but later they were rejected as too stout or too slender, and the ancients devised a column that

> lay between the two extremes. They therefore resorted first to arithmetic, added the two together, and then divided the sum in half; by this they established that the number that lay between 6 and 10 was 8. This pleased them, and they made a column 8 times the width of the base, and called it Ionic (IX, 7, p. 309).

The same procedure determined the Doric column as 7 modules high (6 + 8 = 14 ÷ 2 = 7) and the Corinthian as 9 modules (8 + 10 = 18 ÷ 2 = 9).

Most usually, columns are arranged in rows, and may be free-standing, as in a portico, or attached and placed adjacent to a wall surface. The required width and height of the portico or wall relates to the size of rooms within the building. This in turn influences the size of the columns and the distance between them. The column type and its proportions are determined by building type. The correct proportions of rooms within the building were arrived at by applying the formula of the 'mean and two extremes' used to size the ideal column types to a room's width, length and height. Each relates to the other according to a ratio derived from the ancient Greek musical scale.[69] This had been determined by the relationship of four similar strings, of a proportionally related length, expressible as the progression 6:8:9:12. Pythagoras was supposed to have found that when these strings are vibrated, under equal tension, the sound (wavelength) interval between them creates consonant tones, which correspond to ratios of whole numbers. Doubling the string length (1:2) creates an octave (called by the Greeks *diapason*); a ratio of 2:3 creates a difference in pitch of a fifth (*diapente*); a ratio of 3:4 creates a fourth (*diatessaron*). Alberti describes the favoured tones in detail, and he explains that:

> the musical numbers are 1, 2, 3 and 4; there is also *tonus* [. . .] where the longer string is one eighth more than the lesser.

Architects employ all these numbers in the most convenient manner possible: they use them in pairs, as in laying out a forum, place, or open space, where only two dimensions are considered, width and length; and they use them also in threes, such as a public sitting room, senate house, hall, and so on, when width relates to length, and they want the height to relate harmoniously to both (IX, 5, p. 305).

Alberti did not conceive of these ratios as linear dimensions but as flat surfaces, or *areae*, which combine with one another to create harmonically proportioned spaces.[70] These *areae* may be classified as 'short', 'medium' and 'large', and any ratio of two properly proportioned planar surfaces achieves a 'musical' consonance. Each *area* is defined first as a square which may then be turned into a rectangular plane by reducing or extending one of its sides according to the application of preferred numbers, and where the number of one side is in ratio with the number of the other side.[71]

Alberti makes it plain that while oratory and musical composition are instructive to the architect, the analogy should not be taken too far. Yet, the architect 'should forsake painting and mathematics no more than the poet should ignore tone and meter' (IX, 10, p. 317). The effects of light, shade and colour, and of forms placed in measurable relationships, were matters that should properly concern the architect.

This promotion of painting and mathematics over music and oratory is significant: the need to represent objects accurately through measured drawings obviously requires quite different skills to the 'measured' composition of music and speech. Common to the success of all four disciplines is finding an appropriate mental or visual encapsulation with which to communicate the essential idea or concept. A formula or theme was required by mathematicians, musicians and orators, which would be memorable and could then be recollected at will. In a painted composition the concept is relayed through *historiae*.[72] Architects need, however, to select the appropriate building type, with its particular configuration of rooms related to use. Thus, there are obvious formal distinctions to be made between buildings dedicated to sacred and secular use: those intended for worship, commemoration, city administration, family occupation and bathing (VII, 13–14; VIII, 1–10, pp. 228–90). While there exist model examples of such building types (mainly in antiquity), immediate circumstance and opportunity will suggest deviations from the ideal:

> should [the architect] find anything anywhere of which he approves, he should adopt and copy it; yet anything that he considers can be greatly refined, he should use his artistry and imagination to correct and

put right; and anything that is otherwise not too bad, he should strive, to the best of his ability, to improve (IX, 10, p. 316).

In her book on early humanist architecture Christine Smith, by emphasising the influence of oratory and ancient rhetoric on Alberti's treatise, has defined the constituents of *concinnitas* as measure, metre and rhythm; as type, figure and content; and composition.[73] While I am broadly in agreement with this definition, my preferred reading of *concinnitas* as number, outline and position is determined by Alberti's emphasis on combining manual dexterity with the intellectual demands of painting and mathematics, and by the evidence of his architectural theory in practice, to which I will now turn.

Ultimately, I believe that Plato's influence may be discerned in Alberti's rendering of this term, particularly as his message was filtered through the doctors of the Christian church. As St Augustine wrote:

> Plato emphasises that God constructed the world by use of numbers, while we have the authority of Scripture, where God is thus addressed, 'You have set in order all things by measure, number and weight'. And the prophet says of God, 'He produces the world according to number'.[74]

THEORY INTO PRACTICE

It is uncertain when Alberti first had an opportunity to translate architectural theory into practice. It is improbable that he built anything of substance in Rome during Pope Nicholas V's reign, though he at least had the opportunity to observe the progress of numerous building projects then under construction. The coffered entry vault in Palazzo Venezia, Rome (formerly Palazzo di San Marco: first designed in 1455, but not begun until 1466), has been attributed to him, though there is no documentary support for this notion, and no convincing stylistic evidence.[75] According to Vasari, the now destroyed Trevi Fountain in Rome was restored for Nicholas V by Alberti and Bernardo Rossellino working together.[76] But while there are numerous documents to support Bernardo's active role in the various building projects undertaken for the pope, in and outside Rome, there is nothing equivalent with which to confirm Alberti's architectural involvement. His relationship with Rossellino is difficult to fathom. While Alberti had opinions on the Vatican project and may have been critical of Rossellino's design for the Constantinian basilica of St Peter's, their names are traditionally linked with the façade of Palazzo Rucellai in Florence which was more surely designed by Alberti.

Unravelling the nature and extent of Alberti's role in several major building projects outside Rome is the primary purpose of the following chapters. Besides his work in Florence, he became involved with the ruling families of three key northern city states, the Malatesta of Rimini, the Gonzaga of Mantua and the Montefeltro of Urbino. The Malatesta and Gonzaga were connected through blood and common interests; the Malatesta and Montefeltro were close neighbours, but separated by a long and bloody feud. Yet Alberti inspired the leaders of all three families, their common ground being a passion for architecture *all'antica*, and their respect for his exceptional expertise as both an intellectual and architect.

There is evidence of his leading role in architectural projects in those places, and in the chapters that follow I shall attempt to identify the principal ideas and processes that translated the architectural theory contained in *De re aedificatoria* into monuments of considerable significance.

VI

SIGISMONDO MALATESTA
AND THE TEMPIO MALATESTIANO
IN RIMINI

THE MALATESTA DYNASTY AND THE CHURCH OF SAN FRANCESCO IN RIMINI

THE DISTANT ANCESTRY OF THE Malatesta of Rimini is uncertain. The claims of various members of the family, or rather those of chroniclers on their behalf, that they were descended from famous historical figures − Noah or Scipio Africanus, or, less specifically, from the peoples of Tarquinia, or from the Germanic lands of the north − cannot be substantiated.[1] It is, however, possible to chart their rise to prominence from the second half of the twelfth century. They acquired land in the Romagna of Italy, though their right to ownership was much disputed and the territories were fought over constantly. To retain such contested possessions at this time required authority backed by the threat of force. Indeed, it was as men of action, and through their considerable military skill in particular, that the Malatesta were able to assume and then hold on to a precarious power-base in Rimini and the Romagna for several centuries (fig. 33). During this time the Malatesta formed a strong alliance with the Gonzaga of Mantua, and became a bitter rival of the Montefeltro of Urbino.

The church of San Francesco in Rimini became of dynastic importance to the Malatesta when the first Lord of Rimini of that name, Malatesta da Verucchio, was buried there in 1312. He was an extraordinary and fortunate man who, despite being a great warrior, lived for more than a hundred years. His main rival in the Romagna was Guido da Montefeltro in neighbouring Urbino, who fought under the banner of the Ghibelline party. For his efforts on behalf of the Guelphs and faithful devotion to the church Malatesta was commended by the pope and the Malatesta *Signoria* was born.[2] He remained throughout his life a pious Christian, and among the many bequests he made to religious houses he emphasised his affection for the Order of St Francis, and provided for the holding of a General Chapter of

the Franciscans in Rimini. When he was buried in their church of San Francesco he was clothed in the habit of a Tertiary.[3]

The tribe grew strong over successive generations and the city attained some prominence at the end of the fourteenth century under the leadership of Carlo Malatesta.[4] The bitter family feud with the Montefeltro continued almost without break throughout that century and into the next.[5] Several positive alliances were made by Carlo for his family and, in 1393, his sister Margarita was married to Francesco Gonzaga[6] and Carlo acted as an intermediary to prevent the escalation of a potentially ruinous disagreement between the Gonzaga of Mantua and the Visconti of Milan. With the death of Francesco Gonzaga in 1407, responsibility for his twelve-year-old son, Gianfrancesco, fell to the Malatesta and the Republic of Venice jointly, though it was Carlo Malatesta who honoured this bequest. Carlo took charge of Mantua and oversaw the change of government there. This allowed him to forge an alliance between his family, the Gonzaga, the Este at Ferrara and the Venetians.[7] Carlo's power-base was extended further when, on the death of Giangaleazzo Visconti in Milan, his brother Pandolfo stood for the Visconti in a city troubled by anarchy. In 1408 Carlo reinforced his brother with troops there and the Malatesta were briefly a power with which to reckon in northern Italy.

The Malatesta were courted not only by the great ruling families in Italy but by the papacy, who used the local authority of such families in their attempt to maintain the central region under their jurisdiction. Carlo was a staunch supporter of papal power and during his early years as ruler of Rimini this alliance was fostered by Urban VI and his successor Boniface IX.[8] Moreover, Carlo was praised for his erudition by leading humanists: Poggio Bracciolini, Leonardo Bruni and Flavio Biondo commended him for his virtue and 'gravitas'.[9] However, he was also condemned as anti-humanist: in 1397 he reportedly had a statue of Virgil in Mantua thrown into the river, an action prompted by his concern that local people were actively involved in pagan idolatry.[10] He was consistent in his retribution: in Rimini he legislated to punish blasphemers and idolaters, and to make sure that holy days were properly observed. His Mantuan wife, Elisabetta Gonzaga, was no less devout, and the son of his younger brother Pandolfo, Galeotto Roberto, followed their pious example to austere extremes.[11]

On the death of Pandolfo in 1427,[12] Carlo brought up his three surviving illegitimate sons, Galeotto Roberto (1411–32), Sigismondo Pandolfo (1417–68) and Domenico, later known as Malatesta Novello (1418–65). As Carlo Malatesta was otherwise childless, Galeotto Roberto was groomed to inherit the Malatesta *Signoria*.[13] He did not find his dynastic responsibilities easy to bear. From an early age he made it known that he wished only to become a 'povero di Cristo', and that he sought salvation in heaven, not power and authority on earth. He died at the age of

twenty-one, probably as a result of fasting and privations from which even the pope had failed to discourage him.[14] Sigismondo Malatesta succeeded Galeotto Roberto in 1432 and, at the age of fifteen, was commanding papal troops, engaging and defeating a joint force of the Count of Urbino and a rival faction of the Malatesta of Pesaro.[15]

While a cardinal, Gabriel Condulmer (later Eugenius IV) had built up a close relationship with Carlo Malatesta.[16] Soon after having become pope in 1431, Eugenius fled Rome to establish the papal court in Florence, and, as he had some influence over his native Venice, he persuaded both cities to side with Sigismondo in Rimini.[17] At first all went well. In September 1433 a knighthood was bestowed on Sigismondo by his namesake the Holy Roman Emperor Sigismund, who was *en route* from Rome to the Council of Basle: Sigismondo was then aged sixteen.[18] Three years later he was among the papal dignitaries at the consecration of Florence Cathedral.[19] But Sigismondo was less constant than Carlo; all too regu-

33   Pierre Van der Aa, map of Rimini, *Galerie agréable du monde*, Leiden, 1729. The campanile (bell-tower) and church of San Francesco are visible immediately to the right of the oval-shaped piazza, and the Arch of Augustus is placed close-by, within the city walls, and straddles the main road (the ancient via Flaminia) entering the piazza from the left.

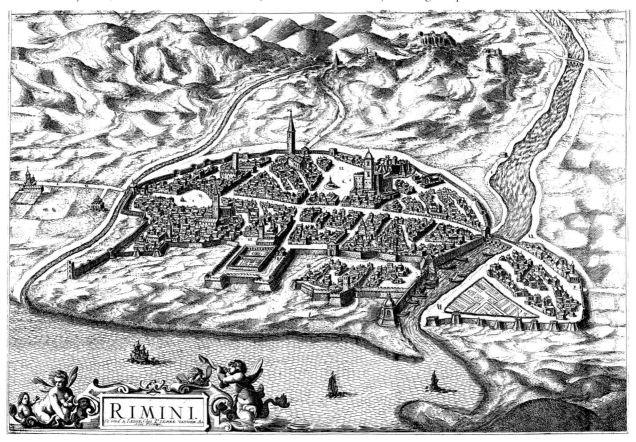

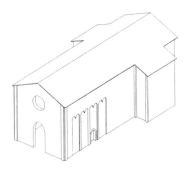
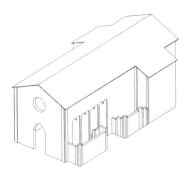
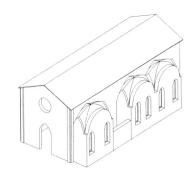
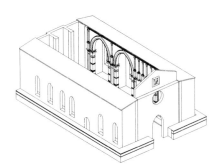
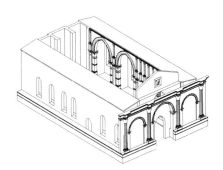
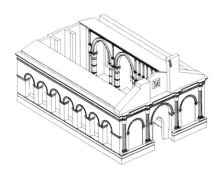

34 Tempio Malatestiano, Rimini. Reconstructions of former church pre-Alberti: (a) San Francesco; (b) with lower walls of new southern side chapels; (c) vaults; and implementing Alberti's design for the exterior: (d) plinth; (e) façade; and (f) side arcades (Olivetti/Alberti Group).

larly his allies turned enemies. Indeed, his faults were many and he has been described as 'impulsive, imprudent, precipitate and mutable in action'.[20] He underestimated the power of his rivals, and soon antagonised the papacy to the extent that a new pope wished the Malatesta destroyed. Sigismondo was excommunicated by Pius II on 25 December 1460, and condemned as a citizen of hell.[21]

It is through the vehement condemnation of Pope Pius II that Sigismondo's notoriety has spread. In his *Commentaries* Pius labelled him a heretic, whose worst atrocities included murder, violence, adultery, incest, sacrilege, perjury and treachery.[22] There can be no doubt he had upset the pope,[23] and there is probably some truth behind the hyperbole for, unlike his older brother, Sigismondo was no saint. His only constancy was his total devotion to his mistress Isotta degli Atti, whom he made his third wife, probably in 1456.[24] She became an essential part of his life, which he honoured by making available to her a sanctuary within the family church of San Francesco in Rimini for her burial. The subsequent remodelling of San Francesco by Alberti, who turned the exterior of the church into a fabric *all'antica*, and created, as Vasari honoured it, 'one of the

most famous temples of all Italy', is a monument to God, the city and to Sigismondo in particular.[25]

FROM CHURCH TO TEMPLE: TRANSFORMING SAN FRANCESCO INTO THE TEMPIO MALATESTIANO

The interior of San Francesco was developed in a piecemeal way, chapel by chapel: the northern chapels were probably modernised within their thirteenth- and fourteenth-century structure first, and work began on the southern chapels during the 1440s (fig. 34).[26] Alberti conceived the later envelope of the existing church as structurally and stylistically independent both of the old building and of its new interior. The only continuity was that the same team of masons and sculptors probably worked on both the inside and the outside, and they were led, most famously, by Matteo de' Pasti and Agostino di Duccio.

The chapels were remodelled with pointed arches and groin vaults which echoed current northern (Lombardic and Venetian) buildings. Fluted stone pilasters and capitals were overlaid on this framework

35   Arch of Augustus, Rimini, *c*.27 BC (photo/author).

interior chapels, the arcaded sides of the building are left open to reveal the walls and windows of the older chapels within. These side arcades join the façade at right angles, of which only the lower half was finished; the upper storey above the finely detailed entablature over the entry portal has an incomplete central arch and only partially built supporting 'wings'. Similarly, the side arcades were left unfinished at their ends, since in 1461, Sigismondo fell from power and building work stopped. How the church was intended to appear in its complete state is a matter of some debate.

There is physical evidence, then, of two distinctly separate stages in the fifteenth-century development of San Francesco. The first involved the repair and remodelling of the old fabric internally by Matteo de' Pasti and Agostino di Duccio. The second stage concerned the encasing of the church as a temple under the supervision of these two men, and according to a radically new design by Alberti for the exterior (fig. 37).[28] The involvement of the same supervisors ensured that there

36   J.B.L.G. Seroux d'Agincourt (1847; I, pl. 51), etching displaying elevations and details after Alberti's Tempio Malatestiano.

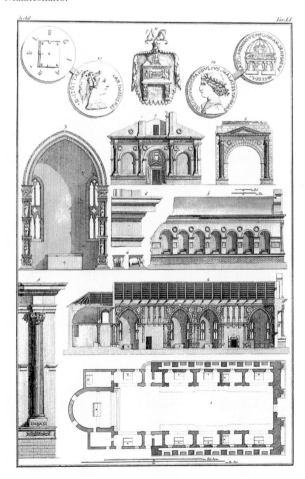

and combined with sumptuous stone decorations to give an effect of building *all'antica*, but without any of the metrical precision and discipline of ornament with which it was being developed by Brunelleschi and his followers in Florence.

In contrast, the exterior of the church is severe and strict in its adoption of ancient Roman ornamentation, and deliberately adapts the ornamental features of the triumphal Arch of Augustus nearby (fig. 35). Only the capitals are obviously different, being Corinthian on the arch and Composite on the church – the kind of column type identified by Alberti as specifically 'Italian' – 'to distinguish it from all foreign imports'. The Italic 'combines the gaiety of the Corinthian with the delight of the Ionic, and [. . .] has hanging volutes; the result is graceful and thoroughly commendable' (VII, 6, p. 201). This was the first use of this type since antiquity, and the four semi-detached columns, combined with distinctive mouldings, relief and inscriptions on the frieze in the ancient manner, transforms the elements of the former triumphal arch into the first modern temple: this is the main reason why its renaming as the Tempio Malatestiano has endured.[27]

Built of large blocks of Istrian stone, the new enclosure literally cloaks the earlier brick structure of San Francesco: while respecting the need for light of the

37 (*above and following pages*)   Leon Battista Alberti, Tempio Malatestiano, Rimini. Photographic views of the façade, sides and details (photos/R. Schofield and author).

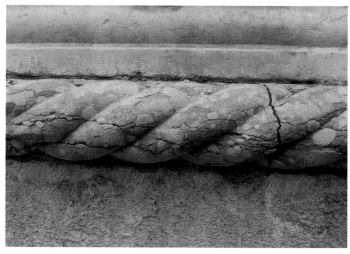

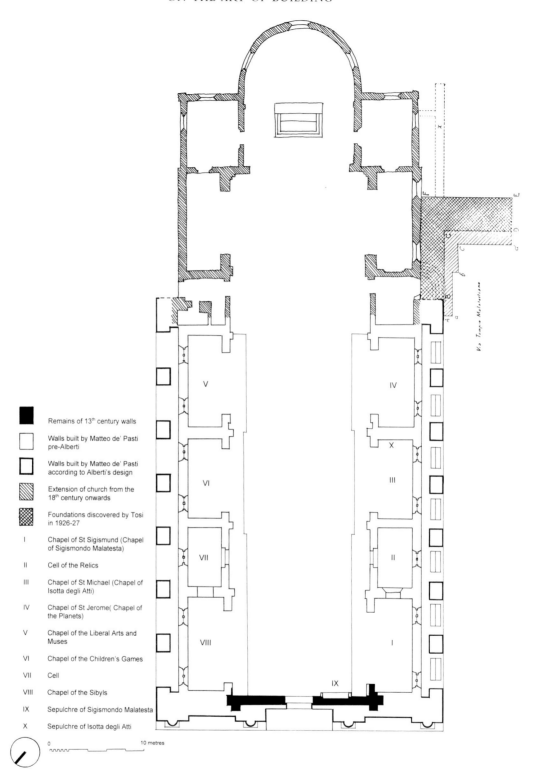

■	Remains of 13th century walls
□	Walls built by Matteo de' Pasti pre-Alberti
□	Walls built by Matteo de' Pasti according to Alberti's design
▨	Extension of church from the 18th century onwards
▩	Foundations discovered by Tosi in 1926-27
I	Chapel of St Sigismund (Chapel of Sigismondo Malatesta)
II	Cell of the Relics
III	Chapel of St Michael (Chapel of Isotta degli Atti)
IV	Chapel of St Jerome(Chapel of the Planets)
V	Chapel of the Liberal Arts and Muses
VI	Chapel of the Children's Games
VII	Cell
VIII	Chapel of the Sibyls
IX	Sepulchre of Sigismondo Malatesta
X	Sepulchre of Isotta degli Atti

38 Plan of the
Tempio Malatestiano
(drawing/author).

0   10 metres

was an efficient use of labour and materials, though for
modern historians the continuity this provided has
served to blur the distinctions between the separate
phases of development, and has led to considerable difficulties in determining from the patchy documentation

that survives what the building was meant to look like
in its final form.

Sigismondo certainly became actively involved with
remodelling the southern chapels in the 1440s, and
he probably intended to build one for himself next

to that of his mistress. The privilege of internment in the family church was extended to Isotta while Sigismondo's second wife was still living,[29] and on 12 September 1447 Pope Nicholas V issued a papal bull to allow Isotta to endow the Chapel of the Angels (now called the Chapel of St Michael) in San Francesco, so that it may be 'repaired and remodelled' (*reparari et reformari*).[30]

Isotta's chapel is on the south side of the nave, between that of St Jerome to the east, and the Cell of the Relics and the Chapel of St Sigismund to the west (fig. 38). It was built during her lifetime. She donated money for its construction in May 1448 when it was further recorded that the moneys were for the chapel 'to be constructed or otherwise repaired and enlarged'. Its subsequent enlargement may well refer to the repositioning of the outer wall so it aligned with that of the adjacent chapel.[31] Isotta's own tomb was placed on the wall at the eastern end of the Chapel of the Angels, and marked with an inscription that translates as 'To Isotta of Rimini, for beauty and virtue the honour of Italy. 1446', a formula that appears also on medals of

Isotta made by Matteo de' Pasti (fig. 39).[32] Some unknown event is being commemorated, as 1446 precedes the papal bull by one year and her donation by two years, also pre-dating the commencement of the chapel. When Isotta's tomb was finally installed the inscription was covered with a bronze plate bearing the dedication D. ISOTTAE and the date 1450. Much political mileage was made from this by Pope Pius II who objected that the letter D indicated the word DIVAE, a deification not sanctioned by the church, but, he believed, with audacious presumption by Sigismondo himself.[33]

Permission was also granted by papal authorities to found the adjacent Cell of the Relics to the west of Isotta's chapel and its neighbour the Chapel of St Sigismund. The foundation stone of the Chapel of St Sigismund was blessed in October 1447, and was finally consecrated on the saint's feast day, 1 May, in 1452. In the Cell of the Relics, a fresco by Piero della Francesca (bearing the date 1451) shows Sigismondo kneeling before his patron St Sigismund.[34] It is thought that the Chapel of St Sigismund was to have contained

39 Tempio Malatestiano: (a) drawing of the tomb of Isotta degli Atti on the eastern wall of the Chapel of Angels (now Chapel of St Michael) (CMS/Alberti Group); (b) tomb of Isotta degli Atti (CMS/Alberti Group).

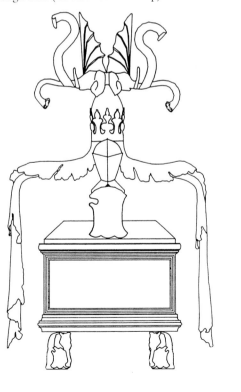

Sigismondo's tomb, not least because Isotta was to be located in the chapel on the other side of the Cell of the Relics.[35] However, some time around 1450 the future development of the whole building and consequently Sigismondo's ambitions for his tomb were changed quite radically. He now wished for the church to be transformed into a 'monument both notable and holy' and the basis for this was his commitment to a vow written in Greek and placed on a panel on the south side of the Tempio Malatestiano. It translates as follows:

> Sigismondo Pandolfo Malatesta, son of Pandolfo, having by fortune's favour escaped with his life from many great dangers in the Italian war, victorious on account of the deeds which he had courageously and successfully accomplished, set up this temple with due magnificence and expense to God immortal, and to the city, as he had vowed when he found himself in those circumstances, and left behind him a monument both notable and holy.[36]

Recorded more prominently on the frieze of the façade is the statement that Sigismondo 'made the building'

40 Matteo de' Pasti (attributed), commemorative medal of the Tempio Malatestiano. Bronze, dated 1450, 40 mm diam. Staatliche Museen zu Berlin – Preussischer Kulturbesitz. Münzkabinett: (a) front elevation of the proposed Tempio Malatestiano, bearing the inscription PRAECL.ARIMINI. TEMPLUM.AN.GRATIAE.V.F.M.CCCC.L; (b) on the obverse, portrait of Sigismondo Malatesta, with the inscription SIGIS-MUNDUSPANDULFUS.MALATESTA.PAN.F.

(*fecit*) in 1450. This same date is borne by the newer inscription on Isotta's tomb, and it also appears on a medal commemorating the foundation of the remodelled church as the Tempio Malatestiano (fig. 40).[37]

Alberti had contributed to the revival of placing dedications on sacred and private buildings, and in *De re aedificatoria* recommends that this ancient practice be continued, stating: 'It has been our own custom to inscribe on our chapels details of their dedication and year of consecration. I approve of this strongly'; dedications may come in two forms, they 'should be either written – these are called epigraphs – or composed of reliefs and emblems' (VIII, 4, p. 256). Both are in evidence at the Tempio Malatestiano, and true to his recommendation Alberti composed epigraphs and emblems for his subsequent buildings for Giovanni Rucellai in Florence, where they are also set into stone friezes.[38] Again, as discussed below, where dates appear in these inscriptions (as on the Rucellai sepulchre), they do not relate to the start or even the completion of building work – hence the uncertainty about when Alberti first became involved in Rimini.

It has been suggested that Sigismondo's vow, made in 'circumstances of great danger', may relate to his victory over Alfonso of Aragon at Piombino in 1448, in which case the date of 1450 on the building and commemorative medal is significant for another reason.[39] Perhaps this year was seen by Sigismondo and Isotta as a turning-point in their relationship, following the death of his second wife in 1449. Alternatively, it may have been prompted by an act of contrition in the Jubilee Year of 1450 set by Nicholas V, or as part of the pope's 'grand plan' for that year: the via Flaminia being conceived as part of the processional route for pilgrims to Rome would thus be marked at Rimini by the Arch of Augustus and Alberti's 'triumphal' façade for the Tempio Malatestiano.[40] The year on the façade of 1450 may thus have been important for several reasons, perhaps including the commencement of the new building enclosure according to Alberti's design.

Comments made at the time do not help to confirm when Alberti's design was begun. According to a contemporary chronicle by Giovanni di maestro Pedrino of Forlì, Sigismondo began 'a magnificent work', 'a magnificent and superb oratory in the city of Rimini at the church of the friars minor, in the name and memory of St Sigismund the king' as late as 1453.[41] Whether or not the Forlivese chronicler is correct, by the end of the following year a letter refers clearly to the temple and 'the thick walls' Sigismondo was having built 'on this side and that'.[42] This is corroborated by other correspondence which suggests that the foundations under the front and side walls were complete, and the ashlar stone walls on top of them were as high as the plinth supporting the arcades; the shape of the arched niches on the façade was still under discussion and had not been finalised.[43]

Progress was slow if the project began in 1450 and rapid if it began in 1453. Certainly, until the Chapel of St Sigismund was completed in 1452, there was still plenty of activity and expense to be met inside the church, and once the external transformation of San Francesco had been decided upon it would have taken some time to acquire the necessary stock of building materials. A steady supply of suitable stone for revetment could not be found locally, and Sigismondo obtained material from outlying regions, not necessarily under his direct control, by means both fair and foul. While still remodelling the interior of old San Francesco in 1448, the Forlivese chronicler, for one, relates how cartloads of ancient stones – marble and slabs of porphry and serpentine – were brought to Rimini from the despoiled ancient fabric of Sant' Apollinare in Classe.[44] The city fathers of Ravenna were outraged and sent a representation to the Venetian government who were employing Sigismondo's services. They retaliated by withholding 3000 ducats of his salary. His authority locally was unquestioned, and there is no report of opposition when he ordered the partial dismantling of the ancient port of Rimini, or the plundering of buildings within the city itself for the benefit of San Francesco.[45] Quantities of stone were also ordered from Verona, and from Istria between 1451 and 1453; the Istrian supply proved unreliable, which may explain his decision to cannibalise ancient structures.[46]

Revamping the church was definitely high among Sigismondo's various building projects, and Istrian stone was diverted to the site in 1450 from a new bridge being built over the River Metauro. This may have been intended for the revetment of the chapels, and a later delivery of Istrian stone was undoubtedly for that purpose. Alternatively, it has been proposed that this material was for the new exterior, with the precious porphyry and serpentine being used for the new entry portal, which would suggest that building work was in progress simultaneously internally and externally (presumably for the foundations and lower walls) in 1450.[47] The re-routing to San Francesco of stone which had been ordered for another project suggests a degree of urgency, though it is unknown why the interior chapels should need their revetment more urgently than the bridge. Clearly, the foundations would need to be deep and sound to take the weighty masonry structure above, and one can imagine that Rimini's impetuous ruler, having accepted Alberti's design, would wish to proceed without delay to ensure his vow was met: 'to set up this temple with due magnificence and expense to God immortal and to the city'. Without further evidence, the date of Alberti's design for the Tempio Malatestiano and its initiation on site will remain uncertain.

What is evident from the documentation surrounding this building venture is the extent of Alberti's involvement in the precise detailing of its design, and the store put on his expertise by those on site. This is represented most clearly in this project through an exchange of letters from around the turn of 1454–5. The best known of these is one Alberti wrote to Matteo de' Pasti from Rome on 18 November 1454 (fig. 41).[48]

CORRESPONDENCE DESCRIBING ASPECTS OF ALBERTI'S DESIGN FOR THE TEMPIO MALATESTIANO

Alberti was resident in Rome during the building of the Tempio Malatestiano. Being such a distance from Rimini when crucial decisions were being made about detailed aspects of its construction caused him some frustration, especially when he received unsolicited comments from an individual for whom he clearly had no respect, and yet who was influential enough to sow seeds of doubt in those who had been entrusted to execute his design. He was determined to remind Matteo, among the other building 'masters' in Rimini, of the reasoning behind his decisions. It is worth quoting Alberti's letter to Matteo de' Pasti in full.[49]

Greetings. Your letters were most welcome in many ways, and welcome in that my Lord [Sigismondo Malatesta] has done what I wanted, that is has taken the best advice from everyone. But when you tell me that Manetto asserts that the dome should be two diameters high, then I prefer to believe those who built the Baths and the Pantheon and all those other great things rather than him; and reason more than any person. And if he relies on opinion, I will not be surprised if he is often in the wrong.

As for the business of the pier in my model, remember what I said to you: 'that façade should be an independent structure', because I find the widths and heights of those chapels disturbing. Remember and keep in mind that on the model, beside the roof, to the right and to the left there is a thing like this: and I did say, I put it here to cover that part of the roof (that is of the covering which will be made inside the church), because that width within cannot be modified by our façade. And one

41 Leon Battista Alberti, letter of 18 November (1454) to Matteo de' Pasti. New York, Pierpont Morgan Library. MA 1734r.

wants to improve what has already been done, not spoil that which one has to do. You see from what the measurements and the proportions of the piers arise: if you alter them, you will make a discord in all that music. And let us consider how to cover the church with something light. Do not trust the piers to carry any weight. And that is why it seemed to us that a wooden barrel vault would be more useful. Now, that pier of ours: if it does not align and tie up with the one of the chapel, it does not matter, because the one in the chapel will not need support on the side of our façade; and if it will need it, it is so close and almost touching that it will get a lot of support. If then you are in agreement, follow the drawing, which I consider all right.

As for the circular windows [oculi], I would like those who claim to be in the know that they understood their craft.[50] Tell me: why is the wall broken up and the building weakened to make windows? Because light is needed. If you can provide more light by weakening [the building] less – then are you not making a great mistake by giving me such trouble? To the left and the right of the oculus [the wall] is broken up, and the weight above is carried as much by an arch as it is by half a circle. Below the work is no stronger if it is an oculus, and that which should provide light is blocked. There are many reasons for this, but this one is enough for me, that never is any building praised by those who understand what nobody understands nowadays:

never, never will you see an *oculus* made if it is not in domes, [and then, only] as if it were a [priest's] tonsure; and this is done in certain temples – those of Jove and Phoebus which are patrons of light; and there is a good reason for their large size. And this I told you to show you from where the truth arises.

If someone will come here [to Rome], I will do my best to satisfy my Lord. As for you, I beg you to consider [all this] and listen to many and let me know. Someone might say something worthwhile. Commend me, if you see him, or write to him, to my Lord, to whom I would like to show my gratitude. Commend me to the magnificent Roberto [Valturio] and Monsignor the Protonotary, and to all those who you think love me. If I find someone trustworthy, I will send you [my book] Ecatonfilea and other things. Farewell.

Alberti is firm and to the point, and critical as ever of those who have nothing to offer but 'opinion'. The 'Manetto' he refers to may have been Giannozzo Manetti, the Florentine envoy in Rimini, and subsequently Pope Nicholas V's secretary and biographer.[51] He represented Florence in Rimini over a number of years, and delivered an enthusiastic speech in support of the Malatesta and their martial skills, conferring on Sigismondo the title of captain-general of the Florentine forces in September 1453.[52] Alternatively, and more probably, 'Manetto' was the architect Antonio di Ciaccheri Manetti, who took over from Brunelleschi at Florence Cathedral. A model of the dome of Florence Cathedral was built under his supervision after 1451, and he later worked on the tribune of the Annunziata in Florence for, or in advance of, Alberti.[53]

Manetti's opinion was probably based on his having seen a wooden model of the proposed Tempio Malatestiano. Alberti refers in this letter to 'my model' and its architectural details, and just over a month later (21 December 1454) Giovanni di maestro Alvise, a mason on site, describes to Sigismondo how, in order to determine the form of the vault internally, the 'front part of Battista's model' was removed.[54]

Alberti recommends in *De re aedificatoria* that wooden models be made of building projects before work starts on site (fig. 42). This provided the architect with the best means by which to check every aspect of the design, its proportions and the quantities of material required (II, 1–2, pp. 33–7). It was also a useful point of reference when he had cause to be absent from the building site for long periods, as Alberti was from Rimini. From the correspondence between his residence in Rome and the masters in Rimini, it would appear that this model provided the basis for minor adjustments to the original design, as the old church was built against, and occasionally cut into.

It must be assumed that Alberti's model bore a close relationship to the design for the Tempio Malatestiano

42 Wooden model of the Tempio Malatestiano, as reconstructed by the Alberti Group, and as exhibited at the Alberti exhibition, Palazzo Te, Mantua, 1994. Two views: front and oblique side view (photos/Giovetti).

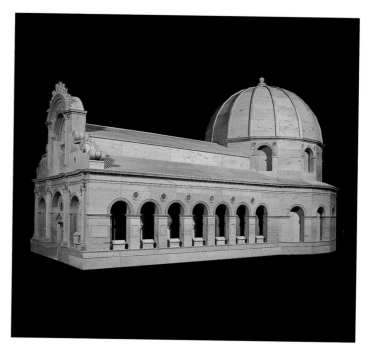

depicted on the commemorative medal. For, although the medal has a diameter of less than 4 cm, and the image is small, its design is carefully delineated and corresponds to what was built of Alberti's façade (as a comparison of the medal and building demonstrates). The similarities between the finished parts of the building and the medal are sufficiently close in detail and general proportion to warrant the notion that the image on the medal was based on the model of the proposed building referred to by Alberti in his letter (fig. 43).

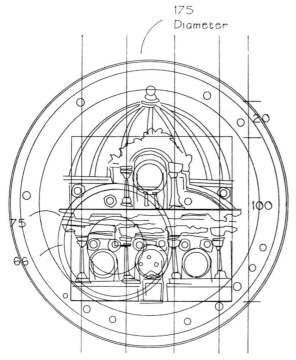

43   Photogrammetric plot of the commemorative medal of the Tempio Malatestiano, Rimini (see pp. xiv and 58, fig. 40a above), with geometrical overlay and dimensions in Roman feet derived from the width of the façade as built (Olivetti/Alberti Group).

Alberti's design for the Tempio Malatestiano, represented by the wooden model presumably kept on site, was undoubtedly altered slightly as building work progressed because of difficulties being encountered. New enclosures around imprecisely built structures invariably present their architects with design problems: Palladio's basilica in Vicenza is an obvious example of a similar challenge, which is recorded through a sequence of developmental drawings.[55] In his letter to Matteo de' Pasti, Alberti stressed the need to keep the structure of his design independent of the relatively thin brick walls of San Francesco:

remember what I said to you: 'that façade should be an independent structure', because I find the widths and heights of those chapels disturbing [. . .]. And let us consider how to cover the church with something light. Do not trust the [existing] piers, to carry any weight. And that is why it seemed to us that a wooden barrel vault would be more useful.

To decide what type of roof would be most appropriate, a drawing was prepared that involved partially dismantling the original wooden model. This is known from Giovanni di maestro Alvise's subsequent letter, dated 21 December 1454:[56]

I inform Your Excellency that my father has shown Pietro de' Gennari, Matteo de' Pasti and those other masters how the vault of the church etc. has to go. He has done so in this way: he has taken away that front part of messer Battista's model, and on it he has made the structure as it is to go, so that one can see clearly, without his having removed anything from the said model.[57] And he has done this to demonstrate that he does not want to depart from the design [ordine] of messer Battista. So that Your Excellency understands it, I am sending you a drawing, assuring you that the design provided by messer Battista in no way prevents the building from being constructed as you will see it in the drawing, nor does one have to take away anything on account of the said covering [coverto], nor does one need to diverge from the style of the aforementioned messer Battista.

This confirms that Alberti's design is being followed earnestly and that Matteo de' Pasti is in agreement with the proposed change. We have further evidence of this from the letter signed jointly by Matteo de' Pasti and Pietro de' Gennari, sent to Sigismondo Malatesta four days before, on 17 December:[58]

And Giovanni di maestro Alvise is writing everything to you, and especially about the roof, and he wants the said roof outside to be one, that is to say that it covers the chapels and the church. And I think that in our area one will find timber suitable for that. But when you come here one can confirm all this work. And, if need be, Giovanni di maestro Alvise and I will go to Rome to spend a couple of days with messer Battista, and we will see what he thinks, so that matters proceed as they should, or indeed [we can] arrange for him to come here. This is for you to decide.

It is certain from this correspondence that Alberti's instruction, that the new roof structure should not be an imposition on the nave walls, and should be light-weight and in timber, had been accepted. His authority was not doubted by the experienced masters in Rimini. Indeed, so anxious were they to follow his design intentions that, Sigismondo willing, Matteo was even prepared to make the journey to Rome with another master to confirm the detailed implications of this decision.

Curiously, none of the roofing options under discussion at this time was followed, and the pre-existing nave walls, contrary to Alberti's reasoning, directly support the timber roof structure.[59] It is puzzling, too, that the term Alberti used to describe its form – 'barrel vault' – was not referred to again by those on site, and that Giovanni di maestro Alvise concludes his letter to Sigismondo with what would appear to be quite a different proposition for the roof:

> If it pleases Your Excellency, I think it would be good to go to Rome to see messer Battista and discuss with him the method of vaulting [*modo del voltare*], and learn his view, and which method he thinks will be best, whether third- or quarter- or entirely acute, so that things turn out in a good way.[60]

It is not known whether Giovanni di maestro Alvise was allowed to make the trip to Rome to discuss this proposal with Alberti. Nor is it clear why the roof, which had been previously described as a barrel vault, was now apparently being conceived of as a succession of timber pointed arches, or even groin vaults like the coverings of the side chapels. Without further documentation this final comment by Giovanni may be read in different ways. I side with those who interpret this to mean that the letter (and associated ones) refers to the position of the barrel vault, piers, windows and tombs:[61] that the masters were not intent on revising the form of the vault, but simply wished to discuss with Alberti how best to support the barrel vault during construction. A semicircular barrel vault in timber would require centring until its form was complete, and this would be made of straight lengths of timber constructed from the springing-point of the barrel vault. Brunelleschi's acclaimed dome for Florence Cathedral was built to be self-supporting at every stage and was an obvious example that the masters would have known about (if only from the interfering Manetti). Once Alberti realised that the temple roof had to be light-weight, some system of centring had to be devised – 'the method of vaulting' – so that no errors were made during the construction process and 'so that things turn out in a good way'.

As work was completed internally, Alberti would have needed to know the exact positions of the walls which were to support the barrel vault and their relation to the façade under construction. The central upper portion of the façade would conceal the roof behind, and the commemorative medal shows it flanked by curved spandrels which were presumably intended to conceal the chapel roofs. Alberti revised the design of these spandrels in 1454, adopting scrolls instead of curves: he sketched the right-hand scroll in his letter to Matteo de' Pasti (see p. 59 above). He perhaps made this change because the levels between the new and existing buildings were not as the surveyors had anticipated they would be; the uppermost part of the scroll was intended to conceal the roof junction behind without raising the whole façade (which would destroy the overall proportions of the composition).[62]

When describing the scroll in his letter to Matteo de' Pasti, Alberti had used the singular (noun and verb) for a device that is one of a pair: his sketch illustrates the scroll on the right-hand side of the façade only. A partial description of this kind would normally have been enough for the experienced men on site, and Alberti refers to other details similarly. According to the same letter, Alberti sent a drawing of just one capital when there are four distinctive Composite capitals on the façade – a type that Matteo de' Pasti would not have seen before.[63] As Matteo wrote to Sigismondo on 17 December 1454:

> Messer Battista degli Alberti sent me a drawing of the façade and a most beautiful capital, and then Your Excellency has sent that same drawing [i.e., a design of the façade] and a letter of Messer Battista, which Piero de' Gennari has shown me. And we have been with all the masters and engineers, and we have seen the said design and considered it well. It is in this form: where the tomb was to go was square, according to the model of messer Battista, in wood, and this design is round, that is to say in the manner of a niche, and the said niche is a most beautiful work, and stronger, and the pier [*pilastro*] is not cut in any way; and if one cut the end of a brick [*una testa de prede cotta*] this does not matter.[64]

It has long been assumed that the drawing showed the niche on the lower right-hand side of the façade and a pier from the façade of old San Francesco, which would be cut into by a square niche but left mostly unscathed by a semicircular one (fig. 44).[65] This has been disputed, again because only one niche and tomb are mentioned in this letter.[66] It is also apparent from the letter that the right-hand niche was under scrutiny because a problem had been encountered. While Alberti's earlier model showed it 'square' (more pro-

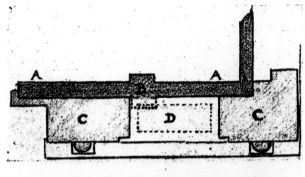

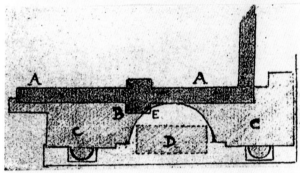

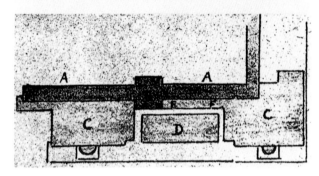

44   Alternative plans for the right-hand niche on the façade of the Tempio Malatestiano, in Ricci (1974), p. 257, figs 297–9.

bably rectangular) in shape,[67] the proximity of the niche to a pier of the existing thirteenth-century façade suggested that a 'round' (or semicircular) niche would be more appropriate, resulting in 'a most beautiful work, and stronger, and the pier is not cut in any way'.[68] As it turned out, neither proposal for the niches proved to be acceptable, and there was a change of mind about their intended use.

The external arcades along the right-hand side of the Tempio Malatestiano contain tombs fashioned like ancient sarcophagi. They contain the remains of the intellectuals and writers Sigismondo admired;[69] presumably, the arcades to the left-hand side were also to have contained sarcophagi. The existing sarcophagi closely resemble those in the mausoleum of Galla Placidia in nearby Ravenna, which were once thought to have been occupied by Galla, Constantius and

Valentian III, who were effectively the founders of ancient Romagna.[70] Galla was the sister of Emperor Honorius, who had removed the imperial court from Rome to Ravenna in the fifth century, and she was famous in her own right for having begun the architectural adornment of that city – a process continued by the Gothic kings Odoacer and then Theodoric (493–526), and particularly by the Byzantine Emperor Justinian and his wife, Empress Theodora. The tomb of Theodoric was also possibly another source for the design of part of the Tempio Malatestiano – the unbuilt rotunda (see pp. 69–72 below).

The side arcades are open to permit light to enter through the irregularly placed windows of the internal chapels, and the tombs in the openings do not shade the interior but draw the eye from the Gothic windows behind them. It is reasonable to assume that the two niches on the façade were also to have had tombs placed in them, and in that position they would have contained the most important remains. The niches share the same base line, and the springing-point of the arches correspond to one another, though those on the front are wider, which is to be expected if they were to have accommodated the principal tombs. It is reasonable to assume that Sigismondo's remains would have been placed in one of the front niches (fig. 46).[71] Indeed, the present position of his tomb, on the back of the façade, squeezed between the entrance door and the screen of the Chapel of St Sigismund, would seem to be an inglorious situation for the initiator of such a grandiose reconfiguration of the family church. Its position is not well composed: it does not align with the ornament of statues and pilasters above; it is not contained in a chapel, like Isotta's sepulchre, or the tomb of the ancestors (fig. 42); furthermore, it is visible only when leaving the church through the main doorway (fig. 38).

Certain examples of the commemorative medal show some kind of surface ornamentation within the frames of the façade niches, but the detail is too small and indistinct to show what, if anything, is being represented.[72] If tombs were to have been placed in these niches, neither option (of 'square' or 'round' niche) proved to be appropriate as building work progressed: a deep rectangular niche would cut into and weaken the old brickwork, and Alberti's semicircular alternative would cause any large tomb placed within it to project out from the opening. The options presented to Sigismondo are set out most clearly by Matteo Nuti, who was attempting to interpret Alberti's design on site. He writes:

I have seen Pietro de' Gennari and Matteo de' Pasti about the drawing which messer Battista has sent

45   Reconstruction of the façade of the Tempio Malatestiano with square niches containing (on left) the tombs of Sigismondo Malatesta surrounded by the Malatesta family 'castello', currently arranged around Isotta's tomb, and (on the right) the tomb of Isotta degli Atti surmounted by the stone carving of a winged angel and associated drapery which is now in the Chapel of St Sigismund (Olivetti/Alberti Group).

regarding the matter of the niches. And I find, according to the drawing, and as I said to your Excellency, on site [*in campo*], that if Your Excellency does not mind that the tomb is partly covered and partly uncovered, it can be done whether you want the round shape, as messer Battista said, or whether you want the square one, because in either of these two forms the work will be strong. But I urge Your Excellency, that if you are happy that the tomb be partly covered and partly uncovered, choose the

square shape, on account of the works that have been prepared and so as not to change the form of the design in any way. And also, in the square shape more [space] is left [*qualche cosa più*] for the place of the tomb, than in the round one.[73]

Several points come across clearly in this letter. Nuti is definitely referring to more than one niche (hence also, presumably, to more than one tomb), and introduces the subject through 'the matter of the niches'. His pref-

46 (a) and (b)   The tomb of the ancestors, in its position on the inside wall of the façade of the Tempio Malatestiano (photo/author).

erence is for a 'square' (rectangular) rather than 'round' (semicircular) one, which (although he is not explicit about this) would have to be shallower than Alberti's original design for a rectangular niche so as not to cut into the pier of the old fabric (fig. 44). As Pasti and Gennari had explained already: 'one could make it [the niche] square, as it was before. But it would be advisable to fill up the thickness of the old pier'.[74] Consequently, in order to strengthen the wall in this area, the depth of the opening would be lessened, and the tomb that was to have been placed in the niche would project from under the arch in either version. Thus, the choice is between two less than satisfactory options, and according to Nuti's argument there was no advantage in changing to a semicircular design.

A further advantage of keeping the niche rectangular was that the ornamental stonework intended for its back wall could still be accommodated. At least, this is one way of interpreting Pasti's and Gennari's comments regarding the 'castello'. As they explain, if it is decided to opt for the 'round' niche:

the 'castello' cannot go in there, as was your intention. But one could put it on the façade elsewhere, in that roundel at the head [*in quello tondo che è una testa*], and it will turn out very well. One could make it [the niche] square, as [was intended] before [. . .] and put the 'castello' inside [the niche] according to the first way. [. . .] But we must inform you, that if your excellency makes the niche, you have more than enough ornamental slabs [*tavole*] for the drapery [*cortine*], because one can make the [semicircular] niche out of any sort of stone; and if you make it square, you need a great quantity of ornamental slabs to make the 'castello' and it will not be as beautiful a work as the [semicircular] niche; and, in either case, the tomb fits there in the same way, and it will be a very fine sight. But I trust in God that your Lordship will come to see this thing yourself before it is done, and that you will decide what is best.[75]

The word 'castello' in this context is troublesome and has led the letter to be interpreted in several different ways. It has been taken literally to mean a castle motif (which is part of the decoration inside the church, and was used as a seal for the city of Rimini), or more liberally as a catafalque.[76] Latin episcopal records, compiled in the later fifteenth century and into the sixteenth, refer to an empty catafalque as a 'castrum doloris' ('castello' being the Italian for 'castrum').[77] The 'castrum' is not the coffin itself, which is referred to as the 'lectus mortuorum', implying that the 'castrum' and tomb together constitute the entire monument. In Rimini, the tomb referred to in the various letters is

termed, by those on site, as a 'sepoltura' (sepulchre),[78] and, from the preceding definitions, 'castello' may here refer to the Malatesta coat of arms which now surround the sepulchre of Isotta: this comprises a stone concoction of mottoes on ribbons, sculpted elephant heads with webbed crests, a crown, helmet and drapery (fig. 39).[79] Alternatively, in the Chapel of St Sigismund a carved stone winged angel holds a canopy of drapery – a baldacchino – yet there is no sepulchre beneath, as one would expect (fig. 45). Could this be the 'castello' mentioned in the letter?[80] It is applied to a flat surface, and could not be adapted to the wall of a curved niche. It is also part of a matching pair, and its counterpart is placed on the opposite wall. They have clearly been adapted to their present situation: an opening has been cut into the drapery to provide a window into the Cell of the Relics on one, and the lower folds of the drapery of the one illustrated have been trimmed by the corner pilaster close to the window wall. Perhaps Matteo de' Pasti and Pietro de' Gennari were suggesting that one of them could have been adapted to fit on the flat surface of the semicircular-headed *tondo*, which was to have been built on the upper half of the façade.[81]

Ultimately, it would appear that Sigismondo would not accept 'that the tomb is partly covered and partly

47 (a) Tempio Malatestiano, drawing of the stone carving of a winged angel and associated drapery in the Chapel of St Sigismund reconstructed behind the tomb of Sigismondo Malatesta (drawing: Olivetti/Alberti Group); (b) photograph of the existing drapery (photo: CMS/Alberti Group).

48 From Basinio de' Basini, *Hesperis*, the Tempio Malatestiano under construction. Oxford, Bodleian Library, MS Canon. Class. Lat. 81, fol. 137r.

uncovered', and no other compromise was reached for its placement externally. The external arched openings on the façade were built filled in, as a miniature showing the temple under construction, which accompanies Basinio de' Basini's epic poem on the Malatesta, the *Hesperis*, demonstrates (fig. 48).[82]

Perhaps, then, Sigismondo's tomb was to have been placed in the rotunda indicated on the commemorative medal (but not built) and so, ultimately, was destined neither for the outside nor the inside of the façade.[83]

RECONSTRUCTING THE ROTUNDA AT THE EAST END OF THE TEMPIO MALATESTIANO

While it is possible to reconstruct Alberti's design for the façade of the Tempio Malatestiano and the roof over its interior with some confidence from documents and the physical evidence of the building itself, there are few facts with which to reconstruct the rotunda. The main clues derive from the depiction of the dome on the commemorative medal, a commission for an east

end built in the sixteenth century (demolished in the eighteenth), and some incomplete foundations excavated in the 1920s.

The medal shows the dome to be the same width as the façade. It has a ribbed surface, the ribs springing from a cornice and rising towards the summit to an orb sitting on an annular base. Part of the drum below the cornice is visible, and there are two roundels placed on it which look similar to those built into the main façade. The structure below the drum is hidden by the façade, though there are no lateral extensions visible, or side supports to the drum and dome. It is likely that the medal depicts the Tempio Malatestiano in elevation, as the cornice of the dome appears perfectly horizontal, without a hint of curvature, and there is no diminution to the building as one would expect to see in an accurate perspective.[84] The façade, as built, is represented quite accurately, except for the later documented change (according to Alberti's instructions in 1454) to the shape of the spandrels on either side of the upper storey opening. It is possible, then, that the original wooden model of Alberti's design was the basis of the elevation on the medal.

The lack of visible support to the drum and dome on the medal has aroused two main responses from historians: that Alberti had designed a circular tribune the full width or slightly wider than the façade; or that the medal is inaccurate and cannot be used as a reliable indicator of Alberti's intentions for the east end of the Tempio Malatestiano.[85] It is known that nothing of Alberti's design was built beyond the ragged ends of the new Istrian stone side walls (figs 37 and 38) and that it was left to two friars to see to the completion of the building, some fifty years after Alberti's last recorded involvement with building operations on site. The friars were Emolo Martelli and Domenico Fassari, who ordered a row of five chapels to be built on 17 May 1503 at the east end of the church facing towards the nave.[86] These were demolished in the eighteenth century and their foundations uncovered after the Second World War: the present east end was rebuilt after wartime bombing destroyed an eighteenth-century structure there.[87]

A report linked to the discovery of some other foundations, of uncertain date and purpose, was published by Alessandro Tosi in 1927.[88] These foundations continue the line of Alberti's side walls on the southern side of the building. They extend the walls eastwards by about 10 m., before turning south for just over 9 m. (fig. 49). Several courses of Istrian stone bear on them for a short distance (about 1.7 m., but they are below ground level and not visible), and there are several courses of brick to a height of 400 mm. Subsequent

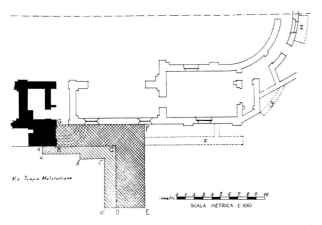

49 Plan diagram from Tosi (1927), p. 233, of excavated foundations at the eastern end of Alberti's southern side wall of the Tempio Malatestiano.

Proportionally, however, Alberti compares his design here with the great masonry domes of antiquity – Roman baths and the Pantheon. The interior of the Pantheon is just over 43 m. high and wide (fig. 51): similarly proportioned structures existed in the complex of forms that constituted public bath buildings in Rome.[94] The rotunda of the Tempio Malatestiano would have compared with the scale of these ancient buildings, with an outer width of at least 30 m. (it is shown the width of the façade on the medal),[95] so it cannot be ruled out that its dome was to have been of masonry, and that the nave roof was built of timber

50 Two views of the Alberti Group reconstruction of the Tempio Malatestiano. Rendered computer model, front and oblique side views (Olivetti/Alberti Group).

excavations by Gino Ravaioli in 1951 found nothing comparable on the north side of the building.[89] The position of those on the south side makes it likely that they were intended to marry with Alberti's design, but does not mean they were placed in accordance with his wishes; it is impossible to date these foundations.[90]

It is possible that a decision had been made after Alberti's involvement to complete the church with a Latin-cross plan. As discussed further below, similar circumstantial physical evidence has led to the conclusion that Alberti designed transepts (and presumably a dome) for Sant'Andrea in Mantua. But these transepts were not begun until about fifty years after his death, and were probably conceived by a subsequent architect.[91] Indeed, when Alberti did complete a domed rotunda at the east end of Santissima Annunziata in Florence it is reported that he resisted local support for a Latin-cross plan, arguing instead for the expressive circularity of the rotunda.[92] Other historians have concluded that the Tempio Malatestiano was to have had a circular rotunda – a notion I support.[93] The Alberti Group reconstruction illustrated here derives from the image on the medal, and on the proportions of the built portion of his design (described below) (fig. 50).

The commemorative medal shows the surface of the dome divided by the curved ribs into six segments – presumably only half the total of twelve are visible. The layering of roofing material indicated on the medal suggests sheets of a metal – perhaps lead – rather than terracotta tiles. The letter from Alberti to Matteo de' Pasti suggests that he was proposing to build a barrel vault of timber and metal over the nave. As the dome would probably have abutted the nave, it too may have been conceived as having a metal-clad timber structure, as was common practice for major churches in the region, including St Mark's in Venice.

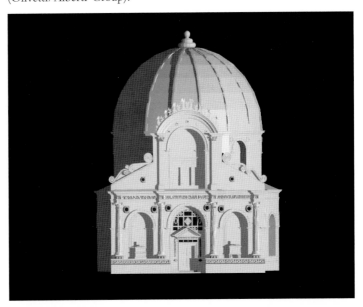

51 Pantheon, Rome, *c.* AD 128,
exterior and interior views:
interior (a) (*above*) attic, coffered
dome and *oculus*; exterior (b)
(*right*) view of lead covered dome;
(c) (*top right*) main entry portal;
(d) (*centre right*) main apse; (e) (*far
right*) a triangular pedimented
aedicule (photos/author).

because of Alberti's anxiety over the bearing capacity of the existing side walls.

The Tomb of Theodoric outside Ravenna has been suggested as a likely source for Alberti's rotunda (fig. 52).[96] This stone structure of *c*.520 is in two storeys and comprises at ground floor a decagonal base and a cruciform chamber with arms of equal length. The base is entered through one face of the exterior polygon. The exterior has a maximum diameter at its base of about 14m., which is set in to about 11m. at the second storey to accommodate a gallery. Within the decagonal walls at this upper level is a circular chamber, which has, as Alberti remarked, 'a single hollowed stone for a roof' (I, 8, p. 21). This massive stone roof slab is

52 Tomb of Theodoric, outside Ravenna, *c*.520, exterior views: (a) (*left*) general view (photo/author); (b) (*above*) detail of stone roof (photo/J. Rykwert).

smooth except for twelve equally spaced protruding
brackets at its perimeter: only six are visible at any one
time. The brackets on top of Theodoric's tomb may be
analogous to the twelve columns positioned around the
tomb of Constantine, the first Christian emperor – on
whom Theodoric modelled himself. For Constantine they represented the twelve apostles: later, at
Theodoric's tomb, the names of the four evangelists and
eight of the apostles were carved on these brackets, and
the upper chamber was used as a church dedicated to
the Virgin, and called Santa Maria Rotonda.[97]

The decagonal arcade of Istrian stone around the
lower floor of Theodoric's tomb is made up of angled
piers supporting semicircular arches whose rectangular,
blind niches powerfully evoke the character of Alberti's
long arcades for the Tempio Malatestiano. In Alberti's
time these were buried by a build-up of deposits as
high as a cornice from which the arches spring, though
he was presumably aware, through excavations, of what
lay below the surface.[98] A famous drawing of the
building by Antonio da Sangallo the Younger includes
the entire basement storey, and this structure evidently
captured the imagination of other Quattrocento architects.[99] Within the cruciform chamber of Theodoric's
tomb a shell motif is used to adorn otherwise quite
plain walls, and it is formed from a stone block arranged
in two pairs across the axes, with the hinge of the shell
lowermost: shells are also placed with their hinge lowermost on either side of the main door of the Tempio
Malatestiano.[100]

A mausoleum to a Gothic king who challenged the
mighty Roman Empire would seem to have been
appealing to Sigismondo. There is also contrition,
however, in his vow to provide the city with a
'monument both notable and holy' which would
honour 'God immortal'. In this context there is another
more universal model, the Holy Sepulchre in
Jerusalem, with which the Tempio Malatestiano may
be usefully compared. Along with the church of the
Holy Sepulchre, or Anastasis (Greek for 'Resurrection'),
and the Dome of the Rock, the Holy Sepulchre itself
was one of the main monuments in Jerusalem to influence the design of small and large churches around
Europe.[101] It was also the basis of Alberti's design for
the Rucellai sepulchre in Florence.[102] Santissima
Annunziata in Florence was also linked with the Holy
Sepulchre; Alberti's circular tribune there concludes the
rectangular body of the church, which bears comparison with what appears to have been the intention
in Rimini. Intriguingly, the Annunziata tribune provides a fitting conclusion to the east end of the Tempio
Malatestiano, as the plan drawing of the two structures,
to the same scale, suggests (fig. 54). By the end of the

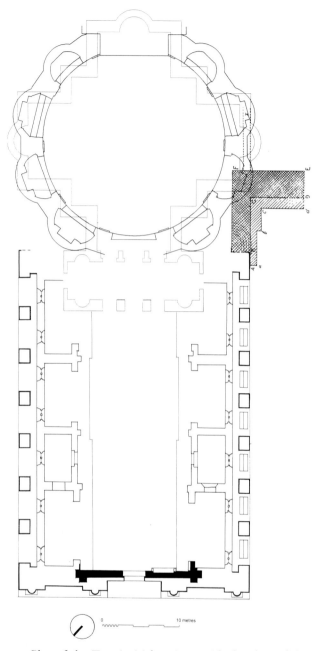

53   Plan of the Tempio Malatestiano, with the plans of the
tribune of Santissima Annunziata, Florence (in bold) and San
Sebastiano (light line) attached to its east end, at the same
scale.

fifteenth century the Annunziata tribune had become
the second largest domed structure in Florence after
Brunelleschi's dome over the cathedral; this was an
exemplar far more accessible to judge than any in the
Holy Land.

★   ★   ★

THEORY INTO PRACTICE: THE PROPORTIONS OF THE TEMPIO MALATESTIANO AND 'TUTTA QUELLA MUSICA'

The interior of the octagonal dome of Florence Cathedral is 72 Florentine *braccia* wide (42.01 m.) and 144 *braccia* high: or 'two diameters high' (fig. 54).[103] The dome Alberti intended for the Tempio Malatestiano while perhaps not quite as large, would still have been a source of wonderment as the second largest dome to be constructed in Italy since antiquity. Alberti undoubtedly admired the achievements of Brunelleschi, and in many ways strove to emulate his success, yet his reverence was not uncritical. At 'two diameters high' the cathedral dome was clearly not Alberti's preferred model for the Tempio Malatestiano (nor, perhaps, were its proportions the natural choice for Brunelleschi, who was working to complement the design of an existing structure with an established ground-plan).[104] With eight ribs marking its exterior (of which only four are visible at one time) and a profile taller than a hemisphere, the cathedral dome differs from the more simply shaped one depicted on the Tempio Malatestiano's commemorative medal. None the less, Florence Cathedral was still a model worthy of emulation and refinement. In his *Profugiorum* of the early 1440s, and presumably while he was still formulating his notions of architectural perfection, Alberti wrote of the 'grace and majesty' of the cathedral, and posed the question: 'who could hesitate to call this temple the nest of delights?'[105] Its consecration would have been memorable for Sigismondo Malatesta and the other dignitaries present both for the visual spectacle and its aural dimension; it has been argued that the motet composed for the occasion, by the Burgundian Guillaume Dufay, has a structure that complements and harmonises with the proportions of the enclosure in which it was performed.[106] Dufay was well known to the Malatesta, and had composed music to celebrate the wedding in 1423 of an uncle of Sigismondo, and Dufay probably composed the ballade *Mon chier amy* for the funeral of Pandolfo, Sigismondo's father, in 1427.[107] A year earlier

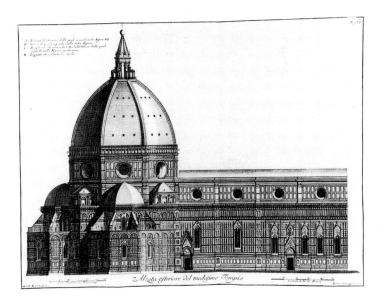

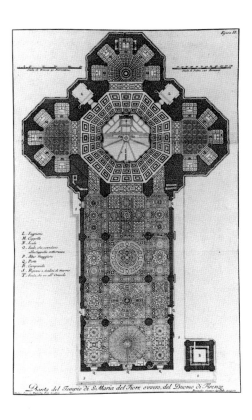

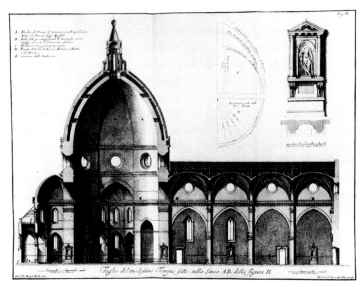

54 Plan, elevation and section of Florence Cathedral, completed 1436. Etchings from Nelli (1733), plates II and IV.

he had written a motet to celebrate Pandolfo's restoration of a church at Patras.[108]

Alberti too was sensitive to the necessary relationship between music and architecture. Again, in the *Profugiorum* he spoke of the qualities of 'voices during mass' in the marvellous setting of the cathedral.[109] He wrote too of the music he had captured in his design for the Tempio Malatestiano, and he communicated to Matteo de' Pasti his anxiety about some proposed modifications which would disturb its composition: 'You see from what the measurements and the proportions of the piers arise: if you alter them, you will make a discord in all that music [*tutta quella musica*]'.[110] The need for correct aural and visual proportion in imitation of nature was something that Alberti had argued for early in *De re aedificatoria*:

> Just as in music, where deep voices answer high ones, and intermediate ones are pitched between them, and they ring out in harmony [*concentum*], a wonderfully sonorous balance of proportions results, which increases the pleasure of the audience and captivates them; so it happens in everything else that serves to enchant and move the mind (I, 9, p. 24).

As their exchange of letters would suggest, Alberti was eager to pass on these ideas to Matteo de' Pasti and others in Rimini, and the wooden model of the complete design was an essential medium through which general design and specific details could be discussed. However, the notion of 'harmony' in architecture is a complex one. It is not identifiable through a single ornament, neither is a musical composition reducible

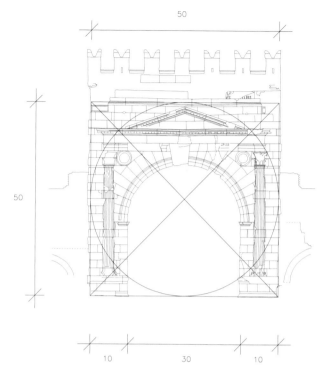

55 (*above*) Arch of Augustus. Photogrammetric drawing overlaid with geometry and with key dimensions in Roman feet (Olivetti/Alberti Group); (*below*) Arch of Augustus and facade of Tempio Malatestiano, Rimini. Photogrammetric drawings to the same scale (but with different ground planes) (Olivetti/Alberti Group).

to a single note or phrase, but is evident from the proper combination of each element of the building. Tampering with just one part may lead to the destruc-

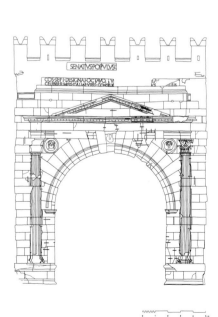

56 (*right and below*) Tempio Malatestiano, Rimini. Photo-grammetric drawings of façade and side elevation with key dimensions in Roman feet (Olivetti/Alberti Group).

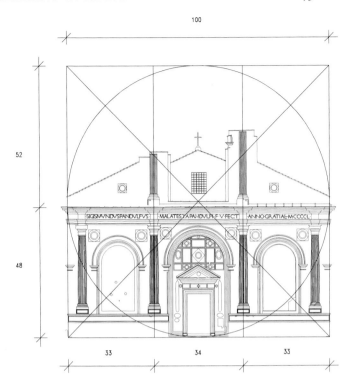

tion of the entire composition. This is why Alberti was so concerned that Matteo was about to wreck 'tutta quella musica' by changing the dimensions of piers.

There is strong evidence to suggest that the numbers Alberti used to determine his design for the Tempio Malatestiano are multiples of the ancient measure used by the Romans in the design for the nearby Arch of Augustus. It is composed of whole number multiples which closely correspond to 50, 40, 36, 30 and 18 Roman feet, a foot being 296 mm in length (fig. 55).[111] So, it should be no surprise that multiples of this measure are evident in the primary composition of the outside of the Tempio Malatestiano: from its 100 *pedes* overall width, to the 6 and 12 *pedes* rhythm of the arcaded piers down its length (fig. 56).[112]

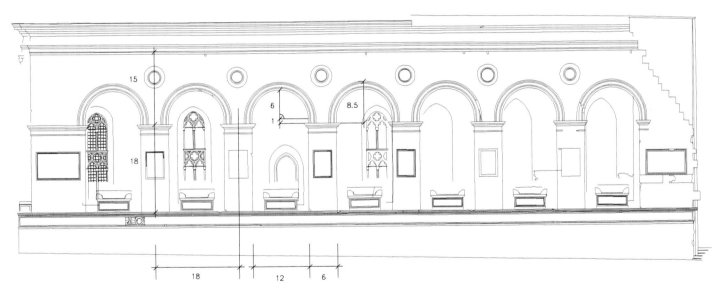

The relationship between number and measure at the Tempio Malatestiano is explained most simply through drawings. A clear process is discernible in this design. The overall width and height of certain elements on the façade are determined by qualitative whole number multiples of the Roman foot. However, the design of the column on the façade does not conform to the 'ideals' described by Alberti in his treatise and, although it shares some of the dimensions of the column on the Arch of Augustus (as do their entablatures), the size of the shaft appears to have been adjusted, and designed to fit within the overall composition of the façade of the Tempio Malatestiano (fig. 57).

What is so obviously missing from the façade is the topmost arched canopy-like element, shown on the medal as being concentric to the upper arched opening. By referring to this small section of arch, the Alberti Group reconstructed this element following the medal as closely as possible, and using a geometrical overlay of a square. The choice of a square was based on Wittkower's observation that Alberti's design for the façade of Santa Maria Novella in Florence 'can be exactly circumscribed by a square': indeed, the façade of Alberti's Sant'Andrea in Mantua is also 'square'.[113] The square used to reconstruct the façade of the Tempio Malatestiano has sides of 100 Roman feet.

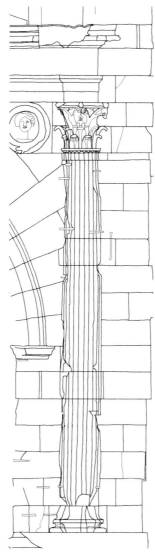

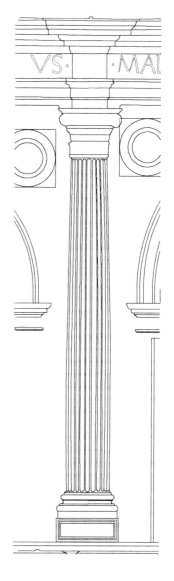

57 (*this and facing page top*) Comparisons: photographs of roundels, capitals and arch imposts on the façade of the Tempio Malatestiano (on the right) and of the Arch of Augustus (on the left) (photos/R. Schofield); and photogrammetric drawings of a column on the façade of the Tempio Malatestiano (on the right) and of the Arch of Augustus (on the left) to the same scale (Olivetti/Alberti Group).

0 1 2 3 4 5 m

Some commentators believe that the rounded pediment is incongruous with Alberti's style, though its form is echoed in Alberti's *ombrellone* above the façade of Sant'Andrea in Mantua (see chapter 8). St Mark's, Venice, may also have been a primary inspiration for this feature, and it was a motif taken up again, later in the fifteenth century, by Mauro Codussi for the façade of San Michele in Isola, Venice (after *c.*1468), thought to have been influenced by St Mark's and Alberti's design for the Tempio Malatestiano (fig. 58).[114]

Alternatively, Alberti was simply echoing in the façade the form of the barrel vault he had intended to be built over the nave: again, at Sant'Andrea, the façade replicates the elevations of the internal side chapels.

With complete harmony as his aim, the incomplete state in which the Tempio Malatestiano was left after Sigismondo's death surely caused Alberti some personal distress. However, his potential as an architect of considerable originality was fulfilled more completely in subsequent projects in Florence and Mantua.

58   Mauro Codussi, San Michele in Isola, Venice, after *c.*1468 (photo/author).

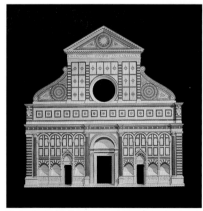 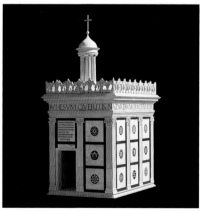 

59   (a) (*top*) Francesco Salviati (attributed), *Giovanni di Paolo Rucellai*. Tempera on board, 119 × 96 cm, early sixteenth century. Private Florence, Palazzo Rucellai, Collection; (b), (c), (d) (*bottom row*) wooden models of the Rucellai buildings in Florence as they appear today, as built for the Alberti Group, and as exhibited at the Alberti exhibition, Palazzo Te, Mantua, 1994: (b) the façade of Santa Maria Novella; (c) the Rucellai sepulchre; (d) the façade of Palazzo Rucellai looking through the Rucellai loggia (photos/Giovetti).

VII

GIOVANNI RUCELLAI
AND HIS ARCHITECTURAL ENSEMBLE
IN FLORENCE

INTRODUCTION

GIOVANNI DI PAOLO RUCELLAI (1403–81) lived his life among his clan in a western part of Florence: the parishes included San Pancrazio, San Paolino and Santa Maria Novella. With a population of more than two thousand inhabitants, the district was dominated by the Strozzi and Rucellai families (fig. 60). According to family tradition, the Rucellai had settled here after moving from northern Europe, following the successful expansion of the wool trade: the name Rucellai is derived from *oricello*, the wool dye orchil.[1] Giovanni was from a wealthy family, and during his early adulthood, through considerable business acumen, he increased greatly the wealth he had inherited. In fact, Giovanni proved so successful that, at the height of his career, he was one of the wealthiest men in Florence (fig. 59a).[2]

In 1448, aged forty-five, Giovanni began to build, lavishing a considerable proportion of his wealth on monuments intended to promote and preserve the family name. His ambitions were modest at first, focusing on improving his domestic accommodation to complement his rising status within the clan. He amalgamated several separate houses into one and carved a new central courtyard from them. Giovanni also proposed building a personal memorial, 'a chapel with a sepulchre like that in Jerusalem, like that of our Lord'.[3] The chapel, and sepulchre in imitation of the Holy Sepulchre in Jerusalem, were to be built either in Santa Maria Novella (perhaps as an adjunct to the existing family chapel), or in the Vallombrosan church of San Pancrazio near his home where Giovanni had an obligation to the main chapel under his grandfather's will.[4] He decided finally on San Pancrazio, where construction began about 1458. By then he was immensely rich, its being recorded that he was the third wealthiest man in Florence, behind the head of the Medici Bank and Cosimo de' Medici himself.[5] His alliance with the powerful Medici family was secured with the betrothal in 1461 of his son Bernardo to Nannina, a daughter of Piero de' Medici.[6] Political respectability ensued, and Giovanni was elected to the Florentine *Signoria* in 1463.[7] His wealth meant that he was not only able to make provision for his tomb and chapel to be built in San Pancrazio, but also to build a novel stone façade for his palazzo and a rich marble facing to Santa Maria Novella. Adjacent to the palazzo he built a family loggia, and both buildings looked on to a newly created public piazza (figs 59b–d).

Each project had its own mason who superintended construction work, and there is no contemporary record that these buildings were conceived by a single architect. However, there is a unity in the quality of their details and of their composition which would suggest they mostly derive from one individual – someone with a highly cultured and original mind. Two documents from the next century state unequivocally that Alberti was their architect. Vasari believed this,[8] and in a less well-known document, also from the sixteenth century, there is a declaration that 'Gio[vanni] di Paolo Rucellai built the façade of Santa Maria Novella which was designed by Leon Battista Alberti', and that 'in 1450 [he] built [*murò*] the palazzo in the via della Vigna and the loggia to a design by Leon Battista Alberti'.[9] While this statement confirms Alberti's role, the date of 1450 raises queries.[10] The surviving documents do not provide comprehensive building records, and it is possible that a design for the palazzo and loggia may have been prepared at this time but started later.

It is also difficult to obtain a complete understanding of Giovanni Rucellai's objectives behind this ambitious building enterprise. He wrote that men have two roles to perform in life: to procreate and build,[11] and that he built to honour God, his city and to perpetuate his name.[12] These earnest sentiments were recorded in his notebook, *Il zibaldone quaresimale*, begun in 1457, which describes a miscellany of significant and

60   Lucanton degli Uberti, the *Carta della Catena*, Florence viewed from the west, 1482. Staatliche Museen zu Berlin –
Preussischer Kulturbesitz, Kupferstichkabinett, inv. no. 899–100.

lesser events in his life.[13] Unfortunately, it provides
scanty information on his building projects and does
not mention his relationship with Alberti at all, so one
can only guess what first brought them together.

We know that Alberti was in Florence from 1434 to
1443 in his role as a papal abbreviator and was actively
involved with the Church Council which met in Santa
Maria Novella for four years, from 1439.[14] The earlier
lifting of the ban on Leon Battista's branch of the
Alberti family would have allowed members of the
Rucellai and Alberti clans to meet freely, and friend-
ships are known to have grown between them over the
years. Giovanni's second son Bernardo enjoyed a close
relationship with Francesco d'Altobianco Alberti, who
became an important family benefactor of Leon
Battista: Francesco owned a villa and garden at Paradiso
and made Leon Battista rector of an oratory nearby in
October 1468.[15] Bernardo knew Leon Battista personally, and wrote of their trip together around the
monuments of Rome, in the early autumn of 1471,
amidst a group of Florentines led by the young
Lorenzo de' Medici (see p. 29 above).[16]

While Alberti was much admired by his contemporaries in Florence for his intellect and writings, it is not
known why Giovanni Rucellai chose him for his
building projects over the heads of established professional architects in Florence; though Brunelleschi,
whom Rucellai had described as 'master of architecture
and sculpture' and as having 'revived the greatness of
antiquity',[17] had died in 1446. By the time Giovanni
was ready to build Michelozzo di Bartolomeo had

become the most sought after architect locally and
was an obvious candidate for a major commission.
Michelozzo had designed a new palazzo for Cosimo
de' Medici around 1444, a building that Cosimo had
earlier asked Brunelleschi to design for him.[18] Indeed,
it was conceived by Brunelleschi as part of an ensemble that included a church, loggia and a piazza; Vasari
describes the palazzo as free-standing, and across a
piazza from the church of San Lorenzo.[19] It would have
been a grand design, but Cosimo rejected it to 'escape
envy rather than expense', a judgement that prompted
Brunelleschi to lose his temper and smash a wooden
model of it 'into a thousand pieces'.[20]

Cosimo de' Medici was widely respected as the
leading citizen of Florence. Giovanni Rucellai, however,
was a major banking rival, and would have wanted to
project himself as his own man. Perhaps Alberti was
chosen because he was an independent man of vision
not affiliated to the Medici or to any other potential
challenger in Florence.[21] Whatever the reasons, it
would seem likely that Alberti became Rucellai's principal architectural adviser for most of his Florentine
buildings.

Accounts relating to the finance and acquisition of
related property suggests that Rucellai could not realise
his building ambitions until after the mid-1450s. Money
for the façade of Santa Maria Novella was made available in 1457–8.[22] At about this time construction began
on remodelling the chapel in San Pancrazio to prepare
it for the Rucellai sepulchre. It is proving increasingly
difficult to date both the start of the Palazzo Rucellai

façade and the extent of Alberti's original design for it.[23] Deciding on these matters has some bearing on the role Alberti played in Giovanni's building enterprises.

THE FAÇADE OF PALAZZO RUCELLAI

The façades of palazzi in Florence had undergone only gradual modifications since the fourteenth century and their composition followed the traditions of the locality.[24] Essentially, they had three storeys, each diminishing in height and demarcated by string-courses. An odd number of doors was preferred (usually one or three), and windows arranged above one another and placed on the string-courses. Bands of rusticated stone texture the surface between the windows, which is often rougher at ground level and smoother above the first string-course. The overall height of city-centre dwellings was regulated to a maximum of 50 *braccia* (about 29 m.) by a city statute dating back to 1325.[25] An annotated design of a palazzo façade, dated to the first half of the Quattrocento, outlines the general rules that builders should follow:

> Note that if you wish to make a façade for a dwelling, first take its diameter, that is, its width, and distribute the doors that you think will be needed. You should know that every dwelling needs one door or three or five or seven or nine or eleven, and [. . .] make the windows correspond above them [. . .] place void above void and solid above solid, noting that the solid needs to be the equal of the void and that in dimensions every window or door should be twice as high as wide, and that means two squares. Also you will make the thickness of the wall diminish every ten *braccia* [as it rises] according to how much space is available in the edifice, and this diminution should occur at the level of the imposts of the vaults or the ceilings.[26]

Changes to this general format were prompted by new legislation, or stemmed from changing notions about the decorum proper to a patrician palazzo. Thus, palazzi usually accommodated shops on the ground floor, until a law was introduced in the early fifteenth century which taxed rental property and discouraged this arrangement.[27] Thereafter, with fewer openings at ground floor, newer palazzi tended to be detached from the activities of the street, with the occupants' business and family life being conducted in and around private courtyards, and at first-floor level, the *piano nobile*. The palazzo Michelozzo di Bartolomeo built for Cosimo de' Medici in Florence after 1444 is an important example of this new type (fig. 61). It has a forbidding rusticated exterior contrasting with delicate *bifore* (round-headed window openings subdivided by three colonettes – small posts or columns, one in the centre and one attached to each jamb – supporting smaller arches) which resemble those of Palazzo Vecchio (Palazzo della Signoria), the city's principal symbol of political power and authority: Michelozzo also remodelled its courtyard about a decade later. Palazzo Medici influenced the next generation of palazzi erected during a construction boom after 1454,[28] and rusticated lower storeys, impenetrable except for an entry portal and perhaps small square windows, became more commonplace. The upper part was hardly changed, the higher windows opening directly above each string-course. While the wealthiest patrons could afford to build an entire façade in coursed stone, a less expensive alternative was to decorate a rendered surface with *sgraffito* having the effect of articulated stone blocks.[29] To cap the whole composition, instead of pronounced overhanging eaves in timber, the newer palazzi of the wealthy were surmounted by grand projecting stone cornices *all'antica*.

Superficially, the palazzo of Giovanni Rucellai was built in the Medici mould, with an arcaded courtyard and a rusticated façade with *bifore* in the upper storeys (fig. 59). But the application of pilasters to its three-storey façade, all in *pietra forte* sandstone, and the insertion of a small entablature above the colonettes within the traditional arrangement of *bifore* set it apart from contemporary palazzi in Florence.[30]

A strikingly similar façade to the Rucellai's was built at about the same time by Bernardo Rossellino for Pope Pius II in the new town centre of Pienza. Known as Palazzo Piccolomini (after the pope's family name) it combines the plan of Michelozzo's Palazzo Medici with a façade that may either derive from Alberti's design for Palazzo Rucellai, or his description of a palazzo façade in *De re aedificatoria* (fig. 60). Some historians even hold that Rossellino designed Palazzi Rucellai and Piccolomini, since his name appears in the building records of both. Surviving documents are not entirely helpful in clarifying the precise design role of each man, though I concur with the view that Rossellino reconfigured the interior of Palazzo Rucellai and Alberti invented its façade.[31]

The conversion of several properties into one new family home is described clearly and straightforwardly by Giovanni Rucellai in his *Zibaldone*: 'from eight houses I made one, three were on the via della Vigna and five were behind'.[32] Six of the properties were purchased between 1428 and the mid-1440s, and were adjacent to his ancestral home at the corner where via della Vigna (or via della Vigna Nuova, as it is now

61–3   (left) Michelozzo di Bartolomeo, part elevation and section through the façade of Palazzo Medici, Florence, after 1444, from Stegmann and Geymüller (1924); (centre) Leon Battista Alberti, part elevation and section through the façade of Palazzo Rucellai, Florence, after 1455, from Stegmann and Geymüller (1924); (right) Bernardo Rossellino, part elevation and section through the façade of Palazzo Piccolomini, Pienza, after 1460, from Stegmann and Geymüller (1924).

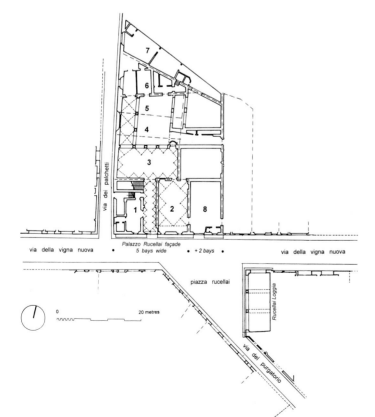

64   Plan of Palazzo Rucellai and existing loggia showing internal subdivision of properties, after Preyer (1981) and Saalman (1988) (drawing/author). The numbers on the plan relate to the property divisions referred to in the text.

called) and via dei Palchetti meet (fig. 64). Tax reports declare that modifications to the interior, principally the reordering of existing rooms around a new courtyard, date from the early 1450s, and that this work was supervised by Bernardo Rossellino (who was also completing work on the Spinelli Cloister at Santa Croce in Florence for other patrons).[33] The façade of the palazzo appears to have been conceived separately from the interior reorganisation of the buildings, and was not started until 1455, or later.[34] It was presumably needed to provide the once separate properties with a united front so that Giovanni's enlarged and enhanced residence would look like a house of substance.

The Palazzo Rucellai façade, with its visual arrangement of pilasters supporting straight entablatures, contrasts with Michelozzo's Palazzo Medici, which is far more plain and severe externally, and depends on the rusticated wall plane, cornices and ornamented windows for its ornamentation. Brunelleschi used pilasters to articulate plain wall surfaces externally, as reconstructions of his incompleted Palazzo di Parte Guelfa and Ospedale degli Innocenti suggest.[35] His architecture is better known, however, for its combination of column and arch, which proved popular with his immediate Florentine successors: the arcuated courtyard of Palazzo Rucellai, that of the Palazzo Medici and the Spinelli Cloister are just some of the many structures built in Florence during the second quarter of the fifteenth century according to the Brunelleschian interpretation of ancient architecture.[36] The visual lightness he sought in his architecture is emphasised in his preference for plain white walls on to which stone embellishment is applied. Conversely, at Palazzo Rucellai, Alberti expressed the homogeneity and integrity of the wall plane by articulating the rusticated stone wall and pilasters as one complete element. Alberti's architecture was different, probably because he had taken a different route *all'antica*. He had knowledge of the monuments of Rome first and Florence second. He knew that the endurance of the Roman remains was due to the solidity of their construction, and he was openly critical of the combination of column and arch as a structural system in *De re aedificatoria*. He argued that good practice demanded arched colonnades be supported on square piers, because 'The work would be defective with round columns, since the springing of the arches could not be fully supported by the solid of the column, and whatever lay in plan beyond the circle contained by the square would rest on nothing but thin air' (VII, 15, p. 236). Nor did the arcuated system carry with it the symbolism appropriate for the finest buildings. Referring to the arrangement of porticoes, he wrote

that 'The portico of the highest citizens ought to be trabeated, and that of the ordinary man arched' (IX, 4, pp. 300–01). He preferred the trabeated system because it is a more durable approach to construction: it places the emphasis on the integrity of the wall, with its bones and panelling, which is later pierced with openings (and weakened) only as necessity demands.[37] By contrast, Brunelleschi's designs are composed of separate architectural elements – columns, arches, beams – which are arranged in an additive manner.[38] Alberti's insertion at Palazzo Rucellai of an entablature between the colonettes and arches of the more usual Florentine *bifora* accords with this philosophy: it also demonstrates his willingness to accept a local and traditional assembly of parts, providing it can be improved upon and corrected (fig. 65).[39]

Brunelleschi had resolved the apparent defect in the column and arch combination differently by inserting what Alberti called a 'quadrilateral plinth', or impost block, between the base of the arch and the capital. This practice, Alberti acknowledged, was known to 'the experienced architects of antiquity', though he does not mention its recent use by Brunelleschi, nor does he rate it higher than a 'remedy'. Not every architect who followed Brunelleschi's lead – like Rossellino – was so well versed in ancient practice; or maybe Rossellino just chose to ignore what he saw. Imposts are absent from the arcades around the courtyard of the Palazzi Rucellai and Piccolomini (fig. 66).[40] He used them only once, inside Pienza Cathedral, but according to Pius they were there to correct an error – one, fortunately for Rossellino, he accepted as a novelty.[41]

Alberti argued in his treatise that columns are the principal ornaments to be applied to a building. When designing public buildings (temples, theatres, etc.) he referred to ancient precedent whereby columns are arranged in an orderly manner: the Colosseum in Rome, for example, has four tiers of columns, starting with the Doric at ground level and rising according to the ancient hierarchy through the Ionic, Corinthian and Composite. With private buildings he believed that architects could take delight in deviating from this established norm and 'a certain licence is possible'; the details (within the bounds of propriety) may achieve some desirable visual 'effects'. As Alberti says:

There are certain features of ornament which you might want to apply in private buildings and that must not be overlooked. [. . .] For the revetment to a wall there can be no project more pleasant or attractive than the representation of stone colonnading [*quam quae lapideae columnationes exprimat*] (IX, 4, pp. 298–9).[42]

65 (*this and facing page*) Leon Battista Alberti, the façade of Palazzo Rucellai, Florence: general oblique view (photo/author), and details (photos/CMS and T. Anstey).

At Palazzo Rucellai the appearance of 'stone colonnading' demonstrated the magnificence of its occupant and physically distinguished it from neighbouring properties; this is often necessary when building in cities, as Alberti acknowledges (IX, 2, p. 294).

As it is likely that the body of Palazzo Rucellai was already completed by the time he designed its façade, Alberti could only modulate the surface skin of the building. Being close to a road, his composition could have no physical depth, and the colonnade had to be fictive (as in a *trompe-l'oeil*) and be integrated with rather than stand proud of the wall, so he worked for the effect described in his treatise when describing a portico 'for the highest citizens':

> The ornament to the beam and the cornices that rest on the column should take up one fourth the height of the colonnading. If there is to be a second row of columns above the first, its height should be one quarter less. If there is to be a third row, its height should be one fifth less than that below. In each case the height of the dadoes and the plinth should be one quarter that of the column they support (IX, 4, pp. 300–01).[43]

Vitruvius describes a two- and three-storey façade for a royal palace when recounting the ideal form of the 'scaena frons' – the front, or elevation, of the stage in the Roman theatre. It has three doorways, a wide central royal door (with double leaves), and on either side single doors leading to the guest chambers (an arrangement adapted in 1580 for the first known permanent theatre of the Italian Renaissance, Palladio's Teatro Olimpico in Vicenza). The proportions of Alberti's 'portico of the highest citizens' are similar to Vitruvius' theatrical 'scaena' in the form of a royal palace, except that Vitruvius has each successive storey one-quarter less in height than that below, and the ornaments of the upper storey are one-fifth of the column height at that level.[44] The Alberti Group reconstructed Alberti's portico and compared it with the details and composition of his façade for Palazzo Rucellai (fig. 67). This revealed some features in common, as well as some marked differences.[45] The pilaster shafts, capitals and entablature built for the lower storey of the palazzo correspond reasonably closely to a tall version of the Doric column type that Alberti describes in his treatise, though their bases are shorter and narrower, and the frieze is shallower. The second and third storeys have Corinthian capitals, and the height of the pilasters is approximate to the taller Corinthian column described by Alberti, although the entablatures have different details (fig. 21).[46] With each successive storey of the façade the pilasters are only

66   Bernardo Rossellino, Palazzo Piccolomini, Pienza. View of the façade (photo/author).

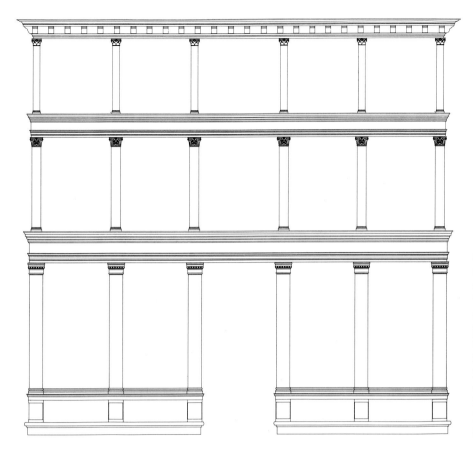

67 (a) and (b) After Alberti, *De re aedificatoria*, IX, 4, the 'portico of the highest citizen' (Alberti, 1988, pp. 300–01), constructed using ornamental details from the façade of Palazzo Rucellai; and compared with (*below*) façade of Palazzo Rucellai, Florence (Olivetti/Alberti Group).

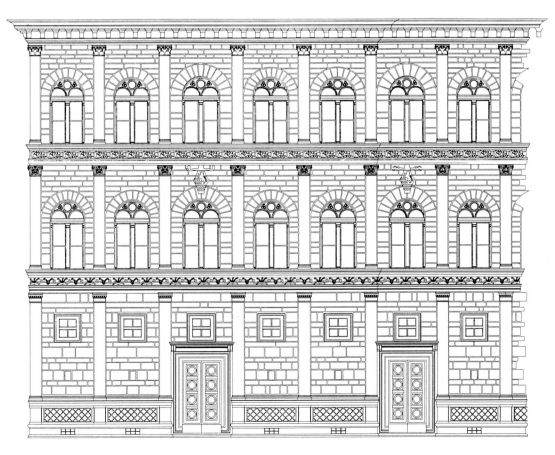

68 (*above left*) The corner stonework of the façade of Palazzo Rucellai, Florence, viewed from·high level, looking along via della Vigna towards the city centre, where it meets the junction with via del Palchetti (CMS/Alberti Group).

69 (*above right*) Part view of façade of Palazzo Rucellai, Florence, as viewed down via del Purgatorio (photo/author).

70 Wooden model of Palazzo Rucellai and the Rucellai loggia, Florence, as viewed down via del Purgatorio (photo/Giovetti): model as exhibited at the Alberti exhibition, Palazzo Te, Mantua, 1994.

slightly shorter and narrower than the one below, and, consequently, are increasingly wider than the arrangement Alberti suggests in his treatise.[47] Alberti certainly accepted that with private buildings there were instances when it was reasonable to deviate from a preferred arrangement of architectural elements 'provided the work is not malformed or distorted. Indeed, sometimes it may be more delightful to stray a little from dignity and calculated rule of lineaments, which would not be permitted in public works' (IX, I, p. 293).

It is possible that the ideal arrangement described in the treatise was a reasoned response to the visual constraints with which Alberti was contending in via della Vigna. Because of the narrowness of the street the new façade would have been hardly noticeable before the piazza was created in front of it (see pp. 119–24 below). With restricted vantage points, the façade would normally be viewed close to, hence obliquely. It is visible frontally from a street opposite, via del Purgatorio, but then only the three bays centring on the left-hand portal can be seen in their entirety (fig. 68). Alberti's concern to achieve the illusion of visual correctness in constrained circumstances may also explain the partial ornament at the corner of the façade. Like stage scenery, the ornament of the street façade is turned around the corner of via del Palchetti for a short distance to give the viewer the effect that the palazzo is more three-dimensional – and therefore grander – than it actually is (fig. 69). This device works especially well with the present spatial arrangement in front of the palazzo. As one approaches it, the eye is soon distracted away from the corner and drawn towards the loggia and piazza at ground level, and only the keenest observer is aware of the deceit.[48] Again Vitruvius had prepared the way for such a situation:

> The look of a building when seen close at hand is one thing, on a height another, not the same in an enclosed place, still different in the open, and in all these cases it takes much judgement to decide what is to be done. The fact is that the eye does not always give a true impression [so] I think it certain that diminutions or additions should be made to suit the nature or needs of the site by flashes of genius, and not only by mere science.[49]

As the façade was not composed to be appreciated *in toto*, Alberti may have created instead the *effect* of a well-proportioned composition designed to be seen from key viewing positions. He might therefore have compensated for the distorted proportions received by the eye when viewing the façade from an acute angle by exaggerating the height and width of the pilasters. This would explain why the upper pilasters do not

diminish in width or height according to this rule. In any case, Vitruvius had suggested the need to cope with 'ocular deception' when designing columns. Describing the appropriate width of columns relative to intercolumniation he argued for a thickening of column shafts according to a set of defined proportions,

> on account of the different heights to which the eye has to climb. For the eye is always looking for beauty, and if we do not gratify its desire for pleasure by a proportionate enlargement in these measures, and thus make a compensation for ocular deception, a clumsy and awkward appearance will be presented to the beholder.[50]

Similarly, Alberti argues for amendments to the normal proportions of columns and for a reduction in the slenderness ratio of the upper shaft according to the distance of the column from the eye:

> Some maintained that the bottom should be one and a quarter times as thick as the top. Others, realising that objects appear small, the farther they are away from the eye, sensibly decided that with a tall column the top should not be reduced as much as with a short column (VI, 6, pp. 201–2).

Further support for the notion that the façade of Palazzo Rucellai was composed pictorially is found in the trabeated, post-and-lintel frames around the windows. Had the pilasters and entablatures been proportioned as Alberti describes the ornament of the private palace portico in *De re aedificatoria*, the rusticated zone above each window on the Rucellai façade would have been less high, and the windows more tightly framed.

The need for distortion, so that buildings 'look' correct, was to be explained most clearly by the artist-architect Sebastiano Serlio.[51] Serlio illustrates the discrepancy between elevation and perspective when viewing a building from normal eye height and close to, and the need to exaggerate the height of columns the further they are from the eye (fig. 71). Though not as explicit as Serlio, the discrepancy between the storey heights of the ideal palace and the Rucellai façade does suggest that Alberti chose to compensate for the unsatisfactory effects of 'ocular deception'.[52]

ARCHITECTURE IN PERSPECTIVE

If this interpretation is correct, and Alberti composed the façade of Palazzo Rucellai pictorially, how then did he achieve this effect? What comes immediately to mind is the famous account by Brunelleschi's bio-

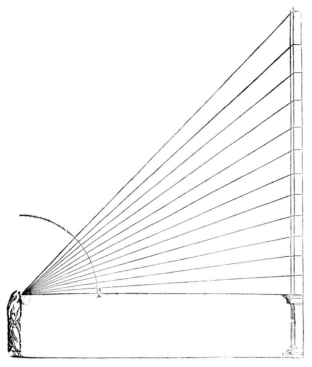

71   Sebastiano Serlio, geometry, and the relationship of eye to distance (column height) to ensure acceptable proportions. After Serlio (1996), I, I, p. 18.

grapher, Antonio di Tuccio Manetti, of a panel, about a foot square, on which an image of the Florentine Baptistery was created.[53] In order to fix the viewpoint for the observer, Brunelleschi made a hole in the panel,

> on which the picture was painted [. . .]. On the picture side of the panel the hole was as small as a bean, but on the back it was enlarged in a conical shape, like a woman's straw hat, to the diameter of a ducat or slightly more [23 mm . . .]. Looking at [it . . .] it seemed as though one were seeing [not a painting but] the real building. And I have had it in my hand and looked at it many times in my days, and can testify to it.[54]

According to Manetti, the reverse side of the small painted panel was placed against the head and one eye aligned with the single aperture. Through this hole was seen a mirror-like surface which was held in the observer's other hand, and was used to reflect the painted image facing it and the sky (preferably animated by passing clouds). The mirrored surface was moved by the observer, to and fro, so that the reflected image could be adjusted to the apparent size of the building.[55] Lorenzo de' Medici owned a picture on 'wood painted with a view [prospettiva] with the Palazzo de' Signori and the Piazza and Loggia and houses just

as it is' and a 'picture on wood, painted with the Cathedral [recte Baptistery] of S. Giovanni', perhaps the panel painted by Brunelleschi.[56] According to Vasari, Alberti also painted urban scenes, including a 'picture of Venice in perspective'.[57] Other fifteenth-century artists were yet more experimental with perspective (such as Piero della Francesca and Andrea Mantegna) and their works were intended, as Leonardo da Vinci later put it, to 'give the effect of the real thing and you will not be able to make people believe that the things in it are painted'.[58]

Conceit of this kind reflects the impact of the illusion-making device described in the *Vita anonima*:

> [Alberti] wrote *On Painting* in [three] Books. Later on, by means of this very art of painting, he also created effects that had not been heard of and were deemed unbelievable by the viewers. These pictures, which were contained in a small closed box, he exhibited through a tiny aperture. There you would have seen very lofty mountains and broad landscapes embracing a huge bay of the sea, and in addition regions very far removed from sight, so remote as not to be seen clearly by the viewer. He called these things 'demonstrations', and they were such that experts and laymen contended that they were looking not at pictures but at the true natural objects themselves. The demonstrations were of two kinds. He called one of them 'daytime' and the other one 'night time'. In the night time demonstrations you see Arcturus, the Pleiades, Orion, and twinkling constellations of this kind, and the moon, rising above the tall tops of hills and cliffs, shines forth, and the nocturnal planets glow. In the day time demonstrations the immense earth is illuminated far and wide by that brilliant light which follows the rainbow-creating dawn, as Homer calls it.[59]

An anonymous panel in Berlin depicting an imaginary city (fig. 72) is a daytime perspective in the manner of Alberti's painted 'demonstration'.[60] Besides a city view and seascape, it shows buildings that closely resemble Giovanni Rucellai's extraordinary palazzo and loggia in Florence. Both the detailing of the palace on the left-hand side and the loggia through which it is seen are consistent with Alberti's stance on architectural ornament.[61] Also, on the water's edge is what looks like either a mausoleum or perhaps a watch-tower, a structure that Alberti calls a 'mole' and describes in detail in *De re aedificatoria* (VIII, 3 and 5) (and see fig. 21c). Apparently, the post-and-lintel arrangement he promoted for the ideal palace was accepted not only by Pius and Rossellino in Pienza, but by the artist of this ideal city representation. Even the ships on the water

72 Anonymous, architectural view, late fifteenth century. Staatliche Museen zu Berlin – Preussischer Kulturbesitz, Gemäldegalerie, inv. no. 1615.

conform to Alberti's description (v, 12, pp. 136–8).[62] Alberti was obviously a source of great inspiration for this work, as he has been for others in this genre.[63]

Alberti had described in *De pictura* how an artist can draw an accurate representation of a three-dimensional object or scene distant from him, by using the veil (*velum*) of translucent material stretched across a rectangular frame, and placing this within reach of the artist's hand, and between his motionless eye and the object or scene to be depicted (see p. 7 above). Alberti considered the rectangular frame to be like a window on to a view, and that lines of sight emanate from the single eye of the artist and are intersected by the window. He recommends that the veil is subdivided by a grid of lines so that the artist can accurately trace what his eye sees on to its surface.[64] His viewing or 'show box', described in the *Vita*, also relies on the veil, since a painting is made on a translucent material and back-lit, and viewed through an aperture. For describing this device Alberti has been credited with the invention of the *camera ottica*,[65] more than a century before Giambattista della Porta described its more commonly known and more precise variant, the *camera obscura*.[66] As a development of Alberti's invention of 'a small closed box' the *camera obscura* has the advantage that it can be enjoyed communally.[67]

Moreover, in *De pictura* Alberti advises painters to judge the final effect of a painting by looking at it in the reflection of a mirror.[68] And if the façade of the Palazzo Rucellai was adjusted pictorially to suit the physical constraints of its location, I would suggest that Alberti used a combination of his 'show box' and a device similar to Brunelleschi's, whereby a mirror

would be moved to and fro, and angled, until the elevation looks correct when viewed from a particular position. The 'adjusted' elevation could then be redrawn within the show box, or on a veil placed between the observer's eye and the reflected mirror.[69]

PRECEDENTS FOR THE PALAZZO RUCELLAI FAÇADE

There are many surviving examples from antiquity of colonnading on public buildings, but none that relates to a private house: according to the *Mirabilia* the baths were ancient palaces, though Alberti knew their true purpose. In fact, there were no authentic remains of an antique palace façade for Alberti to examine at first hand, and there was some confusion as to what constituted a Roman palace façade. As mentioned above, Vitruvius had described the 'scaena frons' of the ancient theatre as taking the form of a royal palace façade, but it is unlikely that Alberti had seen an ancient 'scaena' intact.[70] He may, however, have seen the remains of a Roman villa near Anguillara Sabazia, though he never mentions this extraordinary concrete structure.[71] It is rectangular in plan, with sides of 15 and 20 m.; faced with yellow brick walls pierced with round-headed windows, it has red brick pilasters arranged in three storeys – a combination of elements similar to those found on Palazzo Rucellai. There are three bays to the short faces, and four to the longer walls which incorporate a stair. There is one large centrally placed door into its interior.

In Rome, the Septizonium, although not built as a

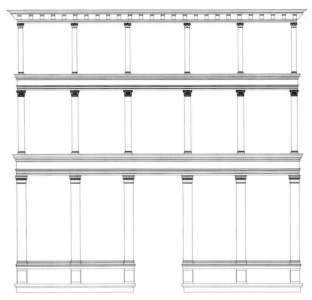

74   After Alberti, *De re aedificatoria*, IX, 4 (see fig. 67a).

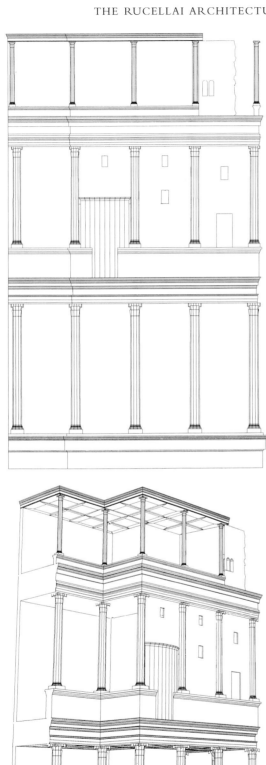

house, was thought by many of Alberti's contemporaries to be an ancient example of one (fig. 73). Constructed from columns attached to a wall, each of the three storeys of the façade was originally divided into seven bays or 'zones', a composition from which its name derives;[72] its appearance would have been not unlike that of Palazzo Rucellai. It was situated on the south-east corner of the Palatine, and Giovanni Rucellai mentions it in the *Zibaldone* as a 'palazzo' linked to Virgil, probably because of the medieval tradition that it had been the location of the School of Virgil.[73] This could have been no more than hearsay: other contemporary writers believed it was once the house of Severus Afer, or even a Temple of the Sun.[74] Before its destruction at the end of the sixteenth century it was variously used as habitation and even as a prison.

Alberti would also have known the biblical description of Solomon's 'house of the Forest of Lebanon': 100 cubits long, 50 wide and 30 high, it had a porch across its width 30 cubits deep and an internal courtyard. The palace had cedar pillars and beams arranged in three rows of fifteen, and 'there were windows in three rows' and 'all the doors and posts were square with the

73   Septizonium of Septimius Severus, Rome, AD 203: (a) (*facing page*) Giovanni Antonio Dosio, view of the Septizonium, late fifteenth century. Florence, Galleria degli Uffizi, Gabinetto dei Disegni e delle Stampe, inv. no. 1774 A; (b) (*above left*) in elevation (Olivetti/Alberti Group) and (c) (*left*) reconstruction drawing of the same, an oblique view (Olivetti/Alberti Group).

windows [i.e., arranged one above the other], and light was against light in three ranks'.[75] The pilaster-articulated palace façades in some paintings of the Virgin's Presentation at the Temple, for example Gaddi's in Santa Croce in Florence, were surely inspired by this description, as was the similar architectural setting for the bronze panel depicting the Meeting of Solomon with the Queen of Sheba on Lorenzo Ghiberti's casting for the Baptistery doors. Ghiberti's Joshua and Joseph panels for the Baptistery also have palaces articulated by pilasters.[76] Some Quattrocento descriptions of Florentine festival buildings reinforce the notion that there was a biblical source for this imagery: during the important city celebrations of the Feast of the Epiphany in the late fourteenth century the three storeys of pilasters of the Baptistery signified Herod's palace.[77]

But why would a palazzo façade articulated by pilasters be appropriate to Giovanni Rucellai, and if it was so potent a symbol of antiquity, why did no other noble family in Florence demand that their palazzi take on this character? The answer to this may derive, in part, from Rucellai's pretensions for his family and himself. For it is worth noting that, from the mid- to late fifteenth century, most of the other patrons who identified with this façade format were churchmen: Pius II who built Palazzo Piccolomini; Cardinal Riario who built what became the Cancelleria (papal chancellery) in Rome; and Cardinal Adriano da Corneto who built a palazzo in the Borgo (now called Palazzo Giraud-Torlonia). Of course, Giovanni was not a cleric, though he claimed to be descended from a 'Templar', the traditional protectors of Holy Relics. The specificity of this palazzo type may explain why so few were built.[78]

PALAZZI PICCOLOMINI AND RUCELLAI COMPARED

It is probable that Pope Pius II knew of Alberti's design for the façade of Palazzo Rucellai and his description of the ideal palazzo portico from *De re aedificatoria*. For he had passed through Florence in late April or early May 1459, having recently left Corsignano where he was already acquiring land to rebuild its town centre.[79] He stayed at Santa Maria Novella in Florence, the façade of which was then under construction according to a design by Alberti, and it is likely that Pius would have enquired after Rucellai's other local projects. He is known to have received Giovanni Rucellai's banking colleague Benedetto Toschi while there, though there is no indication this was for reasons other than business.[80]

Pius was *en route* to Mantua, where the Gonzagas were to host the Church Council he had called; it lasted from 27 May 1459 to 19 January 1460, and Alberti took part in the proceedings in his role as a papal abbreviator.[81] Alberti and the pope were not on close terms: when Pius wanted to read Vitruvius during his stay in Mantua it was Ludovico Gonzaga who asked Alberti to lend the pope his copy.[82] Dated 13 December 1459, this request just precedes the start of building work on Pius's venture in Corsignano.[83]

Palazzo Piccolomini is placed adjacent to a piazza fronted by a cathedral and loggia (fig. 75). It has a main façade three storeys high and seven bays wide. One large door, placed centrally, connects the main street, running east-west through Pienza, to the internal courtyard. The side elevations are each eight bays wide with two doors (one open, one blind). The bay widths are uneven: for example, the bay to the right of the main door on the north façade is some 400 mm wider than its neighbour, so as to accommodate the main stair immediately behind it.[84] This contrasts with the discipline of the Palazzo Rucellai façade, in which the rhythm is less dependent on the internal spatial layout: although it has rooms of differing widths along the street frontage, the bays have a consistent width, and only the door bays are wider. Surprisingly, considering that Palazzo Piccolomini was a completely new building, Rossellino's design appears to concede to utility first, and proportional perfection second.[85]

The heights of Palazzi Piccolomini and Rucellai are similar, although they were probably designed using different measuring standards (fig. 76).[86] Pius proudly

75　Bernardo Rossellino, Pienza Cathedral, with the Palazzo Piccolomini (on the right) and piazza, seen through the loggia of the Palazzo Comune. Partially rendered computer model (Olivetti/Alberti Group).

76 Comparison of the façades of the Palazzi Piccolomini and Rucellai to the same scale: (a) part elevation of the façade of Palazzo Piccolomini adjacent to the cathedral; (b) the façade of Palazzo Rucellai. Partially completed photogrammetric drawing (Olivetti/Alberti Group).

describes the physical character of Palazzo Piccolomini in his *Commentari*, relating its dimensions in *pedes*, and by comparing his measurements with those of the building itself his 'foot' can be calculated. It is close to 277 mm, which bears no relation to any other official foot measure in the region, though it may have been derived from Pius' own foot.[87] The standard of measure used by Alberti to design the Palazzo Rucellai façade has not been identified with any certainty, though the pilaster and bay widths are subdivisible by multiples of a unit of measure close to 582 mm (i.e. about 2 mm shorter than the official Florentine building measure, the *braccio da panna*). This slight reduction of a standard measure may have been necessary if the 'ideal palace' façade was to fit the physical constraints of its site in via della Vigna: the bay widths may have been narrowed fractionally to cover the property that Giovanni Rucellai already owned, much as the storeys appear to be 'stretched' vertically to compensate for acute viewing positions.

The other main difference between their two façades is that the pilasters of Palazzo Piccolomini narrow with each successive storey while those of the Palazzo Rucellai are, to the eye at least, the same.[88] In other words, while the façades appear similar at a glance, they are in fact detailed quite differently. Indeed, Palazzo Piccolomini is closest to Alberti's account of the proportions of the private palace in *De re aedificatoria* than

the Rucellai. It would seem to me that, for the Piccolomini façade, Rossellino was filtering his reading of Alberti's text through the details of Palazzo Rucellai; and he referred to the plan of Palazzo Medici for its overall form. Whereas Alberti's design for Palazzo Rucellai derives directly from his interpretation of ancient sources, as well as the very specific physical constraints of the site. Ultimately, I would argue that what distinguishes Alberti from Rossellino is his erudition and greater command of architecture *all'antica*, which enabled him to invent a façade that appeared antique to his contemporaries. While it can probably never be proved absolutely, there is no doubt in my mind that Alberti's design for the Palazzo Rucellai façade informed Rossellino's palace design for Pope Pius II, but that Alberti had no direct involvement in the design of Pius's ensemble of buildings in Pienza.

PALAZZO RUCELLAI EXTENDED

Of the separate houses that Rossellino combined to form Palazzo Rucellai three were situated on via della Vigna and five were behind.[89] Five bays of Alberti's façade would have been sufficient to cover the first two properties Giovanni owned along via della Vigna, starting from the corner of via del Palchetti. The door central to these five bays leads directly to the internal loggia and courtyard built by Rossellino. Alberti's façade was probably widened once Giovanni was presented with an opportunity to expand his accommodation and to incorporate the neighbouring home of Jacopoantonio Rucellai, who had owned the third property on via della Vigna. Following his death in 1456, it became available for purchase in 1458; it was clear to the parties interested in the purchase negotiations, even before the bids were shown, that there was 'someone who would gain great convenience from the house', and this led to a much inflated asking price.[90]

The five-bay façade may have been complete at this time, for as a contemporary document relates: 'From his old house [. . .] Giovanni [. . .] is building [. . .] a large and agreeable edifice [. . .] which is understood to be not yet completed, at least in breadth, and which he will be able to complete together with the above-mentioned house [of Jacopoantonio] which is being bought'.[91] The Florentine goldsmith and architect Antonio Averlino (c.1400–69), called Filarete, cites the Palazzo Rucellai façade 'built in a new street called La Vigna' in his *Treatise on Architecture* of c.1460–64, written while Filarete was resident in Milan; he reports having seen a 'complete façade composed of worked stone in the antique manner'.[92] Alternatively, if the five-bay façade was not yet complete when the extension was being considered, Giovanni may have decided to adapt, rather than radically alter, what had been built.[93] From variations in the façade ornamentation it has been suggested that the five-bay façade had reached no higher than the first-floor frieze when the opportunity came for Giovanni to extend his house.[94]

Any further plans Giovanni may have had to acquire additional properties along the street were not realised in his lifetime. While the façade was extended to cover Jacopoantonio's house, its interior was not altered substantially and the second door on via della Vigna (which the façade extension incorporates) still leads directly into the old house and does not link directly with the courtyard that Rossellino had built already. In 1492, after Giovanni's death, it was proposed that the palazzo be subdivided in order to provide separate accommodation for two of his sons. The party wall between the five-bay façade and the adjacent house became the line of division since, according to the logic expressed in the relevant legal document, 'the house was made and constructed in two stages, namely the large and the small house, which are at present [. . .] one house, [and] are being used as one house'.[95]

This subdivision halted any further plans for expansion for two hundred years, when family descendants bought the property beyond the ragged and incomplete edge of the façade (fig. 77).[96] Had the façade been

77   Incomplete edge to the façade of Palazzo Rucellai (CMS/Alberti Group).

extended to cover this as well, the effect would have been truly monumental, with an elevation at least eleven bays wide and three entry doors onto the street; during the eighteenth century there was a rumour that Giovanni had planned a façade fourteen bays wide with four doors.[97] By then, of course, such grandiose extensions were more commonplace. Palazzo Medici was extended to the north and west in the mid-seventeenth century, after the Riccardi had bought the building, and the join between the old and new building is seamless. The same is true of Palazzo Pitti which developed from a width of seven window bays into a gargantuan structure of twenty-three. Such was the flexibility of the regularly composed Renaissance palazzo façade, and the skill of Florentine masons, that, in practice, the original rhythm of bays or windows could be repeated to almost any size that was practical and affordable, as if it had been so planned from the start (fig. 78).

★   ★   ★

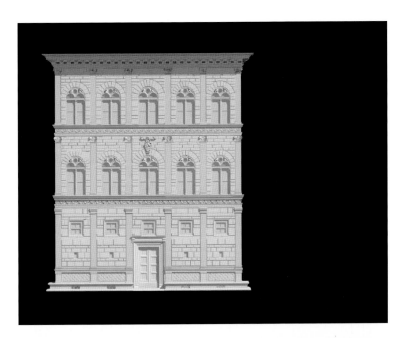

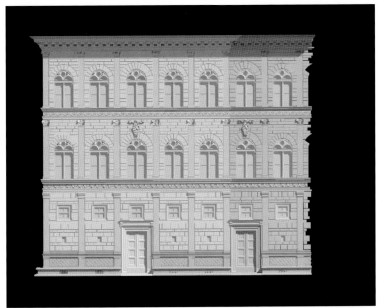

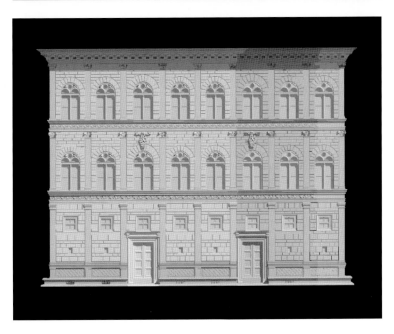

78 Computer reconstructions of the façade of Palazzo Rucellai with: (a) five bays; (b) seven bays, as it is today; (c) eight bays (Olivetti/Alberti Group).

THE FAÇADE OF SANTA MARIA NOVELLA

When the papal court resided in the cloisters of Santa Maria Novella between 1434 and 1443, it was one of the most celebrated Dominican centres in Christendom.[98] By the time of the Decree of Union in 1439, the light spacious interior of the church (a combination of a tall central nave with side aisles) already contained Masaccio's fresco of the *Trinity*, and possibly Brunelleschi's *Christ Crucified*.[99] The splendour of the church was dimmed only by its incomplete condition, since, in the fifteenth century, it was still lacking a façade.

The body of the church dates from the late thirteenth century, when the lowest portion of the main façade was under construction; only the *avelli* – the tombs along the base and their protective polychromed arched canopies – were completed. Above, a large rose window was inserted by Andrea di Bonaiuto around 1365; the walls were left bare until Giovanni Rucellai commissioned a new design for the façade.

Giovanni financed its construction through his part-ownership of the Poggio a Caiano estate, situated to the south-west of Florence. He had come by this property in 1431 through his marriage to Iacopa Strozzi. Her father, Palla Strozzi, was exiled to Padua three years later, and in order to ease a censorious taxation liability placed on him by the authorities, Palla sold Giovanni the estate (and other property) with the proviso that the income gained from it be used to patronise ecclesiastical building. Both families had donated chapels within Santa Maria Novella, but it was Palla Strozzi's misfortune that allowed Giovanni to promote the Rucellai name so visibly on its façade. According to a dedication written by Fra Giovanni di Carlo, a friar at the church, to Cristoforo Landino, Alberti designed the marble inlay on the façade, and this was executed by Giovanni di Bertino, a mason skilled in this art.[100] This attribution is confirmed by Vasari, who wrote that Giovanni Rucellai 'consulted Leon Battista, his close friend; and receiving not only advice but a design [*disegno*] as well, he resolved to have the work done as a memorial for himself'.[101]

Alberti, it would seem, reinforced his advice with a design of some kind. This may have been a combination of a letter and a drawing (which accompanied unsolicited advice he was later to offer Ludovico Gonzaga in Mantua; see chapter 8), or an annotated drawing (like his proposal for a bath building which he supplied to an anonymous patron; see chapter 9). Presumably a wooden model was built of the façade. Indeed, it is possible that models were made of all the buildings Giovanni planned to build in Florence, and that they were designed by Alberti as an ensemble, at the same time.[102] The models would have provided the masons on site with details of Alberti's designs well into the future, and would have allowed Giovanni to employ different masons for each project, when he was ready to build. This may be a factor that has contributed to the uncertainty surrounding Alberti's role in Giovanni's projects.

The chronology of the ensuing building progress is unclear. The inscription on the uppermost frieze of the church façade boldly delivers the name of its benefactor, 'Giovanni Rucellai son of Paolo', and includes the date 1470, the significance of which remains unknown; it does not denote the start of construction, which was 1458, when Giovanni was also purchasing the house next to his palazzo.[103] In 1478 work was still to be done on the entry portal and right-hand scroll.

In its arrangement of architectural elements (a pedimented temple-like upper storey with triangular panels and scrolls placed on a broad base) and the rich geometrically patterned marble inlay surface, in white and dark green marble (the latter known as *verde di Prato*), Alberti's design resembles the general ornamental qualities of the Florentine Baptistery of San Giovanni, and especially the twelfth-century façade of San Miniato al Monte which overlooks Florence (fig. 81). As Wittkower has written:

> the façade contains definite elements borrowed from S. Miniato and from the Baptistery in Florence. The Baptistery supplied some details, such as the pillars at the corners with their horizontal incrustation. And S. Miniato was the model for the disposition of the façade in two stories, of which the upper one screens only the nave and is crowned by a pediment.[104]

Also, the late thirteenth-century design of Santa Maria del Fiore, the Cathedral of Florence, by Arnolfo di Cambio (1245–1302), may have been an influence on Alberti. In both churches the internal modulation of nave-to-aisle width is as in the ratio 1:2, and the external surface decoration of regularly proportioned rectangular encrustation on the sides of the cathedral and the lower third of its original façade, before it was demolished (the present façade was built in the nineteenth century), was similar to the surface patterning adopted by Alberti for the façade of Santa Maria Novella:[105] the pink stone Alberti used for the portal is the same kind that had earlier been used at the cathedral, and on Giotto's adjacent campanile.[106]

Alberti adjusted the proportions of the façade of Santa Maria Novella by widening the lower storey,

79   Detail of the façade of Santa Maria Novella (photo/author).

80 (*this and facing page*) General and detailed views of the façade of Santa Maria Novella (photos/author, CMS and T. Anstey).

81   (a) the façade of Santa Maria Novella; (b) the façade of San Miniato al Monte, twelfth century; (c) the Baptistery of San Giovanni, exterior facing completed in the thirteenth century (photos/author).

building thick pillars at either end: these are banded in white marble and green *verde di Prato* and are paired with giant Corinthian columns (with shafts of *verde di Prato*), which match those framing the central portal – an arrangement also apparent at the Baptistery. The Baptistery was significant for its assumed antiquity. Although its present physical appearance dates from around the late twelfth century, it was commonly thought to have been an antique Temple of Mars, built when the city was founded by the Romans.[107] As Giovanni da Prato wrote, around 1425, 'this temple can be seen to be of a singular beauty and is built in a most ancient form according to the custom and ways of the Romans'.[108] It was thought to have been modelled by the Roman colonists of Florence on the Pantheon.[109] The central portal of Santa Maria Novella is certainly Pantheon-like[110] – it has fluted pilasters framing the door, supporting a coffered entrance vault decorated with rosettes – and Alberti's design is perhaps even more elegant and refined than its ancient counterpart (compare figs 51 and 82).

The four giant Corinthian columns of the lower storey support a cornice and a deep attic. This arrangement is reminiscent of Alberti's description of the ancient triumphal arch in *De re aedificatoria* (VIII, 6, pp. 265–8) (see figs 21a and 148a), an account probably influenced by the well-preserved remains of the Arch of Constantine in Rome, according to which the prototype has three vaulted passageways, the central one

being larger than those on either side, and with four giant free-standing columns supporting a cornice and a high attic: 'along the face of the wall inscriptions and carved *historiae* should be added in square or circular panels'. There are no *historiae* on Santa Maria Novella, only Rucellai insignia. The cornice on which the entrance vault rests displays on its frieze ringed feathers tied by ribbon (a motif also found on the lower frieze of the Palazzo Rucellai); the attic is decorated with squares containing discs patterned with geometrical inlays (similar to those on the Rucellai sepulchre); and the frieze of the lower cornice carries the Rucellai emblem of the billowing sail, the 'vela gonfiata' (also displayed on the Palazzo Rucellai, and on the Rucellai sepulchre; see pp. 106–19 below).[111] This culminates in the uppermost storey of the whole composition, which is arranged like the front of a classical temple, with a triangular pediment supported on four pilasters; its frieze bears Giovanni Rucellai's name and the date 1470, which contrasts in its directness with the Rucellai emblems more subtly incorporated elsewhere on the façade. The temple top is slightly under half the width of the lower storey, and is tied to its base by triangular side panels containing large inlaid discs: their outer edge is gently rounded by scrolls with more discs and flower-like emblems. They are like the scrolls Alberti had proposed for the façade of the Tempio Malatestiano, and similarly they were designed to conceal the roofs over the side aisles behind.

In the façade Alberti successfully combines the themes of sacred temple, triumph (presumably the Christian triumph of eternal life over death; see also the discussion of Sant'Andrea, pp. 179–87 below) and antiquity, with pre-existing medieval elements.[112] The precise extent of the original revetment of the lower façade is uncertain, as it is incorporated so completely within Alberti's overall design. It is recorded that by the early fourteenth century the revetment had reached as high as the round-headed arches 'in the middle of the façade', though some scholars maintain that Alberti designed these arches to harmonise the *avelli* at the base within the overall composition of his design.[113] However, it is likely that the façade had reached at least as high as the cornice now supported by the end pillars and giant columns, which Alberti introduced to frame and contain the fabric already in place. Evidence for this is documentary and visual. The Baldesi family, the successors of Turino di Baldesi who undertook to provide Santa Maria Novella with a façade in the thirteenth century, claimed the privilege then being sought by Giovanni Rucellai to complete the original bequest. They lost the court action that ensued, but managed to extract the concession from Giovanni that 'the part that had been done already, from the first cornice down, should be left just as it was when carried out with the bequest'.[114] The 'first' cornice was presumably in a position similar to the one now supported by the end pillars and giant columns. That the columns were not there originally is evident because the outer ones are placed over the original revetment and so conceal the fact that there were formerly five arched tombs on either side of the central door: the curve of the round-headed arches just below the cornice can still be seen rising behind the Corinthian capitals of Alberti's outer columns. As well as removing the end tombs and niches Alberti remodelled the original thirteenth-century portal with its fluted pilasters and barrel vault *all'antica*. Clearly, Giovanni did not honour the concession claimed by the Baldesi family to the letter.

The changes Alberti introduced were resolved with the pre-existing fabric by developing the Florentine-style ornament into the more disciplined Roman manner he preferred. The elements of the entire composition were then framed through the rigorous application of number and geometry. As Wittkower observed, the 'whole façade of S. Maria Novella can be exactly circumscribed by a square. A square of half the side of the large square defines the relationship of the two stories. The main storey can be divided into two such squares, while one encloses the upper storey'.[115] More accurate surveys indicate that the façade lacks a precise symmetry, but there can be little doubt that

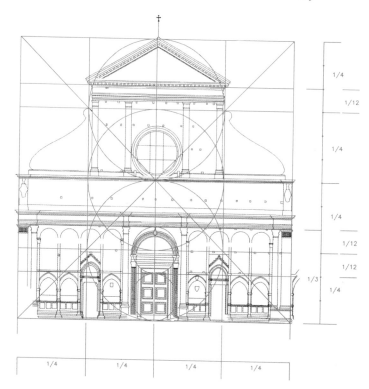

82 Elevation of Santa Maria Novella, Florence, overlaid with geometry and proportions derived from an encompassing square. Photogrammetric drawing (Olivetti/Alberti Group).

Alberti intended the composition of number and geometry to be regarded as perfect.[116] The façade fits within a square of 60 Florentine *braccia* – wider and higher than the body of the church behind.[117] Within this geometry the elements of the San Miniato façade are refined and rearranged to fit the constraints imposed by the larger size and existing elements of the front wall of Santa Maria Novella. Indeed, the main width and height dimensions of Alberti's design are about one and a half times larger than those of San Miniato al Monte (fig. 83).[118] It was enlarged to cover the existing west wall of Santa Maria Novella, and perhaps to provide the final design with a discernible square geometry.[119]

Alberti had to incorporate a pre-existing circular rose window within the upper storey, and a modern observer may consider it to have been positioned too low in relation to the pedimented 'temple top' that now frames it; when seen from ground level and close to the entry door, the lower part of its surrounding moulding is lost from view and it is difficult to discern its details. However, the string-course on which the rose window rests is the midpoint of the façade as Alberti designed it. Above this is a low plinth from which the pilasters rise. On either side are the triangular panels edged by scrolls, each containing an inlaid disc with a wheel

83 (*this and facing page*) Elevations of Santa Maria Novella and San Miniato al Monte, Florence, to the same scale (Olivetti/Alberti Group).

pattern. Slightly smaller in diameter and similar in effect to these is the circular motif of a sun-burst placed at the centre of the tympanum.[120] The three discs appear to orbit the rose window, and they combine to establish a coherent visual order independent of the vertical pilasters which constitute the 'temple' motif. The barrel-vaulted entry portal is the same width as the rose window, and this design draws the eye down along a vertical axis, which the rose window and sun-burst disc straddle; there is in effect a notional cross-axis con-necting these motifs, arranged like a crucifix, with the sun-burst and face at the 'head' and the main door at the 'foot' of the composition. Visual complexity of this kind assists in combining the old and new features of the façade, and provides it with a vitality not found again until the interweaving of motifs in Alberti's later Sant'Andrea, or in Palladio's overlay of a tall narrow temple format on to a broad low base in his Venetian church façades.[121]

There is another body-related reading of the façade

which centres on the rose window. Its central point measures 36 *braccia* above the height of the entry platform within a façade 60 *braccia* high. The number relationship of 36:60 appears in Alberti's *Tabulae dimensionorum hominis*, where the 'ideal' man 60 inches tall has a navel 36 inches off the ground. However, while an association between the body of man and the 'body' of the church was made most memorably by Francesco di Giorgio later that century,[122] the analogy of rose window to 'umbilicus' is not entirely appropriate when applied to the façade of Santa Maria Novella, that of 'oculus' better fitting this kind of aperture. Pope Pius II described a similar circular window on the façade of Pienza Cathedral as 'a great eye like that of the Cyclops', such that the façade of the church is a clear representation of a 'face'.[123] But for the rose window to be appreciated as 'an eye' at Santa Maria Novella, it would need to be set higher; this would have required a much lower design for the façade, presumably no higher than the apex of the nave roof, and would have resulted in a rectangular, non-square composition. However, the 36:60 *braccia* relationship is also the 'perfect' 6:10 ratio emphasised by Vitruvius, and Alberti would surely have recognised this as a satisfactory by-product of the square geometry which was the starting-point for his design.

In whatever way Alberti intended the visual and numerical intricacies of this design to be understood by an observer, the essential qualities of San Miniato al Monte appear to have been adjusted for Santa Maria Novella through the application of geometry and number. This process of scaling and refining the compositional elements of a revered building type to meet the demands of its situation recurs in Alberti's other design projects.

84   Leon Battista Alberti, the Rucellai Chapel and sepulchre, San Pancrazio, Florence, after 1457. View north from entrance atrium of San Pancrazio, according to Grandjean and Famin (1837), before subsequent alterations.

THE RUCELLAI SEPULCHRE IN SAN PANCRAZIO

Porta San Pancrazio was built as part of the second circuit of defensive walls around Florence, and was the city's gateway to the west: the church of San Pancrazio is situated close by, just behind Palazzo Rucellai. Unlike Santa Maria Novella this was a building of no great religious or architectural significance, and was attached to a monastery which passed in 1235 from Benedictine hands into those of the Vallombrosan (one of the congregations of the Benedictine family). Don Lorenzo Toschi, who was abbot there between 1429 and 1460, developed the monastery into a place respected for its learning, and it was during this apex in the intellectual life of the community that Giovanni Rucellai chose to remodel a chapel in the church and place within it his own sepulchre.[124]

The main fabric of what is now known as the Rucellai Chapel dates from the beginning of the fifteenth century.[125] It was situated immediately on

85 (*facing page*)   Rucellai sepulchre, San Pancrazio, Florence, after 1457. View of the front of the sepulchre (photo/Scala).

86 (*facing page*) (*top left*) Wooden model of the Rucellai sepulchre, Florence, as it is today (photo/Giovetti): model as exhibited at the Alberti exhibition, Palazzo Te, Mantua, 1994. (*bottom row, left pair*) Pilaster capitals as built on one side and corner of the sepulchre; (*bottom row, right pair*) columns and entablature' that originally framed the opening between the atrium of the San Pancrazio and the Rucellai Chapel (but which are now placed at the entrance of the former church); (*top right*) a window in the main external wall of the Rucellai Chapel, and associated ornament; and (*middle right*) a detail of the lettering on the frieze and entablature of the Rucellai sepulchre (photo/author).

87 (*above left*) Foreshortened view of the vault and cornice of the Rucellai Chapel; and (*left and below*) ornamental discs on the outside of the Rucellai sepulchre: (*anti-clockwise from top left*, and see p. 228, n. 139) the 'vela gonfiata', or billowing sail; 'mazzocchio'; and a geometrical inlay (photos/author).

the left when entering San Pancrazio and, from the late 1450s until the early nineteenth century, was visible from an entrance atrium to the church through a colonnaded opening. The chapel is constructed of stone of irregular size, faced with dressed stone towards the piazzetta in front of the church, and rendered along via della Spada which runs along one side.

According to a restoration of the chapel in the late 1970s, when a close examination of the fabric was last possible, it was evident that the Rucellai Chapel was made by remodelling an existing chapel, by slightly

raising its floor and by opening up the long wall adjacent to the entrance atrium (fig. 84).[126] Two columns were positioned in this new opening to support a cornice and a new brick barrel-vault over the chapel. On the long outside wall opposite, three new windows were opened to admit light from via della Spada. Otherwise the new internal ornament was applied to the existing wall surface and does not break into the existing fabric, the internal cornices being cut in by the minimum depth required for their stability.

The chapel was first restored in the mid-eighteenth

century when alterations were also made to the church.[127] The changes were short-lived as the Vallombrosan community was suppressed during Napoleonic times and the church deconsecrated in 1808.[128] The columns that formerly articulated the Rucellai Chapel opening were removed and placed in their present location on the church façade and the chapel opening towards the atrium bricked in (figs 87–9), thus destroying the spatial composition of what Vasari considered to be Alberti's best work.[129] Nevertheless, the sepulchre itself remains one of the most exquisite monuments in Florence.

Vasari's attribution of the Rucellai Chapel and sepulchre to Alberti cannot be verified by surviving documentation, and there are no precise records as to when work started on the chapel. A date around 1457–9 has been offered,[130] and work was concluded in 1467 according to an inscription over the door of the sepulchre (though such statements are not always reliable). This was about the time that the Rucellai loggia is presumed to have been finished (in time for the marriage of Giovanni Rucellai's second son Bernardo in 1466). It is also uncertain who executed the design. Giovanni di Bertino has been suggested on the basis of his recorded involvement with the façade of Santa Maria Novella, and the similar quality and type of marble inlay work on both monuments.[131] Whoever supervised work over the ten years or so, the eighteenth-century chronicler Giuseppe Richa is adamant that Alberti was its architect.[132]

The way in which the chapel was remodelled certainly corresponds to Alberti's views on architecture. For example, he was always concerned to work with what existed and not destroy existing structure unnecessarily: 'I would prefer you to leave all old buildings intact, until such time as it becomes impossible to construct anything without demolishing them' (III, 1, p. 62). The skilful insertion of pilasters and a new vault into the chapel did not destabilise the existing fabric, either physically or visually.[133] While the opening of the Rucellai Chapel on to the atrium of the church was a radical intervention, it was presumably required by Giovanni Rucellai to make conspicuous his donation to the church.

Giovanni does not mention his architect, but in a letter to his mother he records that he sent a team of surveyors to Jerusalem to obtain the exact measurements of the Holy Sepulchre on which his own sepulchre is based.[134] There is some doubt about the authenticity of this letter, and there is a suggestion that it is no more than a fabrication by an over-enthusiastic archivist of Rucellai family history.[135] To send a party of men to Jerusalem at this time would

have incurred not only considerable expense but time and danger; since the fall of Constantinople in 1453 the whole of Christendom – and this area in particular – was in a precarious position. It would have been easier to have based the design on one of the many copies already built in Europe or on verbal reports. Giovanni's banking partner, Stoldo Frescobaldi, had a kinsman who visited Jerusalem in the late fourteenth century and made a record of its monuments. There were also Eastern delegates at the Council of Florence in the 1430s with whom it would have been possible to discuss the monuments of the Holy Land; furthermore, Cosimo de' Medici had established an open line of communication between Florence and Jerusalem.[136] Whether or not a team was sent to examine the Holy Sepulchre, it is certain that Giovanni needed more than surveyors to translate its dimensions and form into a monument worthy of his name and high ambitions. Drawings of its present state show how Alberti refined the original model for its Florentine situation.[137]

The Rucellai sepulchre was positioned at the centre of its chapel (which was subsequently extended at one end; fig. 88). Both its length and width are one-third less than those of the chapel, and its height, to the top of its surmounting ciborium, is half the total height of the space. It is half the size and a geometrically 'perfected' interpretation of the Holy Sepulchre in Jerusalem. Such improvements were necessary because, by Quattrocento standards, the Holy Sepulchre had been badly built, with irregularities in its formal geometry; as a result of its age and venerability it had been 'restored' and 'improved', and additions had been made. A drawing published in 1619 gives an impression of its appearance at that time (fig. 89c).[138] The main differences between the Holy Sepulchre and the Rucellai concern the articulation of the rounded end and the ornamental details (figs 90a and b).

The Rucellai sepulchre is rectangular in plan with a semicircular apse at one end. Its exterior is articulated by rhythmically placed fluted pilasters with Corinthian capitals. An ornamental marble inlay is set in squares between the pilasters, each containing discs mainly of geometricised stars in white, serpentine and crimson. Other discs contain heraldic devices of the Rucellai and Medici, the Star of David and Solomon's knot.[139] The pilasters support an ornate entablature and a frieze carrying an inscription which circumscribes the sepulchre. Above is a crown of Florentine lilies, and a ciborium composed of a ring of slender columns supporting a circular entablature, above which is a dome decorated with a spiral relief and supporting a cross-on-orb.

The apse is narrower than the main rectangular body of the sepulchre by two pilaster widths, and is curved,

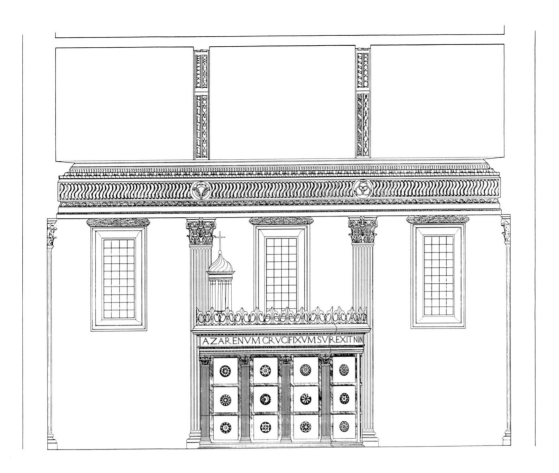

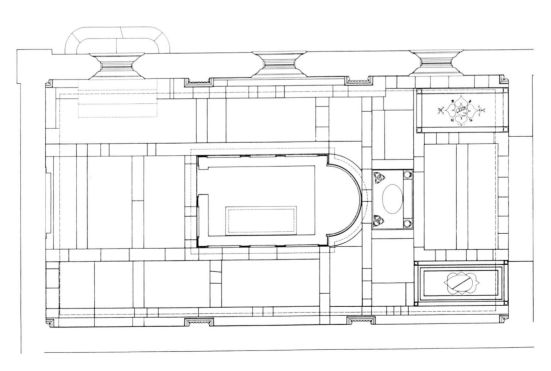

88 Plan and side elevation of the Rucellai Chapel and sepulchre, Florence, as it is today. Drawings by Prue Chiles for Olivetti/Alberti Group.

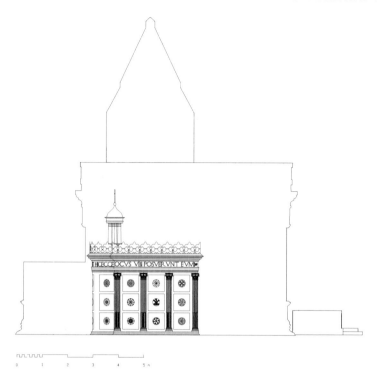

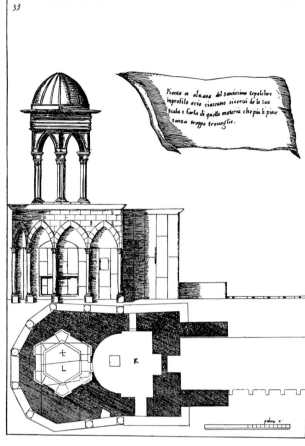

89   (*above*) Side elevations, to the same scale of the Rucellai sepulchre (in detail: Olivetti/Alberti Group) and the Holy Sepulchre, Jerusalem (in outline: after Biddle); and (*right*) plan and side elevation of the Holy Sepulchre, Jerusalem, published in 1619, Amico (1953).

whereas the side walls of the Holy Sepulchre have a polygonal ending. There are no pilasters on the Rucellai apse, probably because of its steep radius, and it is articulated instead by three bays of geometrical marble inlay; the polygonal end of the Holy Sepulchre is articulated by five bays: the side walls of each sepulchre have four pilasters or columns; these form arched recesses on the Holy Sepulchre and are trabeated on the Rucellai sepulchre. The balustraded parapet on top of the Holy Sepulchre has its equivalent in the lily motif which links to form a crown around the top of the Rucellai sepulchre. The most marked differences between their respective outlines is that the Rucellai sepulchre lacks a plinth and does not have arched recesses between the pilasters; its ciborium is half the size of the original and is at the front of the construction instead of at the rear.

Alberti may have decided not to include arches and to change the proportions of the ciborium for reasons of composition. It was presumably desirable that the Rucellai ciborium was visible in its entirety when viewed from the atrium, which directly preceded the nave of San Pancrazio, of which the newly framed opening formed one side. Otherwise the ciborium would have appeared to be cut off, and the view flawed

(fig. 84). The present location of the ciborium, over the vault to the internal chamber, is probably incorrect. The vault is buckling under its load, when there is a much sounder base for it at the midpoint of the semicircular apse which is of solid masonry. Indeed, it would appear from the posthumous sixteenth-century portrait of Giovanni Rucellai, surrounded by his buildings (fig. 59a), that the sepulchre has its ciborium set over the apse, as on the Holy Sepulchre. It may have been moved to its present position as late as the nineteenth century, to improve the visual composition of the sepulchre when the open colonnade Alberti created was bricked in, and access to the chapel restricted to a door entering off via della Spada.[140]

The front elevation of the Rucellai sepulchre is divided into two bays, with the door to the internal chamber placed off-centre (figs 77 and 91). The Holy Sepulchre is entered centrally and has two sepulchral chambers, one in front of the other, the first (outer) of which contains a stone slab, set like a bed against one wall; there is a similar slab in the single chamber of the Rucellai sepulchre, on the right, immediately on entering (the door is off-centre because the slab takes up half the width of the chamber). The chamber of the Rucellai sepulchre is frescoed (possibly by Alesso

90 Computer reconstruction of Alberti's design for the Rucellai Chapel and sepulchre, San Pancrazio, Florence. Rendered views of the computer model: (a) obliquely, and closer to the rear of the sepulchre; (b) from the centre of the former atrium of San Pancrazio (Olivetti/Alberti Group).

91   Rucellai sepulchre, Florence. Front and side elevations with the ciborium repositioned to the rear of the selpulchre (Olivetti/Alberti Group).

0   1   2   3   4   5 m

Baldovinetti, 1425–99) and depicts scenes of the *Descent from the Cross* (fig. 92). On the wall by the stone slab Christ is flanked by two angels; scenes in the lunettes of the barrel vault portray, at the far end, Mary Magdalen (dressed in red and poised over the corpse of Christ), and over the entrance, the Virgin kneeling before the corpse of Christ. The barrel vault is in deep blue and is highlighted by stars which were originally spangled (some traces of gilt remain). Around the Rucellai sepulchre the pavement of the chapel is composed of rectangular panels of white marble bordered by plain *pietra serena* strips. In the fifteenth century, only one floor panel bore an inscription, that is the one placed just behind the apse of the sepulchre.[141] It can be lifted to gain access to a vaulted space beneath and, according to the inscription, it marks the place where the body of Christ was placed for cleansing and embalming before the entombment. It would appear that Giovanni was concerned not only to mirror the form of the original shrine but wished also to capture

its sacred qualities, and perhaps even to re-enact rituals associated with that place. The sepulchre achieved sacramental status in 1471 when a bull from Pope Paul II granted worshippers who visited it, on Good Fridays and Holy Sundays, seven years plenary indulgence.[142] This was a considerable honour for Giovanni Rucellai, and was in keeping with a family tradition. In his *Zibaldone* Giovanni drew attention to an earlier Rucellai, Messer Ferro, 'knight of the Order of Knights Templar', an order devoted to the protection of pilgrims and holy places. This was an inheritance of which Giovanni was proud and he believed the family deserved the epithet it had acquired, 'de' Tempiali'.[143] But to achieve sacramental status for the sepulchre Giovanni had to be careful not to over-personalise it. Consequently, he paid for its construction indirectly by donating several farm estates to the Money-Lenders' Guild in Florence, of which he was a member. The Consuls of the Guild were to share in his honour in perpetuity, providing they 'visit the chapel every year in

92 Attributed to Alesso Baldovinetti, detail from a fresco in the cycle *Descent from the Cross*, after 1457. Rucellai sepulchre, Florence (photo/author).

Procession on the Sunday after the feast of St Pancras'.[144] The procession began in the hall of the guild, moved to Orsanmichele to pay respect to an image of the Virgin Mary, and then on to San Pancrazio. On arriving, four consuls were followed to the chapel by members of the Rucellai family and Mass was said. The ceremony ended at the high altar where donations were made, and the Vallambrosan monks presented flowers in return. A small, painted wooden box, now in Monselice, has been linked with the sepulchre because of its appearance: it is entirely rectangular (without an end form equivalent to an apse), and though it lacks the Florentine lilies above the cornice and the ciborium of the sepulchre, it

93 Anonymous, wooden box in imitation of the Rucellai sepulchre. 38.5 × 45.6 × 29 cm (h × l × w). Monselice, Società Rocca di Monselice (photo/courtesy H.A. Millon).

has similar geometrical decorations painted on it. Its purpose is unknown, though it may conceivably have been used as part of these ceremonials, perhaps to contain offerings (fig. 93).[145]

Sharing the honours with the Money-Lenders' Guild had another purpose. Giovanni reflected in his *Zibaldone* that the making and spending of money are two of the greatest pleasures in the world.[146] But banking at that time was akin to usury in the eyes of the church, and was frowned upon unless this wealth was redistributed or dedicated to the glorification of God.[147] Giovanni sought expiation of guilt – his own salvation – and this he gained through the sepulchre in his name and its blessing through the papal bull. As a Latin inscription over its entrance proclaims: 'Giovanni Rucellai son of Paolo gained his salvation from the place where Christ was resurrected for all, for which reason this shrine was constructed on the model of the Sepulchre in Jerusalem. 1467'.[148] Far more dominant and integral with the sepulchre is the Latin inscription that runs around its frieze, in a script influenced by antique Roman examples but entirely original in character.[149] It reads YHESVM QVERITIS NAZARENVM CRVCI-FIXVM SVRREXIT NON EST HIC ECCE LOCVS VBI POSVERVNT EVM: 'You seek Jesus of Nazareth who was crucified: he rose: he is not there: this is the place where they put him'. It is taken from key biblical quotations which have been abbreviated and combined in a new way. It most closely quotes the Gospel of St Matthew.[150] The Holy Sepulchre in Jerusalem no longer bears an inscription, though one was briefly visible on it in the fifteenth century. When it was rebuilt in 1555 the rock beneath the tomb was opened up. According to an eyewitness at the time, inside the tomb 'One could make out two painted angels [. . .] one with the superscript "He has risen; He is not here," and the other, pointing to the tomb [and saying]: "Behold the place where they laid him." Both images, as soon as they were exposed to the air, mostly disappeared'.[151] Giovanni's informants or emissaries surely knew of this painting and inscription, as the painting inside the Rucellai sepulchre and Alberti's inscription externally have reinterpreted it – unless the correspondence of words was taken from the biblical story itself.

The format of the message on the Rucellai sepulchre was determined by the height, length and articulation of the frieze (fig. 94). The passage begins over the entrance to the sepulchre (YHESVM QVERITIS N) and continues down the side (AZARENVM CRVCIFIXVM SV), with the succeeding letter (R) placed directly over the pilaster where it turns the corner; REXIT NON EST HIC ECCE runs around the apse, with the next letter (L) over the corner pilaster and OCVS VBI POSVERVNT EVM

94 (*above and facing page*)   (a) the inscription on the frieze of the Rucellai sepulchre: rubbing of the original made by Prue Chiles, scanned and plotted by computer (Olivetti/Alberti Group); (b) letters from the above arranged as an alphabet by the author.

completing the length. Apart from the letters R and L on the return to the apse, the shortest length of frieze is over the door. It bears fifteen letters and two spaces (i.e. seventeen units), while the two sides and apse each carry twenty-two units.[152] In order to achieve this balance Alberti had little latitude in which to mano-euvre the letters, and they are positioned less by eye, or any perfect geometrical formula, than by necessity. The letters themselves are entirely regular and nearly conform in their geometry to a process later described in an alphabet by Luca Pacioli, which appeared in man-uscript form in 1498, and was published eleven years later in *De divina proportione* (Venice, 1509).

Luca Pacioli (*c.*1445–1517) is best remembered as a mathematician. More notoriously he was also a plagia-rist, and *De divina proportione* is a close adaptation of writings by Piero della Francesca, especially his *Libellus de quinque corporibus regularibus*.[153] Thieves invite suspi-cion, and one is left wondering about the originality of the alphabet he claims to have invented.[154] As the

younger man, he would certainly have benefited from Alberti's approach to epigraphy, and he resided with Alberti in Rome for a short while. As Pacioli wrote in *De divina proportione*: 'I was a guest of our fellow citizen Leon Battista Alberti for many months in his house in our beloved Rome in the time of Pope Paul, and he always treated me well. He was undoubtedly a man of very great intelligence and learning in the humanities and rhetoric.'[155] Pope Paul II was elected in 1464 and died in 1471: and he signed the bull which granted the Rucellai sepulchre sacred status.

The design of letters which occupies a large part of *De divina proportione* is set out as a series of instructions: the designer should first describe a circle with a com-pass, then mark diagonals with a rule and compass to define a square.[156] The letter to be drawn is placed within the square, which has its sides subdivided into nine equal parts; the thicknesses of its limbs are multi-ples of this fraction, as are the cross-limbs and serifs. The curved parts of each letter are sections of circles

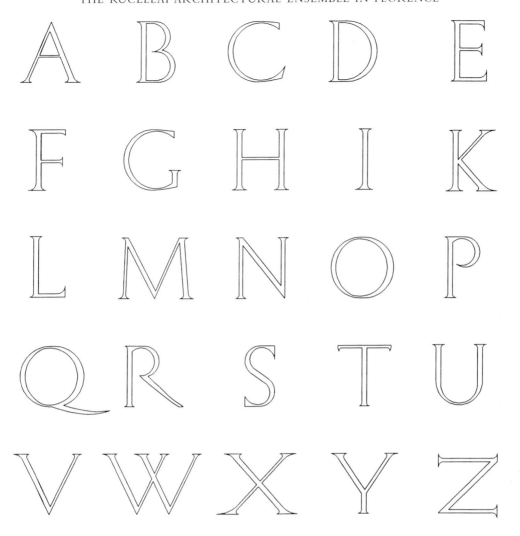

drawn with a compass, and their centres are positioned according to a ninth division of that enclosing square (fig. 95). While Alberti's letters are contrived from a square, unlike Pacioli he does not derive his letters from a ninth of the square, but a twelfth. The following description of the letter A on the sepulchre is based on the mode of presentation adopted by Pacioli:[157]

Describing the letter A:
Describe a square with its diagonals from a circle.
The apex of the letter is at the midpoint of the top side.
The thickness of the right hand limb is one-twelfth, that of the left-hand half of one-twelfth of a side of the square.
The right-hand limb is set in one-twelfth from the right edge of the square, the thinnest two thirds of one-twelfth from the left.
The cross limb is set down one-twelfth from the midpoint of the square and up one third of a twelfth.

The left-hand serif is composed of two circles, the largest has a diameter of three-twelfths, and the smallest one-twelfth.
The right-hand serif has circles of three-twelfths in diameter and one and a half twelfths.

While the process of design may have been similar, the final appearance of Alberti's and Pacioli's alphabets differ. Pacioli's letters appear better shaped to the modern eye, with pronounced serifs, whereas Alberti's letters are much plainer and have a geometrical, almost austere purity about them. These differences may reflect the medium being used. Pacioli's letters were to be printed in ink, and he would have been influenced by the earlier attempts at designing a lucid, non-Gothic script of Coluccio Salutati, Niccolò Niccoli and Poggio Bracciolini. Their letters were shaped by the use of a pen and Romanesque precedent: the tablet recording the Council of Florence of 1438, in Florence Cathedral, shows this clearly.[158] Similarly, the form of the lettering on the sepulchre has been categorised as the

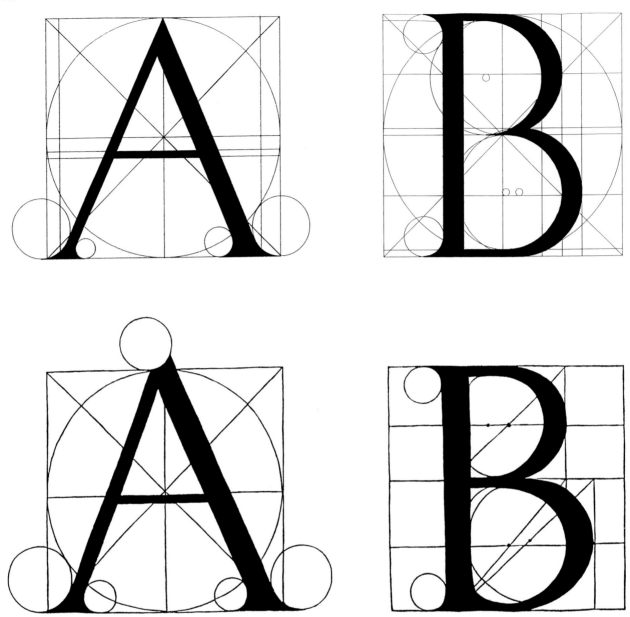

95   Comparison of alphabet styles: the letters A and B by (a) Leon Battista Alberti, the Rucellai sepulchre, San Pancrazio, Florence, after 1457 (Olivetti/Alberti Group); and (b) Luca Pacioli, according to *De divina proportione*, Venice, 1509.

'Romanesque Florentine Capital'.[159] However, it is never easy to pigeon-hole Alberti, for whom geometrical reasoning appears to have prevailed over visual or political conventions. His lettering on the frieze of the Tempio Malatestiano, by contrast, is based on Roman stone inscriptions found on the Arch of Augustus,[160] while that on the sepulchre is more likely a blend of ancient practice and modern theory: it was more likely influenced by the *Alphabetum romanum* of Felice Feliciano of Verona, the first treatise on the design and proportion of capital letters. Derived from Feliciano's first-hand observations of ancient characters,[161] the trea-

tise is dated 1463, just four years before the completion of the Rucellai sepulchre.

Feliciano was the first to expound the notion, in writing, that correctly proportioned letters should be derived from the square and circle.[162] Consequently, his z, for example, looks like the letter N on its side. The z of the Rucellai sepulchre inscription is contrived similarly. Rather than apportioning one-twelfth or one-ninth of the height of the square to the thickness of the letter, Feliciano states that the letters should be formed by 'the perfect number' ten: Albrecht Dürer used the same proportion for his alphabet design.[163]

The authority of the square and circle, while important to the proportional theory Vitruvius had expounded for architects, would have been hardly visible in the ancient inscriptions Feliciano and Alberti had scrutinised. In antiquity, lettering was largely a balance of geometry, proportion and eye.[164] Surviving Roman examples only approximate to the square and circle, and there are many formal variants which developed out of the pragmatics of brush calligraphy and stone carving. Yet Feliciano was concerned to find a rational basis for an alphabet whose letters were to be penned and, in particular, appropriate for the new printing presses. Alberti had reduced the complexities of the form of the Holy Sepulchre to a more rational, geometrical proposition. The alphabet he devised for the Rucellai sepulchre showed that even lettering can be integral with the architecture to which it is attached, and that the smallest ornaments should – and can – be truly a part of the whole.

THE RUCELLAI LOGGIA

Loggias built in Florence during the fourteenth and fifteenth centuries were usually privately owned, by individuals or families; otherwise they were owned by guilds (fig. 96). Such buildings were the focus of significant events in family and working life, and stood as permanent reminders of the potent authority of families and institutions. The most public loggia in Florence was the fourteenth-century Loggia dei Lanzi, situated close to the seat of the city government, the Palazzo della Signoria.[165] It is a huge free-standing structure composed of three tall arched bays and overlooks the city's main public piazza. The much smaller, slightly older loggia incorporated into the Bigallo, adjacent to the Florentine Baptistery, is where foundlings were presented for identification or adoption. A family loggia was incorporated into the corner of the new Palazzo Medici designed by Michelozzo di Bartolomeo in 1444; a double cube in shape, it was 12 *braccia* square and 6 *braccia* high (approximately 7 × 3.5 m.).[166] In 1470 there were at least seventeen loggias still standing within the city ambit, though few were built after that time: Michelangelo walled up the Medici loggia in 1517.[167]

The building of the Rucellai loggia in the 1460s coincided with a period when changes in social life were being reflected in a different kind of architecture (fig. 97). As the city grew, extended families were fragmenting, and public unity was sought instead through city-wide festivals which often focused on leading political figures.[168] By the second half of the fifteenth century, the colonnaded courtyards of palaces and

96 Anonymous, *Libro di matematica di Giuliano de' Medici*. A representation of a family loggia. Florence, Biblioteca Riccardiana, MS Ricc. 2669.

loggias adjacent to private gardens were the preferred settings for family celebrations and recreational events, not the open street or loggia.[169] Even if new loggias were becoming rare, some Florentine families continued to rebuild their ancestral loggias; the Rucellai loggia, set at right angles to the façade of the palazzo, remained serviceable until being walled up in 1677.[170]

Vasari and an anonymous sixteenth-century chronicler of the Rucellai buildings attributed the design of the Rucellai loggia to Alberti.[171] While there is good cause to believe that Alberti was behind Giovanni Rucellai's other buildings in Florence, there remains some uncertainty about his role in the design of the loggia. Its composition is awkward and unoriginal, with three bays of vaulting faced by a triplet of arches on columns and half-round columns, backed by a wall; the pilasters and columns are Corinthian and, while the columns are well proportioned, the pilasters appear to be exceedingly tall (fig. 98). Internally, the columns support segmental arches which span across to corbels and, in the corners, engage with quarter-round

97 Antonio di Migliorini Guidotti, the Rucellai loggia, Florence, after 1464 (photos/author).

columns set in from the end piers. As the external arches to the front and sides are semicircular, the separate segmental and semicircular arches in the end bays look awkward from the interior: this led to Vasari's damning censure of Alberti as a theoretician who lacked practical experience.[172]

It is certain that Alberti shared Giovanni Rucellai's belief in the importance of family life, his *Della famiglia* having been written to celebrate familial bonds. It is also known that in 1421 his kinsman Alberto d'Adovardo rebuilt the ancestral Alberti loggia in Florence, which had been destroyed after many members of the family had been banished from the city.[173] In 1460 Alberti designed a new loggia for Ludovico Gonzaga, though this came to nothing.[174] However, the family loggia is not one of the building types described by Alberti in *De re aedificatoria*, and while he describes porticoes as the setting for casual social encounters, and as a place where young men can let off steam, he considers the private domestic atrium and salon the nearest equivalents to sheltered public enclosures adjacent to the urban forum and public square: the salon was 'where the gaiety of weddings and banquets took place', and the atrium or hall 'where the prince may sit on the tribunal and give judgement', activities and uses that had traditionally taken place in the family loggia (v, 2–3, 119–21).

Pope Pius II had two loggias built during the early 1460s: the Piccolomini Logge del Papa in Siena, built in 1462 by Federighi; and a loggia in Pienza overlooking the new cathedral square, designed by Rossellino. Both are similar in size to Giovanni Rucellai's loggia and are also composed of round arches supported on columns; while Alberti was not completely averse to the combination of column and arch (he proposes this arrangement in large basilicas where colonnades with larger than normal spans were necessary and so made a trabeated system unsound) he certainly preferred columns to support beams directly (VII, 14, p. 232).[175] For the column and arch system to be acceptable in Alberti's terms required an impost to be inserted between the columns and the arches they support. This element is present in the Rucellai loggia in a compressed form, much as Alberti describes it (but is missing from Pius II's two loggias). This detail was widely employed in Florence by Brunelleschi, who combines free-standing columns and arches with compressed imposts (in the broad loggia of the Ospedale degli Innocenti), or with imposts the depth of a full entablature (as in the interior colonnades of San Lorenzo and Santo Spirito).

I find it difficult to believe that Alberti would have approved of the use of ornament on the Rucellai

98   Rucellai loggia, Florence. Side and front elevations, drawing by Prue Chiles (Olivetti/Alberti Group).

loggia.[176] The Rucellai sepulchre, for example, uses a trabeated system of ornament even though it was modelled on the Holy Sepulchre in Jerusalem which has arcuated side panels; and it is the rigorous application of trabeation on the façade of Palazzo Rucellai that makes the arcuated loggia look alien to Alberti's approach. Apart from using the same stone, the only ornamental feature common to the Rucellai façade and loggia is the diamond pattern cut into the stonework: this can be seen on the palazzo façade between the plinths of the pilasters at ground level, and at the same height along the back wall of the loggia. Its shape derives from 'opus reticulatum', an ancient form of wall construction described by Alberti in his treatise (II, 10, p. 52).

There is also documentation that seems to refute the attribution by Vasari to Alberti. Giovanni Rucellai apparently built two separate loggias across from his palazzo, the first of which was destroyed in late 1463 or early 1464 to make way for the creation of the present loggia and piazza; and it is possible that Alberti may have designed the first one, but Vasari was aware only of the second.[177]

The site for the first Rucellai loggia was a gift to Giovanni from Ugolino di Francesco Rucellai, a distant relation, who donated his shop 'for the honour of our family' in April 1456, a year before his death.[178] An associated document grants permission for the internal ceiling of the shop to be raised, presumably so that it could be turned into an effective loggia.[179] The conversion may have been completed within a month, to coincide with a clan gathering held in the street outside

to celebrate the marriage of Giovanni's eldest son, Pandolfo Rucellai, to Caterina Pitti.[180] It is probable that Giovanni had persuaded Ugolino to donate the shop and permit specific alterations so that the loggia would be ready for the occasion.

The gift of Ugolino's shop in 1456 coincided with the death of Giovanni's neighbour, Jacopoantonio. This proved fortunate for Giovanni: not only was there the potential now to extend the width of his palace along the street, but by gaining a foothold in Ugolino's shop he would also have some leverage over Ugolino's heirs. With Ugolino's land he could improve the setting of the palace by building a new piazza and an even grander loggia, which would make the purchase of Jacopoantonio's house, at an inflated price, more palatable.[181] To acquire the domestic property above and behind the former shop-cum-loggia, Giovanni had first to wait for the death of Ugolino's widow and convince the other heirs to part with their inheritance. She died some time after March 1461 and Giovanni owned the complete site by the end of 1463.[182] He must have started to clear the site and so form the piazza almost immediately, as a year later, according to Giovanni's *Zibaldone*, work started on the loggia – that is, the second loggia that stands there today.

The second loggia was not completed until the marriage celebrations of Giovanni's second son Bernardo to the sister of Lorenzo de' Medici in June 1466.[183] By then the palace formed one side of a triangular piazza, and the new larger loggia was placed in its present position, at right angles to it (fig. 100). Documents relate how the via della Vigna was closed to traffic for the festivities, a temporary triangular platform, presumably of wooden boards, being set off the ground by 1.5 *braccia* (876 mm) linking the palace and loggia together. Here the wedding guests were able to enjoy the event in the open, yet above the dirt of the thoroughfare. Seats and benches and the platform itself were covered in rich cloth and tapestries, and decorated with garlands, roses and leaves, and the emblems of the Rucellai and Medici families, and the guests protected from the sun by a deep-blue awning of cloth.[184] The newly weds presumably benefited from the grandly framed setting of the new loggia along with their immediate family.

The model for the second loggia was made by Antonio di Migliorini Guidotti. This information comes from Antonio Billi, who also attributed a model of the Palazzo Rucellai to Bernardo Rossellino.[185] Guidotti was a moderately wealthy business- and craftsman whose son married a ward and niece of Giovanni Rucellai. His family had interests in banking as well as woodworking, and were members of both guilds. While Guidotti and Rossellino may each have provided Giovanni with a model for the building work they were to oversee, this does not necessarily mean they also designed those buildings: it is also recorded that Guidotti provided a model for the church of Santo Spirito in Florence, and he was certainly not its architect.[186] Of course, to extend the original five-bay palace façade did not require an architect. It would have been easy enough for any experienced stonemason to take details from the original wooden model or from the palace itself. Similarly, the details of the Rucellai loggia are so unexceptional that Guidotti may have done no more than copy parts of Brunelleschi's loggia for the Ospedale degli Innocenti with which it bears comparison in particular.[187] It was not unusual for designs to be acquired in this way, though it took an architect of Alberti's abilities to do more than copy the examples his patron admired.[188] Giovanni had openly based the design of his sepulchre on the original in Jerusalem, and Alberti perfected and so transformed its form and ornament that his design reflects the qualities, while not imitating the exact details of the Holy Sepulchre. Likewise, although the façade of San Miniato al Monte was probably a source of inspiration for Santa Maria Novella, the change in scale and situation demanded that its format be modified, and in the process Alberti turned it into something quite new. The design of the present Rucellai loggia does not appear to have been developed in this way, and its lack of resolution in detail (which Vasari complained about), and Brunelleschian references overall, make it unlikely that Alberti contributed to its design.

It is impossible to establish why Alberti should not have been consulted for the second Rucellai loggia (he does not seem to have been involved in Giovanni's villas at Quarachi and Poggio a Caiano either).[189] Perhaps, after initiating so many building projects, Giovanni felt confident enough in this instance to proceed without his expert advice. Also, it may have been a decade or more since Alberti had made the designs which were then translated into the wooden models for the Rucellai ensemble of buildings. Instead of turning to Alberti for further advice, Giovanni may have decided instead to combine his own knowledge of architecture with the skills of the local building craftsmen he had come to know over the years.

Alberti's advice may have been sought for the design for the first Rucellai loggia.[190] Its construction in 1456 is close enough to that of the palazzo façade and the initiation of the other Rucellai buildings in Florence with which he is more positively linked. Speculating on its form, Brenda Preyer has highlighted the loggia-like qualities of the chapel surrounding the Rucellai sepulchre in nearby San Pancrazio. In its composition of three bays opening on one side towards an atrium, its form and ornament resembled the Praetorium depicted in Piero della Francesca's small painting of the *Flagellation of Christ*.[191] Preyer also notes that the Rucellai Chapel was similar to the loggia depicted in the panel in Berlin (fig. 72). There are differences: the Berlin loggia has arched openings at either end and a flat (possibly timber) panelled ceiling, though the first palazzo on the left (seen through the loggia) is practically identical with the Alberti Group's reconstruction

99   Wooden model of the Rucellai loggia as exhibited at the Alberti exhibition, Palazzo Te, Mantua, 1994 (photo/Giovetti).

100   Palazzo Rucellai and second loggia, Florence. Axonometric of the palazzo façade reconstructed with eight bays, and in relation to the loggia built post-1464 (Olivetti/Alberti Group).

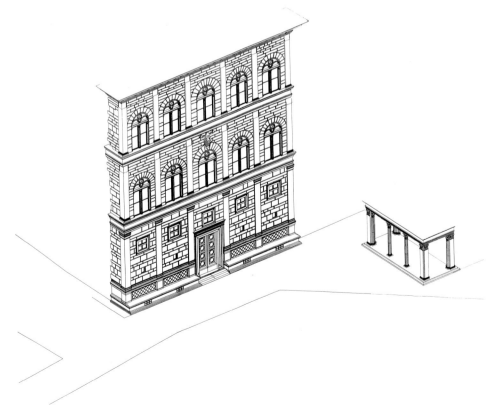

101   Palazzo Rucellai and loggia, Florence. Axonometric suggesting the relationship between the palazzo façade with five bays, and in relation to the loggia built pre-1464 (Olivetti/Alberti Group).

of Alberti's 'ideal' palace (fig. 63), and has a single central door and a five-bay façade similar to the arrangement suggested for the first Palazzo Rucellai on via della Vigna (fig. 78a). Indeed, the pilasters on their façades appear to be the same width at each storey (unlike those on Palazzo Piccolomini in Pienza). While this view is a *capriccio*, and bears little or no relation to an actual vista, it may nevertheless be composed of real and fantasy buildings.

It should also be pointed out that the loggia depicted in Salviati's portrait of Giovanni Rucellai differs in detail from the Rucellai loggia that was built. While only half the loggia is visible in the painting, this is sufficient to recognise the motifs on the frieze and the corbels supporting the internal vaults, and that instead of free-standing columns supporting arches, pilasters rise to support the entablature, between which are arches supported on half-columns. Thus, if the depicted loggia was entirely visible, the front elevation would probably have four pilasters supporting the entablature, with three arches inbetween, each resting on two half-columns. This general arrangement would surely have been more acceptable to Alberti than the present Rucellai loggia. A loggia constructed from a combination of pilasters and arches is structurally stronger, and could be larger than a trabeated one: and the pilasters on the loggia would have corresponded more closely with the visual language of the palace façade. Whether it represents his design for the first or second loggia, whether either of these was made available to Salviati for the portrait, or whether the paint-

ing represents the artist's improvement of the built loggia, must remain a matter for speculation. It is possible, then, that Alberti provided designs for two different sizes of loggia across from Palazzo Rucellai, that the smaller one would have been trabeated with columns (like the original Rucellai Chapel arrangement, or the loggia in the Berlin panel), and the larger would have been designed like that depicted by Salviati. Unfortunately, not enough is known about the first loggia in via della Vigna to be more positive about its relationship with either painted version. All that is known is that the existing shop ceiling had to be heightened to accommodate the loggia inserted into it. Its potential width and depth can be gauged only by comparison with other property boundaries at that time. The widths of the houses that Giovanni Rucellai bought along via della Vigna to make up his palazzo varied in width between 7.5 and 11 m, and were up to 13 m. deep.[192] The triangular site owned by Ugolino opposite was subdivided into at least four properties: the shop-cum-loggia, along with accommodation for at least three of his heirs.[193]

Until the existing piazza is excavated to reveal the foundations of these properties, their boundaries will remain concealed. In the meantime, there are two obvious reconstructions to be made of the first loggia: one facing the palazzo across via della Vigna, the other at right angles to it, perhaps set forward of the present Rucellai loggia, and equivalent in scale to the former Medici loggia, which was tucked under a corner of the palazzo and just 3.5 m. high (fig. 101).[194]

VIII

LUDOVICO GONZAGA AND ALBERTI
IN MANTUA AND FLORENCE

INTRODUCTION

MANTUA WAS A FLOURISHING ISLAND CITY in the fifteenth century, surrounded by lakes fed by the River
Mincio, which issues from Lake Garda before entering
the Po (fig. 102). The Gonzaga family took the city by
force in 1328 and dominated its history for three
hundred years until imperial troops sacked it of its
treasures in 1630 and Mantua fell into decline.[1] The
stability of Gonzaga rule was built on a network of
powerful allegiances. Their ties with the Malatesta of
Rimini were particularly important. Francesco Gonzaga
(1366–1407) was married to Margherita Malatesta,
and after his death his young son Gianfrancesco
(1395–1444) was protected by Margherita's brother
Carlo Malatesta and his Gonzaga wife, Elisabetta.[2] Carlo
maintained his ward's interests and oversaw the change
of government in Mantua, and in so doing helped the
Malatesta to consolidate their power base in northern
Italy.[3] This was of mutual benefit, as neither family
had the aristocracy of lineage enjoyed by the Este of
Ferrara, or the Visconti of Milan, nor the great wealth
of some patrician dynasties in Florence. Their strength
was founded on allies obtained through military success
and marriage: Gianfrancesco later married Paola
Malatesta, maintaining the links between the two
families.

As I have already mentioned, a decade earlier Carlo
Malatesta had exerted his influence more controver-
sially by ordering a statue of Virgil to be thrown into
the river in an attempt to quell the fervent idolatry of
the poet.[4] It is true that as a native of the city Virgil
had become a cult figure locally, but the Mantuans had
much else of which to be proud. They could also boast
Etruscan roots, as well as the sacred relic of the Blood
of Christ which attracted Christian pilgrims to the city
from across Europe.[5]

Gianfrancesco Gonzaga was highly regarded for his
military glories, intellect and good marriage.[6] As an
ardent supporter of the arts Alberti sought his patronage and dedicated *De pictura* to him.[7] Vittorino da
Feltre, professor in rhetoric at the University of Padua
and a product (like Alberti) of Gasparino Barzizza's
school, was brought to Mantua by Gianfrancesco and
in 1423 founded his own school, the Casa Giocosa,
where he taught until his death. The education he
offered covered poetry, oratory, Roman history and
the ethics of Roman stoicism as well as mathematics,
astronomy, music, physical exercise and the martial arts.
Among his pupils were Ludovico Gonzaga (1412–78)
and Federico da Montefeltro of Urbino, both of whom
were later to welcome Alberti to their courts. Ludovico
reinforced his family's links with the Holy Roman
Empire by marrying Barbara of Brandenburg in 1433,
when he was also invested as Marquis of Mantua by
Emperor Sigismund. Their son, Federico, married
Margaret of Bavaria in 1463. It was at the prestigious
Council of Mantua, held in the second half of 1459,
that Alberti's relationship with Ludovico Gonzaga
matured sufficiently for him to be asked to demonstrate
his architectural skills for the great benefit of the
Gonzaga family and their city.

The Council Pius had summoned was intended to
rally support from across northern Europe against
the Turks, who had a strategic stronghold in
Constantinople and were threatening Western
Christendom. For the convenience of the northern
representatives the Council was to have been held in
Udine, close to Trieste and Venice. However, the
Venetians were unhappy with this choice and Pius
settled on Mantua as a more neutral location, given its
geographical position between the more powerful and
larger Venice and Milan. Its links with the Holy
Roman Empire must have also been in the city's favour.
It certainly was not chosen for the environmental qualities of the area. These the pope's cardinals deplored:
they complained that the city was marshy and
unhealthy; the summer heat intense; fever rife; the
wine flat; and nothing was to be heard there except
the croaking of frogs.[8] Pius's view of the city was more

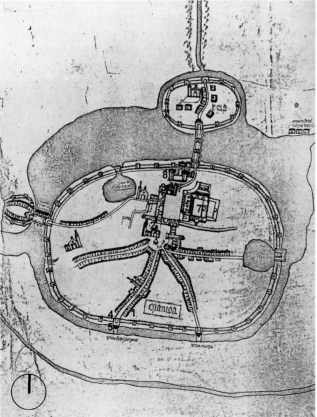

diplomatic: he praised Mantua for its many splendid houses and palaces, though he pitied its inhabitants for having to endure summer dust and winter mud.[9]

Pius entered Mantua with his cavalcade of councillors on 27 May 1459, and processed from the city gate (where he received the keys to Mantua from Ludovico, also on horseback) to the cathedral, along streets covered with mats (which disguised their dusty condition) and lined with welcoming crowds, the buildings adorned with flowers and fine cloth.[10] Pius, in return, greeted the city, making reference to its heritage as the birthplace of Virgil, and made play on his own name, Aeneas Silvius Piccolomini: 'The Mantuan Virgil sang of the Trojan Aeneas. Aeneas of Siena has enriched Virgil's homeland'.[11]

Whether prompted by Pius's rebuilding of Corsignano, by the presence in Mantua of such an august expert on architecture as Alberti or by the derogatory comments on the condition of Mantua during the months of the Council, Ludovico began a major renewal of his own city. This lasted for nearly two decades, until his death in 1478. He saw to the paving of streets in the central area and the piazza (now known as piazza Erbe) between the old monastery and pilgrimage church of Sant'Andrea and the round church of San Lorenzo. Indeed, he had ambitious plans to demolish these two structures and to rebuild them anew. The resistance of the Abbot of Sant'Andrea frustrated Ludovico's plans for more than a decade, and when papal permission was granted to remove San Lorenzo Ludovico was fully committed financially to other projects.

The full extent of Alberti's involvement in this large-scale renovation of the city's public spaces is uncertain, though he undoubtedly made designs for new buildings in the central area, and on an approach road from the south, soon after the Council had concluded its deliberations.[12] On 27 February 1460 Alberti wrote to Ludovico that 'the designs for San Sebastiano, San Lorenzo, the loggia, and of Virgil are done'.[13] It has been suggested that Alberti's new design for San

102 (*above left and left*) (a) Anonymous, topographic map of Veronese territory, fifteenth century. Venice, Archivio di Stato di Venezia, *Miscellanea mappe*, dis. 1438, no. 1; (b) detail, showing Mantua and the locations of Alberti's subsequent churches which are indicated on the map as follows: (1) San Sebastiano; (2) Sant'Andrea, and other buildings; (3) Cathedral of San Pietro; (4) Palazzo di San Sebastiano; (5) Porta Pusterla; (6) San Lorenzo; (7) Palazzo Ducale; and (8) Castello.

Lorenzo was connected to the loggia, which has been interpreted as a proposal to colonnade the edge of the resurfaced piazza, in the centre of which a new statue of Virgil was to be placed.[14] The idea for the statue had come from Platina, but no immediate action followed Alberti's design for it, or his proposals for the adjacent buildings.[15] However, within just a few months the church of San Sebastiano was under construction on the south-western edge of the city.

A BUILDING HISTORY OF SAN SEBASTIANO IN MANTUA

The idea to build the church of San Sebastiano came to Ludovico Gonzaga in his sleep, though neither the details of his dream (or nightmare) nor its date were reported. The feast day of St Sebastian is 20 January; the first documented evidence that Ludovico intended building a church dedicated to this saint came a month later, in the letter from Alberti dated 27 February 1460. Immediately, it would seem, a site was chosen in a southern district of the city called Redevallo, just inside the city walls and close by the Porta Pusterla, a southern gateway into the city. The urgency to build was such that materials intended for the rebuilding of the gate were diverted to the new church straightaway.[16]

Tradition has it that an ancient oratory dedicated to San Sebastiano already existed there,[17] but there are no reports of demolition taking place. There was a pestilential marsh nearby, the Pajolo, and as St Sebastian was often invoked against epidemics (and disease generally), the church may have been built to protect the city from plague.[18] Ludovico had the marsh drained, at considerable expense, in only four days by 3500 men, and the foundations were dug in March 1460. Ludovico's commitment to build must have been obvious to all, but his haste, and the poor drainage of the area, were to the detriment of the long-term condition of the building.

No first-hand descriptions of Alberti's original conception for San Sebastiano survive, and the building was completed by others after his death in 1472, abandoned, and then 'restored'. Surviving correspondence between Ludovico, Alberti (who had returned to Rome) and the leading figures on site gives details of certain aspects of progress on the project.[19] These missives can only be read in the context of the fabric of the church (which was left in a ruinous condition, and is the worst preserved of Alberti's buildings) and of three sixteenth-century designs which purport to illustrate its plan and proportions.[20] A design by the architect Antonio Labacco also describes the heights of the main physical elements of the building and is accompanied by

an incomplete and very sketchy elevation of the exterior.[21] Even though Labacco probably never visited San Sebastiano in person, and his drawing copies another drawing, or is based on a model, it remains one of the most useful documents available as it probably reflects Alberti's original intentions for this church (fig. 103; see also pp. 136–43 below).

Labacco drew the plan of San Sebastiano in the manner of a Greek cross, with a central square and four projecting chapels, slightly narrower than each of its sides. Three semicircular apses articulate the outer walls of three of the chapels, and a broad portico is attached to the fourth. The chapels are barrel-vaulted and, according to his description, the central space was to have been surmounted by a dome (fig. 104).

The condition of San Sebastiano in the sixteenth century (and today) is quite at odds with the image Labacco drew (fig. 103). The church is set high on a crypt and access to it is by three separate staircases: one at the side has Quattrocento details, almost certainly added after Alberti's involvement in the project;[22] the other two lead to openings in the portico and are the invention of Andrea Schiavi, who renovated what remained of the church in 1925 as a war memorial (cf. fig. 107).[23] Schiavi also reconstructed the interior, rebuilding the brick groin vault over the main space which had collapsed as a result of neglect during the nineteenth century.[24] He modernised the ornaments of the interior by exposing bare the brickwork, removing pilasters and their bases from the four corners that supported the central groin vault, and by replacing three sets of Serliana windows (probably of post-fifteenth-century origin) above the three apses with large circular openings (fig. 107, p. 132 top right). By detaching the west and south sides of the church from an adjoining monastery he created an open memorial garden.[25] Schiavi left the building in a sound condition structurally, which it had not been for many years, though its present state is unlikely to have appealed to Alberti. Externally, the portico (restored in the 1990s) retains a covering of render but there is little about its composition to commend: a row of openings, some round headed, others square, sit on the raised ground-floor level of the portico. The frames of these openings overlap four slender pilasters which support a deep and crudely formed entablature. The entablature is broken at its centre by a window and reconnected by an arch. Behind the portico there is a low pyramidal roof of terracotta tiles covering the main central space of the church where the dome described by Labacco was intended. How the building contrasts with the compact centralised church depicted by Labacco! What went wrong?

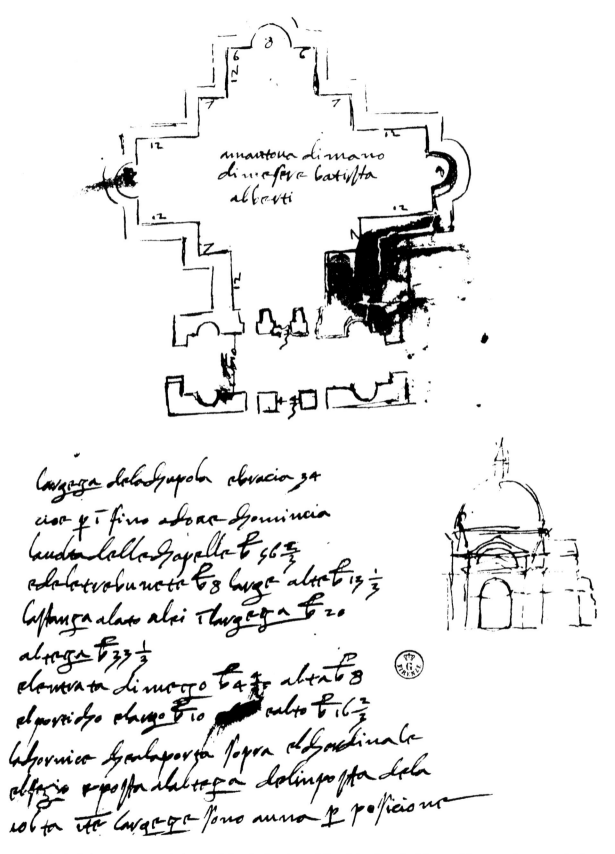

103 Antonio Labacco, annotated plan, and sketch elevation of San Sebastiano in Mantua, 'di mano di messere batista alberti'. Pen and ink on paper, 24 × 17.9 cm (max. dimensions). Florence, Galleria degli Uffizi, Gabinetto Disegni e Stampe, 1779A.

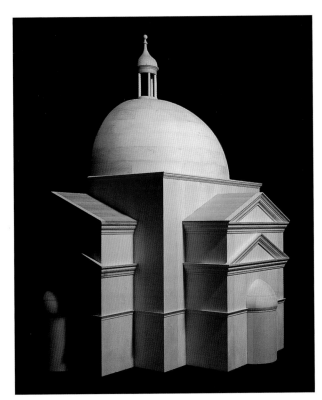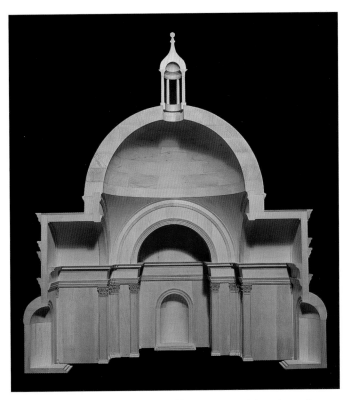

104   San Sebastiano, as reconstructed by the Alberti Group after Antonio Labacco: two views, oblique rear and interior, of the wooden model exhibited at the Alberti exhibition, Palazzo Te, Mantua, 1994 (photos/Giovetti).

Until 1979, only a few historians had risked providing an account of the church beyond a simple description of the outward appearance of the building and its place, as an early centralised Renaissance church, in the history of that period. In that year two detailed monographs on the church were published, as well as an account of the activities of the Gonzago court architect Luca Fancelli in Mantua.[26] Their interpretations of its building history turned out to be quite different. A primary disagreement concerns the amount of work completed during the first few years of construction. One view extends Wittkower's reading of the relevant documents, that building work 'after a quick start progressed comparatively slowly'.[27] Thus, while the lower walls of the church were soon completed, nineteen years later when Fancelli abandoned the project, the church was still without a roof. The contrary argument is that work progressed rapidly at first and the walls reached the height of the proposed dome within three years, and that the building was complete (excluding its decoration) five years after the foundations were dug; necessary repairs and design changes kept Fancelli employed on the building, on and off, for the remaining period.[28]

The documents covering the first few years of building work are not numerous: six mention San

Sebastiano directly during the first year, four the second and only one in the third. This may imply a falling-off of activity and commitment, but secondary sources, describing the stockpiling of building materials during 1461, would suggest otherwise.[29] Clearly, the letters are not conclusive in themselves and need to be interpreted with caution.

Fancelli reported to Ludovico Gonzaga, on 31 March 1460, that the foundations of San Sebastiano had been dug.[30] The construction of the foundations and lower walls appears to have been the responsibility of another mason, Gianpietro de Figino. Within six weeks Figino informed his patron that half of the walls were up to the height ordered, and that soon the other half would also be up to a height 'above ground level', as would 'li pillastri' and the portico.[31] By the end of May the prescribed level was inadvertently exceeded by three brick courses, and Figino expressed his uncertainty about Alberti's intentions for the stairs 'at the head of the portico' and for the doors which he understood were to be 'in the antique manner'.[32]

How work progressed over the rest of 1460 is unknown, but a flurry of correspondence survives from early 1461 relating to the supply of tens of thousands of bricks and other building materials for San Sebastiano and the nearby Porta Pusterla, perhaps

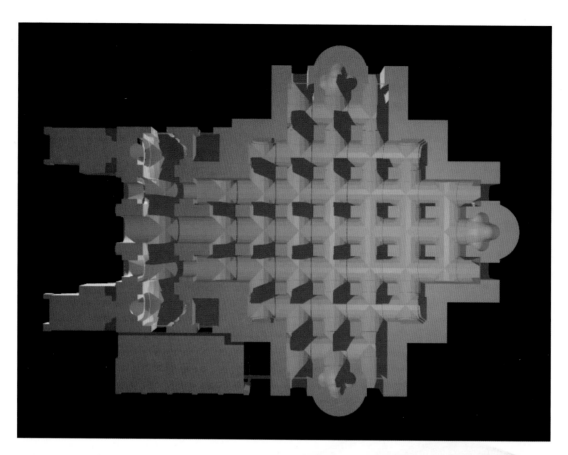

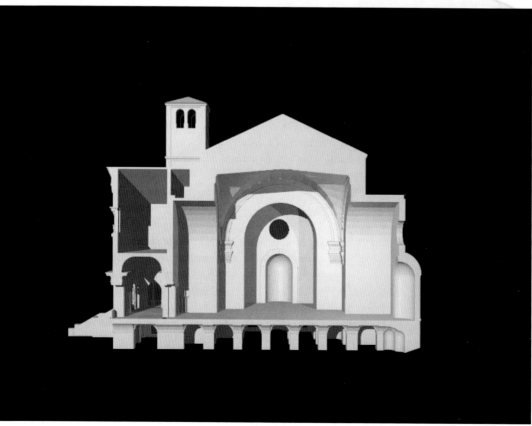

105   San Sebastiano, as it stands today: two views of the rendered computer model, plan of the undercroft, supporting piers and worm's eye view of the internal vaults; and long section in perspective of the existing interior (Olivetti/Alberti Group).

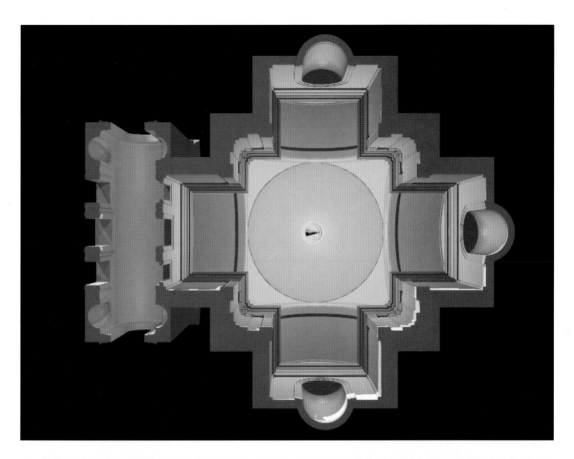

106   San Sebastiano, as reconstructed by the Alberti Group after Antonio Labacco: two views of the rendered computer model, plan and worm's eye view of interior, and long section in perspective (Olivetti/Alberti Group).

107 (*this and following pages*) Leon Battista Alberti, San Sebastiano, Mantua, begun 1460, and as it stands today: general and detailed views of the exterior and interior (photos/author).

(*left*) The façade of San Sebastiano by
Andrea Schiavi in 1925.

I MANTOVANI
MORTI
PER LA PATRIA
QVI
VIVONO

(*left*) The church interior before the 1925 restoration.

(*facing page bottom row, left and centre*) The vaults of the undercroft to the portico, and the internal vaults and piers of the area under the church floor.

brought about by the delivery of 3000 ducats promised to Ludovico on 18 August 1460 for the building of 'that church'.[33] But, less than two years into construction, difficulties were being encountered on site and it had become apparent that action had to be taken to remedy signs of premature deterioration in the condition of the building fabric, and completed vaults were now in need of protection from rainwater.[34] From a report by Fancelli, it would appear that Alberti's remedy to this potential catastrophe was to cover the walls and vaults with mats and 20,000 *coppi* (curved roof tiles) to prevent further damage. It transpires, the following summer, that the lower parts of walls were also damaged, presumably by flood waters or rising damp, and were also in need of repair.[35] The area had remained notoriously marshy despite Ludovico's best efforts, and was also susceptible to seasonal flooding.

The height of the building at this stage is uncertain. Progress had either been so steady that there was little need for correspondence, or the confusion caused by an outbreak of plague – which probably brought building work to a standstill in the autumn of 1463 – meant that key documents have been lost.[36] There is a reference to some vaults having been completed in less than two years, but this could be either the many small groin vaults forming the roof of the crypt, or the four large barrel vaults to the apses. Arguments have gone both ways. They depend largely on an estimate of what could have been built by that time. My own view is that enough time had elapsed for the building to be almost complete. The entire structure of Santa Maria delle Carceri in Prato, which is similar in scale and form to San Sebastiano, was finished, including its dome, within two years of starting in 1485 (see pp. 139–42 below).[37] Also, Alberti designed the very much larger and complex Sant'Andrea in Mantua a decade after San Sebastiano was begun, yet Ludovico Gonzaga remained confident that it would be complete within two or three years (see pp. 159–60 below). At San Sebastiano we know the foundations had been dug and the walls were above ground level within two months. Over the next twelve months a quantity of building material was brought into the vicinity sufficient to build the entire structure, and it is reasonable to assume that the walls and main vaults could have been completed within two years. It is even possible that a dome was begun in 1463 over the main central space by the engineer Giovanni Antonio d'Arezzo, who first repaired (and possibly strengthened[38]) the walls. Luca Fancelli was away selecting stone at this time to ornament the portico, which was the other main area still under construction.[39]

In 1488 the building was in danger of becoming a ruin and repairs were undertaken. These may have been demanded after a visit to the church early that year by Pope Innocent VIII, when he gave indulgences to the faithful in the *sotterraneo* or undercroft (for it is not underground), now usually referred to as the crypt of San Sebastiano.[40] The undercroft cannot have been ideal for this purpose, and the pope would hardly have been visible in the tiny spaces left by numerous piers, except for a small part of the congregation. While far from ideal, this may have been the only covered space available, as the upper church probably lacked a roof, or was full of debris from collapsed material: it was another eleven years before a groin vault was begun over the main space. By then, there appears to have been no intention of building a dome.

The papal visit in 1488 is the first recorded mention of the *sotterraneo*, which is neither indicated on the sixteenth-century drawings of San Sebastiano nor mentioned in Labacco's proportional account of the church. Yet, it has generally been assumed that the crypt was intended as an integral part of the church. The existence of the crypt and its piers provides the main support for this assumption, along with a letter dated 15 May 1460, which refers to the raising of 'li pillastri' to the height of the rest of the church.[41] Some historians have taken this to mean the main piers of the crypt, though this may simply be a reference to the four piers framing the inner and outer sets of doors into the church, the same doors 'in the antique manner' that were under discussion two months into the building programme.[42]

Those who believe that the crypt was an integral part of Alberti's design from the start have argued that water-damaged vaults, mentioned in December 1462, are those between the piers of the crypt, which support the floor of the upper church.[43] This is unlikely. Alberti advised that the vaults be protected with mats and 20,000 curved roof tiles, which would have served no useful purpose in this location, even as a temporary expedient. They would be too fragile to walk on, and without being raised and laid to an incline, rainwater would pool and continue to saturate the vaults – there would be nowhere else for the water to go, unless numerous holes were made in the perimeter walls. Alternatively, I believe it more probable that a raised hollow floor (now known as the crypt) was not considered until the summer of 1463, and that previously the floor was much lower, and had reached a height just above ground level where the mats could be used to soak up rain and flood water. This would imply that the walls of the main body of the church were at full height by the end of 1462, with the main vaults over the chapels complete, for only then would it have made

108   San Sebastiano: plans, elevations and sections of the fabric today (drawings/author).

sense to give the vaults a permanent roof covering of tiles as quickly as possible.

No timber was required for this roofing (and none is mentioned in correspondence). Later, at Sant'Andrea, Alberti designed the main nave vault to be covered with roof tiles laid directly on a dry bedding material. The damage caused to the lower walls would have been less easy to remedy. If the ground was saturated with water after a period of heavy rain or winter flooding, and water was being drawn up the walls through capillary action, Alberti would have had three main options: either to improve drainage locally (which Ludovico had failed to do), render the lower walls impervious to water (the techniques were not then available without first taking down the full height of the walls), or to raise the ground floor higher than had previously been planned. A well-ventilated hollow floor

would be more effective than raising the ground level with rubble – an operation that would have required large quantities of material – as the fabric would have remained susceptible to ground moisture. Also, by raising the floor of the church with piers and vaults, and cutting permanent openings into the external walls at this level, the fabric would be dried by cross-currents of air passing through the void. The side openings would admit light into the void too, but an insufficient quantity for it to become useful liturgically. Consequently, I doubt that this space deserves the status of 'crypt' it has recently acquired.[44] Indeed, the undercroft remains damp and under used despite Alberti's drastic remedy.

Once the undercroft is recognised as a later insertion into Alberti's original scheme, the similarities and differences between the plan drawn by Labacco and the

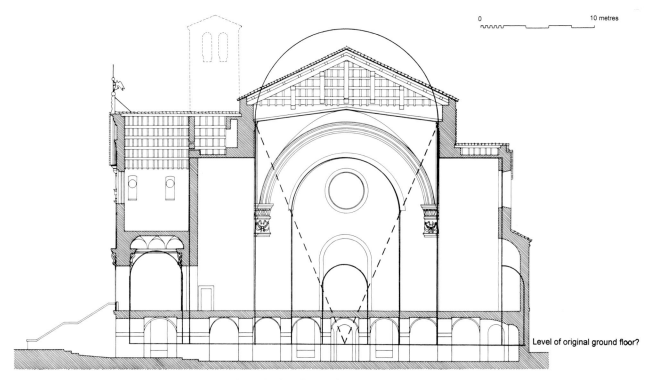

0   10 metres

Level of original ground floor?

109   San Sebastiano, Mantua, long section through church, overlaid with the proportions described by Labacco (in bold and pecked lines), and indicating the probable ground floor of the original design by Alberti (drawing/author).

present 'upper' ground-floor plan of San Sebastiano can be understood more clearly, particularly when the 'ideal' height measurements of the church, recorded by Labacco, are compared with survey measurements of the existing building.[45] From Labacco's notes it is evident that the vaulted spaces he describes are related proportionally. That is, when a cross-section of the church is drawn out as Labacco describes it, their springing-points can be connected by two lines that converge on a common point. When this diagram is overlaid on to an accurate cross-section through the existing church at the same scale, there is an obvious misalignment which suggests that: either the floor level and apses are the only elements to have been built in the correct position, and the vaults of the chapels have been lowered; or the floor and apses have been raised relative to the height of the chapels (fig. 109).[46]

If Labacco was describing the proportions of San Sebastiano that Alberti recommended, and if the undercroft was to be incorporated from the beginning, why does the existing building only partially reflect Alberti's intentions? And why did the height relationships indicated by Labacco have to be altered? If, however, the decision to build the undercroft was made much later, when the side chapels were already vaulted and the walls were up to roof height, then Alberti would have been forced to face the prospect of either destroying

several years' work or of compromising the original design. I believe he chose the latter, and that the 'ideal' proportions recorded by Labacco were lost, the hollow raised floor inserted, and the three apses rebuilt and set at a higher level while leaving the chapel vaults untouched.[47] If this interpretation is correct, the height of the floor as it was originally set by Alberti is where the lines of the sectional diagram through the church, taken from Labacco's description, converge (Fig. 109).

Raising the floor level when the building was almost complete meant that the main doors into the portico would also need raising. If the heads of these doors were formerly square (to take the all'antica ornament now fitted to the main central doors above), then modifications would have had to have been made to the piers on either side of them so that the arches there now could be fitted. These were probably the same piers that were recorded as being at the height of the surrounding walls early in 1460,[48] and it can be seen that slithers of piers are attached to them, effectively reducing their width. Perhaps this is 'the diminishing of the piers of the portico' (el minuire quelli pillastri del portico) referred to in 1470.[49]

It is likely, then, that the undercroft of San Sebastiano was a brilliantly improvised expedient, quite independent of Alberti's original conception for the church. Had this space been considered essential before construction work was so advanced, it is tempting to suggest that Alberti would have designed a spacious crypt, less cluttered by piers, with the emphasis on wider vaults, so the space could be better utilised.[50] An obvious ancient reference for a large vaulted crypt with a domical structure above was the Tomb of Theodoric (as it was for the tribune of the Tempio Malatestiano; see pp. 71–2 above). Alberti had observed that this had been 'one-quarter buried by the sheer force of time' (I, 8, p. 21). Other exemplars may have included the two-storey, cylindrical Tor de' Schiavi just outside Rome.[51] But the constraint of what had been built already at San Sebastiano, and of maintaining reasonable proportions within a limited height, meant that Alberti had little room for direct quotation. He could not even trust the bearing capacity of the existing perimeter walls in their dilapidated state, and the ends of the chapels as well as the corners of the main space had to be strengthened by increasing their thickness, perhaps as part of the remedial work of 1463.[52] Repairs to the walls and the late inclusion of the undercroft (whose expensive vaulting required Giovanni Antonio d'Arezzo's engineering skills)[53] seem to have drained the project's resources and may explain why there is no dome there today. This work was probably meant to have been guided by a new model of San Sebastiano which Alberti sent to Ludovico Gonzaga in July 1463, but which left both engineer and patron uncertain about what was now intended. Ludovico urged Alberti to return to Mantua 'because before proceeding higher [. . .] we need to understand your advice better'.[54]

Work may have begun on remedial work soon afterwards, as correspondence up to the end of 1463 deals mainly with walling and associated materials. After 1463 the focus switches to the building's ornament and letters refer to the quarrying and placement of stone: the brick portico is rendered, the *all'antica* doors are detailed in stone, as is the cornice under the vault inside the portico. Alberti was ill during the summer of 1464 and, wishing him well, Ludovico encouraged him to return the following spring, 'to see with your own eyes what has been done, I am sure you will not be disappointed'.[55] Alberti was in Mantua again in the autumn of 1465; and he received a visit from Fancelli on at least one occasion.[56] By the close of 1466 work was being done 'to the cornice that goes over the door of the portico vault'; this was the last progress report for four years.[57] Work continued, however, and Alberti sent some designs to Mantua from Rome in 1468.[58]

There is no evidence of Alberti's presence in Mantua again until the autumn of 1470.[59] By then Ludovico Gonzaga was in a position to initiate the rebuilding of Sant'Andrea in Mantua. A scheme had been prepared

for this already, by 'Manetti': if this was the same Antonio di Ciaccheri Manetti to whom Alberti may have been referring in his letter to Matteo de' Pasti in 1454 (see pp. 59–61 above), the design would have been at least a decade old, as Manetti had died in 1460. In any case, Alberti sketched out a proposal for the church and sent it with a letter to Ludovico by the third week of October 1470. A week earlier Fancelli had written to Ludovico concerning Alberti's decision to alter the 'pillastri del portico' of San Sebastiano, and Alberti sent Ludovico information relating to it. This has been lost, though it was probably little more than a sketch, because at the end of November Ludovico asked Alberti to send Fancelli 'those measurements and templates' of the portico.[60] So that Alberti should not delay, Ludovico stressed his concern that the form of the portico be considered before all else. The fact that Alberti should turn his attention to the design of the façade ten years into the project bears comparison with Santa Maria delle Carceri in Prato, a building that is much better documented: in the first two years building activity concentrated on walling and vaulting, and the next six years were concerned mostly with interior stone detailing, and it was not until the ninth year that Giuliano da Sangallo, its architect, built a model of the façade.[61]

San Sebastiano was made resplendent with decoration in time for the celebration of the saint's feast day in January 1472, though Fancelli did not finally leave the project until 1479, a year after Ludovico Gonzaga's death. It is uncertain whether he left because his work there was done, or whether interest in the project had waned and it was considered more appropriate that his time be devoted elsewhere.[62] His last recorded report on San Sebastiano was written on 25 May 1479, when he informed the new Marquis Federico Gonzaga that 'this evening we hauled up both of the large cornices of the portico of San Sebastiano'.[63] Such ornamental details often have no structural role, and may be inserted within channels or attached to protruding 'ribs' towards the end of the construction period, when they are least likely to be damaged.[64] The general fabric of the portico may therefore have been largely complete at this time. Internally, however, there was still important work to be done, though it was not until 1488, twenty years later, that a contract was issued to Pellegrino Ardizzoni to build up the walls as necessary, along with the *croceria* (central groin vault).[65] More repairs were necessary by then, because the fabric was described as dilapidated and in danger of falling into ruin – presumably because the church had not had a roof over its main space for some twenty-eight years. Ardizzoni did not have the benefit of direct contact with Alberti or Ludovico Gonzaga, and it is not known to what extent he was following Alberti's revised scheme, or whether he was improvising. The large groin vault he built allowed the upper church to be useful for the newly appointed keepers of San Sebastiano, the Lateran canons, but it bears no relation to the domed covering of Alberti's original plan as recorded by Labacco.

The Lateran canons built themselves accommodation that was attached to the south side of San Sebastiano, but has since been destroyed.[66] It had floor levels that coincided with the upper floor level of the church, and a room above the entry vault over the portico.[67] Once the main space acquired a roof, however, easy access to the upper church was required not only from the interior but from the street outside for public services. Ardizzoni has been credited with the canopied and arcaded staircase still to be seen to the north side of the portico. In order to integrate this with the design of the façade it is likely that he opened up two niches on the back of the façade (they are indicated as such on Labacco's plan), so turning the portico into an arcuated ambulatory, emphasising movement across the façade, rather than frontally from the street, directly into the interior of the church. He may also have completed and roofed the top of the portico, including the entablature, which he broke in its middle to admit light into the room above the entrance. The effect of this window on the façade resembles the motif presented in bas-relief on the side fronts of the Roman arch at Orange in France.[68] The entablature is crudely cut through where the window is presently positioned, possibly a result of Ardizzoni's stylistic preference for the arch motif (developed on the side stair). Alternatively, it may be intended to emphasise and frame the opening to the upper room (which some scholars believe had a significant use on the saint's feast day)[69] or to enable light to enter the upper room so that the Lateran canons could worship separately, above the lay congregation in the church.[70]

Whoever completed the upper part of the façade, it is clear that this was done under severe economic constraint: no elaborate capitals were carved or moulded for the façade, as they were for Sant'Andrea;[71] nor were the pilasters provided with a base or plinth, details that would have improved their proportions. Consequently, as Wittkower observed, 'an unusually heavy entablature rests on unusually thin pilasters', making it a curious, ungainly compromise of a composition.[72]

It is likely the pilasters are a later addition, and were introduced once the stone ornaments around the central doors were in place. This is suggested by a comparison of the two sets of consoles supporting the cornices over the external and internal doors. The consoles on the exterior are partly obscured by the pilasters, while those inside the portico (above the central door leading to the interior of the church) are fully visible (fig. 110).[73] From this observation, it would appear that the external pilasters were added after the consoles were in place.

As to Alberti's original intentions for the façade, it is worth noting that the main doors and windows of Santa Maria delle Carceri are the principal ornaments of that building. Simple triangular pediments highlight the openings, and pilasters are used only to frame the composition; inbetween are panels of contrastingly coloured stone. Perhaps the wall surface of San Sebastiano's main façade was to have been patterned like this, either in stone as at Santa Maria Novella, or painted stucco as at Sant'Andrea.[74]

The building history of San Sebastiano is so complex and full of uncertainties that I offer the following summary of the main events as I perceive them. Work began on the foundations in early 1460 and construction had reached the height of the barrel-vaulted chapels by the end of 1462. To remedy the problems of the high water-table (for which Ludovico Gonzaga may well have taken full responsibility, as he had instructed the area to be drained), Alberti submitted a revised design in July 1463, and the undercroft was inserted between the existing walls. On the exterior the doors and their ornaments were raised to the new upper ground level, as were the apses in the chapels. The main pyramidal roof was probably not constructed until after 1488, when the space was finally vaulted. The side stair was also built then to provide access to the upper level; and the room above the portico was connected with the upper floor of the Lateran canons' new accommodation next to the church. A window was cut into the façade to light the upper room, and this involved the removal of the central portion of the entablature.[75] To complete the ornament of the façade the broken entablature was provided with 'visual supports' in the form of pilasters which were constructed either side of the central door and at both ends of the façade, and an arch was built to span and connect the two halves of the entablature. This provided a frame to the central window. Complementary round-headed windows were placed in the chapels above the apses to light the interior of the church (which, had the dome been built, would perhaps have been lit mainly by a lantern at its summit).[76] Internally, the chapel windows were arranged like Serliana. These were replaced by circular windows during restoration in the 1920s (fig. 111). Externally, provision appears to have been made for an arrangement of double pediments, as banding of brickwork in this shape (to which the pediments would

110 San Sebastiano, Mantua, two stone consoles above the central door on the façade: (a) externally; and (b) internally (photos/author).

111 J.B.L.G. Seroux d'Agincourt, San Sebastiano, Mantua, early nineteenth century. Sectional detail from Seroux d'Agincourt (1847; I, pl. 52).

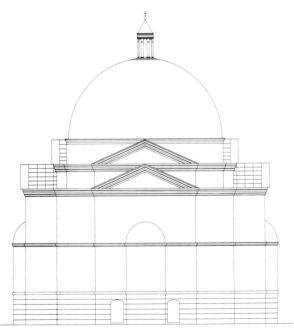

112 San Sebastiano, Mantua, rear elevation with reconstruction of Alberti's design for the double pediment and dome (drawings/author).

have been fixed) is clearly visible as part of the main structure of the church. If such an arrangement had been planned by Alberti, the heightening of the floor level after 1463 may have caused him to decide to raise the pediments too, the lowest being removed and placed above the roof of the chapel (fig. 112).

In conclusion, I repeat my belief that it is unlikely that the church in its present state reflects Alberti's original intentions as represented by Labacco. The plan is the least changed aspect of his sketch, though there are now two additional 'door' openings in the façade (replacing semicircular niches on the plan), a stair loggia, and two small chambers either side of the entrance 'chapel'. Also, when comparing the dimensions of the present walls with the notes left by Labacco, it is apparent that the outer walls have been increased in thickness, especially at the corners of the main space externally, and have reduced the depth of the chapels internally. These amendments may have been made in 1463, when the structure was repaired and strengthened, or as late as 1499. Certainly, they had a detrimental effect on the proportional system Alberti had intended for this design, to which I now turn.

THE ALMOST PERFECT PROPORTIONS OF SAN SEBASTIANO

Labacco wrote on his sketch plan of San Sebastiano that the design came from the hand of Alberti ('a mantova di mano di mes[s]ere bat[t]ista alberti'). It is likely that Labacco's drawing derived from a *modello* requested by Lorenzo de' Medici from Luca Fancelli in 1485. Lorenzo had long admired Alberti's approach to architecture, and he had acquired a manuscript copy of *De re aedificatoria* which became a treasured possession: he lent it to Borso d'Este but requested its return because it was very dear to him and he read it often.[77] During 1485, as the manuscript was slowly turned into the first printed edition of this work, Lorenzo's fervour was such that he demanded to read the printed sheets immediately they came off the press, and they had to be rushed to him by horse when he was out of Florence.[78] The *editio princeps*, with Poliziano's dedication to Lorenzo, is dated 29 December 1485 (see p. 16 above).

During the previous summer, on 1 August 1485, Lorenzo wrote to Luca Fancelli in Mantua asking him for the *modello* of the church of San Sebastiano.[79] The word *modello* can mean a physical model or a drawing. However, as wooden models are expensive to construct (and there is no mention of payment for this work), and as Fancelli writes that he 'made the model' (*fato el modello*) within a matter of weeks of Lorenzo's request,

he may have prepared a careful drawing, made to scale and perhaps with dimensions marked on it.[80] Alberti had sent a *modello* to Ludovico Gonzaga in July 1463, and it may have been this that Lorenzo requested Fancelli to send, or a copy of it (though it is not certain whether this was of a revised scheme for San Sebastiano, or one of the other Mantuan projects with which he was involved).[81]

Lorenzo had had an opportunity to see the church when he visited Mantua two years previously, and its design was probably of particular significance to him now because of the decisions he and his architect had to make in designing the church of Santa Maria delle Carceri in Prato. Giuliano da Sangallo had been appointed project superintendent to the Prato church during late summer, 1485,[82] and its design was approved on 9 October 1485,[83] two months after Lorenzo's request to Fancelli for the *modello*. Not surprisingly, both Santa Maria delle Carceri and San Sebastiano have plans derived from the Greek-cross format (fig. 113).[84]

Giuliano da Sangallo had already used his patron's powerful influence to obtain plans of ancient monuments and important recent buildings, such as the Palazzo Ducale, Urbino, which he had visited in 1481. Fancelli's *modello* would presumably have been a useful reference for Giuliano during the construction process, and would most likely have remained in the possession of the workshop during the building campaign. The drawings were later used by architects associated with the Sangallo workshop, and copies made.[85]

Whether the *modello* Lorenzo received from Fancelli was wooden or drawn, it almost certainly provided Antonio Labacco with the information he recites on San Sebastiano. The plan is annotated by numbers which refer to the lengths of the internal walls, and these are incorporated in his notes at the bottom of the sheet where the major internal dimensions and heights are listed. They are multiples of a *braccio* measure, though Labacco does not specify which one. Several studies of these annotations have been made, and attention has been drawn to a ratio comprising the perfect numbers, of 6:10, which underlies all the integer and integer-fraction number combinations he lists.[86] The perfect number ratios may be arranged in ascending order as follows:

$$4\tfrac{4}{5}:8, \ 8:13\tfrac{1}{3}, \ 10:16\tfrac{2}{3}, \ 20:33\tfrac{1}{3}, \ 34:56\tfrac{2}{3}$$

These number ratios describe the dimensions – width to height – of the main elements of the design: the entrance door, apses, portico vault, chapels and dome. Comparison with recent surveys of the building shows that Labacco was recording the measurements of the

113   Giuliano da Sangallo, Santa Maria delle Carceri, Prato, begun 1485. Plan, section and elevation after Morselli and Corti (1982).

modello of San Sebastiano in Mantuan *braccia*, a measure with which he was probably not familiar.[87] There is no suggestion that he was attempting to analyse what he recorded or to improve on the design by Alberti.[88] Indeed, there are too many similarities between the formal arrangement of the design Labacco outlined and what was built of San Sebastiano to dismiss his drawing as either imagined or only approximate.[89]

Unfortunately, the external appearance of the *modello* of San Sebastiano that Labacco saw cannot be ascertained, so the ancient models to which Alberti may have been referring also remain unknown. Even in 1473, when the revised design by Alberti was presumably almost complete, it was not recognisable to the son of its patron: having just visited San Sebastiano, Francesco Gonzaga commented to his father Ludovico, that while 'in the ancient manner, after the fantastic vision of Messer Battista of the Alberti, I could not tell whether he meant it to look like a church, a mosque, or a synagogue' – and he was a cardinal![90]

The reasons for Francesco's incomprehension may be contained in the first mention of San Sebastiano in February 1460, when Alberti wrote to Ludovico Gonzaga that his designs for San Sebastiano and San Lorenzo (among other buildings) were ready. It is generally assumed that Alberti was referring to the early twelfth-century round church of San Lorenzo, now forming the eastern edge of Piazza Mantegna to the side of the main porch of his Sant'Andrea, though nothing is known of his designs for it.[91] He may have been asked by Ludovico to restore or enlarge it, or provide a decorative programme. Whatever was intended, it was a structure of some significance for pilgrims and the inhabitants of Mantua.

The Blood of Christ, the most revered holy relic of Mantua, attracted vast numbers of pilgrims to the city, particularly on Ascension Day, when a casket containing two phials of the Blood was held aloft in Sant'Andrea to be viewed.[92] The area immediately surrounding Sant'Andrea thus became the religious centre of Mantua, which brought the city considerable commercial affluence as well. This trade benefited the Benedictine monastery attached to Sant'Andrea and, during the eleventh century and the beginning of the twelfth, four additional churches were built as its dependencies.[93] Three were built along the road that runs at right angles to Sant'Andrea's façade: Sant'Ambrogio to the west; and San Lorenzo and San Salvatore to the east. The fourth, Santo Sepolcro, possibly the oldest, was built in the suburb now called Belfiore, on one of the main routes from the west, which entered the city through the Porta Pradella. None of these four structures had a clearly defined liturgical use and no regular priest was attached to them. San Lorenzo once housed the bones of St Longinus, the Roman soldier who brought the Blood to Mantua, while the twelfth-century church of Sant'Andrea was under construction; but the primary purpose of all four was probably to serve as a sacred 'station' for pilgrims converging on Sant'Andrea.[94] By the seventeenth century they had fallen into disrepair, and only San Lorenzo was restored.[95] A late seventeenth-century map of Mantua includes a sketch view of Santo Sepolcro (fig. 114).[96] Clearly, both buildings were circular.

Round churches were popular in northern Italy in the early twelfth century. The accepted reason for this is that they were built in imitation of the Church of

114 (a) Santo Sepolcro, Mantua, possibly late eleventh century (since demolished). Detail of the upper central portion of the *Urbis Mantua descriptio*, a bird's-eye view of the city of Mantua, designed by Gabriele Bertazzolo (published by L. Delfichi, 1628); (b) clock-tower and San Lorenzo, Mantua, possibly early twelfth century. View as rebuilt in 1906 (photo/author).

the Holy Sepulchre in Jerusalem, which had been built to enclose Christ's Sepulchre and had been liberated by the Crusaders in 1099.[97] They share its general qualities: a circular wall enclosing a ring of columns that support an upper wall and gallery, surmounted by a vault or dome;[98] the centre may hold sacred relics, or the whole structure may be hallowed as the place of a vision or martyrdom (the Anastasis itself was known as the 'Great Martyrium'). Alternatively, smaller rotundas may be satellites of a more important site towards which pilgrims were moving, as was probably the case with the four Mantuan structures on the approach roads to Sant'Andrea. The very name of Santo Sepolcro refers to the venerated prototype.[99] It is possible that San Sebastiano may have been built as another sacred station *en route* to Sant'Andrea, being located just within the city walls and by a new gate on an approach road from the south.

Buildings associated with pilgrimage and located on the main routes to and within the Holy Land copied the essential qualities of the sacred buildings of Jerusalem. They share the dimensions of the Anastasis,

the Dome of the Rock and the Church of the Ascension on the Mount of Olives (despite obvious formal differences),[100] or they are exactly half the size of the originals.[101] A principal reason for these commonalities may be found in the wide-reaching influence of the building practice of Roman architects. A catalogue of the major surviving centralised buildings of ancient Rome (published in 1989) reveals that structures were often designed in plan using whole number multiples of 10 or 12 Roman measuring units, with diameters of 50, 100 and even 300 feet or 200 cubits.[102] Similarly, the lengths of columns were frequently standardised as multiples of ten Roman feet: as 10, 15 and 20 feet high.[103] Vitruvius lists such column lengths in his treatise when describing the proportions appropriate to each.[104] Their standardisation enabled architects to achieve concordance in the plan and section relative to the whole building, as Vitruvius strongly advocated.

It must be assumed that Alberti had some direct knowledge of this building tradition. He was familiar with Vitruvius' account of the adjustments to be made to the diameters of columns, and he lists these with some amendments in his own treatise: they fall into size bands of 10, 15, 20, 30, 40 and 50 Roman feet (VII, 6, pp. 201–2). Alberti also knew Santo Stefano Rotondo in Rome well enough, as it was the subject of a major restoration during the early 1450s by Bernardo Rossellino for Pope Nicholas V. The plan of Santo Stefano has three concentric rings of structure, with increasing diameters of 50, 100 and 150 Roman feet (or 100 cubits).[105] It is the largest early Christian circular building in Rome, and may have been in Alberti's mind in his discussion of the perfect format for temples – the circle and its three-dimensional counterpart, the sphere (VII, 4, p. 196).[106]

Introducing the centralised or 'round' temple in *De re aedificatoria*, Alberti stresses that 'Nature delights primarily in the circle'. Not only is the round plan 'defined by the circle', so too must 'many-sided' (or polygonal) plans 'be circumscribed' by one.[107] Many of the surviving temples from antiquity were quadrangular or derived from pure circles,[108] and one of the more intricate centralised designs was under construction in Florence when Alberti was resident there: the oratory of Santa Maria degli Angeli by Brunelleschi (fig. 115).

San Sebastiano has a cruciform plan, and Santa Maria degli Angeli is composed of a regular octagon set

115   Giuliano da Sangallo, drawing of Santa Maria degli Angeli by Filippo Brunelleschi, Florence, *c*.1434. Plan, and part elevation of the interior, and with a plan of a 'Tenpio [*sic*] a Bologna', after Hülsen (1910).

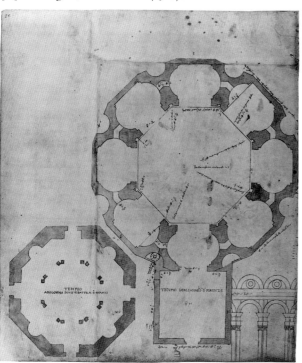

within outer walls having sixteen sides,[109] and while their forms are quite different there are some intriguing dimensional parallels to be drawn between the plans of the two buildings, which have a similar physical width – or 'diameter' – internally and externally. Indeed, had they been constructed as they were described by later commentators, both would have had domes of a similar internal height (fig. 116).[110] These similarities are surprising because the buildings were designed for sites in cities with different standards of measurement, and twenty-five years separates their conception. Yet, the overall physical dimensions of Brunelleschi's oratory are articulated by whole-number multiples in Florentine *braccia* of the perfect numbers 6, 10 and 16; and Alberti manipulated these perfect numbers for San Sebastiano so that the ratio of 6:10 permeates every aspect of its plan and section in Mantuan *braccia*.[111] It would appear that the primary objective of both architects was that their designs should appear 'round', comprise perfect numbers (as multiples of the local measure) and be of a certain size overall.

Although Alberti placed the pure, single line geometry of the circle over the polygon, certain polygons were favoured for their symbolism. It was traditionally held by Christians for example that, not only the circle, but the octagon and the number 8, symbolised regeneration and immortality: it is probably because of this that baptisteries often have circular or octagonal plans.[112] Baptisteries built before the fifteenth century looked like ancient temples to Quattrocento eyes (on the Florentine Baptistery, see p. 102 above). San Lorenzo in Mantua was believed to be antique, and the legend was still circulating in the eighteenth century that it had been a pagan temple which Constantine had converted into a Christian church.[113] Mantuan historians made conflicting claims about the deity to which it had been dedicated: Amadei believed it to have been a Temple of Diana, Donesmondi a Temple of Mars.[114] It is not known what Alberti thought about this issue,[115] or to what extent San Sebastiano was intended to be associated with it. But as the existing sacred stations in Mantua were round, and were generally celebrated as such, the decision to build San Sebastiano in the form of a cross would not have been taken lightly. Ultimately, there is no record that it was used except as a church, and one dedicated to the soldier-saint. It would seem to me most likely, therefore, that it was built to ward off the plague and as a sacred station.

The appropriateness of a particular formal geometry according to specific anticipated uses became the focus of a debate in which both Alberti and Ludovico Gonzaga became embroiled when completing the

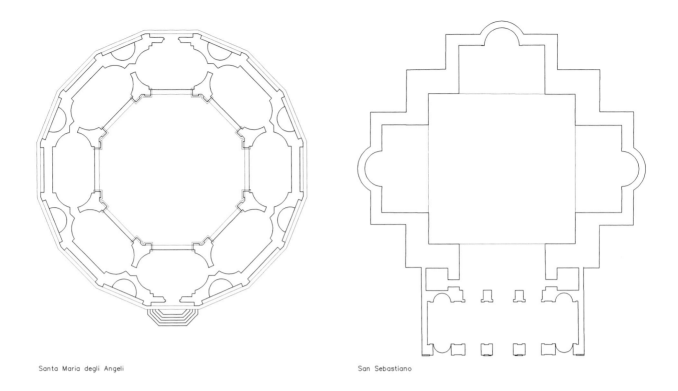

Santa Maria degli Angeli

San Sebastiano

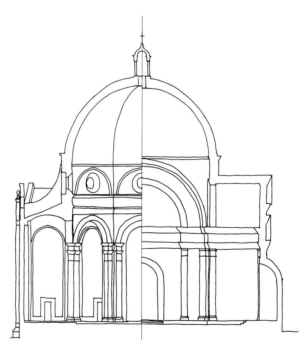

116 Plans and sketch reconstructions of cross-sections (to the same scale) of Santa Maria degli Angeli and San Sebastiano, according to the notations of Agostino Fortunio and Antonio Labacco, respectively (Olivetti/Alberti Group).

tribune of the Santissima Annunziata in Florence. In this instance, they supported the construction of a circular form, when critics demanded it should be cruciform, and their reasoning was recorded.

THE TRIBUNE OF THE SANTISSIMA ANNUNZIATA IN FLORENCE

The church of Santissima Annunziata is visually connected to the spiritual centre of Florence as it is positioned at the end of a long straight road leading north-east from the tribune of the cathedral, known today as via de' Servi. The church overlooks a rectangular arcaded piazza in the direction of the cathedral (fig. 118). On the long eastern side of this piazza is Brunelleschi's Ospedale degli Innocenti with its long arcade of columns. The front of Santissima Annunziata along the northern side of the piazza appears to have

been entered originally through a single door that was framed by a canopy supported on columns. The arcade now in front of it conceals an atrium designed by Michelozzo di Bartolomeo. Internally, the side aisles to the nave were walled in to create large side chapels, the roof was raised, and the fabric of the adjacent convent improved. A marble tabernacle was erected in the nave to enclose the miraculous image of the Annunciation, which brought pilgrims to the church from all over Italy. At the east end Michelozzo began the tribune of Santissima Annunziata in 1444. Like Brunelleschi (whose oratory of the Angeli is nearby), he designed a polygonal structure, though one with twenty sides externally and seven semicircular chapels emerging from its perimeter: a larger one at the head, with three on either side of the polygon on alternate faces (fig. 117). The tribune was being built to incorporate a choir for the Servite Order, which had founded the church in the mid-thirteenth century.

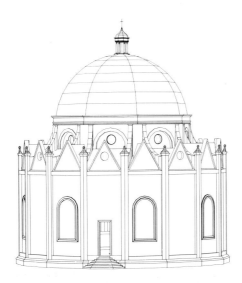

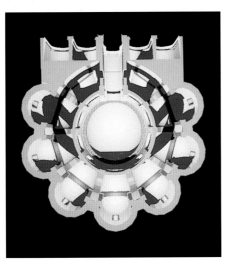

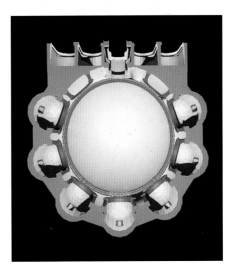

117 (a) Reconstruction of exterior of Brunelleschi's Santa Maria degli Angeli (Olivetti/Alberti Group); (b) the southern tribune of the dome of Florence Cathedral (photo/author); (c) reconstruction of Michelozzo's tribune of Santissima Annunziata (1444), worm's eye view of interior and plan (Olivetti/Alberti Group); (d) reconstruction of Manetti's tribune of Santissima Annunziata (1454), worm's eye view of interior and plan (Olivetti/Alberti Group).

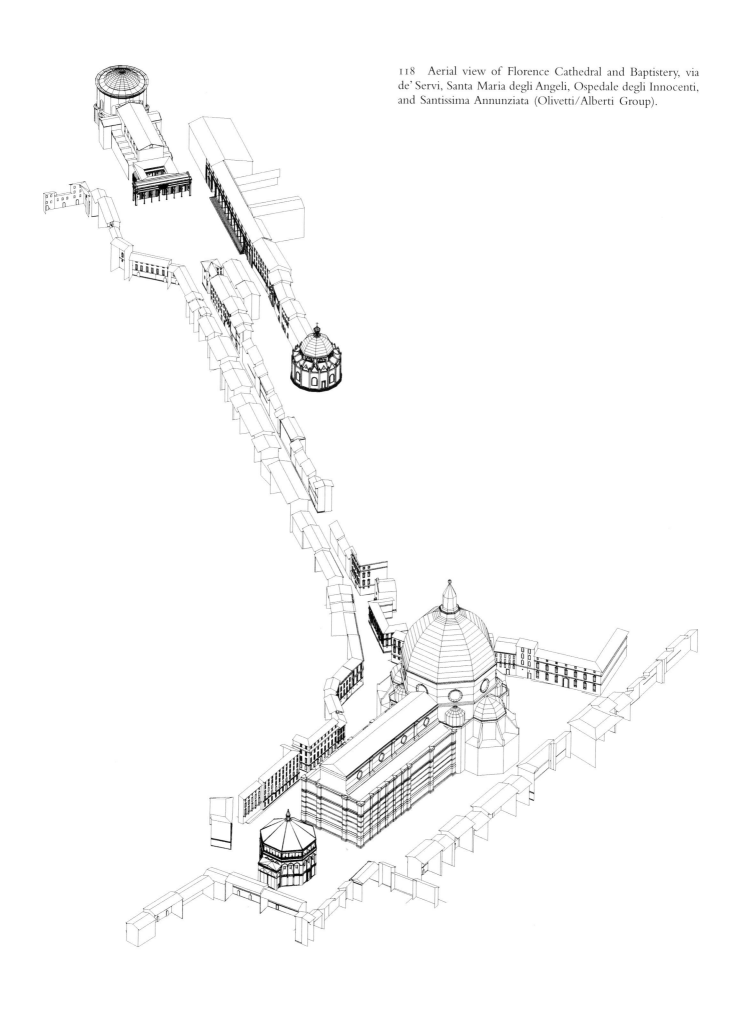

118 Aerial view of Florence Cathedral and Baptistery, via de' Servi, Santa Maria degli Angeli, Ospedale degli Innocenti, and Santissima Annunziata (Olivetti/Alberti Group).

There was no formal precedent in Florence for an amalgamation of church and (almost) circular tribune of the kind designed by Michelozzo. The cathedral has an octagonal tribune with three large polygonal chapels protruding from it, and local churches traditionally had either basilican or Latin-cross plans. Before the alterations by Michelozzo the Annunziata had the plan of a basilica with a large rectangular chapel placed centrally at its east end, flanked by smaller chapels, all of which opened towards the congregation. It has been suggested that the model Michelozzo was adapting for the Annunziata tribune was the rotunda enclosing the Holy Sepulchre in Jerusalem – the Anastasis.[116] As already stated, this was often copied by church builders in Europe during the Middle Ages (see pp. 72 and 120–21 above);[117] and the importance of the Holy Sepulchre for Giovanni Rucellai has also been described (pp. 110–15). Again, the intention was never to produce a direct copy of the Anastasis, but more to commemorate, and to reinforce and exhibit afresh, the original act of Christian veneration. This was particularly apt in Florence at this time, when the desire to rekindle the spirit of the Early Christian church was given a formal boost by the Decree of Union of the Greek and Roman Church at the Council in 1439.

Alberti's early mentor in Florence was Bishop Biagio Molin. As Patriarch of Grado and head of the College of Papal Abbreviators, Molin had appointed Alberti as his secretary in Rome in 1432, and subsequently as a papal abbreviator. It was in his new role as Patriarch of Jerusalem that Molin laid the foundation stone of the Annunziata tribune in 1444.[118] He could not have known that Alberti would later complete the construction he had symbolically initiated.

The pre-Alberti proposals for the Annunziata tribune

To understand the nature of Alberti's intervention at the Annunziata it is necessary to reconstruct what had been completed of Michelozzo's design before his appointment. There have been several attempts at reconstructing his scheme for the tribune.[119] According to Lang, Michelozzo had already completed a 'ring of columns' that formed a central choir within the tribune, and which was designed to carry a dome surrounded by an ambulatory from which the perimeter chapels radiated.[120] The ring of columns, she argues, was destroyed by Antonio Manetti when he replaced Michelozzo as project architect about 1455, as it was then decided to build a larger dome, the full width of the tribune. Lang goes on to suggest that Alberti, the architect of the domed tribune proposed for the Tempio Malatestiano in Rimini (c.1450), was probably

behind this design change; that Manetti's premature death, in November 1460, only six months after he had begun to implement the alterations, led to a temporary hiatus which was protracted by a series of legal disputes and financial shortfalls. The delays led to a complete cessation of building work for almost a decade, until Alberti took personal charge of site work and the tribune was put on course for completion shortly before his death.

The evidence for there having been two different tribunes at the Annunziata comes from descriptions of the structure made in two surveys, in 1453 and 1455; these list materials (both in place and being removed) of which there is no longer any trace.[121] To make sense of these surveys it is necessary to reconstruct what Michelozzo had built, which is where the scholarly arguments begin. The disputes centre on whether Lang's description of a 'ring of columns' as free-standing and intended to support a dome is correct; counterproposals suggest that they were pilasters attached to the inside face of the main external wall of the building, between the chapel openings. Indeed, documents found since Lang first put forward her thesis confirm that there was a central choir, but that this was composed of ten piers, not columns (fig. 119).[122] Two of these piers were taller and wider than the other eight, and were attached to the parallel side walls of the former *capella maggiore* (the main chapel at the head of the nave) which intruded into the choir enclosure. These walls established a

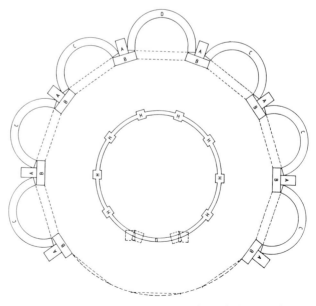

119 Reconstruction of the plan of Michelozzo's design of 1444 for the tribune of Santissima Annunziata based on information from building surveys of 1453 and 1455 (drawing/author) (see description of lettering in n. 125).

narrow visual and physical link between the choir and nave.[123] In Michelozzo's original design, therefore, the central enclosure of the choir was composed of a total of ten piers, and these were probably tied together by a circular wall, having window openings in it, supporting a dome.[124] It is likely then, that the rotunda Brunelleschi had designed for Santa Maria degli Angeli, and Michelozzo for the Annunziata, were similar. Each was probably intended to have a high central dome supported on square piers encircling a choir, surrounded by an ambulatory. In Brunelleschi's scheme the ambulatory ran transversely through the outer rings of chapels, while in Michelozzo's tribune the chapels and ambulatory were probably separate. Numerically, where Brunelleschi manipulated his design with dimensions combining 6, 10 and 16 *braccia* lengths, Michelozzo used multiples of 10 *braccia*: there were ten piers around the choir of the Annunziata tribune; and the choir probably had a diameter 20 *braccia* wide and the tribune 40.[125] Externally, and following modifications to the outer walls of the tribune in 1460, the outer diameter is 50 *braccia*. Its surface is articulated by twenty facets, each 7.5 *braccia* long, providing a measurable total perimeter length of 150 *braccia*.[126]

The redesign of the tribune

After ten years of building Michelozzo's design for the tribune, the newly proposed changes meant that the completed piers and wall around the choir would have to be demolished, and the outer walls of the tribune thickened and strengthened to take the direct weight of a drum and dome. This work was supervised initially by Antonio Manetti but the tribune was eventually completed and vaulted by Piero del Tovaglia. The external scaffolding was finally removed in 1476, though interior work continued for three more years.[127] This involved making a substantial new opening between the tribune and the church so that the interior of the tribune would be visible from the nave, which was achieved by demolishing the remaining side walls of the *capella maggiore* at the head of the nave, as well as the ancillary chapels on either side of it.

It is uncertain whether it was Michelozzo or Alberti who initiated this change of direction. Alberti undoubtedly influenced the final form of the tribune after 1470, when he was at the centre of a bitter dispute about what form would be most appropriate for it. However, the date of his first involvement with the project is unknown; it is conceivable that he had been responsible for its redesign in the early 1450s. Certainly, the Gonzaga had become involved after 1449, when Ludovico formally accepted responsibility for its con-

struction, and indeed earlier still, on his death in 1444, Ludovico's father, Gianfrancesco Gonzaga, had left 200 ducats to the church.[128] That Gianfrancesco's death coincided with the year in which the foundation stone of the tribune was laid probably has no particular significance: building preparations had already been in hand for several years, and the old choir had been demolished in 1443 when the Medici family were the Servite's principal patrons. But in 1449 the building committee had need of Gianfrancesco's still unpaid bequest, and Cosimo de' Medici, realising that any pressure brought to bear on the Gonzaga would be futile, personally requested Ludovico to take the lead in the enterprise, perhaps with the inducement (which emerged as a Gonzaga claim twenty-one years later) that Ludovico could become the official patron of the tribune.[129]

The decision to redesign the tribune had major consequences: not only was its completion delayed (which cannot have pleased the Servites) but the concomitant technical difficulties were immense. Once complete, it would be twice the size of the dome Michelozzo had planned. But when Cosimo de' Medici was replaced by Ludovico Gonzaga as the principal benefactor of the tribune, the time was ripe for a change of direction.[130] Michelozzo's reputation was under a cloud: he had been disgraced in April 1452 when dismissed as *capomaestro* of the lantern of Florence Cathedral because his employers were 'not content with him'.[131] Manetti took over from him on the day-to-day supervision at the Annunziata, as he had done at the cathedral.[132]

Manetti, though considered by some of his contemporaries as self-seeking and pugnacious in manner, was an obvious substitute for Michelozzo.[133] He was experienced technically and familiar with the Annunziata project, having modelled Michelozzo's design in 1447. But whether he was the author of the changes being undertaken or supervising a design by Alberti is not known. Certainly, the demolition of the central choir in the 1450s would suggest a move towards the sound constructional principles of a more massive wall architecture, an approach advocated by Alberti, and away from the Florentine predilection (which Manetti shared with Michelozzo) for a lighter columnar approach to architectural form.

The first design by Michelozzo probably met the Servite's requirements iconographically and functionally.[134] In the introduction to the building survey of 1453, it is recorded that 'the chapels and the tribune [. . .] are [dedicated] to the honour of the Virgin Mary',[135] and the Virgin was often associated with 'round' sacred buildings. There was ancient precedent for this. As Alberti wrote of the goddess Vesta, being

associated not only with fire but with earth, the
ancients made her temple 'round like a ball' (VII, 3, p.
194). As early as 1400, a parallel had been drawn
between Vesta and the Virgin Mary, and during the
Renaissance twenty-six of the sixty new Italian centralised churches were dedicated to the Virgin.[136] The
cult of the Virgin was possibly nowhere more passionate than in Florence. The Florentine calendar began
with the Annunciation, and the Virgin was proclaimed
as greater than any of the saints; Girolamo Savonarola
claimed that she had been granted power over the city,
and in 1412 the cathedral was rededicated to her
name.[137]

If Michelozzo's circular design was suitable symbolically, functionally the Servites required a choir where
they could be heard and not seen and to which they
could gain access independently of the main body of
the church. It was also important for the glory of the
Gonzaga name that the tribune reflected the extent of
their benefaction, and this is possibly where the first
design by Michelozzo failed. For although the tribune
was large, its impact internally and externally would
have been minimal: the opening between the choir and
tribune through the *capella maggiore* was narrow and
obscured by the altar, so that very little of its interior
would have been visible from the nave. As the first
design would not have enhanced the reputation of this
prestige-seeking foreign patron, it is most likely that the
physical changes emanated from both Ludovico and
Alberti.

Some idea of the revisions being made between 1453
and 1455 may be deduced from a bird's-eye view of
the Annunziata in the Codex Rustici (fig. 120).[138] Of
course, the accuracy of this drawing is difficult to ascer-
tain, and the tribune would have been no higher than
the vaults of the radiating chapels when it was drawn,
so that its artist would have had to rely on descriptions
or a model. Indeed, he appears to be depicting a fusion
of two different designs. A slit-like window cut into a
curved wall protruding from the tribune is visible, and
recalls the design by Brunelleschi for Santo Spirito in
Florence: the outer facets of the *tondo* are also indi-

120 An artist's impression, *c*.1457, of the tribune of
Santissima Annunziata. Detail from the Codex Rustici,
Florence, Biblioteca del Seminario, fol. 11r.

cated, and their angles extend upwards over the dome
as ribs; the dome itself is drawn the full width of the
tondo and is surmounted by a lantern. It is reminiscent
of the tribune seen on the foundation medal of the
Tempio Malatestiano: both tribunes, it would seem,
were intended to be 'round' and capped by ribbed
domes. Indeed, the two buildings might have shared
almost identical outer dimensions, with a difference of
less than one Florentine *braccio* between their respective
widths.[139] The depiction of the Annunziata does not
show the drum that was eventually built, nor the upper
storey windows which were introduced to light the
central space.

The Rustici illustration is unlikely to represent a
design by Manetti, for without a drum the width-to-

121 Comparison of the 1444, 1454 and 1470 designs for
the Annunziata tribune. Outline drawings in cross-section
(drawing/author).

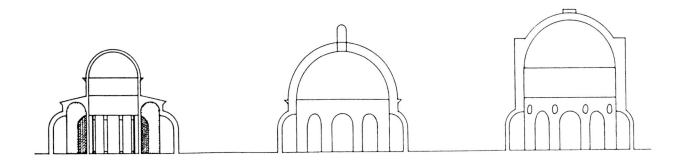

height ratio inside the tribune would have been less than 1:1, a proportion that he had declared inappropriate when reviewing Alberti's proposed design for the tribune of the Tempio Malatestiano.[140] Alberti's models for the Tempio Malatestiano were the ancient baths and the Pantheon, which has massive outer walls and an internal space proportioned so that its height and width are equal, while the Florentine preference was for an internal height that was greater than its width: consider Brunelleschi's designs for the Old Sacristy, the Pazzi Chapel and the crossing of Florence Cathedral.[141] The Annunziata tribune was to be provided with the first Pantheon-shaped dome of the Renaissance, which is stepped with a flat curvature externally: quite unlike Brunelleschi's dome for Florence Cathedral. If Alberti had been responsible for the design of the Annunziata tribune from as early as the mid-1450s, his rebuke to Matteo de' Pasti about Manetti's criticism is particularly tantalising. Could Alberti have sent the disapproving Manetti to Rimini to see his proposals for the Tempio Malatestiano tribune in order to prepare him for the redesign of the Annunziata? If so, Manetti could never have been more than a somewhat reluctant supervisor of works.

While the roof covering of the Annunziata tribune looks remarkably Pantheon-like, proportionally, its interior is slightly taller than wide, with a width-to-height ratio of close to 3:4 (fig. 125c).[142] This exaggerated height may have been in response to the set-back position of the tribune,[143] Alberti's patron wishing the tribune to be visible from the street and piazza leading up to the Annunziata from the cathedral (fig. 122). Heightening the dome also meant that a second storey of clerestory windows could be inserted above the protruding chapels and that their tall narrow windows, evident from the Rustici illustration, could be filled in and the lower walls strengthened (fig. 123). Internally, the clerestory windows lighten the visual weight of the dome and provide the interior with plenty of illumination, making a lantern unnecessary.[144] Externally, the Pantheon-shaped dome of the tribune made a new contribution to the character of the city skyline, as a late fifteenth-century view of Florence suggests (fig. 60).

Alberti improved on the apparent rotundity of the interior of the tribune by reversing two chapels on either side of the former *capella maggiore* which were facing the nave. These were made to face into the tribune, and were given a semicircular plan. The space occupied by the former *capella maggiore* was widened to create a stronger visual link between tribune and nave. This widening constrained the width of the two new chapels so that their diameter is narrower than the others around the tribune. Their reversal meant that the chapel rhythm within the rotunda would be more complete, and there was only a single opening (formerly occupied by the *capella maggiore*) when looking towards the tribune from the nave.[145]

If the Baroque excrescences from the interior of the tribune are stripped away, one can gain some idea of the strength of Alberti's design, in which a robust simplicity was created out of the more complex delicacy of Michelozzo's architecture. Before the semicircular chapels of the tribune were redecorated they were framed by *pietra serena* arches supported on Corinthian pilasters. On the piers inbetween the arches were placed large discs bearing Gonzaga arms and emblems: a coat of arms with its quarters of imperial eagles alternated with a sun motif (fig. 124). Above, a continuous cornice binds the interior of the rotunda together, and a large arch springs from this line, monumentalising the opening link between tribune and nave.[146] This is very similar to the arched opening connecting the portico with the interior of the Pantheon, and there can be

122   View north along via de' Servi towards Santissima Annunziata at street level (photo/author).

little doubt that this was Alberti's primary model for the Annunziata tribune (cf. figs 51 and 125).

Had Vasari been aware of what Alberti had salvaged from the existing constraints, he may have been more forgiving of the end result. As it is, he criticised the arches over the chapels which, he states, 'lean forward' because of 'the concave shape of the tribune', and that 'Leon Battista would have been better not to try it'; more personally, he argued that 'Alberti would not have done this if his practical experience of architecture had matched his theoretical knowledge'.[147] But the tribune was not originally conceived by Alberti, as Vasari had been led to believe, and he had adapted an earlier, partially completed design, creating a rotunda that is, arguably, visually stronger and geometrically and spatially more pure than Michelozzo's design.

Alberti, however, was no stranger to criticism, and he knew how to parry contrary viewpoints of this kind with well-informed, reasoned conviction. When the first moves were made to implement his proposals in October 1470, a number of Florentines were roused

123 (*above and below*) Two external views of Santissima Annunziata: (a) side view of exterior of the Annunziata tribune (photo/author); (b) Bartolomeo della Porta, late fifteenth century, drawing of side of church, and to the right Brunelleschi's Ospedale degli Innocenti.

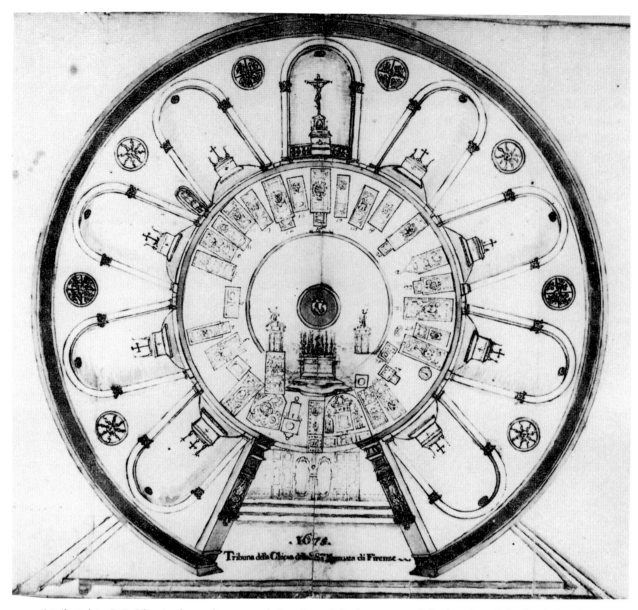

124   Attributed to P. F. Silvani, plan and out-spread elevation of the lower part of the interior of the Santissima Annunziata tribune, before its redecoration, 1625. Florence, Archivio di Stato, Conv. soppr. 119, b. 1273, fol. 27.

into opposition. It should be remembered that little or no building work had taken place for ten years, and the project was now in its twenty-seventh year. There had been opposition to the design from the early days, resulting in legal actions and delays. Most prominent among the new generation of complainants were a minor architect who had completed some of Brunelleschi's projects, Giovanni da Gaiole, and a Florentine merchant, Giovanni Aldobrandini.[148]

Giovanni da Gaiole favoured a rebuild with a Latin-cross plan, and he argued why in a letter written to Ludovico Gonzaga on 3 May 1471. He referred to criticisms that Brunelleschi had raised against the first

tribune designed by Michelozzo (before 1446), which was:

damned by Filippo [Brunelleschi], our Master, for several reasons: first of all because it was erected so close up against the church that there remains no proper crossing for the nave and body of the church.

125 (*facing page*) Reconstruction of the interior of Santissima Annunziata in the late fifteenth century, according to Michelozzo's overall schema for the church, and as completed by Alberti: (a) plan; (b) internal axonometric; (c) long section (Olivetti/Alberti Group).

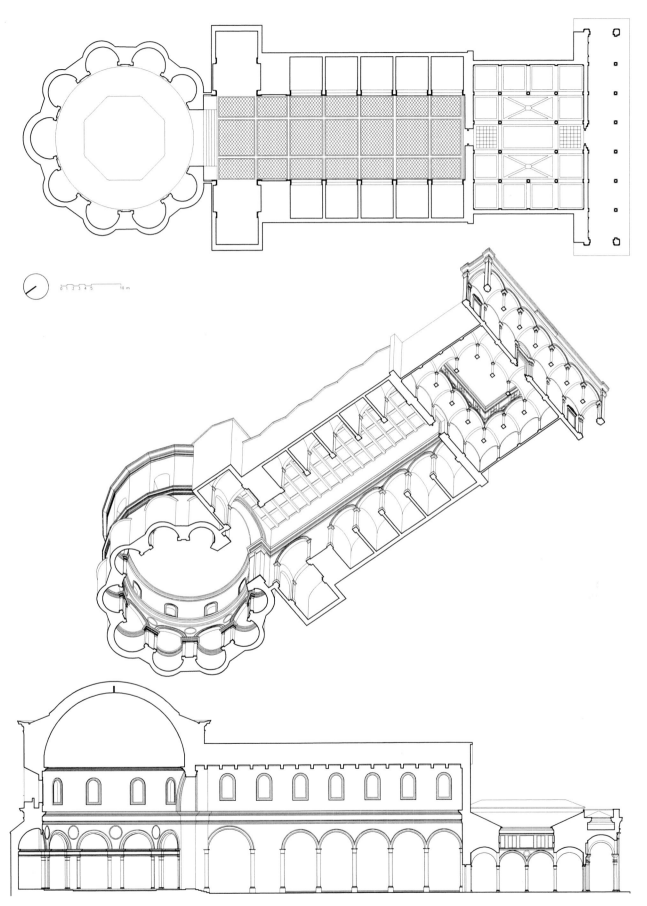

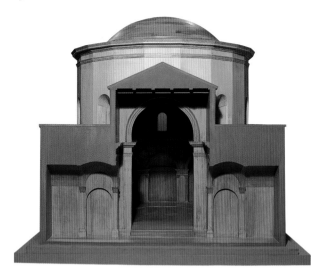

126   Wooden model of the Annunziata tribune as reconstructed by the Alberti Group and exhibited at the Alberti exhibition, Palazzo Te, Mantua, 1994: cross-section through church with tribune behind (photo/Giovetti).

127   Santa Costanza, Rome, *c.* AD 350. Interior view of drum, clerestorey windows, and supporting columns (photo/author).

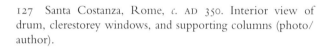

[. . .] And it does not work, either in itself, or in relation to the whole, which is why this work is condemned in its entirety.[149]

Aldobrandini levelled criticisms that were functional and iconographical, and he felt strongly enough about the Michelozzo–Alberti design to propose an alternative cruciform plan based on the crossing of Brunelleschi's San Lorenzo.[150] Besides listing the functional defects of rotundity, Aldobrandini thought the design was inappropriate on two further counts: similarly shaped structures in Rome were imperial mausolea, having four or six chaplains (*capellani*) officiating – they were not extensions to monasteries; also, they were ornamented with mosaics and other fineries, while the Annunziata tribune was to be white, and without any ornament from the chapels up. The tribune would appear plain and stripped, and would not complement the rest of the church.[151] His argument served to delay the project and Alberti's design

128   Tempio di Minerva Medica, Rome, fourth century (AD). Interior view (photo/author).

129 (*facing page*)   Detail of interior of wooden model of the Annunziata tribune shown in fig. 126.

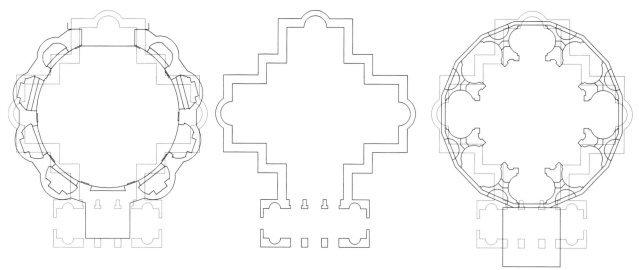

130   Comparison of the plans (to the same scale) of: (a) the Annunziata tribune (overlaid on to San Sebastiano); (b) San Sebastiano; (c) Santa Maria degli Angeli (overlaid on to San Sebastiano) (Olivetti/Alberti Group).

was probably executed in full only once it received Lorenzo de' Medici's personal blessing.[152]

The comparisons Aldobrandini made with ancient mausolea were pertinent. Michelozzo's first design, with its central circular choir, had possibly been based on Santa Costanza in Rome (fig. 127). Even though this ancient mausoleum is in fact circular, not polygonal, it has alternating semicircular and rectangular niches around its perimeter, an ambulatory supported on outer walls and an inner line of paired columns; above these columns a drum punctuated with windows supports a central dome. Again, I am not suggesting that Michelozzo's design for the Annunziata tribune was intended to be an exact copy of this venerated mausoleum, but as a variation on the centralised theme, a tradition to which Santa Maria degli Angeli and San Sebastiano also belong (fig. 130): that is, it is antique and round in shape, and so ideal for a tribune to be dedicated to the Virgin; and its dimensions approximated well to valued multiples of the Florentine *braccio* in which the tribune was to be built.[153] The composite plan of Florence Cathedral would have been the most obvious point of reference locally, not least because it was dedicated to the Virgin.

It has been suggested that Alberti's redesign of the tribune resembles the ruins of the so-called Tempio di Minerva Medica in Rome,[154] which has a main decagonal chamber flanked by two semicircular exedrae (fig. 128). It was thought to be a bath building during the early Quattrocento, and was known as the Terme di Caluce; Biondo erroneously reasoned it was the Basilica of Caius and Lucius, a notion generally adopted into the next century.[155] However, Alberti made it clear in his treatise that the ancients built decagonal temples, and as this is the only major monu-

ment having this form to have survived from antiquity, he would surely have considered it to be an appropriate model for the Annunziata (VII, 4).[156] Ultimately, though, as he wrote to Matteo de' Pasti, 'the Baths and the Pantheon' were his primary inspiration for large domical chambers of this kind: and the Pantheon certainly left its mark on this design. To look for just one model for this or any of the other Quattrocento centralised forms, however, will only serve to divert attention from the real issue here. Aldobrandini's criticisms

131   Wooden model of the Annunziata tribune as reconstructed by the Alberti Group and exhibited at the Alberti exhibition, Palazzo Te, Mantua, 1994: oblique view (photo/Giovetti).

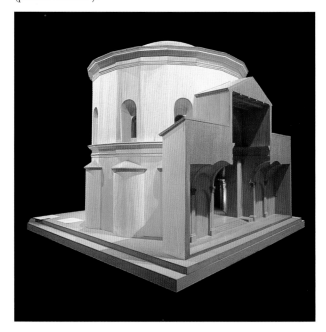

were not based on a comparison with any particular Roman mausoleum but all 'buildings in this form' (*edifitii in questa forma*) because of their pagan associations: erroneously, Santa Costanza, which had been built for the daughter of Rome's first Christian emperor, was thought to have once been a Tempio di Baccho.[157] In contrast, leading architects appear to have been aware of the universal qualities of centralised buildings, expressed in their articulation of specific numbers, size and form.[158] This must have been privileged information that even Piero da Tovaglia, who had the task of building Alberti's design for the Annunziata tribune and was caught up in the ferment about its qualities, did not know. His comments about Alberti's design for the Annunziata (in a letter to Ludovico Gonzaga of 27 April 1471) share something of the bemusement shown by Cardinal Francesco in his response to the design of San Sebastiano two years later:

> Messer Battista continues to say that it will be the most beautiful construction ever built, and that the others cannot understand it because they are not used to seeing such things, but that when they see it built, they will say that it is much more beautiful than a cruciform plan.[159]

Ludovico Gonzaga continued to support Alberti's approach to architecture at the Annunziata. At the same time he accepted a design from Alberti for the new church of Sant'Andrea in Mantua, which was to become one of the most influential church buildings of the Italian Renaissance.

A BUILDING HISTORY OF SANT'ANDREA IN MANTUA

Two letters outline Alberti's design intentions for Sant'Andrea: one from Alberti to Ludovico Gonzaga; and the other is the patron's response. In the former Alberti addresses a proposal to build anew on the site of the Benedictine abbey church of Sant'Andrea (fig. 133). He opens by mentioning some inscriptions on which he is working with Luca Fancelli for a tower, presumably in Mantua, and then continues with the true purpose of the letter: 'I have also learned [. . .] that Your Lordship and your citizens have been discussing building here at Sant'Andrea. And that the chief aim was to have a large space where many people could see the Blood of Christ'.[160]

An earlier proposal for the church had been made by Manetti, but progress on it had been prevented by Abbot Nuvoloni who was vehemently opposed to Gonzaga changes in the existing building. 'Over his dead body' was the phrase he used. The abbot died in March 1470, and the project had obviously been discussed soon after, since Alberti's letter is dated October of that same year.[161]

Alberti goes on to offer his judgement on the design which had already been drawn up for the new church:

> I saw Manetti's design and I liked it. But to me it does not seem suitable for your purpose. I thought and conceived of this, which I send you. It will be more capacious, more eternal, more worthy, more cheerful. It will cost much less. This type of temple was called an Etruscan shrine by the ancients. If you like it I will see to drawing it out in proportion. Your servant, Baptista de Albertis.[162]

The esteem in which Alberti was held by the Gonzaga court is beyond doubt, and Ludovico replied promptly, a day or so later. His letter suggests that Alberti's proposals will override Manetti's earlier one.

> We have also seen the design which you have sent us of that temple, which in principle pleases us; but as we cannot properly understand it for ourselves, we shall wait until you are in Mantua, and then when we have spoken with you and explained our idea [*fantasia*] and understood yours, we will do what seems best.[163]

Alberti had described a scheme with 'a large space where many people could see the Blood of Christ'. Presumably this was something that the existing church lacked: little is known about its form, except that it had a two-storey loggia in front which faced on to a small piazza. The relic, dried and contained in two crystal phials, was displayed inside to the pious assembled there on Ascension Day: 'in the church of Sant'Andrea, above the podium of the church itself'.[164] Clearly, with certain antique models in mind, Alberti believed that the Etruscan temple would provide a more suitable space for this setting. Virgil had recorded the tradition that his city was founded by the Etruscans, and symbolically for Alberti there could not be a more appropriate antique prototype for the Mantuan church than the Etruscan temple. Yet what attracted him to its form is not immediately apparent. His description of the Etruscan temple in *De re aedificatoria* (VII, 4, p. 197) has not proved easy for readers to reconstruct as a diagram, and it differs from Vitruvius' own account of this temple type.[165] The principal difference relates to the arrangement of chapels (*cellae*) within the plan: in Vitruvius' account there are three chapels immediately behind the portico and their respective entrances face forward; in Alberti's there are six chapels, three on either side of a central space entered from one end behind a portico, with a semicircular apse at the head of this main space and at the back of the middle chapels.

One explanation for the disparity is that Alberti was interpreting Vitruvius' account of this type of building through the ruins of the ancient Basilica of Maxentius close to the Roman Forum. This building has the proportions and formal properties that Alberti describes as essential to the Etruscan temple (VII, 4, p. 197; see also pp. 169–76 below). Several historians have commented on their formal similarities.[166] In particular, Richard Krautheimer has observed that at the basilica and in Alberti's Etruscan temple:

> the proportion of the plan, width to length is roughly five to six; the entire structure is vaulted in all its parts; the nave is flanked on either side by three niches; their openings are roughly five times as wide as the separating piers; a vestibule leads from the short side into the nave; an apse terminates the nave to the east and a second apse is joined to the centre niche to the north.[167]

Clarifying the origins of Alberti's interpretation of the Etruscan temple helps make sense of the relevant passage in *De re aedificatoria*, but Krautheimer's description reveals a marked discrepancy between the appearance of the Etruscan temple and Sant'Andrea as it stands in Mantua today, with its Latin-cross plan and great dome at its crossing (figs 132–3). This has prompted speculation about the form of Alberti's original design: the existing nave, flanked on either side by three large chapels, resembles the general arrangement of the Basilica of Maxentius, but what of the transept and crossing? Were they intended by Alberti, or do they constitute a later extension by another architect?

A controversy has grown around this issue: whether Alberti designed Sant'Andrea as a nave-only structure, or as a much larger church with a Latin-cross plan (and presumably a dome) has been hotly debated.[168] However, a letter written by Ludovico Gonzaga to his son Cardinal Francesco has considerable bearing on this matter. It was written some two years after his initial correspondence with Alberti, and concerns the progress of the project. At the time of writing, 2 January 1472, Ludovico had every right to feel optimistic. After ten years of struggle he now had the wherewithal to demolish the old structure, providing his son could obtain the necessary papal permission, and the letter was intended to expedite his son's negotiations with Pope Sixtus IV. Ludovico reminded the cardinal of the importance of the project not only to the family but to the city. Anxious that his son should not see the project as a problem, he reiterated information given to him, presumably by his architect: that it should be complete within two or three years; a large workforce and two million bricks had been prepared; it would justify

itself and attract more money; according to the new plan the project should not take as long or cost as much as previously had been thought, so that he, Ludovico, hoped to live to see it finished.[169]

Ludovico was then sixty years old and certainly wanted to see this ambitious project realised: Francesco had stressed the previous year that the family did not want to carry the burden of a Milan Cathedral, then still incomplete nearly one hundred years since it had been begun.[170] With a well-considered design and good planning, both father and son would have been aware that a two- or three-year building programme was feasible. They knew, after all, that Pope Pius II had completed an equally ambitious project for the redevelopment of Corsignano into Pienza in a comparable span of time.[171] As Sant'Andrea was to be constructed in brick (whereas Pius's project was of dressed stone) and a brick-kiln was to be set up close to the site specifically for this venture, then, with the building process thought through, and God willing, Ludovico's confidence was well reasoned.[172]

Alberti was probably the source of this confidence. He had already emphasised the need to plan carefully before undertaking to build any major project, and he commended the ancient practice whereby builders made drawings, paintings and wooden models of the project in hand since, he explained, from a model the cost of the enterprise can be calculated accurately (II, 1, pp. 33–4). Accordingly, as Ludovico made reference to the quantity of bricks required for the project, and if construction started on site six months later, detailed plans and perhaps a model would have been completed by the time of writing. That is, the design must have been resolved over a fourteen-month period, between autumn 1470 and the end of 1471; Alberti died in the spring of 1472.[173] Indeed, Ludovico refers in the letter to his son to 'un modello ch'e facto',[174] which may mean a model or a drawing, and Fancelli specifically mentions the 'disegno' of a building he had received from Ludovico that spring (though there is some uncertainty whether this relates to Sant'Andrea).[175]

There can be no doubt Alberti deemed it necessary 'to consider and review every particular of a design thoroughly in his mind' before starting building (II, 1, pp. 33–5).[176] Of the various preparations Alberti believed an architect should make, calculating the number of bricks required was certainly important.[177] The size of the proposed brick-kiln at Sant'Andrea would be determined by the quantity of bricks to be produced each year, especially since there was a three-year target date for completion. Indeed, that a figure of two million bricks was mentioned by Ludovico is a useful indication as to the intended size of the church

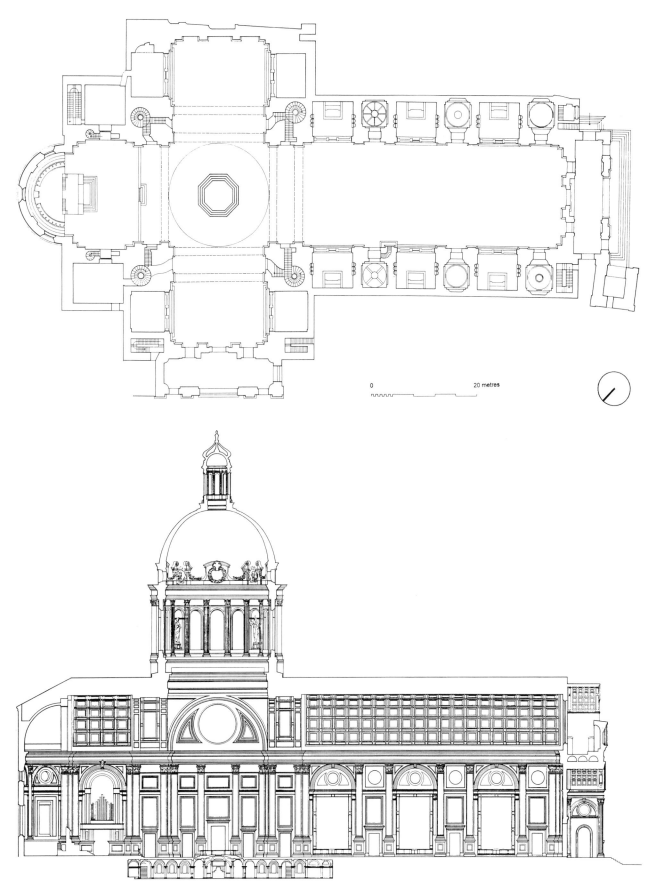

132   Sant'Andrea, Mantua, begun according to a design by Leon Battista Alberti in 1472, and subsequently extended. Drawings in plan and section by Prue Chiles, after Ritscher (1899) (Olivetti/Alberti Group).

133 (*this and facing page*)   Sant'Andrea, Mantua, as it stands today: general and detailed views of the exterior and the coffered vaults of the portico (photos/author and CMS).

at the end of 1471. By making survey drawings of the building as executed (as substitutes for the architects' lost drawings or model) and calculating the volume of brick used for the fabric, the quantity of brick needed to build either the nave-only or Latin-cross structure can be ascertained, with certain allowances.

This calculation is possible because Italian city-states controlled their own weights and measures and building bricks were a regulated commodity. Brick standards were controlled by comparing the products of local kilns with an official mould in bronze. In Mantua, the brick was dimensioned by the local *braccio* and had a size equivalent to $320 \times 160 \times 80$ mm.[178] The moulded clay was stored outside to dry off before firing. Natural shrinkage and firing reduced the size of the finished brick; and at Sant'Andrea the bricks are about $294 \times 140 \times 64$ mm in size (about ten percent smaller than the official standard) and are laid with a mortar joint equivalent to about 10 mm.

Sant'Andrea would not have been constructed solidly of brick: the need for economy of material so 'it will cost much less', and the ancient building practices favoured by Alberti in *De re aedificatoria* would suggest otherwise. Alberti favours building up two parallel skins

of wall separated by a cavity (III, 6 and 9). The skins are tied at horizontal intervals with courses of stone or brick and, as the wall is built up, the cavity is filled in with rubble. This was considered good practice by others too. A purveyor (or site foreman) for the new sacristy at San Lorenzo, Florence, carefully scrutinised every part of the building work and demanded to see everything with his own eyes 'in order that the wallers do not use brick where they could use rubble'.[179] It is a form of construction evident in dilapidated parts of Alberti's earlier San Sebastiano in Mantua and it has been estimated that about two-thirds of the fabric was brick, the remainder rubble infill.[180] At Sant'Andrea, it is therefore reasonable to assume that the debris of the former Benedictine church would have been put to good use.

Economies were also made through the expedient use of niches inside the church, and externally between the buttresses to the roof and on the façade. Alberti explained the purpose of niches in his architectural treatise. They provide 'a dignified and appropriate setting for statues and paintings [...] and [...] they contribute as much, however, to reducing the cost, as they do to improving the appearance of the work, in

134 Leon Battista Alberti, Sant'Andrea, Mantua, begun 1472: (*left*) the façade; (*below*) view of the nave; (*bottom row*) details of two of the four main pilasters as restored in the nineteenth century (photos/author).

that fewer stones and less cement are used to complete the wall' (I, 12, p. 30). With these material and constructional considerations in mind, one can calculate that the fabric of Sant'Andrea as a nave-only structure incorporates about two million bricks, while the present Latin-cross structure (even assuming a more modest dome at the crossing than exists there at present) uses nearly double this number: the volumetric disparity between the nave-only and Latin-cross fabrics is so great that Ludovico must have been describing a structure no larger than the existing nave of Sant'Andrea.[181] It would seem most likely, therefore, that Alberti's design for Sant'Andrea resembled the model of the 'Etruscan shrine' characterised by the Basilica of Maxentius.

By about 1494, or at the end of what has been called the first building campaign at Sant'Andrea,[182] twelve chapels had been consecrated and dedicated, and Mantegna had frescoed the roundel on the west portico's tympanum. The 'third' and final part of the vault was under construction, and Alberti's design of about twenty years earlier was, at long last, almost complete (fig. 134).[183]

There are some clues as to Alberti's intentions for the east end of the church. A survey drawing by Cesare Pedemonte in 1580 shows a temporary wooden screen, which he notates as being at the 'head' of the church, the screen being in need of repair (fig. 135). The drawing is made from the outside of the church in an area described as 'under construction', and the pedimented *capella antica* (as Pedemonte referred to it) protruded into this zone. A brick wall is drawn on either side of this 'old chapel', extending as high as its cornice but lower than the springing-point of the nave vault. Since no apertures are indicated externally the chapel presumably opened into the nave.[184]

Historians of the church have argued that this chapel was not part of Alberti's design, but either a remnant of the former Benedictine church or a temporary structure that would permit the use of the church during building operations.[185] There are problems with the former suggestion in particular. According to Pedemonte's elevation drawing, the chapel was ornamented with a cornice and pediment in the antique style, and the formal coincidences – its perfect axiality to the new nave and the apex of the pediment as springing-point to the new vault – all suggest it was designed later than the Benedictine church.[186] Furthermore, for a 'temporary' chapel, why build walls in a permanent material like brick, and to so great a height on either side of the chapel as Pedemonte indicated, when timber boarding (as seen at high level) would have been adequate?[187] My preferred reading,

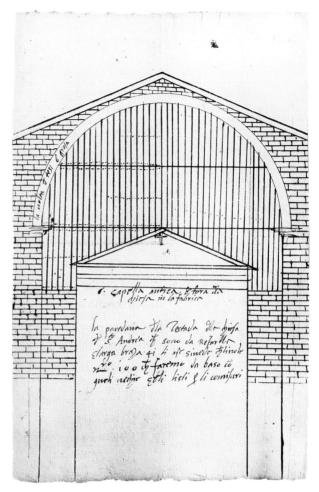

135 Cesare Pedemonte, sketch of the east end of the nave of Sant'Andrea from the outside. Attached to a letter dated 3 December 1580. Mantua, Archivio Gonzaga, F. 111.8, b. 2611.

therefore, is that the chapel drawn by Pedemonte was in fact the main chapel at the head of Alberti's fifteenth-century design and was square or rectangular in plan (fig. 136a).[188] Alternatively, if it was a temporary structure, I would concede that a semicircular apse may have been planned to be built over and around it, to provide a more spacious area for the choir, in which case the semicircular east end of San Martino a Gangalandi, built according to Alberti's will, may offer some indication of what he had in mind for Sant'Andrea (cf. figs 20 and 136b and c).[189] Whatever Alberti had intended here, a building programme was begun around 1530 that transformed the original nave-only structure.

The new building programme coincided with the rule of Federico Gonzaga, 5th Marquis and 1st Duke of Mantua.[190] Federico is remembered as a phenomenal patron of the arts. He did more in his twenty-one years of rule to enrich Mantua as an artistic centre

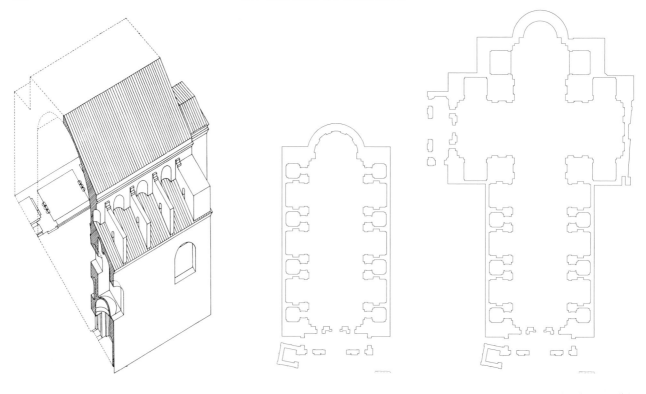

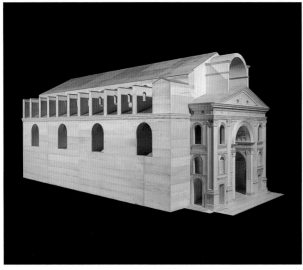

136 Reconstruction of the east end of Alberti's nave-only design for Sant'Andrea: (a) (*top left*) axonometric showing the nave and a small side chapel in section, the exterior window of a large chapel, roof buttresses, and the protruding east end altar chapel after Pedemonte's sketch (drawing/author); (b) (*top right*) plans comparing the nave-only scheme (with a semicircular apse) with the present plan of Sant'Andrea (Olivetti/Alberti Group); (c) wooden model as reconstructed by the Alberti Group, and as exhibited at the Alberti exhibition, Palazzo Te, Mantua, 1994. Two views: front and oblique side and interior view (photos/Giovetti).

than any of his predecessors (even including his mother, Isabella d'Este) or successors. He had spent several of his formative childhood years in Rome at a time of enormous artistic activity: Michelangelo was painting the Sistine Chapel ceiling, Raphael the Stanza della Segnatura, and Bramante was designing the new basilica of St Peter for Pope Julius II. Federico, five

years after he became marquis, succeeded in convincing Giulio Romano to leave Rome and settle in Mantua as architect to the court.[191]

Giulio was soon involved in several architectural projects which, coupled with his abilities as a painter, brought him great acclaim.[192] Work started on the second phase of construction at Sant'Andrea under the direction of three 'superiors', of which Giulio was the most noted. He supervised an extensive programme of decoration in the nave chapels, and his architectural influence must have been considerable. In 1526, two years after his arrival in Mantua from Rome, building preparations were made and vaults built in the north porch and possibly the transept chapels.[193] Work stopped prematurely following the death of Federico Gonzaga in 1540 and Giulio Romano in 1546.[194]

The extension, and church in general, was completed and achieved its present appearance from the beginning of the eighteenth century (fig. 139). It is well integrated with Alberti's original church, repeating the internal rhythm that he had established, and the new north porch takes the form of Alberti's original façade to the church. That Giulio Romano should be credited as architect of the Latin-cross plan is supported to some extent by his intimate knowledge of architectural events in Rome. Indeed, just before his death, Giulio was invited to return there and take over from Antonio da Sangallo the Younger as architect of St Peter's.[195] He declined, possibly because of his poor state of health, and the task fell to Michelangelo.

137 The eastward extensions to Sant'Andrea: Giulio Romano's transept and north porch (sixteenth century), and Filippo Juvarra's drum and dome over the crossing (eighteenth century).

The new St Peter's was required to accommodate thousands of pilgrims and celebrate the site of the apostle's tomb. This double demand was met architecturally by combining a basilican form for the pilgrims with a centralised space over the tomb, an arrangement that Bramante had first developed as a conflation of two ancient and revered buildings, the Basilica of Maxentius and the Pantheon.[196] Alberti's design had been concerned to fulfil Ludovico Gonzaga's 'principal intention' to provide 'a great space where many people would be able to see the Blood of Christ'. There had been no requirement for a Gonzaga 'pantheon' and it would appear that it was Federico Gonzaga who now wished Alberti's design to be extended, inspired perhaps by the designs being considered for St Peter's. Federico may have been concerned to mark the site where Mantua's holy relic was stored more obviously, though it was not until the end of the sixteenth century that the underground space reserved for it also became a Gonzaga mausoleum.[197]

In transforming Sant'Andrea, the east end *capella antica* had to be removed, and the remainder of Alberti's design was remodelled slightly. An indication of the façade in its original polychromed state can be gained from the drawing by Hermann Vischer the Younger in 1515, and an eighteenth-century painting (showing some subsequent changes above the main door), by an unknown artist (figs 138–9).[198] Vischer's drawing shows the west porch in the early sixteenth century to have been much as it is today, except that he exaggerated the height of the arched canopy above the pediment, perhaps because the drawing was made from approximate sketches, or was made from memory rather than on the site. As the façade faces south-west this canopy, or *ombrellone* (as it is familiarly called in Mantua), literally 'shades' the interior from strong direct sunlight. It is prominent from a distance but is barely visible from the piazza immediately in front of the church. The window protected by the *ombrellone* is the only one on this face to light the interior, and the two rectangular round-headed windows between the paired giant pilasters light rooms within the portico. From observations of changes to the fabric internally, it would appear that similar round-headed windows were placed between the giant pilasters of the interior, and that the window under the *ombrellone* was not circular as it is at present, but only round-headed, like the others.[199] Giulio Romano's extensive programme of decoration to the church is recorded, but not in detail, and it is not known whether the circular windows (*oculi*) date from his intervention: certainly they do not reflect Alberti's judgement on the form of windows (see the letter from Alberti to Matteo de' Pasti, quoted on p. 60).

138   Hermann Vischer the Younger, façade of Sant'Andrea in 1515. Pen and ink on paper, 322 × 214 mm. Paris, Musée du Louvre, *Inventaire général des dessins des Ecoles du Nord*, II (1938), no. 333.

The natural lighting of the interior concerned successive generations of architects, and more or less illumination was demanded for the interior at different times. According to the visual information recorded by the anonymous German painter, an additional window was inserted above the main door which clashed with the cornice above.[200] This was subsequently filled in and covered over, and today the main door tends to be left open to admit light, with a fine mesh across it to bar entry to people and birds. Modifications such as these have increased the general level of illumination internally, though Alberti advocated the creation of dimly lit church interiors in his treatise, and would probably have thought these changes undesirable (VII, 12, p. 223).

However, it has been suggested that Alberti intended the six large chapels of Sant'Andrea which open on to the nave to be lit by thermal windows, in the Roman manner, and that Giulio had infilled these except for a central *oculus* (fig. 140).[201] Thermal windows are indi-

139   Anonymous (eighteenth century), view of Sant'Andrea. Painting, 77.5 × 100 cm. Berlin, Technische Universität, Plannsammlung.

cated in these positions by Leandro Marconi, in a rendered drawing of 1788. But Marconi also shows other modifications, and the west porch is drawn without its *ombrellone*, 'improvements' to Sant'Andrea that were possibly proposed by his mentor Paolo Pozzi, but were not implemented.[202] From the photograph of the exterior it can be seen that the brickwork along the nave is shaded by differential weathering of the surface in the shape of semicircles. There is, however, no evidence that structural arches were built in the outer wall to allow for windows. Also, in that position large openings would destabilise the structure by undermining the downward line of force from the regularly placed external buttresses above, which run at high level and at right angles to the nave. Such an arrangement would be contrary to good building practice and inconsistent with Alberti's own standards. Indeed, any form of window would be inappropriate directly beneath this buttress, making an *oculus* in this position as unlikely to be part of Alberti's design as the thermal window.[203] It would seem more probable that the nave would have been lit by eight rectangular round-headed windows between the giant pilasters, like those seen today on the west porch. They would have admitted more light than is presently available internally, as their open area is greater than that of the *oculi*.[204] Below these windows are large rectangular painted panels which obscure Alberti's niches. These niches were presumably meant to be visible, along with the rectangular and round-headed windows above them, so as to repeat the articulation of the façade.

As to the external decoration, from Vischer's sketch and the German painting of the façade, shell motifs are indicated in the niches above the side doors. This

140 External view of north side of the nave of Sant'Andrea (photo/CMS).

painted embellishment can still be seen in a niche to the side of the west porch, which was covered by a building around 1500 and so survived the ravages of climate and a nineteenth-century neo-classical restoration of the church (figs 141–2).[205] Since the stucco was frescoed before 1500 it belongs to the first phase of building and decoration and, as such, may have been devised by Mantegna who frescoed the roundel of the tympanum in 1488.

Some polychrome fresco decoration has also survived on the side wall of the façade; and further traces of colour were found on the vault to the entrance. Also, the original stone capitals of the smaller pilasters (now in the Palazzo Ducale, Mantua) bear traces of a red ground, against which the relief decorations were probably coloured a contrasting blue:[206] internally, the vaults of the large chapels display the same colours. Since the building was to be in brick and decorated with stucco and fresco, it can be assumed that Alberti would have found this polychrome decoration acceptable.

Stone is used sparingly at Sant'Andrea, being found only on the pilasters with the fluted shafts (their shafts, capitals and bases being composed of stone), the frame

to the main door of the church, and the jambs of the side doors. Elsewhere, details are of terracotta, except the giant order capitals to the façade which were of lime and crushed brick.[207] Many details, such as these capitals, were replaced with white marble during the nineteenth century, when the lower portions of the pilasters and the entry porch pavement, formerly of terracotta and brick (like those of the later north porch), were also replaced.[208]

ALBERTI'S INTERPRETATION OF THE ETRUSCAN TEMPLE FOR SANT'ANDREA

Ippolito Donesmondi provides an early record of the dimensions of Sant'Andrea in *Dell'istoria ecclesiastica di Mantova*, published in 1616. Raphaël du Fresne incorporated these into his biography of Alberti of 1651 (Fresne (1651)). Just over a century later the renowned local historian Giovanni Cadioli checked these dimensions for his *Descrizione delle pitture, sculture ed architetture [. . .] di Mantova*, published in 1763, in which he

141 (*above and facing page*) Views of side of west porch of Sant'Andrea, in general and detail, showing evidence of original polychromed surfaces (photos/author and L. Volpi Ghirardini).

rebuked the earlier authors for 'some errors in their measurements',[209] principally the length they ascribed to the nave. Donesmondi described the nave as 104 Mantuan *braccia* long,[210] while Cadioli found it to be 120.

It must be remembered that by the time of their respective surveys the building had already been extended beyond Alberti's original design, so both men are referring to the nave in relation to the present Latin-cross plan which dates from the sixteenth century. The discrepancy between their surveys may be due to remodelling of the transept piers during the eighteenth century, and it has been suggested that Donesmondi 'considered the crossing to be distinct from the nave'

and so exempted the final pier from the nave length he recorded.[211] However, the Alberti Group's photogrammetric survey of the church shows the existing nave to have an internal length dimension closer to 115 *braccia*; it is difficult to account for Cadioli's error, unless he arrived at his measurement of 120 *braccia* by multiplying the dimensions of several of the small and large chapels with their piers, rather than measuring the length of the nave itself.[212]

Both authors agree on the nave width of 40 *braccia*, and Cadioli described its height as 60 *braccia*: dimensions that are confirmed by modern surveys.[213] Intriguingly, if the nave had been conceived as 120 *braccia* long, the combined dimensions of the nave

142 Elevation of the west façade of Sant'Andrea with the outlines of the original patterned surface indicated (Olivetti/Alberti Group).

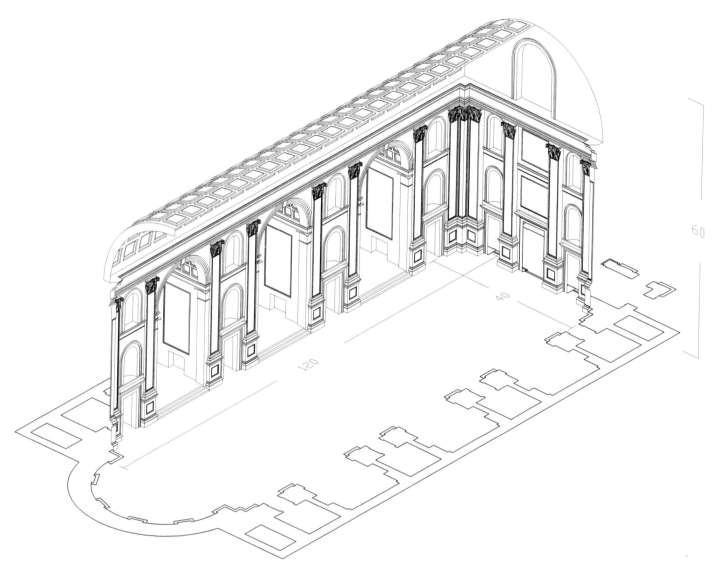

143   View of the interior of Alberti's nave-only design for Sant'Andrea with its width, height and length dimensions indicated in Mantuan *braccia* (Olivetti/Alberti Group).

(width-length-height) would have been 40 × 120 × 60 *braccia*, or the highly significant proportion of 2:6: 3 known as the perfect musical consonance (fig. 143).[214] As discussed above (pp. 46–8), Alberti used the musical analogy to explain the numbers underlying the visual proportions of buildings (IX, 5, p. 305) and the perfect musical consonance is embodied in many Western church buildings. This is because biblical accounts state that the Temple of Solomon, the principal model for churches, had an inner chamber measuring 20 × 60 × 30 cubits overall – dimensions very similar to Cadioli's for Sant'Andrea.[215] The Mantuan church shares other correspondences with the descriptions of the biblical temple: both are entered through a vestibule or porch narrower than the main building behind; from the 'inner chamber' access is gained through doors to

smaller 'chambers' to the north and south; both interiors are decorated with carved 'knops and open flowers' and articulated by pilasters;[216] cherubs appear prominently (on the internal and external friezes of Sant'Andrea) as does the palm tree motif (on the capitals of the pilasters framing the entrance arch; fig. 144).[217] It would have been uncharacteristically perverse of Alberti to have achieved so many correspondences, yet to have designed the length of the nave slightly shorter than the internal length of the biblical temple. It would be more likely, therefore, that Cadioli revealed the intended numbers and proportions of the main space of the church, even if they were not achieved in its building, or were lost with subsequent changes at the east end of the church.

By imitating the essential proportions of the Temple

144 (*this and facing page*)
Sant'Andrea: (*this page*) details of
pediment and of smaller and main
capitals on the west porch, as
restored in the nineteenth century;
(*facing page*) cornice, moulding
details and head of main door on
the porch (photos/author).

of Solomon Alberti can be seen to have been part of a long building tradition. Early cathedrals embody them, as does the Sistine Chapel in the Vatican, and it was made explicit at the consecration of Brunelleschi's dome for Florence Cathedral that the whole structure had been designed to reflect the temple's proportions.[218] Similarly, into the next century, a programme was described for the Venetian church of San Francesco della Vigna that 'resembled the proportions of the Universe transmitted through the Mosaic tabernacle and Solomon's Temple'.[219]

Alberti's interpretation of this archetype in Mantua was tempered by the local measure, the materials available to him and the physical constraints of the site – especially the existing position of the campanile, which restricted the width of the entry porch so that in relation to the nave behind it is narrower, like the biblical archetype. But if this reading is correct, why did Alberti refer to the 'Etruscan temple', not Solomon's, when describing his initial proposal for the church? Alberti's familiarity with the monuments of antique Rome may hold the key, and in particular the Basilica of Maxentius – the model for his description of the Etruscan temple.

Following the collapse of the Roman Empire and the destruction of its monuments, the true identity of the Basilica of Maxentius was forgotten and it was taken for the adjacent Temple of Peace until the early nineteenth century.[220] Consequently, the basilica was referred to erroneously as the 'Templum Pacis' or the 'Templum Pacis et Latonae': Alberti (1, 8, p. 22 and n. 83) called it the 'Templum Latona'.

The Temple of Peace was described by Pliny as one of the three most beautiful buildings of Rome.[221] It had been founded by Vespasian to commemorate the quashing of the Jewish revolt of AD 70, during which Titus, his son, razed the Temple of Jerusalem. This event is recorded on the bas-reliefs of the Arch of Titus, close by the southern corner of the Basilica of Maxentius, on the via Sacra. They depict the carrying of the plundered sacred treasure of the temple in triumphal procession, an image that proved to be influential for Renaissance painters, notably Mantegna, whose canvases of the *Triumphs of Caesar* were painted for the Gonzagas in Mantua.[222] As Rome had housed remnants of the destroyed Temple of Jerusalem, and other holy relics, the church claimed Rome as successor of the earthly Jerusalem.[223] This claim was especially relevant by the mid-fifteenth century, when Jerusalem and Constantinople were in the hands of the advancing Muslim Turks. Pope Nicholas V was reported to have said that the original Constantinian basilica of St Peter was based on the biblical temple, and that so have 'many churches on earth been built'.[224] The pope's biographer, Giannozzo Manetti, went further: Nicholas V's vast building programme for the Vatican and the new basilica of St Peter was itself to be compared directly with the biblical account of King Solomon's temple and palace.[225]

Alberti would have been sympathetic to the biblical

associations made by the pope, though he probably differed with him as to how such qualities should be translated into a building designed to replace Old St Peter's (see pp. 18–25 above). In *De re aedificatoria* (I, 10, p. 26) he was critical of the condition of the Constantinian basilica and of that constructional format in general, where a nave is framed by a high wall pierced by many windows and supported on a colonnade. For churches, he favoured a stronger and heavier 'wall' and 'temple-like' architecture without colonnaded aisles. These architectural characteristics were shared by the biblical Temple of Solomon and the Basilica of Maxentius, and are evident in Alberti's design for Sant'Andrea.[226]

Solomonic associations are also evident in Brunelleschi's church of San Lorenzo in Florence, which resembled 'the various representations of the Temple of Jerusalem in Trecento frescoes of the Presentation in Santa Croce'.[227] Brunelleschi's biographer, Antonio Manetti, describes how Filippo set himself to building the church with three aisles (without side chapels), 'placing the body of the church in the middle so that it is a uniting of three aisles like Santa Croce and Santa Maria Novella'.[228] He enlarged the principal chapel at the head of the church so it could accommodate a choir,[229] and made it the same width as the nave: an arrangement characteristic of the Florentine church plans of Santa Maria Novella, Santa Trinita and Santissima Apostoli.[230] The design 'Manetti' (presumably Antonio di Ciaccheri) had submitted for Sant'Andrea in Mantua, in advance of Alberti, is likely to have been made in this Florentine manner. This would explain why Alberti was moved to offer Ludovico Gonzaga an alternative design: one that was 'more capacious, more eternal, more worthy, more cheerful'.[231]

DESIGNING SANT'ANDREA AS AN ETRUSCAN TEMPLE

It is now possible to reassess Alberti's description of the Etruscan temple in *De re aedificatoria* more completely.[232] It runs as follows:

> Here and there are temples that, following the ancient Etruscan custom, have small chapels along the walls on both sides, instead of a tribunal. These temples are laid out as follows: in plan, their length, divided into six, is one part longer than their width. A portico, serving as the vestibule to the temple, takes up two parts of that length; the remainder is divided up into three, to give the width of each of

the three chapels. Then the width of the temple is divided into tenths, three of which were given to the chapels on the right, and likewise the left, and the four remaining were taken up by the nave in the centre. A tribunal was added to the head of the temple, and to the middle chapel on either side. The width of the wall at the openings to the chapels was one fifth the intervening gap (VII, 4, p. 197).[233]

His process of design begins, therefore, with a geometrical outline of a square of 5 × 5 units which is then extended by an additional unit on two opposite sides of the square (top and bottom; or, by starting with a square 6 × 6 units and making the two opposite ends one unit less). The layout of the temple is then described within the boundaries of the initial square, as follows: two-sixths of the plan length are given over to the portico; the remainder is divided into three side chapels separated by thick walls one-fifth of the chapels' widths; the five-unit width of the temple is also divided into three parts, with two-fifths (or four-tenths, as he puts it) for the nave width and the remainder split between the depth of the side chapels.

While Alberti took the width-to-length ratio of 5 : 6 for the overall plan of the Etruscan temple from Vitruvius,[234] instead of dividing 'the length into two equal parts' (as Vitruvius stipulates) so that the depth of the portico and the *cellae* behind are equal, Alberti divides the *width* of the temple into two equal parts. Thus, Alberti's version of the Etruscan temple has two sets of three *cellae* facing each other across a long nave, while Vitruvius' has only one set of *cellae*, which are entered directly from a deep portico.

Alberti may have chosen to deviate from Vitruvius' account because it made no sense to him, and bore no relation to any surviving temple he knew. Indeed, it was only from the evidence of nineteenth-century archaeological excavations that the typical Etruscan temple was understood to have had just three rectangular *cellae*: that is, one central *cella* flanked by narrower ones; their lengths placed side by side; with openings at one end, and entered through a portico composed of two rows of four columns.[235] In ignorance of this, Alberti may have chosen to interpret Vitruvius' words more freely, which led him to identify in the Basilica of Maxentius the characteristics of the Etruscan temple.

As mentioned above, this basilica was known to Alberti incorrectly as the 'Templum Latona' through a combination of legend, a misreading of ancient texts and, perhaps, because it is unlike the layout of most known basilicas which had colonnaded aisles, such as the Constantinian basilicas of St Peter, Santa Maria Maggiore and St John Lateran. The Etruscan charac-

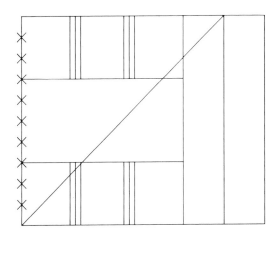

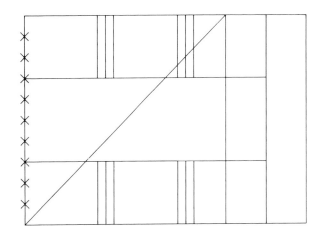

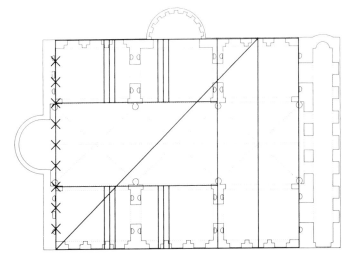

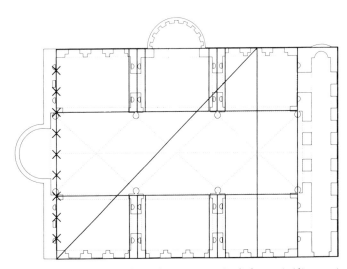

145   The Etruscan temple described by Alberti 'corrected' and overlaid on to the plan of the Basilica of Maxentius (in light pen) (diagram/author).

teristics that Richard Krautheimer identified according to Alberti's definition of this type (see p. 160), along with the formal similarities evident in the Basilica of Maxentius and the nave of Alberti's Sant'Andrea, show that each building was designed with two sets of three large chapels facing each other across a large vaulted rectangular space (fig. 146).[236] Sant'Andrea was not a direct copy of the Basilica of Maxentius, as Krautheimer observed: 'the proportions differ, there are no columns in front of the piers and the nave is covered not with groin vaults, but with a barrel vault. Comparatively small windows light the nave'.[237] In fact, I suspect that the proportions differ mainly because Alberti's description of the Etruscan temple contains an error. This is apparent when the diagram for the temple's plan, which Alberti described, is overlaid on the plan of the Basilica of Maxentius (fig. 145).[238] This comparison shows that,

while the nave and overall widths of the plans correspond, there is a considerable discrepancy in the lengths of their naves and the positions of their respective *cellae*. This displacement occurs because Alberti assigns two-sixths of the plan length to the porch width of the temple: 'In plan, their length, divided into six, is one part longer than their width. A portico, serving as the vestibule to the temple, takes up two parts of that length' (VII, 4, p. 197). However, if, through a simple transposition of numbers, this were meant to read, 'In plan, their length, divided into six, is *two* parts longer than their width. A portico, serving as the vestibule to the temple, takes up *one* part of that length', then the match between Alberti's description of the Etruscan temple and the plan of the Basilica of Maxentius is much closer. Could Alberti have made such a slip? Well, yes, according to his own admission:

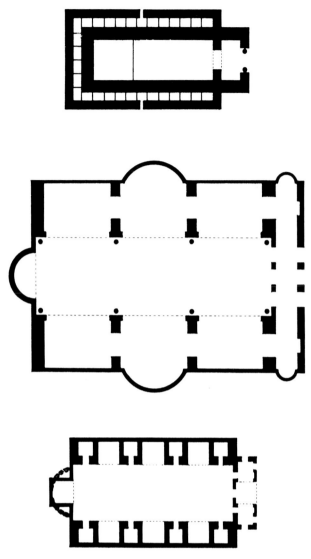

146   Plans of the Temple of Solomon, Basilica of Maxentius and Sant'Andrea (as a nave-only structure) to the same scale (drawing/author).

I can say this of myself: I have often conceived of projects in the mind that seemed quite commendable at the time; but when I translated them into drawings, I found several errors in the very part that delighted me most, and quite serious ones; again, when I return to drawings, and measure the dimensions, I recognise and lament my carelessness; finally when I pass from the drawings to the model, I sometimes notice further mistakes in the individual parts, even over the numbers (IX, 10, p. 317).

That Sant'Andrea is not an exact replica of Alberti's Etruscan temple type is probably due to the physical context in which the building was to be situated, for he had to contend with a dense urban setting, and

incorporate the bell-tower from the former church on that site into his design. In terms of physical size, the Basilica of Maxentius is roughly a third longer and twice as wide as Alberti's design for Sant'Andrea, while the plan of Solomon's Temple has a similar length and width to Sant'Andrea (depending on the length Alberti assigned the biblical cubit),[239] though its nave is smaller and therefore less suitable for displaying Mantua's holy relic, the Blood of Christ.[240] Perhaps these constraints and the specific functional demands required of the building suggested to Alberti the need to modify his model of the Etruscan temple. It may even have been Ludovico Gonzaga who urged him to follow the Temple of Solomon format more closely.[241] Either way, Alberti combined the Etruscan-Latona and Solomonic models to create a totally new kind of church, quite unlike any other that had been built in Italy since antiquity.

THE FAÇADE OF SANT'ANDREA AS 'TRIUMPH'

Alberti describes the triumphal arch in *De re aedificatoria* as 'a gate that is continually open' (VIII, 6, p. 265).[242] He does not refer to its appropriateness as a portico, or façade, to a church. Yet he considered its qualities to be relevant to the façade of the Tempio Malatestiano in Rimini, which was inspired by the form and dimensions of the nearby Arch of Augustus, and for the façade of Santa Maria Novella in Florence, which was influenced particularly by the Arch of Constantine in Rome. His belief in the appropriateness of this ancient building type probably reflects the Christian triumph over death, represented through the Resurrection of Christ.[243]

At Sant'Andrea Alberti employed the triumphal arch as a three-dimensional expression for the first time. Here it provided a backdrop to the many pilgrims who spilled from the church's interior into the piazza outside; it was also the only point of entry and exit before the Latin-cross extension of the church was begun (fig. 147). Its position at the entrance of the church not only reinforced the 'triumph' of the Resurrection, but its placement at the city centre, overlooking a piazza at the intersection of four major routes, is reminiscent of a passage in his treatise: 'The most suitable place to build an arch is at the point where a road meets a square or forum, especially if it is a *royal* road (the term I use for the most important in the city)' (VIII, 6, p. 265).

Geometrically, the elevations of Sant'Andrea and his archetypical triumphal arch (which is similar to the

Arch of Constantine, Rome) are bounded by a square (fig. 148). There are other correspondences: each design is penetrated by three main openings at ground level; they have four columns or pilasters placed on pedestals; and a horizontal cornice weaves behind these vertical elements to support the arch of the central opening. According to Alberti's description, the triumphal arch should be no wider than 50 cubits; the façade of Sant'Andrea is 50 Mantuan *braccia* square. They differ in their depth, however: the triumphal arch has a depth half of its width, while Sant'Andrea is 15 *braccia* deep; also, the principal arch of Sant'Andrea is wider and taller than that of the triumphal arch he describes. But, again, the model Alberti chose had to be adjusted to site and use, and the proportions followed these initial considerations. As Alberti wrote to Ludovico when submitting his sketch design: 'If you like it I will see to drawing it out in proportion'.[244]

Alberti related the exterior of the church to its interior by repeating the motif of a large arch flanked by paired pilasters and doors. Consequently, while the three vaulted chapels along each side of the nave resemble the three giant *cellae* of the Basilica of Maxentius, the much thicker walls between them accommodate smaller chapels: these are 10 Mantuan *braccia* square in plan, and the passages which lead to them are 6 deep.[245]

Alberti's selection of the triumphal arch for a church portico, and the direct resolution of façade with interior, was entirely original. It had a profound influence on the design of church architecture for successive generations of architects: from Bramante and Vignola in Rome, to Palladio in Venice.[246] In this instance, however, the portico may have been required to provide an entrance that was more than symbolical. An account of an Ascension Day service at the old Sant'Andrea in May 1401 records that the phials of Blood were carried from a location below ground level, and 'shown above the podium of the church itself' to the many pilgrims assembled there.[247] Presumably, the services occurred within the interior of the old church, and the phials were taken to a position high enough for all to see. This tradition may have been incorporated into Alberti's design, since the 'chief aim was to have a large space where many people could see the Blood of Christ'.[248] And a suitable location for the display of the Blood in his design would have been the platform that exists above the entry arch, and immediately behind the pediment of the façade, under the shelter of the *ombrellone*.[249] A recent excavation in that general area has revealed symmetrically arranged passageways, stairs and chambers which link the platform to the ground by the two main stair towers on either side of the portico.[250] It shows too that the *ombrellone*

truly does shelter that area from the worst of the elements.[251] The large circular window now separating this platform area and the interior of the church is a late eighteenth-century addition, replacing a rectangular window which, in turn, was a modification of a smaller *oculus*.[252] Perhaps before this *oculus* was built (presumably along with the others by Giulio Romano in the sixteenth century), the external elevated platform was entirely visible from the nave through a round-headed opening, and part of the ceremony on Ascension Day was conducted there so that the crowds in the nave could clearly see and hear the rituals taking place. This arrangement must have been abandoned once the Latin-cross extension of Sant'Andrea was completed, as Giulio Romano's much larger church could hold many more people and offer more internal vantage points.

Also curious are three circular openings formed in the barrel vault over the nave of Sant'Andrea: their outlines in the surface of the vault are still visible (fig. 149). They are placed at roughly equal intervals down the length of the church, and the middle of the three aligns with the middle of the three main chapels on either side of the nave. Their purpose is unrecorded, and they are no longer used. While Alberti disapproved of round windows cut into a vertical wall he approved of an *oculus* in a vault: 'never' he wrote to Matteo de' Pasti, 'will you see a round window [*occhio*] except like a tonsure in the summit of domes; and this is done in certain temples, dedicated to Jove or Phoebus, who are patrons of light, and they have a special justification in their great size' (see pp. 59–61 above) Thus, an obvious precedent for the apertures at Sant'Andrea is the large central *oculus* at the summit of the Pantheon's dome. But as they are small, we must assume that Alberti was less concerned with admitting light here.[253] Perhaps, therefore, they were used to vent humid air from the interior for the physical comfort of the tumult celebrating the Ascension. They would have become redundant once Juvarra's large dome was built over the crossing of the church, as it draws warm air upwards far more effectively (as well as providing a surfeit of light over the crossing). Presumably, once they were no longer necessary, they were blocked over with plaster panels and concealed by the *trompe-l'oeil* coffering that was repainted over the extent of the main vault in the late eighteenth century.[254]

Beneath the crossing of Sant'Andrea is a crypt where the sacred phials are displayed. They may have been kept in a similar location before Sant'Andrea was extended, and were perhaps visible, as is the tomb of St Peter today, below the level of the church floor, behind a *confessio*, reached by curved stairs placed in front of a high altar dais. Such an arrangement was not

147 Computer-rendered views of the portico of Sant'Andrea in its urban context: (a) from San Lorenzo; and (b) from the piazza in front of the church (Olivetti/Alberti Group).

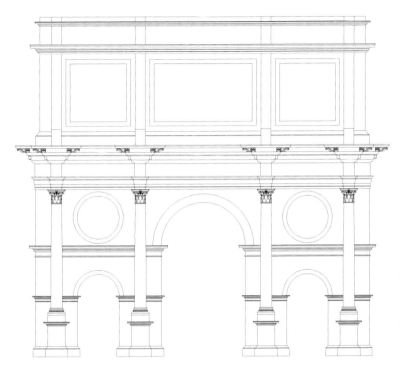

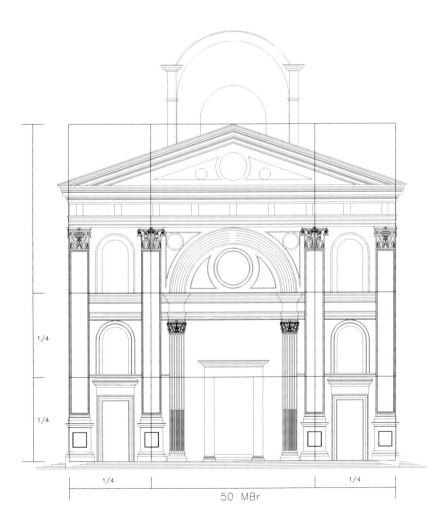

148 Elevations of (a) the triumphal arch, after Alberti's
description in *De re aedificatoria*,
VIII, 6; and (b) Sant'Andrea,
with a geometrical overlay of a
50 Mantuan *braccia* square
(Olivetti/Alberti Group).

1/4

1/4

1/4

1/4

1/4

50 MBr

149   Views of two of the three circular discs obstructing apertures at the ends of the main barrel vault over the nave of Sant'Andrea (photos/author).

common in Italy until the late sixteenth century, though there is some physical evidence at Sant'Andrea that the present crypt may have been adapted from an existing below-ground structure. The west end of the crypt is curved in plan, while the other three ends of this cruciform space have flat ends: the Alberti Group tested through drawings whether it is curved because it once contained two curved staircases leading down to a *confessio*. Such an arrangement could have been effective here, physically and functionally (as the reconstruction suggests), but it cannot be established whether this is consistent with Alberti's thinking (fig. 150).

With this hypothetical reconstruction of Alberti's Sant'Andrea in place, it is appropriate to speculate on the course of the Ascension Day ceremony in the late fifteenth century. On retrieving the phials from the crypt, and processing up the stairs to the altar, the officiating priest turned towards the congregation and led a procession of dignitaries down the middle of the nave, stopping under the vault of the portico where the Blood would be presented to those assembled in the piazza outside. The procession would then lead up the stair towers to the platform above the portico. From here the Blood would be made visible to all those below in the nave, and the service that ensued on the upper platform (perhaps supported by choral music) would be audible from inside and outside the church.[255]

The *ombrellone* on such an occasion would have taken on the role of a baldacchino, to heighten the entire spectacle as well as to provide a dignified setting for the ceremonials (fig. 152). It is also a permanent all-year-round marker of the Ascension Day event, being visible within Mantua and from a considerable distance away, a beacon of sorts for pilgrims before a Latin-cross church with a high dome was contemplated.[256] The triple-stacked arrangement of external balconies with arched canopies (*logge*) on the Palazzo Ducale, Urbino, which overlook the approach road to the city from the south-west, arrest the eye in a similar way. There the upper two canopies are coffered and supported by side walls faced with columns. They are attached to a flat

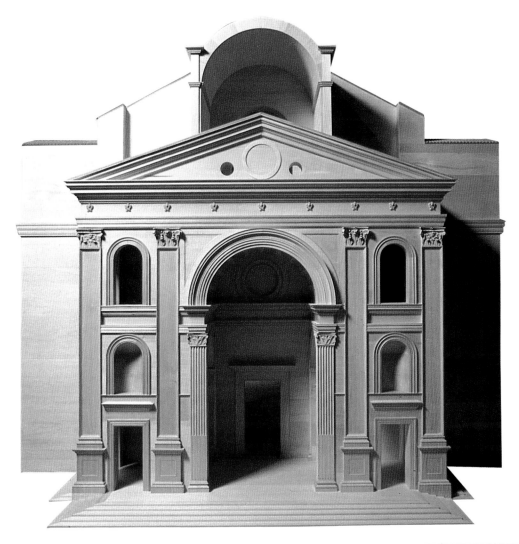

150 Sant'Andrea, Mantua: (a) wooden model of the façade; (b) interior view as reconstructed by the Alberti Group for the Alberti exhibition, Palazzo Te, Mantua, 1994 (photos/Giovetti); (c) computer-rendered reconstruction of the east end, main altar and *confessio* as viewed from the platform above the west porch (Olivetti/Alberti Group).

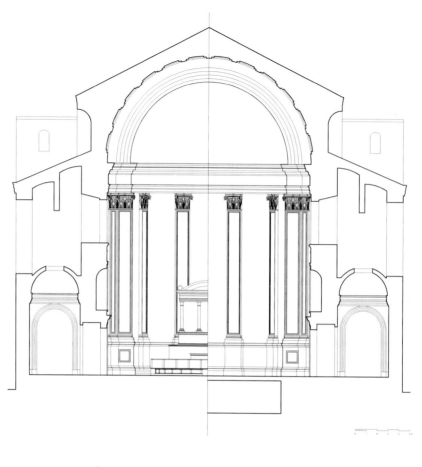

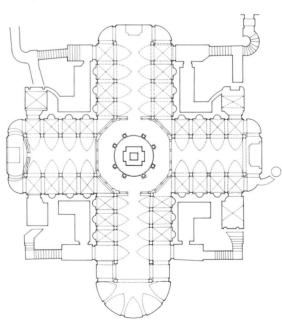

151 (*this and facing page*) Sant'Andrea, Mantua: (a) cross-section through the nave and small side chapels looking east, showing a reconstructed elevation of the main altar (*centre left*), and (*right*) the level of the crypt beneath (Olivetti/Alberti Group); (b) plan of existing cruciform crypt and its semicircular ended arm extending westward (Olivetti/Alberti Group); (c and d) reconstructions in plan and long-section of the nave-only building. The position of the semi-circular part of the existing crypt relative to the nave is indicated on the plan in outline. Alternative east end configurations – a semi-circular apse and a square apse – are also indicated on the plan (though the long-section is reconstructed with the former).

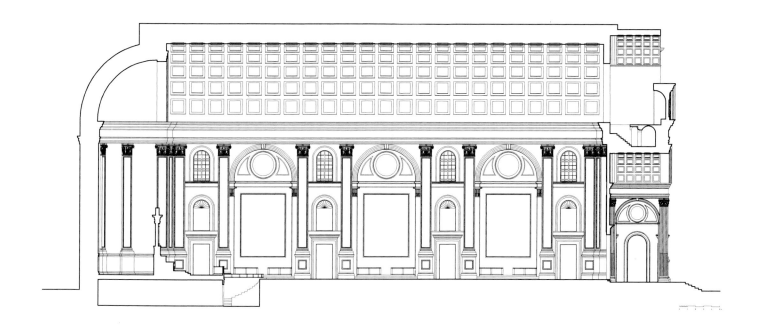

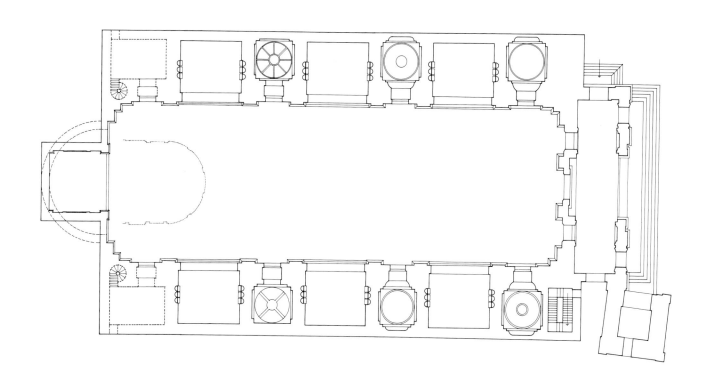

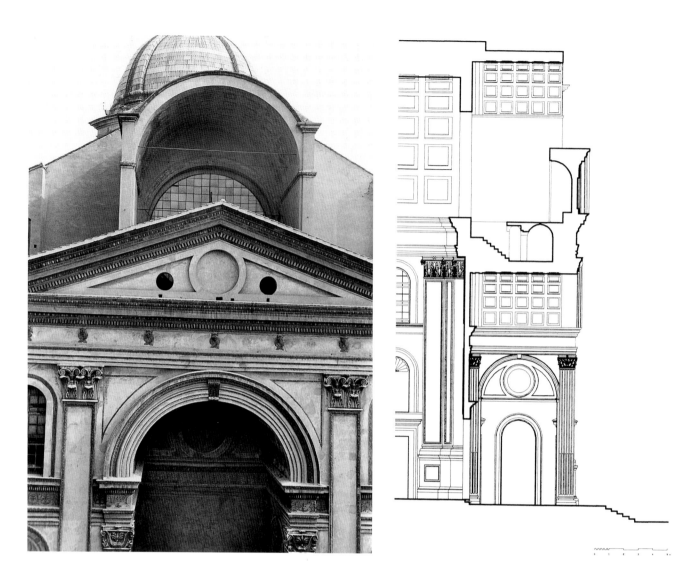

152 Sant'Andrea, Mantua: (a) (*top left*) high level view of the *ombrellone* and pediment over the west porch (photo/author); (b) (*top right*) detail of section through the west porch showing stairs and platform (Olivetti/Alberti Group); (c) hypothetical long section through Alberti's nave-only design with an east-end chapel based on Cesare Pedemonte's external elevation of 1580 (Bearman/Alberti Group).

brick wall, punctured by windows framed with pilasters and entablatures, and flanked by two great *torricini* (circular towers capped with conical roofs). Of course, an arched canopy is evident on the commemorative medal of 1450 of the façade of the Tempio Malatestiano. With each arched canopy, the vertical side walls supporting it rise higher than the springing-point of the semicircular arch itself: at the Tempio Malatestiano

these supporting elements are each covered by a pilaster; and in his drawing of Sant'Andrea, Vischer also shows the canopy flanked by pilasters.[257] Whatever it was intended to signify, the appearance of this motif and the triumphal arch at Rimini and Mantua – buildings separated by as much as twenty years – points to a consistency in Alberti's approach to church architecture.

153   Close view of the Facciata dei Torricini and the projecting balconies of the Palazzo Ducale, Urbino (photo/H. Daher).

154 Urbino: view east towards the cathedral and Palazzo Ducale (photo/J. Rykwert).

IX

FEDERICO DA MONTEFELTRO OF URBINO AND ALBERTI'S DESIGN FOR A BATH BUILDING

THE BENEVOLENT PRINCE

ALBERTI HAD A STRAIGHTFORWARD BELIEF in the respect that powerful leaders should command: they are 'the most exalted', being 'entrusted with supreme power and judgement' (IV, 1, p. 117). He categorised two main kinds of leader, the benevolent prince and the ruthless tyrant. He made this distinction not because he wished to judge these men (that was for God to do), but because the physical environment they inhabit needs to be shaped to suit their temperament and style of government.

> [the leader] is the sort who governs reverently and piously over willing subjects, motivated, that is, less by his own gain than by the safety and comfort of his citizens, or one who would wish to control the political situation so that he could remain in power even against the will of his subjects. For each building and even the city itself should differ when under the rule of those called tyrants, as opposed to others who take up their command and care for it like a magisterial office conferred on them by their fellows. For the city of a king it is sufficient defence to be capable of holding off an enemy attack. But for a tyrant, his own people may be just as hostile as outsiders, and he must therefore fortify his city against foreigner and fellow citizen alike (IV, 1, p. 117).

Alberti knew Sigismondo Malatesta as the archetypal tyrant whose authority was under constant threat. He lived in a castle on the edge of Rimini, guarded by high castellated walls, a moat, gate-house and a single wooden drawbridge. While the living quarters within these defences may have been richly furnished, their outward appearance, celebrated on personal insignia and medals, intentionally exhibited the authority of military strength, not urbane grace and beauty.[1]

By contrast, Sigismondo's arch-rival in the region, Federico da Montefeltro (1422–82) – who had also built his fame and fortune as a *condottiere* (mercenary) by fighting for Venice, Naples, Florence and the Papacy – ruled benevolently. He became *Signore* of Urbino in 1444, and he was granted the status of Duke by Pope Sixtus IV in 1474: King Edward IV of England made him a Knight of the Garter in the same year.[2] In his residence Federico was concerned less with the outward display of might and more with the provision of comforts for himself and his guests. He was in agreement with Alberti (VI, 2, p. 156) that beauty is the best form of defence.[3] Consequently, Federico chose not to inhabit an existing castle (Fortezza Albornoz, placed on the spur of land across the valley to the west of the present Palazzo Ducale), but to develop the family palazzo by the main piazza at the very heart of the ancient city: the former public Forum of ancient Urvinum.

Urbino had been founded as a Roman colony and was named Urvinum Mataurese because of its proximity to the River Metauro, which flows from the Apennines into the Adriatic.[4] It is set on a hill some 500 m. above sea-level and benefited from the natural strategic advantages of its elevation as well as a cooler climate in summer. Situated close to the via Flaminia connecting Rome with Fano, Pesaro and Rimini on the Adriatic coast (some 40 km away), it commanded access to mountain passes and the coastal route, and prospered. During the fourteenth and fifteenth centuries Urbino expanded north and north-west on to an adjacent hilltop, and at its centre Federico transformed the modest family palazzo into a grand residence that was to rival many in Italy for its sumptuousness (fig. 154).

Being perched on the edge of a steep valley, the Urbino palace stands out when one approaches the city from the south-west. Travellers are greeted at first by the elegance of the Facciata dei Torricini, two tall and slender brick towers with conical roofs which flank projecting balconies stacked one above the other (fig.

153). The lowest balcony is blind, while those above admit light and air into the interior of the palace, and frame outward views: they each have arched canopies and well-wrought stone loggias set above them. The façade on the city's main piazza is partially faced in stone and with finely ornamented windows *all'antica*. The entrance is through a vaulted passageway which leads into a large rectangular courtyard, arcaded at ground level, and with walls articulated with pilasters and fine windows above. Cornices running around the full extent of the courtyard bear inscriptions in the ancient manner, advertising Federico and the Montefeltro name (fig. 155). Internally, the spacious and numerous rooms of the palazzo are linked by bright passageways leading to broad stone staircases. The sumptuous rooms include a richly panelled study for the duke, and even his own private rooms for bathing. The palazzo was to contain every convenience to be found in a civilised city: even Lorenzo de' Medici in Florence and Federico Gonzaga in Mantua requested to see drawings of it (fig. 156).[5] In short, and as Baldassare Castiglione famously suggested in *Il cortegiano* (1506), it is like a city in the form of a palace,[6] an analogy promoted by Alberti in *De re aedificatoria*: 'If (as the philosophers maintain) the city is like some large house, and the house is in turn like some small city, cannot the various parts of the house – atria, *xysti*, dining rooms, porticoes, and so on – be considered miniature buildings?' (I, 9, p. 23).

FEDERICO AND ALBERTI

Federico surrounded himself with leading artists, architects and intellectuals, who were drawn to his hospitality and patronage and were impressed by his substantial knowledge of the arts. He built up an impressive library, composed entirely of manuscripts (as he deplored the arrival of printed books and would not house them); by his death he had 1100 volumes, including Giannozzo Manetti's biography of Pope Nicholas V, with its account of the pope's vision for Rome and the Vatican, and treatises on architecture by Vitruvius, Alberti and Francesco di Giorgio.[7] Federico had an active interest in architecture. According to the memoirs of Vespasiano da Bisticci, a principal supplier to

155   (a) Corner junction in the main courtyard of Palazzo Ducale, Urbino; (b) the main axis of the courtyard looking north towards the main entrance and the cathedral beyond (photos/author).

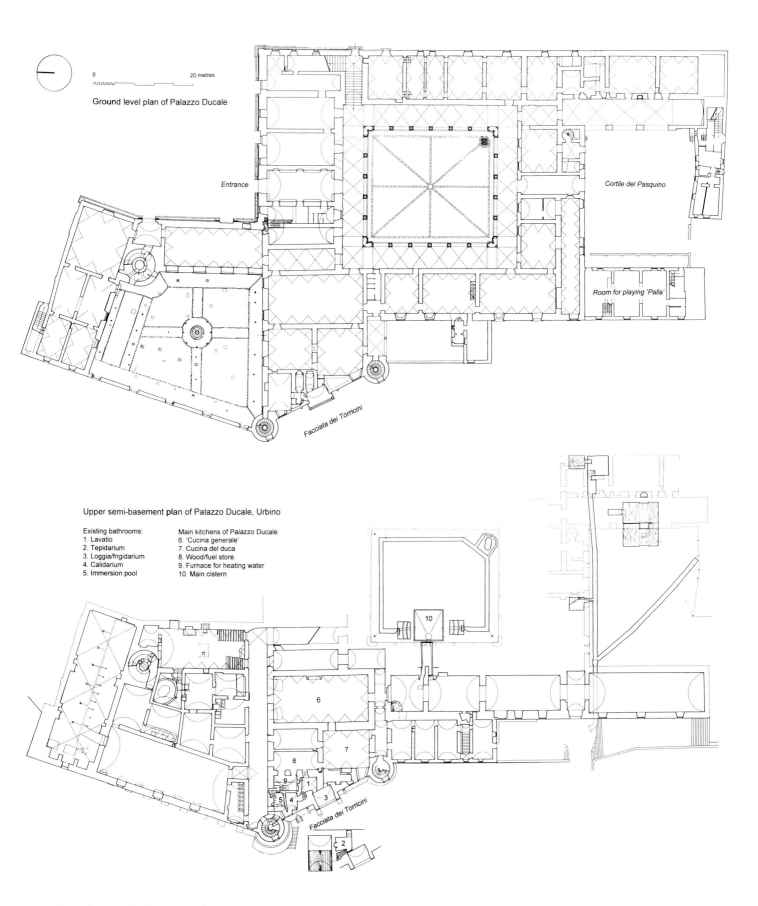

Ground level plan of Palazzo Ducale

0   20 metres

Entrance

Cortile del Pasquino

Room for playing 'Palla'

Facciata dei Torricini

Upper semi-basement plan of Palazzo Ducale, Urbino

Existing bathrooms:
1. Lavatio
2. Tepidarium
3. Loggia/frigidarium
4. Calidarium
5. Immersion pool

Main kitchens of Palazzo Ducale
6. 'Cucina generale'
7. Cucina del duca
8. Wood/fuel store
9. Furnace for heating water
10. Main cistern

Facciata dei Torricini

156   Ground plan of Palazzo Ducale, Urbino, with key; and upper semi-basement plan of Palazzo Ducale, Urbino, with Federico's bathing rooms indicated numerically (drawings/Polichetti 1985).

Federico of the highest quality manuscripts, he not only studied architecture but was involved in the smallest details of the building projects he initiated. Federico's secretary, Francesco Galli, even compared his master to Vitruvius.[8]

An amicable relationship developed between Federico and Alberti during the 1460s.[9] This may have been kindled initially through their mutual connections with the Gonzaga court in Mantua where Federico had studied.[10] Intellectually, they had much in common, sharing a passion for learning, the arts and architecture. According to Bernardino Baldi, a member of the Urbino court and himself a commentator on the writings of Vitruvius, Alberti had intended to dedicate his books on architecture to Federico, but after his death a kinsman of Alberti 'was persuaded by Angelo Poliziano to make a gift of them to Lorenzo de' Medici'.[11] The increasing closeness of their fellowship is reflected in the dialogues of Landino's *Disputationes Camaldulenses* (1474).

The *Disputationes* record a debate prominent in humanist circles at that time: whether the man of virtue should lead an active life in society, the 'vita activa', or retreat to contemplation and writing, the 'vita contemplativa'. The dialogues on this theme are purported to have been between Lorenzo de' Medici and Alberti at the monastery of Camaldoli, high in the Apennines, midway between Florence and Urbino. In the *Disputationes*, Alberti argues for the contemplative virtues and the pursuit of wisdom through scholarship, while Lorenzo recites the benefits of active engagement in political action. In one passage Alberti remarks on the hospitality of Federico da Montefeltro: 'every year, for my health and rest, I escape the Roman autumn and seek pleasure with him, and it seems to me as if I have left the suppers of Sardanapalus for the banquets of Alcinous, and have met a Socratic host'.[12] In mid-August 1464, when Alberti is recorded as *en route* to one such 'banquet', Ludovico Gonzaga wrote to his wife that 'messer Baptista di Alberti was on his way to visit us [in Mantua] and was taking the Marches route [from Rome] and was going to stay at Urbino for some days' (although Alberti did not complete the journey to Mantua because of illness).[13] Ludovico was monitoring Alberti's travels because he was concerned about progress at San Sebastiano in Mantua, which was then at a crucial stage of construction (see p. 139 above). It has been conjectured that Alberti was also advising Federico on the design of his palazzo at Urbino at this time.[14]

★   ★   ★

BUILDING AND BATHING

The Palazzo Ducale was built by Federico in three distinct phases.[15] Work began on it during the 1450s when a Florentine master, Maso di Bartolommeo, first started to expand the existing accommodation through the provision of new wings. What is visible today, however, was overseen mostly by Luciano Laurana (1420/25–79), who was invited to Urbino by Federico in 1465, and was officially appointed architect of the palazzo three years later.[16] Laurana, a Dalmatian, had spent a short time in Mantua and Pesaro immediately before his appointment in Urbino; he was considered suitable because of his experience and because Federico considered that there was no one in Tuscany who could take on this role.[17] Laurana supervised the building of the Palazzo Ducale until 1472, when he left the city and moved south, to become artillery master of the Castel Nuovo in Naples. On his departure there was a hiatus of building work that lasted for around two years, until the Sienese artist and architect Francesco di Giorgio (1439–1502) continued Federico's grand project. Francesco di Giorgio is credited with the design of a range of works there – including a marvellous spiral ramp, large enough to allow Federico to ride a horse up to the base of the palazzo from the parade-ground cum marketplace and stables below – a vertical distance of some 30 m.[18]

Federico's major building works at the Palazzo Ducale had not started by the time Alberti completed *De re aedificatoria*, which refers to the city only in connection with its geology and water supply:

> At Fiesole, and also at Urbino, water is found as soon as you dig, despite the fact that they are hilltop cities: this is because the ground is rocky, the stone being compacted with clay. Also some clods of earth contain little pockets of the purest water within their lining (x, 3, p. 327).

The importance of a ready water supply to the inhabitants of a hilltop city needs no explanation. Federico had several large cisterns built beneath the palace, including one under the main entrance courtyard which collected rainwater not only to supply the daily consumption needs of his household but to allow for his pleasure in bathing, a suite of private bathing rooms being accessible directly from his private apartments in the palace.

Federico's was the first private bathing complex to be purpose-built in a palace that century. A few decades earlier Pope Nicholas V had built a grand detached bath building at Viterbo, known as the Bagno della Crociata (the Bath of the Crusade); he had been a frequent visitor to the town for some years to treat his chronic gout, and the spa waters there were favoured by other prominent members of the church.[19] Nicholas was there in May 1448, with his mother and sister, a year after his election, and the new bath building was ready when Nicholas visited them in 1454, not many months before his death. They were soon destroyed, and their layout and designer is unknown: their attribution to Bernardo Rossellino by Vasari is doubted.[20] It is recorded that they had two floors of sumptuous interiors, with fine windows, and chimneys to vent the heat and steam; the roof was crenellated and the building had towers at either end.[21] Ludovico Gonzaga met Pope Pius II (who also suffered gout) at the spas of Macereto and Petrolio, just south of Siena, in May 1460, soon after the Council in Mantua.[22] Ludovico more frequently visited Acqui, north-west of Genoa, where he and other members of his family attempted to relieve their many inherited ailments by immersing themselves in the hot steam baths and mud of the spa.[23] His treatment, recorded in September 1458, began each day with half an hour in a hot bath followed by a douche to his shoulder; after dressing he had steam treatment in his ears and then his head douched; in the evening his day of therapy was concluded with a mud bath. He also frequented Corsena, near Lucca, where he took the water, drinking there in 1464 nine and a half beakers daily: this, he claimed, made him feel half his fifty-two years.[24] Petriolo was a favourite of Ludovico, however, and he had intentions of improving the facilities there: Federico da Montefeltro also favoured this spa for his aches and pains, as many military leaders had done since the early fifteenth century.[25]

Federico had a suite of bathing rooms built in his own palace, presumably because balneotherapy had proved beneficial for him. They are thought to have been designed after 1476 by Francesco di Giorgio,[26] and consist of what, in ancient times, would have been called a *lavatio* (for rubbing down the body and anointing it with oils); a *tepidarium* with a pool of warm water for soaking in; a heated *calidarium*, or a chamber for sweating in with wet heat; and a plunge bath for totally immersing the body.[27] According to Federico's biographer Bernardino Baldi, writing in 1480, the duke used these rooms after playing *palla* or *pallacorda* (an early kind of tennis) in an adjacent building.[28]

Federico's bathing rooms are placed in a triangular area, and are situated at the level of the courtyard cistern (at what is now known as an upper semi-basement level) and have direct and level access to the lowest placed of the loggias in the Facciata dei Torricini (fig. 156). They are quite small: each room is like a cubicle, with plan dimensions roughly 2 × 3 m. The *lavatio* is equipped with a basin for washing in; and the cubicle containing the *tepidarium* is set immediately above and is accessible by a stepped ramp. The *tepidarium* and *lavatio* have access to the external loggia which, with its splendid south-westerly views (fig. 157), may have been the equivalent of the ancient *frigidarium*: contemplation of the landscape views from the loggia, and fresh air, may have been essential elements of the bathing process.[29] Traditionally the *frigidarium* contained a cold water pool, but the loggia at Urbino is well shaded and admits a cooling breeze to the interior: in winter the wind would of course be cold, though the loggia is open to southerly winds, not the chilling northern ones. The *tepidarium* is positioned between the *frigidarium* and the *calidarium* and acts as a small 'heat lock'.[30] The *calidarium* has its own raised floor which was heated with warm air as in a Roman *hypocaust* from a furnace immediately between the bathrooms. This

157 North-westerly view from the uppermost balcony and loggia of Palazzo Ducale, Urbino (two floors above Federico's bathing rooms) (photo/H. Daher).

furnace also heated the water to the temperature required. Next to the *calidarium* is the immersion pool, and steps lead down into a roughly square basin. Around these rooms are the main kitchens of the palace and the wood stores which provide the fuel for the furnace. The practicality of placing a private bathroom adjoining the kitchens to benefit from its supply of heat was commented on by Vitruvius, who includes descriptions of both public bathing spaces and private baths in his treatise.[31]

Alberti was influenced by Vitruvius' accounts, which he judged against the imposing physical remains of ancient bath buildings in Rome. These consist of very large vaulted rooms, with separate accommodation for men and women, arranged around open-air courtyards (VIII, 10). In *De re aedificatoria* he also alluded to the ancient writers Celsus and Galen, who recommended washing and dry and damp heat atmospheres for health and hygiene,[32] and to Pliny the Elder, who had written of the medicinal properties of waters in the *Natural History*.[33] In Alberti's own times Michele Savonarola, who was professor of medicine at Padua and Ferrara, where he was also the principal court physician, wrote a full account of the benefits of bathing in 1440 (his treatise was printed in 1485).[34] While Alberti describes the spaces of grand public baths, he does not mention private bathrooms.

A DESIGN FOR A BATH BUILDING ATTRIBUTED TO ALBERTI

A design for a bath building drawn in plan has been attributed to Alberti (fig. 158). The design is significant for its subject-matter, and the fact that, if the attribution is correct, this is his only surviving planimetric drawing. According to the plan and its annotations, the design is for a large semi-detached bath building that could accommodate 'guests' who would approach it from adjacent quarters along an *ambulatio*, a covered and (as the distance between the piers on the plan suggest) probably arcaded route.[35] The plan is carefully delineated (a straight-edge and compass were evidently used) and was intended to be understood by others: an annotation written on it states that this project 'will be seen with the greatest pleasure', recalling the wording of Alberti's letter to Ludovico Gonzaga when proposing a design for Sant'Andrea in Mantua.[36]

The drawing was found in a collection of over three hundred drawings and sketches (including some autograph ones by Francesco di Giorgio) believed to have been compiled by Muzio Oddi, an architect practising in Urbino during the early seventeenth century.

Its design and annotations were attributed to Alberti by Howard Burns, and he also suggested its provenance was Urbino: notions disputed subsequently by Gustina Scaglia, though I find her reasoning and counter suggestions unconvincing.[37] There is uncertainty about the plan: the date of its design is not recorded, and the annotations do not indicate where or for whom it was destined. Nevertheless, I am persuaded by Burns that the drawing is Alberti's and that, because of its association with Oddi, and Federico's interest in bathing, it probably came from Urbino. Indeed, it is conceivable that Federico's palazzo was to have incorporated a more major bath building than exists there at present, one that would be suitable for his guests, and that Alberti made the design for Federico during, or soon after one of his visits to Urbino.[38]

This begs the question whether Alberti's design was intended for a site in or adjacent to the new palazzo. Detailed plans of the palace and an accompanying description of room uses at different stages in its history, published in 1985, have greatly facilitated this line of inquiry.[39] This material would seem to suggest two possible locations for Alberti's bath building: at the southern end of the palace adjacent to a courtyard called the Cortile del Pasquino; or adjacent to Federico's own apartments, and close to where the existing baths were subsequently built by Francesco di Giorgio after Alberti's death.

A bath building as an adjunct to the Cortile del Pasquino

Guest rooms at the Palazzo Ducale were contained in two rectangular blocks, placed at right angles to one another, which formed two sides of the main courtyard immediately to the south of Federico's own apartment.[40] The ambulatory that leads away from the southernmost guest wing is unfinished and is left with a ragged end wall, because development south of the palace was halted and not completed (fig. 160). Consequently, the buildings peter out around an ill-formed courtyard known as the Cortile del Pasquino, where a circular mausoleum was once planned to mark

158 (*facing page top*)   Attributed to Leon Battista Alberti, plan of a bath building, with notations. Pen and ink on paper, 27.3 × 38.5 cm. Florence, Biblioteca Mediceo-Laurenziana, Cod. Ashb. 1828, App. cc. fols 56v–57r.

159   Bath building plan redrawn with a millimetre scale and modules indicated, after Burns (1979) (drawing/author).

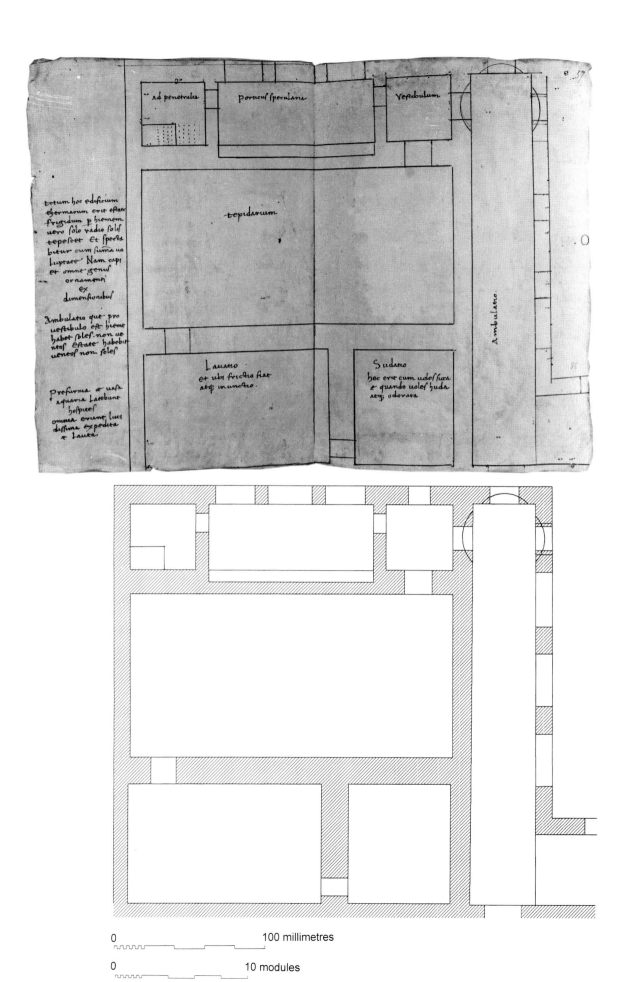

0   100 millimetres

0   10 modules

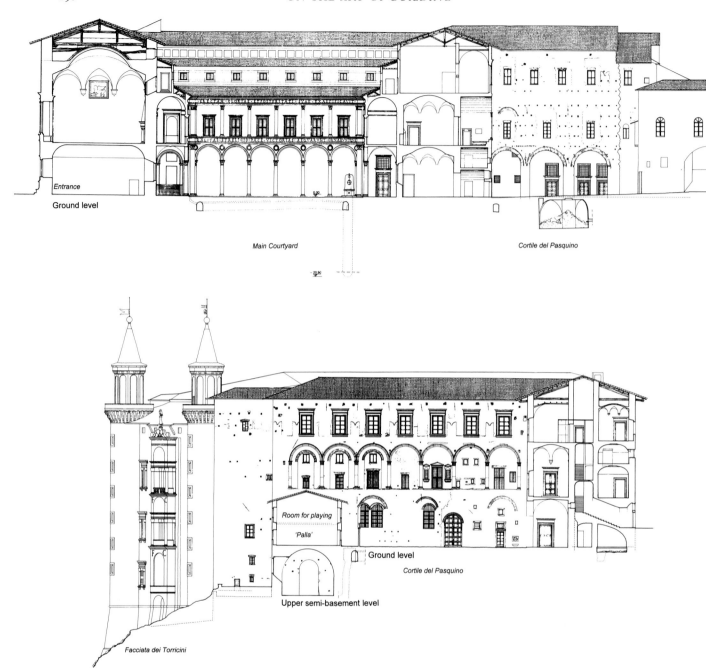

160   (a) (*top*) Sectional elevation running north-south through the main courtyard of Palazzo Ducale, Urbino, looking east;
(b) sectional elevation running west-east through the Cortile del Pasquino of Palazzo Ducale, looking north
(drawings/Polichetti 1985).

the remains of the Montefeltro family.[41] The courtyard was made into a garden in the fifteenth century, and its western edge, next to the steep valley, was closed by Federico's tennis court.

It is recorded that the area to the east of the courtyard was neither 'finished, nor begun'.[42] The southern construction of the palazzo was terminated suddenly in 1472, when Luciano Laurana left Urbino; no further

building work was entertained until the appointment of Francesco di Giorgio. Federico's wife Battista Sforza died in 1472 while giving birth to their son Guidobaldo, and it has been suggested that a grieving Federico no longer had the will to complete his ambitious building project.[43] However (and acknowledging that this is a less romantic proposition), as Alberti died in the spring of 1472, it is also possible that work stopped on the palazzo because Federico had lost his partner in architecture.[44]

To test whether Alberti's design was intended to complete the area to the south of the courtyard, it is first necessary to gauge the size of the building he was proposing. Its minimum size can be determined by the door widths on the plan (which need to be wide enough for the easy passage of its users), and the depth of tread of the service stairs which, as he notes, lead down to the furnaces.[45] Howard Burns estimated the scale of the drawing at about 1:100 of life-size, a proposition made without reference to a particular site (fig. 159).[46] To be able to connect Alberti's design with the partly built southern ambulatory of the Palazzo Ducale also imposes a scale on the drawing; that of 1:100 would seem to fit well. It is reasonable to assume that Alberti had drawn the plan to scale, as he is confident in his annotations that the type of ornamentation appropriate to each space could be understood from its dimensions.[47] Baccio Pontelli obliged Lorenzo de' Medici's request for a copy of the plan of the Palazzo Ducale in 1481, with a scale divided into ten parts, each 10 feet in length.[48] The measure used locally in Urbino was the *piede*; its length is recorded as equivalent to 410mm, though Baldi seems to be using a smaller foot of 334mm in his descriptions of the palazzo.[49]

Alberti's drawing is not precise enough to determine the exact sizes of the spaces he drew, though at a scale of 1:100 the piers of the *ambulatio* have a depth similar to those built along the eastern edge of the Cortile del Pasquino.[50] By attaching Alberti's plan to the incomplete ambulatory of the palazzo at a scale of 1:100, it can be seen that the complete *ambulatio* would have run around two sides of the Cortile del Pasquino, without projecting over the steep escarpment to the west; and the bath building itself would not have collided with Count Antonio's neighbouring palazzo, the only other major property in this area (fig. 156).[51]

Other aspects of the plan work well with this location. The *porticus specularia*, where bathers would probably have disrobed before entering the *tepidarium* and relaxed after bathing – like the loggia or *frigidarium* that Federico built as part of his private baths – would have had an impressive westerly aspect through three large openings. In the summer the duke's guests could have basked in the gentle rays of the late afternoon sun, while in the winter it would truly have been a chilly space. As there were open views from its windows bathers would not have been overlooked, and as the ground under the site falls towards the valley there would have been space under the south-western part of the baths suitable for the 'furnaces and cauldrons of

water'. Below ground (*ad penetralia*), and hidden from the guests, there would have been no need for expensive excavations or a podium to the building. In this suggested location Alberti's bath building design would have been a useful adjunct to the guest wing of the palace, and well matched to the natural topography of the site.

As to the environment around the bath building, Alberti annotated his plan with the following comment: 'this whole bath building will be cool in summer, but in winter will be warmed by the rays of the sun'. Thus, the thick and massive walls would ensure that the entire building would enjoy equable temperatures by excluding the summer heat, retaining its internal warmth in winter. As to its orientation, Alberti's comments would appear at first reading to contradict the siting I have suggested. He states that 'the *ambulatio* which is in front of the vestibule will have sunshine not winds in winter; in summer it will have winds not sunshine'.[52] But the westerly aspect was favoured locally, and other loggias in the palazzo face this direction, as did the greenhouse in the Secret Garden, situated on the northern side of the palazzo (the garden is enclosed by walls and concealed from outside views – hence its name). Vitruvius believed that bathrooms and dining rooms should have a south-western exposure to take advantage of the evening light, and because the setting sun looks splendid and lends a gentler warmth to that quarter in the evening.[53] Similarly, in *De re aedificatoria* Alberti twice mentions the desirability of a westerly aspect for baths: 'make the baths and spring dining rooms face the sunset' (V, 18, p. 153); and 'it is best to make libraries face Boreas, and baths the setting sun' (IX, 10, p. 317). Only when he is writing about a large public bath, 'surrounded by open space', does he recommend that the entrance to the main atrium of the complex be approached through a vestibule with a south-facing façade (VIII, 10, p. 287). In Urbino, the palazzo is entered from the north and, hierarchically, the bath building was unlikely to precede the ducal or guest accommodation. Instead, it would need to be approached internally, through covered arcades, where the sun would not trouble the eyes.

The covered arcade in Alberti's design has three main openings, of equal width. The existing (unfinished) arcade along the eastern edge of the Cortile del Pasquino also has three openings of a similar size to Alberti's. Combined with the guest wing of the palazzo, the Cortile del Pasquino would have been square in shape, its width the same as that of the palazzo's main entrance courtyard. In neither run of arcade is the central opening emphasised. Instead, Alberti stresses the end of the ambulatory with some kind of belvedere, characterised by a circular motif in plan. This area marks the entrance to the baths, and if this location is correct there may also have been a link to the tennis court at this point. The belvedere appears to consist of shallow niches, which may relate to a round element above – they correspond in shape to the staircase towers of the Facciata dei Torricini, which have a similar diameter.

Presumably the circular mausoleum that Baldi had described would have been placed at the centre of the square Cortile del Pasquino, where it would have aligned with and so concluded a north-south axis through the centre of the entrance courtyard.[54] The arcaded ambulatory around the Cortile del Pasquino would have acted as a backdrop to the mausoleum. The main façade of the bath building was therefore the one containing the *porticus specularia* which looked over the valley. The middle of its three windows is slightly wider than those on either side to emphasise the centre of the composition, and was possibly arranged in the manner that was subsequently known as a Serliana or Venetian window.

A bath building as an adjunct to Federico's apartment

An alternative site for Alberti's bath building is in an area adjacent to Federico's private baths and immediately east of them. In the late fifteenth century this area was occupied by the palace kitchens, wood store, and bounded by corridors.[55] My attention was drawn to this area because the shape of the *cucina generale* (the general – or more probably, as it is the largest – the main kitchen) and the corridor running along its northern end have proportions similar to those of the *tepidarium* and *ambulatio* in Alberti's bath building drawing. For these spaces to match in size, Alberti's drawing needs to be scaled to one-ninetieth of life-size.[56] Why this scale would have been appropriate to Alberti is not clear. But perhaps instead of scaling the drawing to an existing measure Alberti provided the recipient of the drawing with a measure attached to an accompanying letter. Alternatively, perhaps the recipient was able to identify the scale from key elements in the plan. Howard Burns suggested that the piers of the *porticus specularia* provide the module, or unit of measure, with which the bath building has been designed. As Burns observed, these piers measure between 8.5 and 9 mm on the drawing, and he found that when the rooms in Alberti's plan were subdivided by the lower of these two measures, 8.5 mm, they have proportions that are whole number multiples of this unit: the *ambulatio* is 5 units wide, almost 30 long, and with piers 2 wide and close to 4 units apart; the *vestibu-*

lum and *ad penetralia* are 5 units square; the *tepidarium* close to 12 × 25 units; the *lavatio* 9 × 15; and the *sudatio* 9 × 8 units.[57]

Overlaying Alberti's drawing on to the recent survey plan of the palace at a scale of 1:90 highlights some key dimensional correspondences (fig. 162). Not only is Alberti's *tepidarium* the same size as the main kitchen (approximately 19 × 9 m.), and his *ambulatio* the same width as the corridor running east-to-west and north of the kitchen (3.8 m. wide), but the thickness of the wall between these rooms is identical. Moreover, the circular belvedere drawn by Alberti at the end of the *ambulatio* has the same diameter as the outer diameter of the twin towers of the Facciata dei Torricini, which are almost 5.5 m. in diameter and contain circular stairs. Indeed, if one imagines that Alberti's plan was designed with an axis of symmetry running centrally through the *tepidarium* and *porticus specularia*, and that the belvedere was mirrored across this axis, the distance apart of the two belvederes would be similar to those of the two towers of the Facciata dei Torricini. The loggia of Federico's private baths as built is placed centrally between the Torricini – as Alberti's *porticus specularia* would have been between its two belvederes.

However, there are problems with this suggested location. The angled wall of the Facciata dei Torricini creates a triangular area relative to the main spaces behind it that bears no relation to Alberti's layout; and to the north of the existing kitchens are miscellaneous cellars and storerooms, which would obstruct the view from Alberti's *ambulatio* and severely limit the quantity of fresh air and light to the baths. The Secret Garden is built on top of these ancillary rooms,[58] and only if it had been set at the same level as Alberti's bath building would his design have been viable.

Not that Federico's baths are perfectly arranged: while benefiting from a south-western aspect and a supply of heat from the kitchens adjacent, they appear to have been adapted to the tight triangular space available, rather than planned for that location. The rooms are misshapen and poorly composed, and compared with Alberti's design resemble a rabbit warren. This is probably because Francesco di Giorgio had to fit in with what had been completed already. Pasquale Rotondi, in his detailed study of the building of the palace, identified the orthogonally arranged rooms (which are identified as the kitchens) with Laurana's workmanship, and the baths would have been accommodated by Francesco di Giorgio as space provision allowed.[59]

The late inclusion of baths in the overall scheme of the Palazzo Ducale does not necessarily mean they were an afterthought. It is possible that Alberti's bath

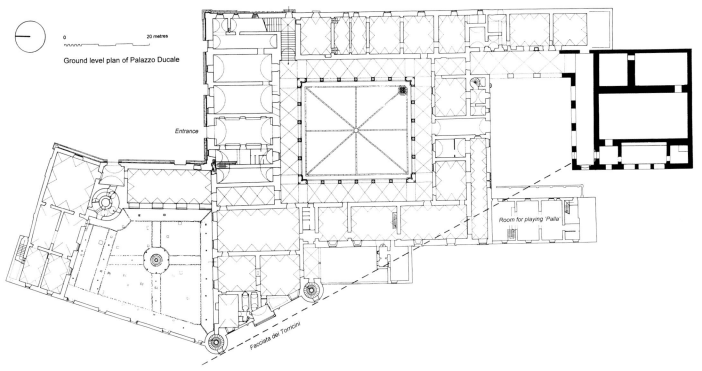

Ground level plan of Palazzo Ducale

Entrance

Facciata dei Torricini

Room for playing 'Palla'

161   Ground plan of Palazzo Ducale, Urbino, with bath building attached at a scale of 1:100 relative to the existing building (drawing/author, after Polichetti 1985).

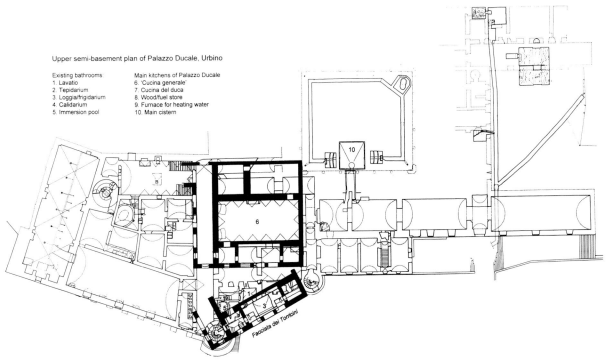

Upper semi-basement plan of Palazzo Ducale, Urbino

Existing bathrooms:
1. Lavatio
2. Tepidarium
3. Loggia/frigidarium
4. Calidarium
5. Immersion pool

Main kitchens of Palazzo Ducale
6. 'Cucina generale'
7. Cucina del duca
8. Wood/fuel store
9. Furnace for heating water
10. Main cistern

Facciata dei Torricini

162   Upper semi-basement plan of Palazzo Ducale, Urbino, with bath building attached at a scale of 1:90 relative to the existing building (drawing/author, after Polichetti 1985).

building design was incorporated into Laurana's original model for the palazzo, and that the *tepidarium* was built (in the position now occupied by the main kitchen) along with the *ambulatio* of the baths,[60] but that after Alberti's death and with Laurana's departure from Urbino, this area was reconfigured by Francesco di Giorgio as kitchens, the baths moved, made private to the duke and reduced in size so they squeezed into the triangular area remaining between the Facciata dei Torricini and the new kitchens.[61] The main kitchen has a fireplace by Francesco di Giorgio, which he may have designed when the function of this room changed from a *tepidarium* to a kitchen.[62] Kitchens, like baths, need and are built to withstand copious amounts of water, hot and cold; at a functional level the exchange of activities here could therefore have been accommodated with relative ease.[63]

Of the two sites which strike me as feasible locations for this bath building the southern end of the palazzo adjacent to the Cortile del Pasquino is, to my mind, more convincing than the alternative area adjacent to Federico's own apartments. Whether or not either proposal is correct, at the very least I would hope to have demonstrated to the reader that this design would have been desirable to Federico and could have been found a place in Laurana's model for the palazzo. The full extent of Alberti's involvement in the overall design of the palazzo can only be guessed at, for it is often hard to separate Laurana's work from Francesco di Giorgio's, and to know how faithful Francesco was to his predecessor's conception for the palazzo.[64] Vasari knew only of Francesco di Giorgio's role there, but thanks to the painstaking scholarship led by Rotondi and Polichetti, the true complexity of the design and building process has been acknowledged, as has the fact that it was probably not the creation of any one individual.[65]

X

THE ART OF BUILDING IN PRACTICE

ALBERTI SPECULATES IN *De re aedificatoria* about the nature of building and the appropriate assembly of material to achieve universal harmony – the 'perfect union of an intellectual idea for a building conceived in the mind of an architect, and the physical realm to which the building is to contribute. In practice, the ideals that frame his text were tempered by the unique combination of circumstances with which his various patrons presented him, including the intended purpose of the buildings' cultural and physical surroundings. Consequently, while Alberti quoted the example of the ancient 'Templum Etruscum' when conceiving his design for Sant'Andrea in Mantua, he modified its ideal form to suit the conditions in which it was to be built and according to the materials available. For the Rucellai sepulchre Alberti adapted information he had received about the Holy Sepulchre in Jerusalem, reducing its size to fit its location in San Pancrazio, and regularising its shape through the rigorous application of geometry and ornament, so as to perfect its appearance. When designing the Tempio Malatestiano in Rimini he may have enlarged the Holy Sepulchre for the form of the entire church, or, indeed, he may have adapted the form of the Anastasis which encloses this most holy tomb.[1] It can be concluded, therefore, that however revered the ancient building types, their example is only ever a starting-point for a design: the complete process will also involve the architect in considering the individual demands of the patron, the peculiarities of the site and the availability of materials. As Alberti observed: 'the greatest glory in the art of building is to have a good sense of what is appropriate' (IX, 10, p. 315). Buildings with quite a different appearance may therefore have been developed from the same precedent.

The perfection Alberti sought in architecture is evident in the proportions of San Sebastiano in Mantua, as recorded by Labacco. The number relationships that Labacco lists, coupled with the plan and intended sectional form of the building, conform with Vitruvius' notion that temples should be the most perfect of building types in number, outline and composition.[2] Labacco shows how the measured outline of

the plan and its extension into three dimensions preceded the application of ornament. This division of beautiful outline and its subsequent embellishment through ornament is further confirmed by the annotations and plan of a bath building which has been attributed to Alberti.

What Alberti intended for San Sebastiano was not realised. The combined effect of perfect form and ornament should have resulted in a building that stimulated a soulful response in individual worshippers: a sense of piety and mystery should lead to a state of contemplation and active worship (VII, 3–4, pp. 194–7; VII, 13, pp. 228–30). It should also have delighted the eye, 'so that one's gaze might flow freely and gently [. . .] and never be satiated by the view'.[3] For variety (*varietas*) 'is always a most pleasing spice, where distant objects agree and conform with one another' (I, 9, p. 24, and Glossary, p. 426).[4] The application of ornament should always be under the architect's control so that it appears to arise naturally from the body-building. In fact, the subsequent interventions at San Sebastiano by other architects have done nothing to fulfil Alberti's total ambitions for this church.

The appearance of the building, and the overall effect it has on the user and spectator, was apparently as important a consideration in the design process as geometrical and numerical perfection. Thus, the final composition should be valid from any viewpoint – intellectually and physically. To achieve this totality Alberti demands that once conceived, a building should be designed from the ground upwards: in plan first, and the elevations constructed from measurements of the plan. He is adamant that the elevations should neither be designed separately from the plan nor use the laws of perspective, because the architect 'desires his work not to be judged by deceptive appearances but according to certain calculated standards' (II, 1, p. 34). However, there will occasionally be instances when this approach cannot succeed, as I have suggested with respect to the façade of Palazzo Rucellai. Here the design had to appear correct in the tight physical circumstances in which it was placed, and perspectival effect provided the means to a visually coherent façade.

The 'calculated standards' the architect must use combine qualities and quantities. For any composition the parts are arranged within a specific geometrical context, like the rectangular veil with its grid of lines which Alberti described in *De pictura*. And the principal elevations of a building are derived from the purest geometries of circle and square. Within these constraints the parts are proportioned, using numbers derived from the width of the square so that they relate to the dimensions of the whole. Alberti adopted from Vitruvius the notion that the ideal body should be circumscribed by a circle and bounded by a square, and he found evidence for this himself in the *Tabulae dimensionorum hominis* appended to *De statua*. He is quite definite about the relationship between body and building in *De re aedificatoria*:

> just as the head, foot, and indeed any member must correspond to each other and to all the rest of the body in an animal, so in a building, and especially a temple, the parts of the whole body must be composed so that they all correspond to one another, and any one, taken individually, may provide the dimensions of all the rest (VII, 5, p. 199).[5]

Only by proceeding in this way, from the whole composition to its parts, and from the general to the specific, can the many different components of the final building be harmonised. This harmony is the building's *concinnitas*: 'the equilibrium of contraries' as Smith has defined it.[6] Alberti called this process of defining the whole building as 'compartition':

> Compartition is the process of dividing up the site into yet smaller units, so that the building may be considered as being made up of close-fitting smaller buildings, joined together like members of the whole body (I, 2, p. 8).

Compartition calls on 'all the power of invention, all the skill and experience in the art of building' (I, 9, pp. 23–4). At a detailed level, compartition can be discerned in the smallest parts of the design, as in the ornamental lettering Alberti designed for the frieze of the Rucellai sepulchre. Each letter is contained by a notional square, the sides of which are then subdivided into equal parts. Multiples, or subdivisions of these parts are used to determine the position of cross-members, the thickness of each element of the letter and the radii of its serifs.

The other ornaments of buildings are disposed within the overall geometry of a façade, in a similar way. Columns – the principal architectural ornament – and their attendant details should be arranged relative to the major openings in a wall elevation or façade (VI, 13, p. 183). Overall, it would appear that the ornaments on his churches, the Tempio Malatestiano, Santa Maria Novella and Sant'Andrea are partitioned – with *decorum*, *dignitas* and *varietas* – so that columns, pilasters and their entablatures have sizes that are in proportion to the enclosing square of each façade, and are so arranged to display the characteristics of the ancient triumphal arch.

The secondary ornaments of these façades are specific to their sites. They may be influenced by the traditional architecture – or style – of the locality, or with which the locals identify: the Baptistery and church of San Miniato al Monte in Florence influenced the revetment of Santa Maria Novella. So too, the materials available in different locations affected the palette: the ancient architecture of Ravenna provided some of the material for the exterior of the Tempio Malatestiano in Rimini, while in Mantua, at Sant'Andrea (and probably at San Sebastiano), Alberti designed pilasters of brick and terracotta, rendered and painted, because there was no ready supply of stone locally. Still, the appearance was meant to be more fabulous than the materials of which it was composed.[7]

Thus, the equilibrium of parts on which *concinnitas* depends is derived from the understanding of an entire process. This starts with the patron, his need to build and the means at his disposal; then comes the architect's selection of an appropriate building type, the adaptation of the ideal form to suit the context and the embellishment of its form through ornament; thereafter the design is given shape and constructed by craftsmen and artists until the building is complete, whole, and in accordance with the patron's and architect's wishes. Only then is it ready for the appreciation and enjoyment of its intended users, and a valuable part of the urban realm – of people, buildings and places.[8]

The art of building was often subject to many calamities, human and physical. Alberti knew this to be so, and expressed it vividly in *Momus*: the creation of the earth was both a source of satisfaction and pain for Jupiter, as building undoubtedly proved to be for Alberti and his patrons. Building will always be thus, which is why Alberti was offering a framework and a process in *De re aedificatoria* – linking thinking and making – with which to mitigate the corruption of the intellectual ideal.

Alberti was successful as a theoretician and as a practitioner, and through theory and practice, he was to associate beauty in architecture with the natural universal laws that govern mankind. He was therefore an inspiration for successive architects, providing them with guidelines for the greatest of human quests, the search for universal harmony.[9] Not many architects have been capable of taking up his challenge, and Alberti remains one of the few to have combined vision and application, the intellectual and sensual, so completely.

QVID · TVM

APPENDIX

CALCULATING THE SIZE OF SANT'ANDREA IN BRICKS

THERE CAN OF COURSE BE NO CERTAINTY as to the precise form Sant'Andrea would have taken had it been designed as a Latin-cross structure by Alberti. The proposals initiated in the 1450s by Pope Nicholas V for extending St Peter's would have been an obvious precedent (see fig. 17, above); and it is unlikely that Alberti would have designed the dome for Sant'Andrea as high as Juvarra did: Alberti's dome for the Annunziata in Florence, for instance, is by contrast considerably lower. Consequently, the most economical Latin-cross form will be used as the basis for the calculations that follow (see fig. 151, above). This includes three porti-coes: the completed western portico, the north porch begun by Giulio Romano and, for a symmetrical arrangement, an equivalent structure at the end of the southern transept. The dimensions used in the calculations are based on the survey by Ritscher (1899) and the Alberti Group photogrammetric survey. Linear dimensions are cited here in metres (m), and volumes as metres cubed (m³). The overall volume of each major element (represented in the diagrams below) is considered first as a total or Gross volume, and the various openings and voids are then deducted from this figure to arrive at the Nett volume.

PORTICO

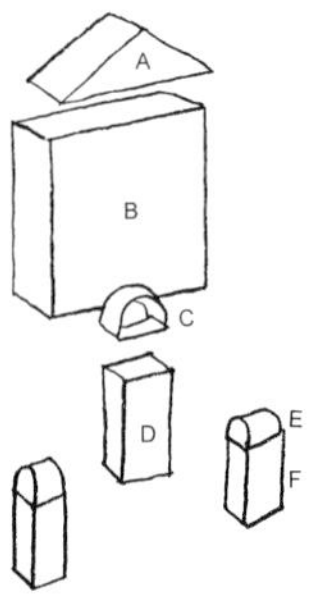

		Width		Height		Depth			Volume
A		$\frac{23.73}{2}$	$\times$	3.8	$\times$	2.2		$=$	99.19
B		23.73	$\times$	19.53	$\times$	8.045		$=$	3728.43
								(A)	**3827.62** Gross volume

Deduct the following voids:

C	$\frac{3.1428 \times 3.55^2}{2}$	$\times$	7.18				$=$	142.19
D	7.306	$\times$	11.9	$\times$	7.18		$=$	624.24
E	$2\left(\dfrac{3.1428 \times 2.55^2}{2} \times 6.634\right)$						$=$	135.57
F	$2(5.17$	$\times$	6.8	$\times$	6.634)		$=$	466.45
Façade doors	$2(1.88$	$\times$	4.22	$\times$	1.205)		$=$	19.12
Nave doors	$2(1.9$	$\times$	4.22	$\times$	1.67)		$=$	26.78
Central door	2.76	$\times$	5.65	$\times$	0.865		$=$	13.49
Side doors	$2\left(\dfrac{3.1428 \times 1.17^2}{2} \times 1.45\right)$						$=$	6.24
Side doors	$2(2.335$	$\times$	3.9	$\times$	1.45)		$=$	26.41
Façade windows	$4(3.1428$	$\times$	0.9^2	$\times$	1.205)		$=$	6.14
Side windows	$4(1.9$	$\times$	3.15	$\times$	1.205)		$=$	28.84
							(B)	**1495.47**

	(A)	3827.62
less	**(B)**	1495.47
Nett volume		**2332.15 m³**

SMALL CHAPELS

A	$7.985 \times \dfrac{2 \times 3.1428 \times 9.15}{2} \times 2^{\star}$	=	227.03
B	$7.985 \times 4.308 \times 1.32^{\star}$	=	45.41
C	$7.985 \times 17.5 \times 8.616$	=	1203.98
D	$2(0.9 \times 4.8 \times 6.3)$	=	54.43

(A) 1530.85 Gross volume

Deduct the following voids:

E	$4.665 \times 2^{\star} \times \dfrac{4.674}{2}$	=	21.8
F	$4.665 \times 16 \times 4.674$	=	348.87
Door	$1.86 \times 4.34 \times 2.712$	=	21.89
Window (arch)	$\dfrac{3.1428 \times 2.05^2}{2} \times 1.38$	=	9.11
Window (rectangle)	$4.1 \times 4.95 \times 1.38$	=	28.01
Clerestorey	$\dfrac{3.1428 \times 1.1^{2\star} \times 2.2^{\star}}{2}$	=	4.18

(B) 433.86

(A) 1530.85

less **(B)** 433.86

Nett volume 1096.99 m³

$\star$Estimated dimension

LARGE CHAPELS

A	$7.185 \times \dfrac{2 \times 3.1428 \times 9.15}{4} \times 2^{\star}$	=	206.62
B	$7.185 \times 4.308 \times 1.32^{\star}$	=	40.86
C	$7.24 \times \dfrac{3.1428 \times 3.93^2}{2} \times 0.65^{\star}$	=	114.21
D	$7.185 \times 17.5 \times 1.38$	=	173.52
E	$0.9 \times 4.8 \times 6.3$	=	27.22

(A) 562.43 Gross volume

Deduct the following void:

F	$7.185 \times 2^{\star} \times 2.337$	=	33.58

(B) 33.58

(A) 562.43

less **(B)** 33.58

Nett volume 528.85 m³

$\star$Estimated dimension

VOLUME OF A BRICK

The official brick size is approximately $32 \times 16 \times 8$ cm., and the mortar joint 1 cm. Thus the volume of one brick and its share of mortar equals $32.5 \times 16.5 \times 8.5 = 4558$ cm³, which equals $\dfrac{1,000,000}{4558}$ or 219 bricks per m³.

VOLUME OF A LATIN-CROSS STRUCTURE ACCORDING TO THE QUANTITY OF EACH ELEMENT

3 Porticoes	3 × 2332.15	=	6996.45
10 Small chapels	10 × 1096.99	=	10969.90
10 Large chapels	10 × 528.85	=	5288.50
			23,254.85 m³ (A)

A Quattrocento style dome at the crossing (excluding a drum and lantern):

$$\frac{4\pi r}{2} \times d = 4 \times 3.1428 \times 9.08 \times 18.16 = \mathbf{1{,}036.45} \ \textbf{(B)}$$

An east end apse:

$$h \times \frac{2\pi r}{2} \times d = 18.82 \times \frac{2 \times 3.1428 \times 9.08}{2} \times 1.38 = \mathbf{741.14} \ \textbf{(C)}$$

Total volume of Latin-cross structure:

(A) + **(B)** + **(C)** = 25,032.76 m³ × 219 bricks

                    = 5,482,174.40 bricks

Less one third rubble   = **3,654,783 bricks**

VOLUME OF A NAVE-ONLY STRUCTURE

1 Portico	1 × 2332.15	=	2332.15
8 Small chapels	8 × 1096.99	=	8775.92
6 Large chapels	6 × 528.85	=	3173.10
			14,281.17 m³

Plus a square east end chapel   **300.00 m³**

Total volume of nave-only structure   = 14,281.17

                                       300.00

                               14,581.17 m³

                            = 3,193,276.20 bricks

Less one third rubble   = **2,128,851 bricks**

In conclusion

It can be seen from these calculations that the nave-only design has about half the volume of the Latin-cross structure. If a third of these totals is assumed to be rubble in-fill, then the nave-only structure has a quantity of bricks much closer to the two million bricks quoted by Ludovico Gonzaga. While a similar reduction to the Latin-cross structure leaves a total number of bricks nearer three and a half million.

NOTES

PREFACE

1 Alberti (1988), p. 1 (foreword by Angelo Poliziano).
2 Landino (1481), fols 10r–14r, in the section relating to the *Apologia nella quale si difende Dante e Florentia da falsi calumniatori*; and see Borsi (1977), p. 263.
3 For an appreciation of the lamentable state of Alberti studies in the mid-twentieth century, see Whitfield (1988), pp. 31–4.

I   THE EARLY YEARS

1 He was christened 'Baptista degli Alberti', but the spelling of his first name is normally regularised to Battista. What follows is generally informed by Mancini (1967); and Ceschi (1948), pp. 191–2. 'Leon' was a name acquired in later life (see p. 33, below). For a broader psychoanalytical reading of Alberti than is pursued below, see also Schneider (1990).
2 For an account of Alberti's natural and stepmothers, see Ceschi (1948).
3 Mancini (1967), pp. 40–44, esp. p. 43 and n. 4.
4 Mancini (1967), p. 43.
5 The letter from Gasparino to Lorenzo is dated 1415, when Battista would have been aged eleven: Mancini (1967), p. 42 and n. 1; Eng. trans. from Borsi (1977), pp. 258–9.
6 Mancini (1967), p. 59 and n. 3; and Burroughs (1994), pp. 143–7.
7 Mancini (1967), pp. 45–6, as translated by Lefaivre (1997), p. 114.
8 Mancini (1967), p. 53. See also p. 50: Lorenzo died in Padua on 28 May 1421, Ricciardo in 1422.
9 It was also known is his lifetime in a corrupt and obscene form, due to the unwarranted insertions of a copyist: Mancini (1967), p. 55. It was published in Venice, in 1588, by the heirs of Aldus Manutius as a Roman work: Lowry (1976).
10 Beccadelli (1824), I, Poem 19, p. 64; Mancini (1967), p. 55; Eng. trans. in Borsi (1986), p. 259.
11 Mancini (1967), p. 67 and n. 2.
12 Mancini (1967), pp. 84–7.
13 Mancini (1967), p. 89.
14 Mancini (1967), p. 89, n. 3.
15 Mancini (1967), p. 277 and n. 1; see also Alberti (1988), introduction by Rykwert, p. xiii.
16 Alberti (1965) and (1987).

17 Translation from *De commodis* in Jarzombek (1989), p. 8. See also Alberti (1976).
18 Alberti (1960–73), I, p. 18; Alberti (1843), III, pp. 246, 252, 255, 266, 365; V, pp. 299–321; see also Alberti (1960–73), I, p. 132; and as translated in Lefaivre (1997), p. 154.
19 Mancini (1967), pp. 26 and 257.
20 Alberti (1969), p. 134; see also Marolda (1988).
21 Tommaso (1972); Westfall (1969).
22 Burroughs (1990) provides a comprehensive account of the social, political and physical reordering of Rome under these pontiffs; see also Westfall (1969).
23 Hollingsworth (1994), pp. 236–8.
24 Alberti (1972), pp. 36–7, and p. 108, n. 2.
25 As cited in Kemp (1991a), p. 17; Rykwert and Engel (1994), p. 423.
26 Alberti (1972), p. 3: Grayson proposes that the Tuscan version was complete by July 1436. And see corroboration for this date by Kemp in Alberti (1991a), pp. 17–18, and in Rykwert and Engel (1994), p. 423.
27 Manetti (1976), pp. 57–60. And see Battisti (1981), pp. 102–13. On the development of Renaissance perspective, see Kuhn (1990) and Edgerton (1991).
28 Saalman (1980), p. 275, doc. 286.3.
29 Battisti (1981), pp. 122–4; see also Saalman (1980), pp. 275–6, doc. 286, 3–4. On the motet composed for the occasion and a proposal, whereby its musical proportions are described relative to Brunelleschi's structure, see Warren (1973); see also Smith (1992), pp. 91–5.
30 Alberti (1972), p. 33.
31 See the comments of Brunelleschi's biographer, thought to be Antonio di Tuccio Manetti: Manetti (1976), p. 48, fol. 295v.
32 Onians (1982), pp. 259–72; Onians (1988), pp. 130–46.
33 For Donatello's rendering of the Basilica of Maxentius in Rome, see Rykwert and Engel (1994), pp. 517–19, and illustration 122.
34 Alberti (1972); Aiken (1980); and Kemp's introduction in Alberti (1991a), pp. 7–17. See also Kemp (1990) and Damisch (1994).
35 See Zervas (1979).
36 Alberti (1972), p. 69.
37 Alberti (1972), p. 69.
38 Alberti (1972), pp. 131 and 135; for the measured relationships Alberti lists, see pp. 134–9. Grayson does not offer a definitive date for *De statua*; for the dates offered here, see Rykwert and Engel (1994), p. 414.
39 Alberti (1972), pp. 129–33; Scaglia (1994), p. 321.

40 On the relationship of *De iure* to Alberti's formulation of architecture, see Magda (1988); and on Italian law in the Renaissance, Kelley (1979).

41 See, for example, Grayson (1960c), pp. 1–28, esp. pp. 13–15; Alberti (1964); Gombrich (1967), esp. pp. 76–82; and Onians (1988), pp. 130–46.

42 Gombrich (1967); Ullman and Stadter (1972); Stinger (1978), p. 272.

43 Stinger (1978), pp. 272–3. Around the time that Brunelleschi was designing the oratory Traversari was in Ravenna and he relayed to Niccoli the impact he felt on seeing the rotunda of San Vitale: 'a marvellous and most magnificent Temple'; Traversari (1759), VIII, letter 52: 'Transivi ad spectandum mirisicum, & magnificentissimum S Vitalis Martyris Templum, rotundum id quidem, & omni genere superioris ornatus insigne musivo, columnis cingentibus ambitum fani marmoreis crustis variis parietes interius vestientibus. Sed habet subspensum, columnisque subsultum peripatum, & aram ex alabastro tam lucidam'.

44 Gombrich (1967), p. 78. It has even been suggested that he was the inspiration for the classicism not only in the architecture of Brunelleschi but also the sculpture of Donatello, but this is unsubstantiated: see Smith (1992), pp. 70–71.

45 Traversari's disciple Fra Girolamo Aliotti first asked Carlo Marsuppini to write the biography, but he declined, and Alberti's response was similar. See partial transcription and Eng. trans. in Borsi (1977), p. 259.

46 Lang (1954), p. 288.

47 Mancini (1967), p. 171.

48 Alberti (1843), I, p. CXX.

49 Jarzombek (1989), pp. 76–7.

50 Alberti (1966), II, p. 71: quoted in translation by Borsi (1977), p. 20.

51 Mancini (1967), pp. 200–06; Gorni (1972), pp. 135–82; Ponte (1981), pp. 182–3; and Jarzombek (1989), pp. 99–100. Alberti wrote a prose dialogue for the event, *De amicitia*, which he appended to *Della famiglia* as its fourth book. Another poem, 'On Friendship', was entered by Michele di Noferi del Gigante. It is aimed with great reverence at Alberti, as the following extract shows: 'Willingly would I see the brow/Of so excellent a man crowned [. . .]/I so yearn to see him leave the cathedral/Accompanied by all the other venerable poets,/Each with a pretty garland on his head,/Their precious little ones of laurel and of myrtle/Enhancing his' (Eng. trans. in Borsi, 1977, pp. 259–60).

52 It is to be found next to a statue of an enthroned Borso d'Este who succeeded Leonello on his death in 1450: the bronzes there today are reproductions of the originals which were destroyed in 1796.

53 Gadol (1969), p. 8; Borsi (1977), pp. 21–4; Alberti (1988), introduction by Rykwert, p. xv.

54 Certainly it lacks any of the principles that were to be enunciated by Alberti in his books on architecture (though his treatise was not in any presentable format until 1452, and may not as yet have even been started).

55 Rykwert, in Rykwert and Engel (1994), pp. 158–61.

56 Alberti (1991); see also Alberti (1890), pp. 238–9.

57 Alberti (1843), I, XCI–CXVIII: *Vita anonima*.

58 Alberti (1972), p. 3.

59 Alberti (1972), p. 35.

60 Hollingsworth (1994), p. 63.

61 Alberti (1965), p. 64: Eng. trans. in Jarzombek (1989), p. 99.

62 Alberti (1960–73), II, Bk I, as cited in Borsi (1977), p. 13. See also Marolda (1988), pp. 71–110.

63 As discussed in Smith (1994a).

64 Alberti (1960–73), II, Bk III; as discussed in Smith (1992), esp. pp. 3–18.

II ROME REVEALED AND RE-PRESENTED

1 Orlandi (1974a and 1974b); Vagnetti (1974); Westfall (1974), p. 89; Scaglia (1994), p. 321.

2 Rykwert and Engel (1994), p. 436.

3 Kahn (1980).

4 In the same chapter that he described the horizon in *De re aedificatoria*, Alberti mentions Eratosthenes' calculation of the earth's circumference. However, the figure for the earth's circumference was left blank and appears in only one manuscript: see Alberti (1988), p. 413, n. 90.

The original reads: 'Terram, qui ista investigarunt, esse aiunt sphericam, tametsi multa ex parte montibus asperam, multa etiam ex parte vestitam mari; sed maximo in orbe vix sentiri aspecitatem, esseque id veluti in ovo, quod, cum asperum sit, tamen in ea ambitus magnitudine minutas illas prominentias non putari; et constare quidem maximum terrae ambitum stadia esse (———); et inveniri montem nullum adeo excelsum neque aquam adeo profundam, cuius perpendiculum milia excedat cubitorum XV' (Alberti, 1966, p. 919, no. 1).

Cosimo Bartoli included Eratosthenes' name in his version of Alberti's text (1550): 'Et è cosa certa, secondo Eratosthenes che il gran' circuito della terra, è dugento cinquanta dua milia stadii, & ce è non si truova monte nessuno tanto alto, ne acqua nessuna tanto profonda che il loro piombo passi .15,000. cubiti'.

Leoni attempted to clarify Alberti's statement by adding that 252,000 furlongs/*stadia* equalled 31,500 miles; see Alberti (1955), Bk X, ch. 7, p. 221. According to Leoni, Alberti wrote: 'Eratosthenes tells us, that the compass of this great globe is two hundred and fifty-two thousand furlongs, or about thirty-one thousand five hundred miles', an interpretation after Vitruvius (1960), I, 6. v, who wrote that the earth's circumference was 31,500,000 paces. While in Orlandi's edition of Alberti (1966), the earth's circumference is left blank because the figure of 252,000 *stadia* in the original manuscript appears to be a later inclusion, but one may conclude that 252,000 *stadia* is the correct figure because it is directly derived from Vitruvius' figure of 31,500,000 paces:

one pace = 5 *pedes*
one stadium = 625 *pedes*

$$\frac{252{,}000 \times 625}{5} = 31{,}500{,}000$$

Although Alberti does not provide his reader with the diameter of the earth, it is straightforward enough to calculate, once we know the value attached to *pi* at that time. Alberti appears to advocate a value of 22/7 or $3\frac{1}{7}$ for *pi*: see Alberti (1568), p. 239; and in his *Ludi rerum mathematicarum* (also known as *Ludi matematici*), Alberti described a circle having a diameter of 14 *passi* which, multiplied by 22/7, has a circumference of 44 *passi*; see Alberti (1960–73), III, p. 155. Piero della Francesca, more precisely, used the ratio of $3\frac{3}{20}$ (or 3.15); see Wittkower and Carter (1953), p. 301 and n. 4. Tantalisingly, by using the value Piero attributed to *pi*, and the circumference of 31,500,000 paces as Vitruvius related it, the earth's diameter is exactly ten million paces:

$$\frac{2(31,500,000)}{2 \times 3.15} = 2 \times 5,000,000 = 10,000,000 \ paces$$

Had Alberti used the same ratio, then the 10-foot-wide horizon would have been exactly one-five-millionth of the earth's diameter. This would imply a link between the horizon (of 10 feet), the ideal height of man (6 feet), and the size of the earth. Regardless of the symbolic overlay, the horizon of course remained a useful tool governed by a sensible integer.

5 Rykwert and Engel (1994), p. 425.

6 Rykwert and Engel (1994), p. 434.

7 Weiss (1969), pp. 108–9, 113–14.

8 Sprague de Camp (1960), pp. 153–9, quoted in Lefaivre (1997), pp. 117 and 267, n. 33.

9 Grayson (1960b), p. 153, and notes 8 and 9, p. 159.

10 Biondo, 'Italia illustrata' (1559), I, p. 326.

11 Burroughs (1994), pp. 151–2.

12 Mancini (1967), p. 278.

13 Alberti (1954); and on *Momus* see Tafuri (1987).

14 Tavernor (1991b), pp. 311–13.

15 For the range of views as to when it was written, see Grayson (1960b), who argues that Alberti wrote the treatise on architecture between 1444 and 1452; and Onians (1988), p. 147, who argues that he continued to refine the text up until his death. See also Krautheimer (1969c).

16 For a more detailed account of the following, see Onians (1988), pp. 74–5 and 147–57.

17 The title-page reads: 'Florentiae accuratissime impressum opera Magistri Nicolai Laurentii Alamani: Anno salutis Millesimo octuagesimo quinto: quarto Kalendas Ianuarias'. This is 29 December 1485 according to modern reckoning. See Rykwert and Engel (1994), p. 462, and cf. Alberti (1988), pp. xviii and xxii, where a date of 1486 was proposed due to a misreading of the Florentine calendar.

18 Alberti (1966), p. 17, and p. 16, n. 1 for Orlandi's re-rendering of the title by changing 'architectus' to 'architecto'. See also Grayson (1960b).

19 Krautheimer (1969c), p. 328, n. 2. Krautheimer suggests that following the death of Leonello d'Este Alberti was persuaded to present *De re aedificatoria* to Pope Nicholas V instead, some time after 1450.

20 Giovanni Rucellai believed that by visiting the basilicas listed he would gain the release from purgatory of ten years for each mortal sin he had committed: Rucellai (1960), p. 67.

21 Westfall (1974), pp. 21 and 174.

22 Rucellai (1960), p. 68.

23 This thesis is developed by Westfall (1974), who cites Alberti as a force who contributed to Nicholas's urban strategy. However, as I shall argue below, I consider it more credible that Alberti was a negative influence rather than a positive contributor to the formulation of the pope's urban ambitions for Rome and the Vatican, as Tafuri has also suggested (1987), pp. 61–75.

24 Weiss (1969), pp. 55 and 147.

25 Bracciolini (1723); see also Weiss (1969), p. 147. Bracciolini had been in the papal chancery in Rome since 1403. He dedicated this work to Pope Nicholas V in 1448.

26 Weiss (1969), pp. 59–72, esp. p. 68.

27 Weiss (1969), pp. 6–15; Krautheimer (1980), p. 198.

28 Vagnetti (1974).

29 For what follows, see Rucellai (1960), pp. 67–82. There is controversy about the dating of the Rucellai buildings in Florence and Alberti's role in their design (see chapter VII below).

30 Weiss (1969), pp. 73–4.

31 Eng. trans. in Westfall (1974), p. 177; from Rucellai (1960), pp. 72–6.

32 Westfall (1974), pp. 175–9.

33 Biondo (1953), III, LXXXVIII, p. 318; Westfall (1974), p. 98 and n. 57.

34 Manetti (1734).

35 Burroughs (1990), pp. 85, 163–7 and 225.

36 Burroughs (1990), pp. 231–4; cf. Alberti (1988), p. 403, and n. 91, p. 402. The bridge had been the scene of yet another Nicholian tragedy when, in the Jubilee Year of 1450, a crowd leaving St Peter's and the Borgo were bottlenecked onto the bridge and two hundred pilgrims lost their lives in the ensuing crush, or were drowned in the Tiber as the balustrades gave way under the pressure of bodies. Nicholas had attempted to upgrade its condition over the years preceding this calamity, and the damage following it was repaired, but the bridge was not restored to its former ancient condition as Alberti may have wished: two small octagonal chapels were positioned on either side of the bridge to commemorate the disaster. One was dedicated to the Holy Innocents, the other to the Magdalene.

37 Vasari (1973), II, p. 546, describes sketches 'showing the bridge of Sant'Angelo and the covering that he designed for it in the form of a loggia'.

38 For a detailed study of Alberti's urban notions, see Choay (1997).

39 See, for example, Rykwert and Engel (1994), p. 430.

40 Alberti (1942 and 1986). For other recent readings of *Momus*, see Tafuri (1987), pp. 69–75; Alberti (1988), introduction by Rykwert, pp. xv–xvi; Whitfield (1988), and cf. Jarzombek (1989), pp. 159–66; and Panza (1994).

41 On the influences on *Momus*, see especially the forthcoming publication by David Marsh, 'Alberti and Apuleius: Comic Violence and Vehemence in *Intercenales* and *Momus*', by the *Société Internationale Leon Battista*

Alberti. In a colloquium in 1995 on which this publication will be based, Marsh mentioned the quote from *Theogenius* (*c*.1442) that the following ancient writers were recommended: 'tutti e' comici, e gli altri ridicoli, Apulegio, Luciano, Marziale e simili facetissimi, eccitano in me quanto io voglio riso'.

42 Begliomini (1972), pp. 267ff.; Alberti (1986), introduction by A. di Grado; and Burroughs (1994), pp. 138–41.

43 Palmieri (1748), col. 241, entry dated 1452; Westfall (1974), pp. 167–71, and his translation of Palmieri, p. 169. See also Tafuri (1987), pp. 61–75, esp. pp. 72–3; Burroughs (1990), pp. 241–4.

44 Manetti (1734), cols 949–50; Westfall (1974), p. 33.

45 The computer reconstruction of the Vatican and supporting research was prepared by Sandra Trkulja, with additional modelling of the terrain by Nigel Hetherington. Both were members of the Alberti Group.

46 Burroughs (1990), pp. 125–34.

47 Porcari's objectives were the capture of Castel Sant'Angelo and Pope Nicholas V, and he was hanged for his attempt. Alberti's *De porcaria coniuratione* is in Alberti (1890). See also Alberti (1960–73), I, p. 707; Fubini and Menci Gallorini (1972); Tafuri (1987), pp. 65–6; and Burroughs (1990), p. 131.

48 Magnuson (1958), p. 170, and notes 23–6.

49 Burroughs (1990), p. 138.

50 A similar conclusion was reached by Burroughs (1990), p. 244.

51 The coronation of Frederick III as Holy Roman Emperor in 1452 prompted Palmieri's entry. And see Burroughs (1990), pp. 241–2, who suggests that the presentation of Alberti's treatise to Nicholas V was made in late 1453 or early 1454. There is, however, no hard evidence to back this suggestion.

52 Nicholas V died on 24 March 1455.

53 Rubinstein (1967); Frommel (1983).

54 Burroughs (1990), esp. pp. 243–5: the Vatican *cantiere* was run largely by Nello da Bologna assisted by Francesco del Borgo. As Burroughs suggests, Rossellino's main responsibility in this workshop was perhaps to prepare architectural ornament.

55 Pius II (1984), II, pp. 1758–71. While Pius was impressed by German hall churches, both he and his architect would have known of a local hall church, the thirteenth-century San Fortunato in Todi.

56 While his role in the collapse of the 'Torrione' in the Vatican is uncertain, he was responsible in Pienza for the collapse of part of the gardens at the Palazzo Piccolomini, and the east end of the church has experienced considerable subsidence. See Mack (1987), p. 77; Pius II, (1984), II, pp. 1758–71.

57 Manetti (1734), III, para. II, col. 938.

58 See esp. Westfall (1974), p. 180, and cf. Magnuson (1958), pp. 91–2. On the relatively small sums of money drawn by Rossellino in the building accounts of Rome during Nicholas' pontificate, see Burroughs (1990), pp. 129–30.

III   ARCHITECT AND VISIONARY

1 Battisti (1981), p. 244.

2 Spallanzani (1975).

3 For Alberti's design process in *De re aedificatoria*, see Battisti (1974), pp. 131–74.

4 For example, it was not possible in the fifteenth century to point to a building that fitted Vitruvius' account of the Etruscan temple (see chapter VIII below).

5 Burroughs (1990), p. 233, and n. 17, p. 295, suggests that 'The drawing may, as Vasari asserts, have been done by Alberti, perhaps in connection with the work on his book; an anonymous later architect may have worked up a drawing on the basis of the description in Alberti's book, most probably after its publication in 1485'.

6 A canon of St Peter's, Mafeo Vegio, complained of the destruction of Christian monuments which were to make way for the new tribune. See Vignati (1959), cited in Burroughs (1990), p. 129.

7 Hollingsworth (1994), p. 63.

8 Mancini (1967), pp. 408–12.

9 Weiss (1958); Zabughin (1909–12).

10 *De Iciarchia* literally means 'a man of excellence and ruler of his family'. Alberti (1960–73), II, p. 132. See also Schneider (1990), p. 268.

11 Lefaivre (1997), pp. 10–11.

12 Lefaivre (1997), p. 92.

13 Lowry (1976), pp. 121–2: quoted in Lefaivre (1997), pp. 98–100.

14 Casella and Pozzi (1959), I:25; Calvesi (1980); Kretzulesco-Quaranta (1986); and Lefaivre (1997), pp. 100–09.

15 Lefaivre (1997), p. 109.

16 The term 'frater' is more generic than the English 'brother', and can be used to mean 'cousin' or, more loosely, 'kinsman'.

17 Lefaivre (1997), p. 80.

18 Kretzulesco-Quaranta (1986), who summarises her view as to the author on p. 450, suggests that Alberti was either the model chosen by Francesco Colonna, as a friend of the family in Rome, or that Alberti was himself the author: 'le pseudonyme cache la personnalité d'un archéologue, L. B. Alberti, l'ami du Cardinal Prospero Colonna? Alberti, comme auteur de l'Hypnerotomachia, selon la convergence des indices recueillis au long de notre recherche, nous semble une hypothèse de travail valable.' See also Smith (1994e), p. 461, entry 53.

19 Lefaivre (1997). The comments made here were made possible because an unbound copy of this book was kindly made available to me in advance of its publication, in July/August 1997, by the author and MIT Press, while my own book was in the editorial stage.

20 Alberti (1972), p. 79.

21 Lefaivre (1997), pp. 64–75.

22 For example, at the level of architectural theory, a study by Onians (1988), pp. 207–15, suggests that the author of the *Hypnerotomachia* holds views that are contrary to those of Alberti, reversing key concepts in *De re aedificatoria*.

23 Bernardo Rucellai had little enough time at this stage in his career to devote to writing and his *De urbe roma* was not completed until around 1496: Valentini and Zucchetti (1953), IV, p. 440; Stinger (1985), p. 70, and Latin extract, pp. 350–51, n. 204. Extracts are also quoted in Borsi (1977), p. 262.

24 The foundation stone of Sant'Andrea was laid on 12 June 1472: Johnson (1975), p. 10; and for the date of Alberti's death see Gaye (1893), I, doc. XCIV, and Mancini (1967), p. 495.

25 Alberti, *Della tranquillità dell'animo*, as translated in Lefaivre (1997), p. 150, and p. 270, n. 109. After Alberti (1843), I, p. 48: 'Oh! Dolce cosa quella gloria quale acquistiamo con nostra fatica. Degne fatiche le nostre, per quali possiamo a quei che non sono in vita con noi, mostrare d'essere vivuti con altro indizio che colla età, e a quelli che verranno lasciargli di nostra vita altra cognizione e nome che solo un sasso a nostra sepoltura inscritto e consignato! Dicea Ennio poeta: non mi piangete, non mi fate esequie, ch'io volo vivo fra le parole degli uomini doti.'

IV SELF-PORTRAITURE

1 Mancini (1967), p. 92.

2 Alberti (1954), p. 65; Eng. trans. by Jarzombek (1989), p. 69.

3 The *Vita Sancti Potiti* is dated 1433 (see Alberti, 1954), and the *Vita anonima* is usually dated as no later than around 1438 because of the period of Alberti's life that is covered, but this is by no means certain: see Alberti (1843), I, pp. LXXXIX–XC. For an English translation of the *Vita anonima*, see Borsi (1977), p. 258.

4 Only three manuscripts of this work are known. They are written in Latin, and are reasonably consistent, one to another, though only one is thought to originate from the fifteenth century. It has been conjectured that the text is actually an autobiography, not least because the author shows a certain enthusiasm for his task. It concludes in the year 1437, when Alberti would have been thirty-three. For those who believe Alberti was the author of the *Vita anonima*, see Watkins (1957); Fubini and Menci Gallorini (1972), esp. pp. 58–60 and 68–78; Marsh (1985); and Jarzombek (1989), pp. 70–73, and n. 18, p. 214. For those against, see Grayson (1956), p. 16, n. 1; and Gadol (1969), p. 11.

5 English translation from the *Vita anonima* in Alberti (1972), p. 142.

6 English translation from Landino in Alberti (1972), p. 142. Three bronze busts of Ludovico Gonzaga were attributed to Alberti, but this is now disputed: see Rykwert and Engel (1994), p. 549, entry 145 (by Rykwert); and for the identification of Alberti as their sculptor, see Badt (1958).

7 Hill (1978): on Pisanello, pp. 36–42; on Alberti, p. 46. See also Pope-Hennessy (1972), pp. 64–9; and Lewis (1994), p. 41. See Hill (1978), p. 46, where the 'two remarkable oval plaque portraits, not, strictly speaking, medals, of the great architect' are briefly described. Hill states that the plaques do not appear 'to me to be the work of a trained medalist; and both betray a certain amateurishness, though it is the amateurishness of genius. Seeing that Alberti confessed to dabbling in sculpture, I see no reason why one, if not both, should not be from his own hand. The attribution of these pieces to Pisanello and Pasti need not be considered seriously. Judging from Alberti's age, they may date from an earlier period than Pisanello's first medal, being possibly as early as the year 1435.'

8 These are now in the National Gallery of Art, Washington, DC, Kress Collection and the Bibliothèque Nationale de France, Paris. They are described in Rykwert and Engel (1994), p. 474, entries 72 and 73 (by Luke Syson): cf. entry 72, in the Louvre, Paris, which was once thought to have been a self-portrait; see also Hill (1978), p. 46. The Washington plaque is an oval, 20.1 × 13.55 cm; the one in the Bibliothèque Nationale, Paris, is probably an aftercast as it is fractionally smaller (19.7 × 13.3 cm), reflecting the 3% shrinkage of an after cast. Otherwise, they are identical.

9 In Rykwert and Engel (1994), p. 487, entries 91a and 91b (by G. Giovannoni).

10 There is another medal showing Alberti's proposed design for the Tempio Malatestiano which bears the date 1450; see fig. 40 below. There has been some dispute as to whether Matteo de' Pasti was the author of the medal bearing this design. Those for include Syson (1994), pp. 46–53, and Giovannoni, in Rykwert and Engel (1994), pp. 484–5, entry 88a–c. Those against include Calabi and Cornaggia (1927), p. 44, n. 15; and Hope (1992), p. 52 and n. 4.

11 Onians (1971), pp. 96–114; Smith (1992); and Eck (1994).

12 The manuscript is in Florence: Biblioteca Nazionale, cod. II.IV.38.

13 Jarzombek (1989), p. 48. From Alberti (1890), pp. 229–31; and see the discussion by Jarzombek (1989), pp. 45–51, esp. the quote from Alberti on p. 50. See also Watkins (1960), pp. 256–8, who suggests that Alberti refers to the emblem as the eye of the eagle – 'oculus alis aquilae insignis'; and Wind (1980), pp. 230–35. Jarzombek (1989), pp. 208–9, n. 116, disagrees with this interpretation.

14 In a similar vein, he argued in the *Anuli* that it is better not to explain the symbol's personal significance in any detail: 'I prefer to be very brief: for to give an exhaustive account of such a compact matter would be prolix; particularly as you yourself, in the measure of your wisdom, will be able, if you apply your mind to it, to perceive the meaning clearly and distinctly'. As quoted in Wind (1980), p. 234.

15 See, for example, Lewis (1994), p. 42. However, when the emblem was drawn in *Della famiglia* these extensions appeared less like thunderbolts and more feathery. Either way, the essential interpretation of the 'all-seeing eye' remains valid.

16 Wind (1980), p. 234.

17 On the obverse Matteo de' Pasti declares his authorship with the formula OPUS MATTHAEI PASTII VERONENSIS.

18 It appears on dedications of his writings in manuscript and first editions, but he normally signed his name 'Baptista de Albertis', and, apart from the one instance on the medal, Matteo de' Pasti addressed Alberti as 'Baptista' in correspondence. It is uncertain, therefore, whether 'Leon' was applied to these works subsequently. See, for example, his dedication of *De equo animante* in 1442 to Leonello d'Este; Alberti (1991b), p. 78, notes 1 and 2, and illustration 22.

19 Poliziano introduced his foreword to *De re aedificatoria* with the opening 'Baptista Leo Florentinus e clarissima Albertorum familia': Alberti (1966), p. 3.

20 For example, by Jarzombek (1989) as 'Leon Baptista Alberti'.

21 Geihlow (1915), p. 36; and see Rykwert, in Alberti (1988), p. xvi. Other readings come from Wind (1980), pp. 231–5; and Jarzombek (1989), pp. 63–5. Gadol (1969), p. 69, quotes Alberti on the Lion, and suggests the emblem may refer to Alberti's concern for insight and 'rational seeing'.

22 'Cupiditate gloriae flagrans, difficillima omnia rite exequebatur ut leonibus omnibus facile praestaret. "Etenim quid insanis?" inquit invidia. "Qui enim huic generi animantium locus debebatur iam pridem merenti consignatus est." Respondit leo: "Sat erit nobis promeruisse"'. Alberti (1984), p. 74, and pp. 44–7 for the dedication to Francesco Marescalchi; Alberti (1989), p. 102, and p. 21 on Marescalchi. Eng. trans. quoted here from Gadol (1969), p. 238.

23 Eng. trans. based on Borsi (1977), p. 258; after Alberti (1843), I, pp. lxxxix–xc.

24 Alberti (1972), p. 61.

25 Alberti (1972), pp. 71–3.

26 Alberti (1972), p. 101.

27 Alberti (1972), p. 101.

28 Alberti (1972), pp. 143–4; Kent (1981), p. 43, n. 4.

29 Vasari (1973), II, p. 547. Giovanni's grandson was Palla Rucellai.

30 Ceschi (1948), p. 192: 'messer Lorentio Alberti, che primma de sposarsi essendo perfecto de chorpo et de viso et anco molto amato per le sue dovitie et richezze da tucti, ebbe da la nobile et bella vidova Blancha Fieschi'.

31 Beccadelli (1824), I, Poem 19, p. 64; Eng. trans. in Borsi (1986), p. 259.

32 Alberti (1972), pp. 105–7, para. 63. For the Italian, see Alberti (1960–73), III, p. 106.

33 See Grayson (1954), pp. 177–8; Berti (1964); Eiko Wakayama (1971), pp. 1–16; Ames-Lewis (1974), pp. 103–4; Johnson (1975), pp. 67–9; Eisler (1974), pp. 529–30; Varese (1985), pp. 181–9; Baldini and Casazza (1990), p. 194 and n. 11, p. 199; Trenti (1991), pp. 62–73; Whitfield (1993), pp. 25–8.

    A capital inside the cathedral of Pienza, built in the early 1460s by Bernardo Rossellino for Pope Pius II, has a head bearing a profile similar to Alberti's and surmounted by wings. However, the face is bearded (when Alberti was probably not). Examples of winged heads are not uncommon (see the Barberini panels illustrated in Borsi, 1977, p. 132, fig. 140); they are carved on the capitals of the Tempio Malatestiano and found on the frieze of Sant'Andrea in Mantua. See Pieper (1994), pp. 54–63.

34 Rome, Biblioteca Nazionale Centrale, Fondo 'Vittorio Emanuele', VE 738. The portrait was uncovered by Cecil Grayson and published as Alberti's self-portrait; see Grayson (1954), pp. 177–8, an assumption questioned by Whitfield (1993), pp. 27–8. Cf. Rykwert and Engel (1994), p. 437, entry 29 (by Lucia Bertolini).

35 This drawing is also referred to by Lefaivre (1997), pp. 157–9, in relation to the *Hypnerotomachia Poliphili*, fig. 22 above.

36 They are identified, respectively, by Berti (1964); Varese (1985), pp. 181–9; Whitfield (1993), pp. 25–8; Ames-Lewis (1974), pp. 103–4.

37 The 'Alberti' by Masaccio in the Brancacci Chapel, Florence, is seen standing between figures identified as Masolino, Masaccio and Brunelleschi (in the *Raising of the Son of Theophilus with St Peter in the Chair*). However, there are some problems with this identification. Vasari describes one of the men as Donatello, but he does not mention that Alberti is among them, yet he knew of a self-portrait by Alberti in Florence (Vasari, 1973, II, p. 547). While Vasari is neither entirely reliable nor comprehensive, it cannot be ascertained whether Alberti's admiration for Masaccio (which he expressed in his dedication of *Della pittura* to Brunelleschi) was reciprocated by the artist in any way: particularly as the Brancacci frescoes were probably painted between 1424 and *c.* 1428 – the year of Masaccio's death – which occurred before Alberti had even visited Florence and begun to make an impression there.

    Alberti has also been identified as the model for Noah in a scene from *The Flood*, by Uccello, in the Chiostro Verde of Santa Maria Novella, Florence. Noah-Alberti gestures impressively with a stern countenance, which recalls Alberti's recommendation (1972, p. 83, para. 42): 'I like there to be someone in the "historia" who tells the spectators what is going on, and either beckons them with his hands to look, or with ferocious expression and forbidding glance challenges them to come near, as if he wished their business to be secret, or points to some danger or remarkable thing in the picture, or by his gestures invites you to laugh or weep with them'.

    The Flood is generally dated to *c.* 1446, when Alberti would have been in his early forties. Yet Uccello was bound to paint a much older figure to fit the biblical description, so that the identification is valid only if it is accepted that he made Alberti look prematurely old for this central role; cf. Eisler (1974), pp. 529–30. Alberti has also been identified among a group of scholars in Cossa's *Triumph of Minerva* (specifically the *Month of March*). The location of the painting in Palazzo Schifanoia, Ferrara (frequented by Alberti), and its theme of wisdom add credibility to the physical likeness of the scholar in profile, in his priestly attire. See Ames-Lewis (1974), p. 103.

38 Since 1912 it has been generally accepted as a portrait of Carlo de' Medici (*c.* 1428–92), but the evidence for this is faulty and has been discounted. The painting is titled *Portrait of a Man* (Uffizi, inv. no. 8540) by Christiansen, in Martineau (1992), pp. 337–9, cat. no. 102; see also Christiansen, in Rykwert and Engel (1994b), pp. 533–4, cat. no. 136.

39 Tavernor (1994c).

40 By the late sixteenth century Mantegna's portrait had become part of the Medici collection in Florence: it was a gift from the Mantuan court, to celebrate the union in marriage of Vincenzo Gonzaga and Eleonora de'

Medici in 1584. Christiansen, in Martineau (1992), p. 337, cat. no. 102, under 'Provenance'; and Christiansen, in Rykwert and Engel (1994b), p. 534. On Alberti and Mantegna in Mantua, see Christiansen (1994a) and Steinberg (1994).

41 On Pisanello and Alberti, see Hill (1978), pp. 36–42 and 46. See also Pope-Hennessy (1972), pp. 64–9. The 'genius and amateurishness' are conflicting attributes remarked on by Sir George Hill with respect to Alberti's self-portrait plaque: see n. 7 above.

42 Kristeller (1902), p. 480.

V BEAUTY IN ART AND BUILDING

1 What follows is derived from Alberti (1972) and is discussed in more detail in Aiken (1980).

2 Aiken (1980), p. 71.

3 For an account of this painting, and related bibliography, see Kuhn (1990).

4 Masaccio is listed as an influence by Alberti in the dedication he made to Brunelleschi of *Della pittura*: Alberti (1972), pp. 32–3, and p. 108, n. 2.

5 Alberti argues against using columns to support an arch (he prefers to use the more solid and wall-like pilasters in this role), and there are no examples of the Ionic column in his buildings. See the discussion of the Rucellai Loggia (pp. 119–24, below).

6 Ragghianti (1977), p. 362 and figs 466–9. Ragghianti observed that the crucifix measured 170 × 170 cm., though the limbs of Christ are bent and would be marginally longer when outstretched. For a modular analysis of this crucifix, see Cassazza (1978), pp. 209–12.

7 Uzielli (1899), p. 14, writes that some authors have supposed the Florentine *braccio da panna* to be double the Roman *pes* (295.5 mm as he records it), though he believed it to be derived from the Palestinian *braccio* (554.8 mm).

8 Vitruvius (1960), III, 1.1, p. 72: 'Without symmetry and proportion there can be no principles in the design of any temple; that is, if there is no precise relation between its members, as in the case of those of a well shaped man'.

9 Vitruvius (1960), III, 1.

10 Augustine (1955), p. 850, and, for the English translation used here, Augustine (1972), pp. 1073–4.

11 Alberti (1972), pp. 134–5. In fact, the human proportions recorded in the *Tabulae* may not have been taken solely from the bodies Alberti had measured and are perhaps an idealised blend of classical and medieval commentaries on human proportions, a conclusion reached by Aiken (1980), pp. 85–8. See also Onians (1988); and Scaglia (1994), p. 321, who argues that Alberti may have been influenced in particular by the Sienese engineer Mariano di Jacopo, called Taccola (*c*. 1382–1453).

12 Alberti (1972), p. 55; Zervas (1979).

13 Alberti states this in *Della pittura*, the Tuscan version of his Latin original. Although he does not state specifically which *braccio* is to be used, there can be little doubt he was thinking of the Florentine *braccio da panna*, 3 of which are man-height. Also, although he describes the height of a man in a painting as 3 *braccia*, Alberti acknowledged Vitruvius' preference for reckoning in feet. See Alberti (1972), pp. 55 and 75.

14 Vitruvius (1960), III, 1.

15 See Wilson Jones (1989b).

16 Vitruvius (1960), V, 1.6.

17 Fernie (1978), pp. 384ff. Even metrological authorities vary in the value they ascribe to the Roman *pes*, and Martini (1883), p. 866 and n. 7, opts for one 295.5 mm long, on the basis of thirty well-preserved standards. On the problems faced by historians when dealing with metrology, see Fernie (1978), and on the Roman foot, p. 384.

18 Uzielli (1899); and Benevolo, Chieffi and Mezzetti (1968), p. 4: 'il braccio [Florentine *braccio*] equivale tradizionalmente a due piedi romani, su campioni trovati, varia tra cm. 29.6 e 29.7 cm; e che nel Rinascimento si usano promiscuamente per l'edilizia le misure in braccia e in piedi'. No further sources were provided by the authors for this tradition. On Florence as a Roman colony, see Rubinstein (1967). So, as an alternative to his 'idealised' measures, Alberti may have taken the contemporary Roman *piede*, or half the Florentine *braccio*, and refined its length when measuring and then making drawings of Roman antiquities. He would have done this presumably by comparing his estimates of the *pes* with dimensions of ancient Roman buildings.

The need to explain antique monuments using their original measures was certainly appreciated several generations after Alberti. Early in the sixteenth century Angelo Colocci, a humanist and curialist, discovered several examples of the Roman *pes* in artefacts and on buildings near the Lateran and Jewish ghetto: Stinger (1985), p. 65. When Philibert Delorme was in Rome during the 1530s he was urged to study examples of the *pes* in the Capitoline collection, as well as among antiquities owned by Cardinal Galli, and to abandon his survey of the ruins with his customary measure, the *pied du roi*. This is discussed by Coffin (1979), p. 12; see also Delorme (1648), V, 1, fols 131*r*–131*v*. A similar process of 'induction' was undertaken most famously by Flinders Petrie (1877). Delorme's contemporaries in Italy were not always as diligent. Serlio appears to have been more interested in the outward appeal of antique monuments than ascertaining the precise measures used, and he offered a rather wayward *piede antico* equivalent to 327 mm (see Lotz, 1982). Lotz believed Serlio's attitude to measure was typical of Cinquecento architects, in that current theories granted human proportions a divine status, so that a surveyor's own foot was as valued as much as any of the official standards then in use. Lotz also believed that there was no need for a unity of measure throughout Italy: the variations of standards in various cities were considered as natural as the variations in human sizes and proportions.

19 See, for example, Baxandall (1972), p. 95.

20 See Smith and Karpinski (1911), p. 128; Baxandall (1972), pp. 95–102; and Goldthwaite (1972), pp. 418–33.

Goldthwaite lists seven courses that were run at the schools in Florence: basic arithmetic; division (three courses); fractions; the Rule of Three; the Florentine monetary system. It had been introduced to Italy through trade with the Arabs, and appeared in Leonardo Fibonacci of Pisa's *Liber abbacci* of 1202.

21 Kidson (1990), pp. 71–97.

22 Similarly, there were correspondences between the *braccio* standards of Mantua and Florence, cities in which Alberti built. Thus, the Florentine *braccio* could be readily adjusted to the size of the local Mantuan measure through a ratio of 4 to 5, the equivalent of 4 Florentine *braccia* being 5 Mantuan *braccia* (a difference of only 1 mm over a length of 2 m.: $4 \times 583.6\,\text{mm} = 2334\,\text{mm}$; $5 \times 467\,\text{mm} = 2335\,\text{mm}$). These correspondences will be described relative to Alberti's other buildings below. For the metrological sources, see Doursther (1840) and Martini (1883); for a discussion of the relative measures in use in Rimini, Florence and Mantua, see Tavernor (1985), esp. pp. 11–18.

23 In the Prologue to *De re aedificatura*, Alberti (1988), p. 5, stated that 'the building is a form of body, which like any other consists of lineaments and matter' and, 'Since buildings are set to different uses, it proved necessary to inquire whether the same type of lineaments could be used for several; we distinguished the various types of buildings and noted the importance of the connection of their lines and their relationship to each other, as the principal source of beauty; we began therefore to inquire further into the nature of beauty – of what kind it should be, and what is appropriate in each case'.

24 'In building a ship, the ancients would use the lineaments of a fish; so that its back became the hull, its head the prow; the rudder would serve as its tail, the oars as its gills and fins'.

25 His assertion that beauty is fundamental to the structure of a building was at odds with the view prevailing throughout the Middle Ages and early Renaissance that beauty is added to a building and resides in ornament. This notion was promoted by Isidore of Seville (1911), XVI, col. 568, and identified as a prevailing view by Schlosser (1896); see also Smith (1994a), pp. 196–215.

26 Alberti makes clear the distinction between structures that are beautiful, and the ornament that embellishes them: 'The city of Smyrna [. . .] is said to have been very beautiful in the layout of its streets and ornamentation of its buildings' (IV, 7, p. 113). Similarly, having described the orientation of temples, he states that 'what remains to be discussed concerns their ornament, more than their use' (V, 6, p. 101).

27 A theme initiated in the Prologue, and stated explicitly in Book IV, chapter 2, where Alberti writes: 'we should follow Socrates' advice, that something which can only be altered for the worse can be held to be perfect' (Alberti, 1988, p. 96). See also Cicero, *De oratore*, 3.45.1792. Because of the association with Cicero it has been argued by Eck (1994), p. 52, and n. 44, p. 308, that 'quin improbabilius reddatur' should be translated more literally, as a rhetorical expression, as 'without rendering it less probable' (instead of 'but for the worse', as in the translation quoted here).

28 Vitruvius (1960), I, 3.2.

29 Cicero had characterised two types of beauty in *De officiis* – *venustas* as feminine and *dignitas* as masculine, whereas for architecture Alberti attaches a moral dimension to beauty (see pp. 43–6, below). To distance himself from Vitruvius' definition of beauty Alberti uses a different Latin term, *pulchritudo*: see Onians (1988), pp. 151–2.

30 Burckhardt (1984), p. 30.

31 In an attempt to fill the gaps left by Alberti, scholars since Burkhardt have interpreted this term variously. However, the nuances they have attached to the three categories of *concinnitas* have proved difficult to verify because the term has been analysed in the abstract – rooted in philosophy and rhetoric – rarely linking it directly to Alberti's design process or practice. This was largely because of the unreliability or incompleteness of existing historical and physical surveys of his buildings. Recent research, however, and the availability of accurate, verifiable photogrammetric surveys have made it possible to suggest more completely than before how Alberti's theory of beauty was to be applied in practice. The photogrammetric surveys made for the Alberti exhibition (Rykwert and Engel, 1994) were carried out by Computer Mapping Services Ltd, of Selsey, near Chichester, England, and the results are archived on computer at the Department of Architecture and Civil Engineering, University of Bath; the Alberti Group web site address is given in the Author's Note above.

32 From: C.T. Lewis and C. Short, *A Latin Dictionary*, Oxford, 1879, rev. edn, Oxford 1969, p. 400; and D.P. Simpson, *Cassell's New Latin Dictionary*, London, 1959; rev. edn, London, 1964, p. 126.

33 See Cicero, *Orator*, 44.149, 49.164 and 65.220; and *Brutus*, 83.287 and 95.325. See also Lücke (1994), pp. 70–95.

34 Cicero's *De oratore* and *De officiis* have been identified as particularly relevant for Alberti, and Onians has shown convincingly how Alberti adapted Cicero's terms for *De re aedificatoria*, and how his rendering of beauty (*pulchritudo*) as 'aesthetic rectitude' accords with Cicero's definition of *honestas* as 'moral rectitude'. See Onians (1971), p. 102, and his development of this interpretation in Onians (1988), pp. 125–6 and 147–57; see also Smith (1992), pp. 82–97; Eck (1994), p. 54; and Gadol (1969), who relates *concinnitas* to Vitruvius' term *symmetria*, a category also taken from ancient rhetoric but not used by Alberti.

35 Plato, *Phaedrus*, 264c. See also Aristotle, *Poetics*, 1459a 17ff, and the discussion in Eck (1994), p. 41.

36 Vitruvius (1960), III, 1.9.

37 Wittkower (1973), p. 33.

38 Vitruvius (1960), III, 1.1, p. 72; and his conclusions to this: III, 1.9, p. 79, and VI, 2.1, p. 174.

39 Vitruvius (1960), III, 1, p. 72; Wittkower (1973), p. 96.

40 Wittkower (1973), pp. 45–6.

41 After Palladio (1570), Bk I. It was Scamozzi (1615), Bk VII, who most clearly systematised the five orders according to a module based on the column diameters.

42 Indeed, Gadol (1969), p. 108, took Wittkower's interpretation a stage further and equated *concinnitas* directly

with Vitruvius' term *symmetria*. However, it should be noted that although Palladio acknowledged Alberti's contribution to architectural theory in the Preface of *I quattro libri*, his mentor Giangiorgio Trissino was critical: 'Leon Battista Alberti wanted to follow in [Vitruvius'] footsteps [. . .] but apart from the length of his treatise, it appears to me that one misses in it many things whilst one finds many which are superfluous'; trans. from Wittkower (1973), pp. 59–60.

43 Wittkower (1973), p. 96.

44 Wittkower (1973), Appx III, pp. 164–6, where 200 such studies are mentioned, made between 1945 and 1958. The list is considerably longer now. The 'concinnitas-symmetria' equation is still upheld by Davies and Hemsoll (1997), pp. 559–60.

45 And not only those dating from the fifteenth and sixteenth centuries: Wittkowerian principles have been applied by subsequent investigators to twentieth-century buildings. See, for example, Tavernor (1995).

46 Alberti (1988), pp. 421–2.

47 Alberti (1988), esp. the Glossary, pp. 421–2.

48 Hersey (1976), pp. 6–7.

49 Westfall (1969), p. 65.

50 Vitruvius, (1960), IX, introduction, p. 252.

51 Vitruvius (1960), V, 6 and 7, pp. 146–52: and as demonstrated most memorably in Barbaro's edition of Vitruvius of 1567; see Vitruvius (1987), IV, 8.

52 Cesare Cesariano, in his commentary on Vitruvius of 1521, drew triangles proportionally related to one another when describing the fourteenth-century design of Milan Cathedral.

53 Wittkower (1973), pp. 160–61.

54 As stated in a letter written by Jacopo de' Barbari addressed to Frederick the Wise, Elector of Saxony: in Barocchi (1971), p. 67; and Davis (1977), p. 82: 'non pol essere proporcione senza numero, ne pol essere forme senza giometria'.

55 Wittkower (1973), p. 110; Westfall (1969), p. 65. In the first complete English edition of the *Ten Books*, published in 1726, Leoni translated this triad as number, finishing and collocation: Alberti (1955), p. 195. Flemming (1916), p. 33, took them to be equivalent to Aristotle's categories of quantity, quality and relation, a view widely adopted and which led 'quality' and 'relation' to be combined as 'qualitative relations': see Gadol (1969), p. 108, n. 27.

56 Lauro in Alberti (1546); Bartoli in Alberti (1550), IX, 5; see also Vagnetti (1973), p. 150, and Alberti (1988), Glossary.

57 Orlandi in Alberti (1966), II, p. 814 and n. 2.

58 Gadol (1969), pp. 108–17.; see also Aiken (1980), pp. 68–95, esp. p. 75.

59 Lang (1965), esp. pp. 333–4.

60 Vagnetti (1973), p. 150.

61 Tommaso (1972), p. 33; Westfall (1969), passim.

62 Tommaso (1972), p. 35; and Alberti (1969), p. 75.

63 Westfall (1969), p. 66.

64 Cf. Vitruvius (1960), I, 1, pp. 5–13 and VI, introduction, pp. 167–9.

65 Smith (1992), pp. 80–96, esp. pp. 82–7.

66 As interpreted by Onians (1971), p. 102.

67 A point made by Vagnetti (1973), p. 141, with reference to *Orator*, 44.149 and 49.164, and *Brutus*, 83.287 and 95.325; see also Smith (1992), pp. 93–4.

68 Alberti, 1972, II, 30, p. 67: 'We divide painting into three parts, and this division we learn from Nature herself. As painting aims to represent things seen, let us note how in fact things are seen. In the first place, when we look at a thing, we see it as an object which occupies a space. The painter will draw around this space, and he will call this process of sketching the outline [*rationem*], appropriately circumscription [*circumscriptionem*]. Then, as we look, we discern how the several surfaces of the object seen are fitted together; the artist, when drawing these combinations of surfaces in their correct relationship, will properly call this composition [*compositionem*]. Finally, in looking we observe more clearly the colours of surfaces; the representation in painting of this aspect, since it receives all its variations from light, will aptly here be termed the reception of light [*receptio luminum*]'.

69 Panza (1994), pp. 155–75; Rykwert (1996), pp. 100–02.

70 This has been clarified by Karvouni (1994), pp. 282–91.

71 Karvouni (1994), pp. 288–91.

72 Grayson (1972), p. 73.

73 Smith (1992), pp. 80–96, esp. pp. 82–7.

74 Augustine (1955), p. 373; Eng. trans. in Augustine (1972), XII, 19, and XI, 30.

75 Tomei (1977), pp. 65, 71–2 and 79, supplies a useful summary of the supporters of Alberti's role in the design of Palazzo Venezia; for a convincing argument against Alberti's involvement here, see Magnuson (1958), pp. 289–96; and Burroughs (1990), pp. 80 and 244.

76 Vasari (1973), II, pp. 538–9; and in support of Vasari's claim, see Burroughs (1990), pp. 96–8 and fig. 33. (Burroughs, p. 244, is generally more circumspect about Alberti's role in Nicholas V's projects in Rome.)

VI   THE TEMPIO MALATESTIANO

1 Jones (1974), p. 26 and n. 1.

2 Jones (1974), p. 33: 'quia semper fuit fidelis et devotus Ecclesiae'.

3 Jones (1974), p. 41. Malatesta di Pandolfo, known as 'Guastafamiglia' (destroyer of families), was the first member of the family to be granted the title of Papal Vicar of Rimini. He founded a family chapel in San Francesco, and was buried there in the late fourteenth century, with due contrition, in spite of his nickname, also in Franciscan habit: Jones (1974), pp. 85–6.

4 Carlo Malatesta was the eldest of four brothers, of whom Pandolfo, Andrea and Galeotto Belfiore controlled other, lesser, Malatesta territories, partitioned after the death of their father Galeotto: Jones (1974), p. 102.

5 Jones (1974), p. 112.

6 Jones (1974), p. 113.

7 Jones (1974), p. 124.

8 Indeed, in the autumn of 1408, Carlo made a gesture to end the papal schism between Rome and Avignon, by inviting Pope Gregory XII to Rimini from Rome, at a time when Gregory was under pressure from his

cardinals to reach an early agreement with the Avignon pope, Benedict XIII. Pope Gregory welcomed the invitation of asylum in Rimini, where he remained until the following spring while deliberations continued; see Jones (1974), pp. 127–8. The efforts of Carlo turned out to be in vain, and reconciliation was long in coming, but the Malatesta commitment to the Roman papacy was clear and very public; it did much for Carlo's reputation as an even-handed and pious man. The latter quality was perhaps instilled in him by his ancestors, several of whom, including Galeotto Malatesta, had made pilgrimages to the Holy Land. See Jones (1974), p. 128, n. 4.

9   Jones (1974), pp. 128–9.

10 Jones (1974), p. 129.

11 Pandolfo Malatesta da Pesaro had been appointed Archbishop of Patras in the north of the Peloponnese by Pope Martin V. St Andrew had been crucified in Patras and Pandolfo restored one of the churches there, an event celebrated in Guillaume Dufay's motet *Apostolo glorioso* in 1426. See Fallows (1987), p. 23; and Jones (1974), p. 129.

12 Pandolfo Malatesta died while on his way to fulfil a vow to visit the Madonna of Loreto and was buried in the Franciscan convent at Fano. It is recorded that although he was contrite on his deathbed, he had earned an unsavoury reputation during his lifetime: he was considered a libertine and the church criticised him for being an active supporter of humanists. See Jones (1974), p. 165, and references in n. 1.

13 Carlo's brother Andrea had also lost his only son. To effect the succession Carlo first needed to legitimise his nephews, and this required a papal bull. Martin V issued it, though not without some opposition, paradoxically, from Guidantonio da Montefeltro, who had legitimised his chosen successor Federico in this very same way. A further bull granted Carlo the power to dispose of his lands by will. The succession had been settled by the time of Carlo's death in 1429, and the government of Rimini was shared by his widow and a regency council of twelve until Galeotto Roberto came of age. Carlo Malatesta was buried in San Francesco, Rimini, dressed in black (as were the rest of the family), and the funeral service was held in the presence of Galeotto Roberto and his brothers: Roberto was aged eighteen, and his brothers Sigismondo and Domenico twelve and eleven. See Jones (1974), pp. 165 and 168.

14 Pius presented more sinister reasons for his death: see Pius II (1984), II, p. 1909.

15 Jones (1974), p. 174. By comparison Galeotto Roberto had done little in his lifetime to extend Malatesta authority territorially, nor did he provide descendants. He had married Margherita d'Este in 1427, at his uncle's behest, but maintained a vow of chastity and devoted himself to the Franciscan Order, of which he became a Tertiary.

16 When pope, and on learning of the death of Galeotto Roberto in 1432, Eugenius wrote to congratulate the surviving brothers on their loyalty to the church: Jones (1974), p. 179.

17 Jones (1974), p. 172.

18 Jones (1974), p. 180.

19 Saalman (1980), pp. 275–6, doc. 286.4.

20 A description of the man made by Jones (1974), p. 177.

21 Jones (1974), pp. 179–83, and esp. p. 228, and p. 229, n. 1.

22 'Homicidia deinde, stupra, adulteria, incestus, sacrilegia, periuria, proditiones et infinita propemodum turpissima et atrocissima scelera eius probata': Pius II (1984), II, Bk VII, 11, p. 1448.

23 Jones (1974), p. 176, suggests this portrait is probably inaccurate and excessively partial, shaped as it is by the pope's own political biases and ambitions for the Church of Rome.

24 Sigismondo and Isotta were probably married in 1456: see Campana (1962). His first two wives were Ginevra d'Este and Polissena Sforza; Jones (1974), pp. 176–7, and p. 177, n. 1; and p. 213, n. 5.

25 Vasari (1973), II, p. 286: 'fece il modello delle chiesa di S. Francesco, e quello della facciata particolarmente [. . .] Insomma, ridusse quella fabbrica in modo che per cosa soda ell'è uno de'più famosi tempji d'Italia'.

26 Hope (1992), pp. 55–6.

27 Although the term 'templum' was interchangeable with 'chiesa' it is unusual for a Christian church to be still referred to as a 'tempio'. On the name 'Tempio Malatestiano' see Ettlinger (1990), p. 133 and n. 5, who says it was first coined in the nineteenth century. On the early applications of ornament *all'antica* in Renaissance Italy, and a suggestion why Alberti used this capital type only once, see Onians (1988), pp. 127 and 182.

28 This distinction between the phases of remodelling the interior and then building a new exterior is made clearly by Hope (1992), pp. 82–93.

29 This privilege of interment was a considerable honour for her, and it was not a favour the Malatesta had granted any of their wives previously. Sigismondo's first wife was placed in a 'magnificent' tomb in the church, but not in her own chapel. His first legitimate son was interred in the same tomb as Carlo Malatesta. See Massèra (1924), pp. 60, 63–4, 74, 81, 119, 121, 128–9, 134–5; see also Ettlinger (1990), pp. 133–43, and p. 134, n. 9. Sigismondo's wife Polissena Sforza died on 1 June 1449: Massèra (1924), pp. 128–9.

30 Soranzo (1926), pp. 17–19. The feast of St Michael, Michaelmas (29 September), is properly called St Michael and All Angels, so the dedication of the chapel has remained constant.

31 On the receipt of Isotta's dowry, see Ricci (1974), p. 585, no. III. On the enlargement of this and the other existing chapel, see Hope (1992), pp. 53–82. In a later bull issued by Nicholas V after March 1448, it is stated that the adjacent Cell of the Relics was being built 'partly in profane and partly in sacred areas of the church of the house of St Francis'. See Ricci (1974), p. 585, no. II; and Hope (1992), p. 59, n. 38.

32 'ISOTE ARIMINENSI FORMA ET VIRTVTE ITALIE DECORI. MCCCCXLVI'. See Ricci (1974), pp. 436–7, and 446–7, figs 534, 535; see also Hope (1992), p. 62 and n. 49.

33 The full inscription reads: 'D. ISOTTAE. ARIMINENSI. B. M. SACRVM. MCCCCL'. As Pius II (1984), I, p. 366, wrote: 'Sacerdotes odio habuit, religionem contempsit. De venturo saeculo nihil credidit et animas perire cum corpore existimavit. Aedificavit tamen nobile templum Arimini in honorem divi Francisci; verum ita gentilibus operibus implevit ut non tam Christianorum quam Infedelium daemones adorantium templum esse videretur. Atque in eo concubinae suae tumulum erexit et artificio et lapide pulcherrimum, adiecto titulo gentili more in hunc modum: "Divae Isottae sacrum"'. Alternatively, and less provocatively, it may have been intended to read as 'Di sacrum', or perhaps the 'D' stood for 'DOMINAE'. On changes to the inscription, see Hope (1992), p. 72 and n. 89.

34 For arguments relating to the history of this chapel, see Hope (1992), pp. 59–61.

35 Mitchell (1978), p. 74; Hope (1992), pp. 75 and 77, fig. 2, where the tomb of Sigismondo is reconstructed by Hope.

36 As translated by Hope (1992), p. 52, n. 5.

37 The inscription on the frieze states that: 'SIGISMVNDVS PANDVLFVS MALATESTA PANDVLFI F[ilii]. V[oto]. FECIT ANNO GRATIAE MCCCCL.'. Also, above the main door, on the altar, and over the arch of each internal chapel is a similar statement bearing the same date. On the foundation medal attributed to Matteo de' Pasti is recorded: 'PRAECL. ARIMINI. TEMPLVM. AN. GRATIAE. V(otum). F[ecit]. M.CCCC.L.', and see p. 211, n. 10, above.

38 Less durable epigraphs were painted internally in Alberti's buildings, as on the frieze of the apse at San Martino a Ganagalandi and (now lost) on the interior frieze of the tribune of Santissima Annunziata, Florence. In Mantua, at Sant'Andrea and San Sebastiano, neither building exhibits a dedication or year of consecration. It is, of course, possible that epigraphs may have been painted on to the decorative fresco externally and not survived the effects of weathering or successive restorations.

39 Mitchell (1978), pp. 74–6, suggested that Sigismondo made his vow in 1448, at the time of a victory over Alfonso of Aragon at Piombino. However, as Hope has stated, this is speculation as the year 1448 is not recorded anywhere in the building: Hope (1992), p. 52, n. 7, and p. 68.

40 A suggestion made by Burroughs (1990), pp. 205–16.

41 Borghezio (1934), II, p. 280: 'El signore miser Gismondo di Malatesti in gli'anni 1453 dè 'l principio a uno magnifico lavoro [...] miser Gismondo sovrascritto con grande amore e sulicitudine faxea lavorare ai prinçipie d'uno magnifico e superbo oratorio in la çitade d'Arimino a la giexa de frade menure, al nome e a memoria de santo Gismondo re: el quale edifiçio tutto venne lavorado de prede, marmore de più fine che lue posse retrovare per Italia e fuora d'Italia. [...] E più mandò a For[lon]puole a charegare çircha X carra de marmore de tagle antighe. Po che le fono garegade, gl'omine de la terra le fè sgaregare, e non le possè avere: adì 24 de novembre 1453'.

42 See Hope (1992), p. 66 and n. 66, Appx pp. 149–54, esp. doc. 7 (letter dated 22 December 1454 from Matteo Nuti to Sigismondo Malatesta).

43 Alberti had sent those in Rimini only a design for the capitals of the columns that month: see Hope (1992), p. 151, doc. 3, and the letter from Matteo de' Pasti and Pietro de' Gennari to Sigismondo Malatesta, dated 17 December 1454.

44 I am grateful to Paul Davies (1992) for the following references on the dating of the second phase of construction: Borghezio (1934), p. 280, Rossi (1572), p. 632, and Clementini (1617), II, p. 368. See also Ricci (1974), doc. IV, p. 586.

45 See Adimari (1616), I, p. 67; Clementini (1617), II, p. 368; Nardi (1813), p. 50.

46 Ricci (1972), doc. VII, p. 587.

47 On the re-routing of this Istrian stone, see Amiani (1751), I, p. 412. It has been argued that this material was intended for the exterior of the Tempio Malatestiano in accordance with a design by Alberti, and has therefore been used to support the notion that Alberti's design was made on or before 1450: Pavan (1975), p. 382. This, however, is questioned by Hope (1992), pp. 95–6, as Istrian stone was still being ordered for the interior four years later; Smith (1994a), pp. 210–11, suggests that the porphyry and serpentine pilfered from Sant'Apollinare in Classe was placed around the entrance portal of the temple.

48 Alberti recorded only the day and month of the letter, but the history of the document and the references it contains point to this year. Alberti's letter was confiscated from Sigismondo's secretary Sagramore Sagramori by the Sienese authorities in December 1454. At this time, Sigismondo was campaigning in Tuscany and Sagramori was returning to him from Rimini with the latest correspondence, and they include several letters referring to building work at the Tempio Malatestiano. These documents were subsequently stored in the Archivio di Stato, Siena, and Alberti's letter to Matteo is now in the Pierpont Morgan Library, New York. It is generally agreed that this too was once among Sagramori's papers, and had been sent on to Sigismondo by Matteo to keep him appraised of developments on site. See Grayson (1957); Massèra (1928), pp. 5–7; and Hope (1992), pp. 96–7.

49 The English translation here is by Joseph Rykwert and Robert Tavernor; see also Grayson (1957); Hope (1992), p. 150, doc. 2; and Saalman (1996).

50 Scholars have made a good deal of Alberti's comments on oculi here. They may relate to the windows intended for the drum of the cupola: these may be the roundels visible on the commemorative medal. Also, depending on how the documents are interpreted, windows would possibly have been located at a clerestorey level, and it is these to which de' Pasti is referring. Alternatively, the twentieth-century rebuilding of Alberti's façade suggests that old San Francesco had an oculus over the main door and it may be that this had provoked a discussion among those on site about the architectural language of Alberti's

redesign of the exterior. In short, the relevance of Alberti's comments here to the fabric of the building itself must remain conjectural. See Hope (1992), pp. 114–15; and Saalman (1996), p. 149 and n. 24.

51 Manetti had been a business partner of Giovanni Rucellai in Florence; see Jones (1974), p. 209. For the identification with Giannozzo Manetti, see Yriarte (1882), p. 243, and Scapecchi (1986).

52 This was a time that Sigismondo was enjoying a run of success: two months later, his illegitimate son, Valerio Galeotto, was one of two children legitimised by Nicholas V, and a few weeks after that, on 24 November 1453, Valerio was appointed to the post of apostolic notary (he is probably the 'protonotary' mentioned in the letter of 18 November 1454); see Giorgio (1742), p. 144; and Battaglini (1794), pp. 633–6. Jones (1974), p. 209 and n. 5, gives further references for this event, and also records that 'Nicholas granted an indulgence to pilgrims visiting the newly consecrated chapel of S. Sigismondo in S. Francesco at Rimini, on the feast of S. Sigismondo and the first Sunday of every month'. See also Hope (1992), p. 97, n. 186.

53 For Antonio di Ciaccheri Manetti, see Mancini (1967), pp. 324f., Ricci (1974), pp. 222–3. For his work at the Santissima Annunziata tribune, see Brown (1981), p. 86 and n. 77, and chapter VIII below. For Manetti, Brunelleschi's biographer, see Manetti (1976).

54 In Italian, these translations read 'nel mio modello' and 'quella parte denancie del modello de miser Batista'; see Hope (1992) p. 150, doc. 2, and p. 152, doc. 5. See also the letter from Matteo de' Pasti and Pietro de Gennari to Sigismondo, dated 17 December 1454, where Alberti's wooden model is mentioned, 'el modello de messer Batista de legno'; see Hope (1992), p. 151, doc. 3; and Ricci (1974), p. 588, doc. IX. The letter of 21 December 1454 is translated and discussed in more detail below, pp. 61–2.

55 Barbieri (1968); and for example, see the discussion on the basilica in Vicenza, in Tavernor (1991a), pp. 32–6.

56 Hope (1992), pp. 152–3, doc. 5.

57 This fact is confirmed towards the end of the letter from de' Pasti and de' Gennari to Sigismondo, dated 17 December 1454; see Hope (1992), p. 151, doc. 3.

58 Hope (1992), p. 151, doc. 3.

59 This is made of triangulated timber trusses, and the present structure is a direct replacement of the original roof destroyed by bombing during the Second World War. The roof design was amended as building work progressed, for reasons recorded by another mason on site, Matteo Nuti of Fano to Sigismondo, on 22 December 1454 (Hope, 1992, pp. 153–4, doc. 7): 'I inform your excellency that I have been with maestro Alvise, who has shown me the drawing [desegno] of the nave that comes in the body of the church, and the drawing [desegno] of the roof [tetto] which comes over the nave, that is to say that the said roof covers the nave of the body of the church and all the chapels on both sides. And the said roof is anchored [vien fermato] on the thick walls which your Excellency is having made on both sides. And it does not give any burden to the

walls or the arches of the chapels, and the weight that is on the said chapels at present will be removed, far from having to support more; because at present there is wood and tiles on them. And with that arrangement there will be no burden except just that [strictly only] of the timberwork of the nave [del legname de la nave schietto], because the said roof goes above the nave and will not provide any burden at all. For three reasons it seems to me that this would be a good piece of work: first, on account of the form, because the roof would appear ample and of very great volume; secondly, because according to the first scheme [el primo ragionamento], the roofs [tecti] of the low chapels would have been damaged by the water coming from the roof [tecto] of the body of the church, because if it [i.e. the tecto] were covered with metal, in the course of time, on account of the continuous beating of the water, it would fail and the said chapels would be damaged, and this would be against the wishes of Your Excellency; the third reason, because above the arches of the said chapel it would not be necessary to put more wall than is there at present, except to install the cornice [cornigiotto]'.

60 Hope (1992), pp. 152–3, doc. 5.

61 Hope's detailed argument proposes that groin vaults were planned over the nave of the Tempio Malatestiano by the masters in Rimini; see Hope (1992), pp. 101–3, and p. 139, fig. 9. However, I cannot agree with this. There is no reason to suspect from any of the surviving letters that Alberti's authority is being questioned by those on site: if he says the roof should be in timber and barrel vaulted, so be it. And while, as he states in his letter to Pasti, 'one wants to help what has been done, and not to spoil what one has to do', it is extreme to suggest that this implies his willingness to adopt the Gothic system internally, for the sake of continuity with what had been built there already. More specifically, there is the matter of the original wooden model. Alvise reports that, in order to determine 'the vault of the church' his father 'has taken away that front part of messer Battista's model, and on it he has made the structure as it has to go'. Equally positively, Alvise goes on to state that this has been done 'without his [father] having removed anything from the said model', and he has done this to demonstrate 'that he does not want to depart from the design of messer Battista'. As the front of the model had to be removed, presumably only the outer shell of the proposed building was represented by it, and the workings of the interior were not constructed. As it was unnecessary to remove anything from the model, but add detail, and as Alberti had reckoned on a barrel-vault structure in his original design, it is difficult to understand how pointed arches could be incorporated without making major changes to the roof of that first model, or without overriding Alberti's decision not to place any load on the walls of the nave. Moreover, Alvise confirms to Sigismondo that no major changes would be necessary: 'I am sending you a drawing, assuring you that the design provided by messer Battista in

no way prevents the building from being constructed as you will see it in the drawing, nor does one have to take away anything on account of the said covering, nor does one need to diverge from the style of the aforementioned messer Battista'.

62   If Giovanni di maestro Alvise's use of the word 'fogliame' means 'scroll', it would appear from his letter to Sigismondo that he was ambivalent about this device (Hope, 1992, pp. 152–3, doc. 5): 'it will be necessary slightly to raise that leaf [*fogliame*] which goes above the façade [. . .] because the more one can raise it, the better it will be, because the effect will be to raise the upper vault [*el volto di sopra*] and it will have more space [*averia più sua raxone*/and it will make more sense]. But nonetheless, even if one does not move that leaf, it can be done exactly as I am sending it in the drawing'.

      Alvise talks about 'that leaf', in the singular, when it is likely that he was referring to one of a pair of elements (or does he mean the mouldings over the upper arch, on top of the façade?). Alberti also refers to this 'thing' in the singular, when writing to Pasti, and draws only one of the pair (Hope, 1992, p. 150, doc. 2): 'Remember and bear in mind that in the model on the side of the roof [*tetto*] at the right and the left there is a similar thing [Diagram: of a double scroll]; and as I said that I put this here to cover that part of the roof [*tetto*]'. Alberti had no name for the scroll (or, if he did, he does not use it here), but there was no need to describe this element twice, because the façade was to be symmetrical, and the other half of the pair would mirror that which was drawn.

63   Alberti's use of the indefinite article ('mandò un disegno de la, faciada e un capitello belissimo') – a capital – reinforces the notion that it is one of a series. The Composite or Italic capital was specifically identified by Alberti in his treatise, and here it is combined with a winged cherub's head.

64   Hope (1992), p. 151, doc. 3.

65   Ricci (1974), pp. 257–9. This is now a shallow rectangular recess in plan, which is arched in elevation.

66   While both Ettlinger (1990), pp. 135–43, and Hope (1992), pp. 110–13, 116–32, and n. 241, agree that only one niche and tomb was to be built, they disagree as to its intended location.

67   The rectangular side arches of the later Porta San Pietro (1473–81) in Perugia by Agostino di Duccio may resemble the sort of configuration Alberti intended for the Tempio Malatestiano. On leaving Rimini in 1457, Agostino also built the oratory of San Bernardino (1457–62) in Perugia: each building there appears to be inspired by the design he worked on for Alberti in Rimini.

68   From a letter of 17 December 1454; see Hope (1992), p. 151, doc. 3. The old façade of San Francesco is described by Ravaioli (1950), pp. 292–4, esp. p. 294; Hope (1992), p. 117, n. 246, argues that the pier was made of stone. Yet both Pasti and Gennari state explicitly that the pier would not be cut by the round niche, implying that with the square design it would be. If this pier had been made of brick their next phrase,

stating that cutting into brick would not matter, would contradict their contention that the round design was superior because the brick pier would not be cut into.

      Hope also proposes that the niche referred to was placed on the back of the façade, inside the church. Yet the opening part of the letter is quite clear about the part of the building under discussion: 'Messer Battista degli Alberti sent me a drawing *of the façade* and a most beautiful capital, *and then Your Excellency has sent that same drawing* and a letter of Messer Battista [my emphasis]'; two sentences later, they write that the niche shown in these drawings is to be found 'according to the model of messer Battista, in wood'. Alvise's letter to Sigismondo, written four days later, shows that it was necessary to remove the front of Alberti's model to test out the position of the vault inside. If the front of the model had first to be removed – Alvise reports that his father 'has taken away that front part of messer Battista's model' (*che ello à tolto quella parte denancie del modello de miser Batista*) – it is improbable it was intended to show anything of the interior, let alone a single niche on the back of the façade. Furthermore, it is certain that the stone façade as built is placed slightly off the central long axis of the old brick church, and that the corners of the former façade coincide approximately with the position of Alberti's blind arches: this argument was put forward convincingly by Ricci (1974), pp. 257–9, and remains entirely credible.

69   The first sarcophagus contains Basinio de' Basini (who wrote an epic poem on the Malatesta, the *Hesperis*); the second, Giusto de' Conti da Valmontone Roma (author of *La bella mano*); the third, Gemistus Pletho (a leading philosopher of the last age of Byzantium); the fourth, Roberto Valturio (native of Rimini, papal abbreviator, and subsequently ambassador of the Malatesta and author of *De re militari lib. XII*); the fifth, Gentile and Giuliano Arnolfi; the sixth is empty, and commemorates Bishop Sebastiano Vanzi of Orvieto; also empty is the seventh and final sarcophagus, dedicated to Bartolomeo Traffichetti da Bertinoro (writer on medicine): Ricci (1974), pp. 287–98.

70   Ricci (1913), p. 57, figs 36 and 37.

71   Wittkower (1973), p. 103, proposes that the two tombs were to have contained the remains of Sigismondo and Isotta. The reconstruction illustrated here (fig. 45) develops his proposal, such that the tomb of Sigismondo (on the left) is surrounded by the Malatesta family arms (which is currently, but perhaps inappropriately, placed around Isotta's tomb), and the tomb of Isotta (on the right) is framed by an angel and drapery as is currently found in the Chapel of St Sigismund: see also figs 46 and 47 and the discussion below. Cf. Seitz (1893), p. 7; and Ricci (1974), pp. 257–9 and 264.

72   Seitz (1893), p. 7; and Ricci (1974), pp. 257–9 and 264. Cf. Hope (1992), p. 116, and n. 244, who believes the niches on the medal do not contain anything. But see the enlarged photograph of the medal in Borsi (1977), p. 95. An obvious, though later, example of a bas-relief

trompe-l'oeil contained within arched frames is found on the façade of the Scuola Grande di San Marco in Venice (1487–90?), by Lombardo and Buora.

The rectangular niches, as originally planned by Alberti, may have been intended to accommodate free-standing statues, but they would not have been suitable locations for windows. The interior is bright enough already, and there would have been practical difficulties in placing windows here. Narrow windows would be awkward to frame within the proportions of the opening; and full-width windows would have clashed not only with the chapel pilasters internally but with Sigismondo's tomb, which is placed on the back of the façade.

73   Matteo Nuti to Sigismondo Malatesta, Rimini, 22 December 1454: Hope (1992), pp. 153–4, doc. 7.

74   Hope (1992), p. 151, doc. 3.

75   Hope (1992), p. 151, doc. 3 (except that I have translated 'tavole' as 'ornamental slabs', as in panels of pre-formed stone, and 'cortine' as 'drapery', rather than Hope's more literal 'curtains').

76   Seitz (1893), p. 7, translates 'castello' as 'catafalque', while Ettlinger (1990), p. 142, and Hope (1992), pp. 123–4, make sense of it as the emblem of a castle, an *impresa* which appears elsewhere in the church, notably in Piero della Francesco's fresco in St Sigismund's chapel.

77   Contemporary use of the Latin root of the Italian word 'castellum' as 'castrum', and in the context of a church, as 'castrum doloris', lends support to the interpretation of this word as 'catafalque'. In the early sixteenth-century 'Diarium Innocentii VIII, Alexandri VI, Pii III et Julii II Tempora Complectens' of J. Burchard (1450–1506), an apostolic protonotary who became Bishop of Orta and Civita Castellana, it appears thus: 'Castrum doloris circa medium basilice predicte supra secundum lapidem rotundum ibidem positum, longitudinus quinque cannarum, et latitudinis quatuor, altitudinis octodecim palmorum usque ad planum suum: tectum habuit satis rapidum, ut congruam portionem ex eo reciperet' (in *Impensis Societatis pro Edandis Fontibus Italicae Historae,* 1854). And in the later 'Caeremoniale Episcoporum Clementis VIII, Innocentii X et Benedicti XIII': 'nisi adesset lectus, seu lectica mortuorum, aut castrum doloris [. . .] nisi alias lectus mortuorum, vel castrum doloris adsit in medio Ecclesiae [. . .] cum quo ibunt ad feretrum, seu castrum doloris. [. . .] Cum pervenerint ad castrum doloris [. . .] in angulo castri doloris [. . .] ad caput lecti, seu castri doloris' (in *Sanctae Sedis Apostolicae et Sacrae Rituum Congregationis Typographi,* Taurini Marietti, Rome, Bk 2, ch. 11). 'Castrum doloris' is used here to mean an empty catafalque – the body of the dead person not being present in the church. 'Lectus mortuorum' is the coffin proper.

'Castello' can also mean an assemblage of parts, such as scaffolding, and a 'castello dell'orologia', for example, refers to the mechanical parts which make up a clock. See the dictionary of S. Battaglia, *La Letteratura italiana*, I, 1971, under 'Castello'. I am grateful to Joseph Rykwert for these various references.

78   By Pasti, Gennari and Nuti; see Hope (1992), p. 151, doc. 3; p. 152, doc. 4; and p. 153, doc. 7.

79   Ricci (1974), illustration pp. 446–7.

80   For an alternative view on this, see Hope (1992), pp. 73–82, and p. 77, fig. 2.

81   According to the commemorative medal: 'quello tondo che e una testa'; see Hope (1992), p. 151, doc. 3.

82   Pächt (1951).

83   A choir would usually be situated at the east end of the church, and an altar placed between the choir and the nave. The tribune of the Santissima Annunziata in Florence which Alberti was to complete towards the end of his life contained a choir and was separated from the nave by an altar under a large arched opening connecting the tribune to the nave. The Annunziata tribune may also provide some indication of the functional potential of the rotunda at the Tempio Malatestiano. It includes chapels of wealthy families who contributed to the cost of the construction (though the lion's share of this burden fell first on the Medici, and finally the Gonzaga). See Ackerman (1980); see also the discussion on the tribune of the Annunziata, pp. 147–59, below.

In his letter to Matteo de' Pasti Alberti compared the rotunda with the Pantheon in Rome. This was an obvious physical comparison for him to make for a rotunda the size of the one projected for the Tempio Malatestiano.

84   Hope comes to a similar conclusion with reference to contemporary medals and their ancient prototypes: Hope (1992), p. 133.

85   Hope (1992), p. 133.

86   Grigioni (1913), pp. 105–8; Ricci (1974), pp. xiv–xv, fig. 10; and Hope (1992), p. 132.

87   Ricci (1974), pp. xiv–xv, fig. 10.

88   Tosi (1927), pp. 231–5; see also Tosi's findings discussed by Hope (1992), pp. 133–48.

89   Ravaioli (1951), esp. p. 126; and Hope (1992), pp. 134–5.

90   Cf. Hope (1992), pp. 132–48.

91   Alberti's design for Sant'Andrea was based on that of the ancient Etruscan temple, as he himself stated, and the transepts were probably designed by Giulio Romano in the sixteenth century: see p. 167, below.

92   See the letter of 3 May 1471, written by Giovanni da Gaiole to Ludovico Gonzaga, cited on, p. 154. In support of the Latin-cross plan at the Tempio Malatestiano, Hope (1992), pp. 132–3, and plate 23b, also cites a seventeenth-century woodcut by Raffaello Adimari (Adimari, 1616, I, p. 67) which illustrates an external view of the temple arranged as a Latin cross; there is nothing, however, to suggest that this was based on anything more than the medal and Adimari's own imagination.

93   Those in support of a rotunda include Salmi (1951), Ragghianti (1965), Mitchell (1973), Verga (1977) and Bacchiani (1987); those against include Borsi (1977) and Hope (1992).

94   Evidence of these would have been fragmentary as they were largely in ruins by the fifteenth century.

95 If the medal shows the building in perspective, the rotunda could have been wider than the façade without having to be visible on the medal. Heydenreich (1937) demonstrates how the façade of Pienza Cathedral obscures the chapels down its sides when viewed from the tight confines of the piazza in front. This is discussed further in Smith (1992), pp. 114–17. Perhaps the image on the medal is based on the wooden model of the Tempio Malatestiano, and was transferred to the medal in the manner that Alberti describes in *De pictura*, using a 'veil' (see pp. 7 and 91, above).

96 Ricci (1974), ch. 10; and Bovini (1977).

97 Bovini (1977), pp. 24–5; and Onians (1988), pp. 70–71.

98 Alberti (1988), I, 8, p. 21; the level of ground build up is evident in an eighteenth-century print illustrated in Bovini (1977), fig. 15, p. 64.

99 The drawing is in the Uffizi, Florence, and was originally attributed to Giuliano da Sangallo: Gabinetto dei Disegni degli Uffizi, 1563. See Rykwert and Engel (1994), p. 25.

100 Bovini (1977), p. 17, and p. 66, fig. 17.

101 Krautheimer (1942/1969); Borsi (1977), pp. 105–25. Penninck (1986) describes a church and family mausoleum in Bruges begun after 1471, which is of a similar size to the Tempio Malatestiano and is clearly based on the form of the Holy Sepulchre. See also Lang (1954), pp. 290–94.

102 Mitchell (1973), pp. 436–7, points to the Anastasis, while also attributing even the exterior form of the Tempio Malatestiano to an idea by Matteo de' Pasti; see esp. Verga (1977), who reconstructs the temple on the basis of Alberti's design for the Rucellai sepulchre (see pp. 106–19, below).

103 Saalman (1980), p. 244, table 1.

104 According to reports of Brunelleschi's design for Santa Maria degli Angeli, the dome was to have been one and two-thirds higher than its plan width (see pp. 145–6, below). On the proportions of Florence Cathedral, see Warren (1973), pp. 92–105.

105 As translated by Smith (1992), p. 80; see also pp. 80–97.

106 See Warren (1973); and Smith (1992), p. 94, who argues against the notion that the cathedral represents a literal translation of music into form.

107 On the motet composed for the occasion and its musical proportions relative to Brunelleschi's structure, see Warren (1973), pp. 92–105; and Smith (1992), esp. pp. 94–5 in the context of Alberti's *Profugiorum*. On Dufay, see Fallows (1987): Dufay, who was born in 1398, wrote the ballade *Resvelliés vous* for the wedding of Carlo Malatesta da Pesaro (cousin of Carlo Malatesta of Rimini) and Vittoria Colonna, 18 July 1423. This commission must have been regarded as something of a coup for the family, as Dufay went on to write the motet *Supremum est mortalibus bonum* for the Holy Roman Emperor Sigismund's entry into Rome, 21 May 1433; as well as the *Nuper rosarum flores* for the consecration of Florence Cathedral, 25 March 1436.

108 See Fallows (1987), p. 23.

109 Smith (1992), p. 80.

110 The English translation here is by Joseph Rykwert and Robert Tavernor; see also Grayson (1957); and Hope (1992), p. 150, doc. 2.

111 According to the Alberti Group photogrammetric survey, the apex of the pediment is 50 *pedes* high, the arch 30 *pedes* wide, and the columns at 40 *pedes* centres.

112 Naredi-Rainer (1977), pp. 104–5, and p. 170, was the first to associate the Roman measures of the nearby triumphal arch with the dimensions employed by Alberti for the Tempio Malatestiano. The small foot used locally in Rimini in the Quattrocento corresponds to this ancient measure, as six *pedes* equal eleven local feet. Through this ratio of 6:11 local craftsmen could work on the building with their usual measuring standards, perhaps even ignorant of the measure Alberti is believed to have used to design it: see Tavernor (1985), pp. 59–63.

113 Wittkower (1973), pp. 46–7 (confirmed by the Alberti Group photogrammetric survey); see also the descriptions of Santa Maria Novella and Sant'Andrea, pp. 99–106 and 179–87, below.

114 McAndrew (1980), pp. 236–61.

VII THE RUCELLAI ENSEMBLE

1 Kent (1981), pp. 16–17 and 32.

2 For a full account of Giovanni Rucellai's life, see Kent (1977 and 1981).

3 Giovanni was at an age when it was considered right and proper to make preparations for death. See, for example, Trexler (1980), p. 73.

4 Kent (1981), pp. 26 and 40.

5 Kent (1981), p. 33.

6 Kent (1981), p. 66. Bernardo's betrothed was Nannina, sister of Lorenzo de' Medici: Kent and Saalman (1988), p. 84 (and not Lucrezia as stated by Hollingsworth (1994), p. 358). The couple did not marry until June 1466.

7 Kent (1981), p. 67.

8 Vasari (1973), II, pp. 541–2. Vasari is wrong however in his belief that Cosimo Rucellai was Alberti's patron for the palazzo and loggia opposite. Cosimo (1468–95) was a grandson of Giovanni and was outlived by his father Bernardo Rucellai (1448–1514) and was not an owner of the palazzo.

9 This was uncovered by Dezzi Bardeschi, in the Vatican library, Barb. Lat. 5002 (LIV. 88) and 5004: this passage is included in a history of Florence by an unknown author which covers the period 1293 to 1527 and is based on, so the author claims, 'varie memorie e notizie spettanti alla città di Firenze' as well as the archives of prominent households. Thus, pp. 148–9 derive from 'memorie de' Rucellai cavate da scritture esistenti in casa il Sig.r Piero e 'l Sig.r Gio. Filippo Rucellai', pp. 376–88 concern the Rucellai directly. See Dezzi Bardeschi (1966), p. 41, n. 54: 'Gio. di Paolo Rucellai fece la facciata di Santa Maria Novella e fu disegno di Leon Battista Alberti'; 'Gio. di Paolo l'anno 1450 murò il palazzo nella via della Vigna e la loggia: disegno di Leon Battista Alberti'.

10 This issue has been hotly debated over the years. For a bibliography and re-reading of Alberti's role in its design and his ultimate intentions for the overall form of Palazzo Rucellai (which I disagree with below), see Saalman (1988).

11 Perosa (1981), fol. 83v; Kent (1981), p. 13.

12 Perosa (1981), p. 121.

13 Rucellai (1960); see also Perosa (1981).

14 Kent (1981), p. 43 and notes 1 and 2.

15 Parronchi (1972), pp. 233–4; Kent (1981), p. 43, n. 3.

16 It has been suggested that Bernardo Rucellai 'showed admiration for Alberti, but did not indicate that his family had a special relationship with the great man': Preyer (1981), p. 192, n. 3.

17 Rucellai (1960), p. 61: 'maestro d'architettura e di scoltura, perfetto gieometrico, di grande ingiengnio naturale e fantasia nelle dette arti quamto niuno altro che fusse mai dal tenpo de' Romani in qua, risucitatore delle muraglie antiche alla romanescha'.

18 Vasari (1973), II, pp. 371–2.

19 Vasari (1973), II, pp. 371–2; and Hyman (1975), pp. 98–120.

20 Vasari (1973), II, pp. 371–2. Vasari also attributes the design of the Palazzo Pitti to Brunelleschi, and recording its beauty he wrote: 'nothing more extraordinary and magnificent has ever been seen in Tuscany. It has two doors, with the opening 16 Braccia [high] and 8 Braccia wide; the windows on the first and second floors are exactly similar to the doors' (p. 373). The attribution to Brunelleschi is in doubt: see, for example, Battisti (1981), p. 352. Vasari's comments about the proportions of its façade are nonetheless still of interest here. As Vasari suggests, there is a repeating module on the façade corresponding to the window width and the wall between each window has the same width as the window. However, the repeating module is not 8 braccia long as Vasari states, but 6$\frac{2}{3}$; the height of the façade is just under 60 braccia high: see the survey in Stegmann and Geymüller (1924). The façade, before it was extended, was consequently 60 braccia high and 100 braccia wide, or the ratio 6:10.

Michelozzo di Bartolomeo's design for the Palazzo Medici is certainly more modest in size than that for the Pitti, though the ratio of width to height is again in the order of 6:10. His façade does not appear to be as carefully ordered as that of the Pitti, and the central portal neither aligns with the windows above, nor their intervals. While a dislocation of this kind, between the ground floor openings and those of the storeys above, is not unusual in Florence in the fourteenth and early fifteenth centuries, it is emphasised by Michelozzo's choice of module, and was presumably therefore premeditated in this instance. For the ground floor he used a module of 5 braccia, and the central portal is 5 braccia wide. The upper storeys have window openings 3$\frac{1}{3}$ braccia wide, half of the module used at the Pitti, and a third less than the 5 braccia opening on the ground floor, while the intervals between the windows are 3 braccia: see the survey in Stegmann and Geymüller (1924). The articulation that results is more complex

than that found at the Pitti and, as the misalignment between the lower and upper storeys suggests, not as well integrated.

The composition of the façade for the Palazzo Rucellai is altogether more complex than those of the Pitti or Medici. A five-bay Rucellai façade is 30 braccia to the centres of the outer pilasters (implying five bays of 6 braccia) and the façade is 36 braccia high, or 6 squared: a ratio of width to height of 5:6, or a minor third on the musical scale. In fact, the door bays are 6.5 braccia wide, and the others 5$\frac{7}{8}$ to pilaster centres.

Michelozzo made the windows of the Palazzo Medici slightly wider than their intervals, and they generate an A-B-A rhythm along the façade, whereas the window to wall rhythm is equal on the other two palaces. This created problems for the overall composition, of reconciling the articulation of the ground and upper floors and, perhaps, of creating a superfluity of windows. Perhaps this is why Vasari (1973), II, p. 372, claimed that 'Cosimo deeply regretted not having followed Filippo's design'.

21 Kent (1981), p. 55, termed this apparent rivalry between these great patrons 'oligarchic jockeying'. Saalman (1966) suggested that Giovanni wanted to avoid the '"everyman a Medici" style'.

22 Kent (1981), pp. 46–51, and p. 62 for the Bankers' Guild's permission which enabled Giovanni to use this income for the church façade.

23 It has even been suggested that the palace façade is a deliberate, incomplete 'ruin': Jarzombek (1989), pp. 175–7. A principal challenger to the accepted view, that Alberti designed the façade of the Palazzo Rucellai, is Mack (1974 and 1987). But see Saalman (1988), p. 89, who continues to argue that Alberti was involved with the design of the Palazzo Rucellai and Palazzo Piccolomini, Pienza.

24 Preyer (1976), p. 149; Hollingsworth (1994), pp. 59–60.

25 Davidsohn (1956–68), V, p. 401.

26 Translated from the transcription of De ingeneis, a manuscript discussed in Prager and Scaglia (1972), p. 202; Eng. trans. from Battisti (1981), p. 351.

27 Preyer (1976), p. 145.

28 Following the easing of a tax burden at the conclusion of thirty years of intermittent wars: see Rubinstein (1981), p. 4.

29 Hyman (1968), pp. 153–64.

30 On Alberti's adaptation of the traditional bifora, see Onians (1988), pp. 182–5. It is possible that pilasters were painted on the rendered walls of palaces (see Preyer, 1981, esp. pp. 202–3). Also, Brunelleschi probably designed pilasters for the upper storey of the loggia and façade of the Ospedale degli Innocenti, and giant pilasters in stone were begun on his Palazzo di Parte Guelfa but not completed: Battisti (1981), p. 54, fig. 35, and pp. 51–2. But even the Florentine Baptistery, which is composed in three storeys with pilasters at each level, differs from the pilaster arrangement of the Rucellai façade: its octagonal geometry in plan demanded robust construction, and heavy corner piers are countered by the lighter articulation of the

arcuated middle storey. Closer in imagery are the three-storey pilastered palaces in bas-relief in the *Fall of Jericho* panel by Lorenzo Ghiberti on the east door of the Baptistery (dated between 1425 and 1452), and the painted representations of this palace type in the later fifteenth century: in Ghirlandaio's much later frescoes in Santa Maria Novella, as well as the famous 'Ideal City' panels in Baltimore, Berlin and Urbino.

31 Preyer (1981), p. 196 and n. 2, and see n. 23 above.

32 Perosa (1981), p. 121; and Preyer (1981), p. 156: 'd'otto chase n'o fatto una, che tre ne respondevano nella via della Vingna e cinque di drieto'. This entry was made by Giovanni Rucellai in 1473, well after acquisition of land for the first building phase of his palace, and therefore represents an overview of the enterprise.

33 Preyer (1981), p. 166 and n. 3.

34 Preyer (1981), pp. 179–84 and 195, proposes a date of 1455; Mack (1974), pp. 517–29, however, proposes 1461 (retained in Mack, 1987). Saalman (1988), pp. 89–90, suggests that Alberti's involvement with Giovanni Rucellai began in 1457–8.

35 Battisti (1981), pp. 46–78.

36 Saalman (1966), p. 152; Preyer (1981), p. 166; and Onians (1988), pp. 136–46.

37 On 'bones and panelling', see Alberti (1988), p. 421. On the weakening of the wall with windows, see Alberti's earlier comments regarding a proposal for circular windows at the Tempio Malatestiano (pp. 59–61, above).

38 For this argument in more detail, see Wittkower (1973), pp. 33–7; Feuer-Tóth (1978); and Damisch (1979), pp. 18–25.

39 Onians (1988), pp. 182–3.

40 For further comparison of the arcading in these courtyards, see Preyer (1981), plates 13 and 15 for the Palazzo Rucellai, and Mack (1987), p. 67, for the Palazzo Piccolomini.

41 On the Pienza project, see Pius II (1984), II, pp. 1758–71; and Mack (1987). In Florence imposts are present in the columnar arcade of the Rucellai loggia, across from the palace façade, but it is uncertain to what extent this structure follows Alberti's original design for a smaller site, set forward of the present loggia (see my account of the Rucellai loggia, pp. 119–24, below). See also Onians (1988), pp. 185–9, for the column types employed by Rossellino for Pienza.

42 The Latin extract is from the parallel Latin–Italian text in Alberti (1966), II, p. 803.

43 Alberti then comments on the character of the pediment, which 'should not emulate the majesty of a temple in any way': Alberti (1988), IX, 4, p. 301.

44 Vitruvius (1960), V, 6.6: 'Let the columns above [. . .] be one fourth less in height than the columns below. [. . .] If the "scaena" is to have three stories, let [. . .] the columns at the top [be] one fourth less than the intermediate, and the architraves and coronae of these columns one fifth of the height as before'.

45 I am grateful to David Vila Domini and Jason Cornish for their researches into Alberti's use of ornament while working for the Alberti Group. Their drawings, illustrated here, greatly aided the development of the following discussion.

46 Onians (1988), pp. 183–5.

47 The built capitals are very similar to Alberti's preferred version, although their necking is longer and the abacus and echinus more compressed. Quite different, however, are the bases of the Rucellai pilasters which are shorter and much narrower than the Doric he describes. The first entablature has a smaller frieze than Alberti's Doric entablature, though the architrave and cornice relate quite closely to the corresponding parts of the taller Doric variant.

For the second-storey pilasters the taller version of the Corinthian column provides the closest fit vertically: the heights of the base and the capital are remarkably close. However, the pilasters are wider, and the Alberti entablature does not relate to what is built. The taller version of the Corinthian he describes also works well with the height of the third-storey pilaster and, again, the widths are much greater. The entablature arrangement is a closer fit than on the storey below. See Onians (1988), pp. 182–5.

48 An alternative reason for this corner rustication is that the façade ornament was to have been carried down the side street – perhaps if Giovanni had been able to purchase property opposite and so straighten out his property boundary. If this is so, it begs the question, if Alberti sanctioned the larger eight-bay façade on via della Vigna, did he also expect that a new principal entrance would be built around the corner, perhaps once additional property had been acquired? This would have had the advantage of creating a separate urban block for the palace, making it physically detached from its surroundings: an argument along these lines is presented in more detail by Saalman (1988). Had it been intended to reorient the Palazzo Rucellai, the existing doors along via della Vigna would have been used to connect the palace more directly to the piazza and loggia on one side; doors on the other side of the palace may have connected more positively with San Pancrazio which, curiously for an ensemble of this kind, is situated at the 'back' of the building. Rossellino connected the palace courtyard of the Palazzo Piccolomini with the piazza directly through a side door, and its twin door has never functioned as such, and abuts a well. His inclusion of a door as a non-functional motif in order to provide the side elevations with symmetry reinforces the notion that Rossellino was adapting an elevation conceived for another situation. See Mack (1987), who argues that the Pienza buildings pre-date those by Giovanni Rucellai, and that it was Rossellino who provided Alberti with inspiration for Palazzo Rucellai; see also n. 23 above.

49 Vitruvius (1960), VI, 2. 2–4, pp. 174–5.

50 Vitruvius (1960), III, 3. 11–13, pp. 84–6.

51 A series of books (known usually, after the title of the collected edition of his writings, as *Tutte l'opere*), which although influenced by late fifteenth-century practice in Rome, was written and mostly published during the sixteenth century: Serlio (1584 and 1996).

52 The notion that Alberti was compensating for 'perspectival distortion' at the Palazzo Rucellai was proposed by Vila Domini and especially by Jason Cornish, based on the Alberti Group's reconstruction after Alberti's description of the portico to a private palace.

53 Manetti (1976), pp. 57–60; Edgerton (1973), pp. 172–95; Parronchi (1964), pp. 226–95; Battisti (1981), pp. 102–13.

54 Battisti (1981), p. 103; for the Italian see Manetti (1976), pp. 57–9.

55 For a full account and illustrations of Brunelleschi's optical instrument, see Battisti (1981), pp. 102–13; and Kemp (1990).

56 These descriptions are found in the inventory of Lorenzo's possessions made after his death, and relate to the contents of the Palazzo Medici on via Larga: Florence, Archivio di Stato, *Archivio Mediceo avanti il Principato*, CCXV, fol. 11; cited in Battisti (1981), p. 357, n. 2.

57 Vasari (1973), II, p. 547.

58 Battisti (1981), p. 103: cited without a reference.

59 Engl. trans. from Pastore and Rosen (1984), p. 260.

60 In fact, there have been two principal arguments regarding the intended use of the panels. The most prevalent is that they were originally painted to be placed on *cassoni* (chests). Perspective scenes in *intarsia* are commonly used to decorate wooden panels in this way, and the Berlin panel is still attached to a chest, an argument supported by Clark (1951), p. 209: 'The picture [in Urbino] was originally the front of a chest. That in [Berlin] is still so placed, and the motif of architectural perspectives is usual in intarsiated chests'. Chastel (1961), p. 141, n. 7, and Sanpaolesi (1949), pp. 322–77, have supported this reasoning. Clearly, paintings are not as durable as inlaid timber and, when attached to furniture, would be very vulnerable to surface damage. Yet the paintings under scrutiny here were surely considered to be of considerable value: they are worked with skill and in great detail. Alternatively, it has been proposed that they were to be placed on *spalliere* (high-backed furniture) since the position of the single-point perspective in their compositions suggests that the panels were intended to be viewed with the eye on the same plane as the vanishing-point, which is consistently placed within the lower third of the composition, and not from above.

However, another suggestion is that they were not made to be placed on furniture, but were intended originally as preparations for stage sets reflecting the Tragic and Comic scenes of antiquity: Krautheimer (1969 and 1994). This notion would be worth investigating further, for it is possible that the positioning of the Berlin panel on a *cassone* was an afterthought (an idea that does not appear to have been entertained previously), perhaps in order that the panel could be made use of once its original purpose had passed, or been forgotten.

61 The five-bay width and vertical proportions of the palace depicted in this panel, and its lack of *bifore*, suggest it is a purer version of the Palazzo Rucellai façade. Similarly, the loggia in the painting is trabeated (with columns and beams), a system of support preferred by Alberti, while the Rucellai loggia is arcuated (with columns and arches).

62 This passage is derived from Alberti's *Navis* (now lost), the manuscript of which was known to Leonardo da Vinci. In his treatise Alberti describes one of the vessels as three squares long in plan, with a mast-height equal to the ship's length. This was reconstructed by the Alberti Group on computer and compared favourably with those ships painted on this panel by Nigel Hetherington of the Alberti Group, with help from a reconstruction in Bonino (1981).

63 The influence of Alberti on these panels has been commented on by various authors. For example, Clark (1951), pp. 230–31, referring to the 'Ideal City' panel in Urbino, wrote that 'the architecture [depicted in the panel] shows very clearly the influence of Alberti, and is almost like an illustration to his Book VII, chapter VI. The rounded temple in the centre is referred to in his Book VII, chapter XV'. More positively, Krautheimer (1994), p. 257, has concurred with the proposition by Morolli (1992), pp. 215–30, that Alberti may have contrived the Urbino panel himself; this essay by Krautheimer (1994) provides a useful summary of discussion on the panels to be mentioned here.

Among the other names often suggested as the author of this panel are those of Piero della Francesca and Luciano Laurana. Reber (1889), II, pp. 47–70, proposed Laurana, as Bernardo Baldi credits him with 'certain scenes [*alcune scene*], drawn and coloured in perspective, on which he put his name and other things in the Slav language'; see Baldi (1724), pp. 44–5. Some scholars have observed the letters 'VRANNA' in the upper corners of the panel, though these marks were invisible to Clark (1951), p. 209, who considered the Urbino panel to be 'far superior to the others both in tone, colouring and technique. It is painted in the blues, greys and whites peculiar to Piero, and the actual handling is closer to his best work'. Kimball (1927–8) remarked on architectural similarities between the amphitheatre at Pola, in Laurana's native Dalmatia, and buildings on an 'Ideal City' panel in Baltimore; see also Allason (1819). For a more complete biographical list containing suggestions for other possible painters of the Urbino panel, see Morolli (1992), pp. 227–8, notes 11–15.

64 Alberti (1972), p. 69.

65 Tiraboschi (1772–82), VI, pt 1, p. 322; and VII, pt 1, pp. 399–400, termed the device *camera ottica*: 'In the history of the preceding century I remarked that Leon Battista Alberti was the first inventor of what is commonly called the Optical Chamber (*Camera Ottica*). By that device, an object painted in fine detail and laid flat is made visible in its natural position by means of well placed crystals and magnified in such a way that it appears as though really before your eyes. Consequently, it is impossible, as some people claim, to ascribe to Porta the glory of this invention. [. . .] Of

course, the invention of the Camera Obscura is due to Porta. This device is a completely dark chamber. A single hole in the window is open, a convex lens being fitted to the whole' (as translated in Pastore and Rosen, 1984, p. 261). Tiraboschi introduced the idea of crystals and magnification seemingly without reference to Alberti's original text. As Pastore and Rosen (1984, pp. 261–2, n. 13) wrote: 'Before Tiraboschi, the terms *camera ottica* (optical chamber) and *camera obscura* were synonomous. For example, Francesco Algarotti (1712–64), the highly successful popularizer of Isaac Newton, regarded them as interchangeable'; see also Algarotti (1752), p. 47.

66 Porta (1558). In their more advanced state, from the sixteenth century onwards, the *camera obscura* took the form of chambers or boxes in which the original image is projected on to a wall or screen, often through a magnifying medium: crystals for the *ottica*; at least one lens and frequently mirrors for the *obscura*; see Hammond (1981), pp. 15–19. Brunelleschi used a mirror in his demonstration, though impressive results could still be produced without optical sophistication; see Battisti (1981), p. 110. Porta describes 'How in a chamber you may see hunting, battles of enemies, and other delusions – and animals that are really so, or made by art of wood or some other matter. You may frame little children in them, as we use to bring them in when comedies are acted; and you must counterfeit stags, boars, rhinoceros, elephants, lions and what other creatures you please'. Porta does not claim to have invented the *camera obscura*, but brought together the 'secrets' of this device for more general consumption, along with certain improvements which he claimed to be his own, especially the way that artificial light may be used instead of natural sunlight to illuminate the painted image, using torch light, to dramatic effect: 'In a tempestuous night the image of anything may be represented hanging in the middle of the chamber, that will terrify the beholders. Fit the image before the hole that you desire to make to seem hanging in the air in another chamber, that it is dark; let there be many torches lighted around about. In the middle of the dark chamber place a white sheet, or some solid thing, that may receive the image sent in; for the spectators that see not the sheet, will see the image hanging in the middle of the air, very clear, not without fear and terror, especially if the artificer be ingenious' (Porta, 1957, XVII, 7, p. 365).

The notion of projecting an image in this way is suggested by the second edition of Kircher (1671), p. 768, where a magic lantern is depicted. This is effectively a *camera obscura* in reverse. See also Pastore and Rosen (1984), p. 267.

67 Waterhouse (1901), p. 272: 'The instrument, judging from the description of it, seems to have been just the converse of the camera-pictures [of the Camera Obscura] being painted on some transparent basis and illuminated from behind, and viewed through an aperture in a dark box'. See also Pastore and Rosen (1984), p. 26 and n. 27.

This conforms to the description in Alberti's *Vita* which is 'closed' and observed only 'through a tiny aperture', yet which allowed night- and day-time images to be created with considerable success. The perspective in the landscapes described would be enhanced by the single-eye view and the isolation of the image itself. The effect of a starry night could be produced by puncturing a dark screen with an arrangement of constellations and illuminating this from behind with a fluctuating light source, which candles provide: this would cause the stars to twinkle realistically. The cenotaph to Sir Isaac Newton designed (but not built) by the French revolutionary architect Etienne-Louis Boullée (1728–99) would have been an enormous show box of sorts, though without the flexibility of Alberti's invention for changing scenes. The painter Thomas Gainsborough had a show box made for his own use (now in the Victoria and Albert Museum, London). See Hammond (1981), pp. 11–13, and Woodall (1996).

68 Alberti (1972), p. 89: 'things that are taken from Nature should be emended with the advice of a mirror'.

69 On the Quattrocento relationship between perspective and the surveying of buildings, and 'the principled interaction of apparent and true dimensions', see Kuhn (1990), esp. p. 118. and p. 121, fig. 2. See also Lefaivre (1997), pp. 144–5.

70 Vitruvius (1960), V, 6.

71 See Lyttleton-Sear (1977).

72 According to the *Mirabilia* it was thought, until the early fifteenth century, to be the seat of the seven sciences or a temple of the sun and moon: Stinger (1985), p. 67 and n. 194. But it had been built by Septimius Severus in AD 203 to greet visitors to Rome who entered from the via Appia; see Weiss (1969), pp. 33–4 and 61–2, where it is identified as the former 'palace' of Septimius Severus. In the thirteenth century it had been used as a fortress of the Orsini, and its columns and beams were cannibalised for buildings before it was finally demolished in 1588/9; see Greenhalgh (1989), pp. 105–6.

73 Rucellai (1960), p. 76, and p. 162, n. 12.

74 Weiss (1969), p. 62; Krautheimer (1980), p. 323, and fig. 258.

75 1 Kings 7: the fourth row mentioned in the second verse might relate to piled foundations. The arrangement of windows in a palace façade is accepted as a general rule by the end of the fifteenth century and extends to the interior arrangement of rooms as well. According to Francesco di Giorgio (1967), II, p. 412: 'a very general rule to be observed without exception [. . . is] that all empty spaces should be above empty spaces: voids above voids and filled-in spaces above filled-in, upright above upright, column above column, and that in general every support or its equivalent should be in a straight line directly on axis above its analogue'.

76 Krautheimer and Krautheimer-Hess (1982), plates 116 and 98, 100, 107 and 111a. I recall this familiar list here because a distinction has been drawn, suggesting that

Florentine painters' and sculptors' representations of palaces of this type were not generally followed for the decoration of Florentine palaces, the Palazzo Rucellai being the notable exception (i.e. Preyer's response to Forster, 1977, pp. 109–13). While this statement is uncontroversial, Preyer (1981), p. 181, n. 2, went on to state that the 'building in one of Fra Angelico's Vatican frescoes [also articulated by pilasters] is probably the artist's own invention, and does not necessarily reflect contemporary buildings'. Yet pilasters also appear on the palaces in Gaddi's Baroncelli frescoes, and later painted and built palaces were also ornamented in this way. It must be assumed therefore that they were not Fra Angelico's invention. The Palazzo Rucellai possibly influenced the late fifteenth-century urban backdrop in Domenico Ghirlandaio's fresco of the *Visitation* (from the *Life of St John the Baptist* in the Cappella Maggiore, Santa Maria Novella, Florence), though this too may be derived from a biblical source.

77 Hatfield (1970), p. 108: 'Herodis autem statio ad sancti Marci edem, in eo qui templo adjacet campo, hac erat arte constructa. Quadrangularem figuram in columnarum morem lignis contextam expresserant, cuius altitudo fere ad xv brachia protendebatur. Longitudo vero quadraginta fere brachiorum fuit. Duodecim autem habebat omnis latitudinis amplitudo'. Even when the route of the procession was later changed, and Herod's palace was relocated in Piazza San Marco, a temporary construction was built, *c.* 1469, 'in columnar style', 15 × 40 *braccia*, and built of wooden beams covered with tapestries and greenery.

78 Federico Gonzaga's new palace attached to the Palazzo Gonzaga in Mantua, the Nova Domus (built 1480–84), has two tiers of pilasters, each extending over two floors, and is not therefore as explicit a reference to Solomon's palace as the others listed here: see Burns (1981a), pp. 30–31. The patron is not known of the small palace in via del Governo Vecchio, Rome – the so-called Palazzo Turci, which is a mini-version of this façade type. On the Renaissance palazzo façade, see Burroughs (1993). As for drawings and paintings of the Palazzo Rucellai type, the architectural treatise (dated *c.*1460–64) of Filarete (see Filarete, 1965) provides examples, as do the famous 'Ideal City' paintings dated to the later fifteenth century; a Florentine example is cited in n. 76 above.

79 Work began in Pienza in 1460: Mack (1987), p. 40.

80 Quoted in Kent (1981), p. 62, n. 5, after Haines, 'Documenti intorno al Reliquiario per San Pancrazio', pp. 264, 266–7 (Kent does not supply a more complete reference).

81 Lamoureux (1979), p. 135.

82 Lamoureux (1979), Appx, p. 166, doc. 1; this letter is also quoted by Mack (1987), p. 40, who suggests that the pope may also have had access to Alberti's *De re aedificatoria*. The only mention by Pius of Alberti is in his commentaries, *c.* 1463, when he applauds his knowledge of antiquity, not his ability as an architect: 'Aquarum conservatoria plurima et ingentia insunt. Baptista Florentinus ex Albertorum familia, vir doctus

et antiquitatum solertissimus indagator, supra xxx inveniri tradidit, quae inter vepres rubosque latitant': Pius II (1984), II, p. 2232.

83 It was also about this time that Alberti designed San Sebastiano (among other works) for Ludovico Gonzaga: Alberti wrote to Ludovico Gonzaga in February 1460 stating that he had completed several designs, including the one of San Sebastiano, and it is reasonable to assume that these projects were under consideration for several months before hand (see p. 126 below).

84 The bay to the left of the central door of the Palazzo Piccolomini, on the main street (north façade), is 4190 mm wide (between the pilasters), that on the right is 4496 mm; see Tavernor (1985), p. 228, and n. 25, and the pull-out drawing at the end, entitled 'Palace Façade Profiles'. For a detailed survey of the palace, see also Stegmann and Geymüller (1924) and for the pope's description of its measures, see Pius II (1984), II, pp. 1758–71.

85 Inconsistencies or even errors in the design may have been forced on Rossellino by the speed at which the buildings were being constructed, or the meddling of others may have brought about unwanted compromises. He complained to Flavio Biondo that he had not been given a free hand during the construction of the palace. Specifically, Biondo records a conversation from September 1462 when the pope's agents 'had not allowed [Rossellino] to construct small portions from the beginning but had persuaded him to add them [later] to the finished work' (*'quas passi principio non fuerant ab eo fieri particulas, perfecto iam operi addendas evicerint'*): see Mack (1987), Appx I, pp. 166–9. This may mean that revetment was applied only when the walls of the Palazzo Piccolomini had been built to their full height – perhaps to safeguard against damage to finished stone during the rapid construction of adjacent buildings, and to prevent the building process from being delayed while quarried stone was being shaped and dressed.

86 See the Alberti Group photogrammetric surveys of both buildings.

87 A male foot of 277 mm fits a British-sized 9 to 9.5 shoe, and is one-sixteenth shorter than the antique Roman *pes* of 296 mm. On the use of the architect's own foot in history, see Lotz (1982) and Kidson (1990). A unit longer than Pius's *pes*, the *braccio*, was commonly used in Florence and Siena; there are two lengths of Sienese *braccia*, 377.6 mm and 600.3 mm. The official length for the Florentine *braccio* is the equivalent of 583.6 mm, while the average lengths of the unit of measure used for the two palazzo façades may be summarised as follows:

Palazzo Piccolomini	Pius's foot	277.4 mm
Palazzo Rucellai	*Braccio*	581.8 mm

I am grateful for a verbal communication by Jan Pieper who has found evidence that the buildings of Pienza were constructed using the contemporary Roman *braccio*, the measure used by Rossellino and his workforce of Roman labourers. However, as neither the Roman nor any other *braccio* appears to bear a relation in length to Pius's 'foot', I can only conclude that Pius was imposing his own preferred dimensions on Rossellino's design out of convenience or ignorance of the true measurements.

88 See the Alberti Group photogrammetric survey drawings for details.

89 Perosa (1981), p. 121; and Preyer (1981), p. 156: 'd'otto chase n'o fatto una, che tre ne respondevano nella via della Vingna e cinque di drieto'. See also Saalman (1988).

90 Preyer (1981), p. 183.

91 Preyer (1981), p. 214, doc. XIII and pp. 182–4.

92 Filarete (1965), I, p. 102, for the English translation (where the editor dates the entry between May 1461 and the end of 1462), and II, fol. 59r for the transcript that follows: 'nella città nostra oggidì un'altra maniera non s'usa ne' pubblici e privati casamenti; et che vero ne sia se none all'anticha tanto in edifici di chiese, tanto se vedete ch'e cittadini privati, facenno fare o casa o chiesa, tutti a quella usanza corrono; in tra gli altri una casa fatta in una contrada nuovamente la qual via si chiama la Vigna, tutta la facciata dinanzi composta di pietre lavorate et tutta fatta al modo antico'. Cf. Mack, who maintains that Rossellino was the architect of the Palazzo Rucellai façade and interior, and that the façade was built after the ensemble of buildings in Pienza and is to be dated 1465: see Mack (1974), pp. 517–29; (1982), pp. 611–12; and (1987), passim and see Saalman (1988).

93 There are two puzzling aspects about the façade which require further comment. The first concerns the capitals of the middle storey of the façade. Describing these (and starting from the left when facing the façade), Preyer (1981), p. 181, wrote that 'Capitals B1, 3, 4, 5 and 6 resemble one another in overall treatment; capital B2 has a different design, but is executed with the same vigour as the other five. Capitals B7 and B8 [of the extension], of the same type as B2, differ from it in handling'. But why should capital B2 be different from the other five 'original' capitals, yet the same type as those of the extension? Preyer continues by observing that 'between the consoles of the cornice, identical rosettes are repeated above the sixth and seventh bays whereas, previously, a number of types of flower were used'. If the cornice was designed for the five-bay façade originally, one would expect its consoles to be placed symmetrically to the axis of the five-bay façade. They are not: a fact illustrated most vividly by Sanpaolesi's own illustration of a reconstructed five-bay façade, verified in the Alberti Group's photogrammetric survey. The 'final' console above the sixth pilaster of the upper storey, C6, counting from the left, is positioned too far to the right on the existing façade, and is omitted from Sanpaolesi's reconstruction: Sanpaolesi (1963); and as reproduced in Borsi (1977), p. 52, fig. 31. Thus, Sanpaolesi shows the cornice commencing on the left with a console, and concluding on the right with a metope.

This last point, especially, would suggest that the document of 1458, where it is stated the façade is 'not yet [...] completed, at least in breadth', is referring to a five-bay wide façade which was perhaps no higher than the second storey when the extension was begun. It would be hazardous to assume too much from the 'deviant' capital, B2, as those above and below it do not differ significantly from their neighbours. For example, there are three different types of capital on the façade of Sant'Andrea: those on top of the giant pilasters are of two kinds, and the outer capitals differ from the inner ones. The third type are on the smaller pilasters framing the central portal. The various types are arranged symmetrically. If this 'logic' were to be applied to the different capital types of the middle storey of the Palazzo Rucellai, then the symmetrical axis of the façade would fall on those vertically aligned pilasters on the extreme right – A, B and C8 – such that a truly symmetrical façade would be fourteen bays and four doors wide! Perhaps the eighteenth-century supposition about the proposed width of the façade was calculated in this way?

94 Sanpaolesi (1963); and Preyer (1981), doc. XIII, pp. 214–15. Sanpaolesi tentatively concluded, before Preyer found the relevant documentary evidence for this purchase of 1458, that Alberti designed a five-bay façade that would exactly cover the street frontage of the palace before the seventh house was bought, and that bays six and seven represent an extension. Preyer's documents substantially support Sanpaolesi's thesis, and she has suggested some superficial evidence in the stonework to support this thesis. She observed that the capitals of bays six and seven are carved more simply, implying they were included at a later date; the sail emblems in bas-relief, below the third-storey windows, are in lower relief in bays six and seven; the rustication field in these final bays is arranged more haphazardly; and the mason's marks on fifty of the stones show that while the same mason worked on bays one–five and six–seven, there are certain marks which are exclusive to each section.

There are also problems about the form of the capitals and their placement. Alberti describes tiered porticoes 'as in a house' (VIII, 7, p. 273). Externally, theatres – such as the Colosseum and Theatre of Marcellus in Rome – display a hierarchical build-up of column types, and have Doric columns below and Ionic and Corinthian (or Composite) above. Yet, the three storeys of pilasters and entablatures on the façade of the Palazzo Rucellai do not appear to be arranged hierarchically. While the lower order pilasters have plain Doric-like capitals, the two storeys above are a form of Corinthian: those of the middle floor each have two ornate and finely carved leaves, while those above have five pronounced curling leaves which are plainer than those below; see also Onians (1988), pp. 182–5. On closer examination there are problems with this reading. Can the lower orders be Doric when similar capitals appear on the façade of Santa Maria Novella coupled with Corinthian columns, and when the entrance doors between them conform to his description of the Ionic portal?; see Heydenreich and Lotz (1974), p. 33, and Rykwert (1996), pp. 367–8. The *bifore* on the upper two floors also appear to contradict the status of their context. The central colonette and flanking two half-colonettes in the window jambs supporting the horizontal entablatures are Composite for the middle storey (the *piano nobile*) and plainer above, the latter being a columnar version of the pilaster capitals at ground floor.

The *bifore* on the upper two floors of the earlier Palazzo Medici have identical Corinthian colonettes on each floor. Also, they support arches directly, without the entablature employed as an intermediary element for the Palazzo Rucellai. The *bifore* of the Palazzo Piccolomini are a simpler, perhaps cruder, version of the Rucellai arrangement, as their entablatures lack any mouldings.

95   Preyer (1981), pp. 176–8.

96   It was purchased in 1654; see Preyer (1981), p. 183.

97   Sanpaolesi (1981), p. 232; and Preyer (1981), p. 223, doc. xxva, where an archivist wrote, *c.* 1722–34, that 'Giovanni di Paolo di Messer Paolo Rucellai built a palace from his house with the other houses from a design by the very famous Leon Battista Alberti. According to various traditions there were to be either eleven windows and three doors or fourteen windows and four doors'. I find it hard to believe that the main façade of the Palazzo Rucellai was ever meant to be eight bays wide, as this would have resulted in only two main doors on to the street; see Saalman (1988), esp. p. 85, fig. 4, for a different viewpoint. An odd number of doors, one or three, is more usual for a main façade, though an even number appears to have been acceptable for the sides, as at the Palazzo Piccolomini.

98   Kent (1981), p. 40.

99   Battisti (1981), pp. 42 and 110–13.

100 Fra Giovanni di Carlo wrote to Landino that 'opera L. B. Alberti celeberrimi architecti marmorea tabulato et monumentorum insigni vallo contenta': Mancini (1967), p. 461, n. 3. On Giovanni di Bertino's involvement at Santa Maria Novella, see Orlandi (1955), p. 307. Giovanni di Bertino is called by some sources Bertano, Bettino, Bertini and Bertoni; see Mancini (1967), p. 460, n. 2; and Morolli, Acidini Luchinat and Marchetti (1992), p. 43.

101 Vasari (1973), II, p. 541.

102 Again, in late 1459 or early 1460 Alberti designed several buildings for Ludovico Gonzaga in Mantua, and he declared that they were all ready at the same time (see p. 126, below).

103 Wittkower (1973), p. 45 (in editions post-1962 only).

104 Wittkower (1973), p. 43. For an elaboration of Wittkower's observations, see Lorenz (1976).

105 The aisles and nave of Santa Maria Novella are 11 and 22 Florentine *braccia* wide; those of the cathedral are just under 15.5 and 31 *braccia*: Weinberger (1941–2), pp. 78–9, and n. 2. Weinberger recorded Santa Maria Novella's central nave and aisle widths as 12.8 and

6.4 m., or 21.93 and 10.97 *braccia*, and the corresponding width dimensions of the cathedral as 18 and 9 m.

106 Smith (1994a), pp. 207–8.

107 Rubinstein (1967), pp. 64–73; Gombrich (1967), esp. p. 76.

108 Gombrich (1967), p. 79 and n. 55: 'Vedesi questo tempio di singulare belleza e in forma di fabrica antichissima al custome e al modo romano'.

109 Campbell (1984).

110 As observed by Wittkower (1973), p. 45.

111 Preyer (1981), pp. 198–201; Saalman (1988), p. 88; and Burroughs (1990), p. 41.

112 On the thirteenth-century capital types on the façade and inside Santa Maria Novella, see Onians (1988), pp. 119–23.

113 V. Borghigiani, *Cronaca analitica del Convento di S. Maria Novella*, quoted without a full reference in Dezzi Bardeschi (1970), pp. 11–13; Wittkower (1973).

114 Dezzi Bardeschi (1970), pp. 11–13; Wittkower (1973).

115 Wittkower (1973), p. 46, and figs 4 and 5; Tavernor (1994b).

116 See the Alberti Group photogrammetric survey drawings: such discrepancies are simple reminders of the difficulty of overlaying a new composition onto an existing, inaccurately built construction and do not detract from Alberti's objectives.

117 Dezzi Bardeschi (1970); drawings republished in Borsi (1977), pp. 66–9. The piers are 1.223 m. wide according to his survey (2.096 *braccia*) and the façade is 35.23 m. high and 35.01 m. wide (60.37 and 59.99 *braccia*). See also the Alberti Group photogrammetric survey drawing.

118 For a precise comparison of their respective metric dimensions, see the Alberti Group photogrammetric survey drawings.

119 Alberti's reasons for using this geometry, and the design process he may have employed, will be described below, pp. 116–19, in relation to the Rucellai sepulchre in San Pancrazio.

120 For an interpretation of the sun motif, see Dezzi Bardeschi (1974).

121 Wittkower (1973), p. 91; Tavernor (1991a), pp. 62–5.

122 See, for example, Wittkower (1973), plate 1a.

123 Pius II (1960), pp. 286–7; and Pius II (1984), p. 1760: 'in morem cyclopis oculum late patentem'.

124 A full account of the parish, the chapel and its contents is in Dezzi Bardeschi (1963 and 1966).

125 See Dezzi Bardeschi (1966), esp. diagrams, p. 7, for a summary of the interventions on this site. The chapel and the structure immediately to the east of it were built between 1400 and 1417.

126 Petrini (1981a), pp. 22–4.

127 Dezzi Bardeschi (1966), p. 2.

128 Thereafter it was used as a 'Lotteria', for the manufacture of tobacco, and as a 'Caserma Militare'. San Pancrazio has since become a museum and is entered from a piazzetta through two columns which were originally placed by Alberti between the chapel and the entrance atrium of the church. These were moved to

129 Vasari (1973), II, p. 543.

130 Dezzi Bardeschi (1966), p. 24.

131 Dezzi Bardeschi (1966), p. 25: Giuliano da Maiano and Desiderio da Settignano as well as Giovanni di Bertino have been suggested on stylistic grounds.

132 Richa (1755), III, pp. 308–26, esp. p. 314; as quoted in Dezzi Bardeschi (1966), p. 24. According to Richa, Giovanni Rucellai 'fece fare per gli ornamenti esteriori il disegno di L. B. Alberti architetto di gran nome il quale vi fabbricò una macchina alta braccia sette e mezza e larga cinque avendo praticata una strada di grande pericolo che fu di forare in più luoghi la volta del pavimento della chiesa'.

133 The chapel was endangered by a fire in 1921 which led to the barrel vault being rebuilt and strengthened. See Petrini (1981a).

134 Rucellai (1960), p. 136: '[Perciò] vi do avviso come ieri finii di fare la spedazione per Terra santa avendo colà inviati due legni a tutte mie spese con ingegnere et uomini acciò mi piglino il giusto disegno e misura del Santo Sepolcro di Nostro Signore Giesù Cristo, e che colla maggior celerità gli sarà possibile in qua ritornino e me le portino, perchè io possa adempire al mio desiderio di farne edificare uno a quella simiglianza qui nella nostra cappella, che nuovamente fo fabbricare nella chiesa di S. Pancrazio nostra cura, quale come voi sapete è buon porto, non mancandovi altro per renderla perfetta che il modello di così ricco e prezioso tesoro'.

135 Preyer (1981), p. 163, n. 3; Kent (1974).

136 Kent (1974), p. 344; Kent (1981), p. 59.

137 I am grateful to Professor Biddle of Oxford University for a photogrammetric survey of the Holy Sepulchre which is presented in outline here (fig. 89).

138 See Amico (1953), pp. 96–111. Restorers undoubtedly made changes to the original structure. Father Boniface of Ragusa, the Franciscan guardian of the Church of the Holy Sepulchre between 1551 and 1560, and 1562 and 1565, undertook its restoration in 1555, and as one pilgrim reported: 'for greater ornament, he added marble slabs and columns, a hemisphere or cupola, and perhaps the middle and eastern side of the vestibule so that it might receive more persons within itself': Peters (1985), pp. 503–4. It is likely Boniface replaced rather than 'added', as earlier illustrations and the Rucellai sepulchre would suggest. See also Amico (1953), pp. 4–5 and 36–7.

139 The 'vela gonfiata', or billowing sail, may be a sign of fortune, or perhaps records the naval victory reported by Paolo Rucellai over the Genoese at Rapallo. The 'mazzocchio', ornamented with three peacock feathers, made in white, red and green, may symbolise the nobility of the Medici. The three linked rings perhaps represent the indissoluble union between the Medici and Rucellai families. The Star of David and Solomon's Knot allude directly to biblical references and perhaps also imply Masonic symbolism. On problems relating to these emblems, and their dates, see Preyer (1981), pp. 198–201; and Saalman (1988), p. 88.

140 The ciborium is now visible immediately on entering the chapel from this side door, and it marks the entrance to the interior chamber of the sepulchre, drawing the eye up towards the vault above.

141 Two others panels were placed in the far corners of the chapel in 1617. They date from the fourteenth century, and were originally in the nave of San Pancrazio; see Petrini (1981), p. 23.

142 Kent (1981), p. 60. The chapel itself was not consecrated until 1485.

143 Kent (1981), p. 59; and see the argument regarding the precedents for Palazzo Rucellai above, pp. 91–4, esp. pp. 93–4.

144 After Richa (1755), III, pp. 315–16.

145 Smith (1994c), p. 456, cat. no. 44. The interior of this box-like object is entered by a key. Its external dimensions are 38.5 × 45.6 × 29 cm (h × l × w).

146 Rucellai (1960), pp. 120–22.

147 See, for example, Thomson (1993), pp. 159–60.

148 IOHANNES RUCELLARIUS/PAULI.F.UTINDE SALUTEM SUAM/PRECARETUR UNDE OMNIUM CUM/CHRISTO FACTA EST RESURECTIO/SACELLUM HOC/ADISTAR IHEROSOLIMITANI SEPUL/CHRI FACIVUNDUM CURAVIT/MCCCCLXVII.

149 See, for example, the brief account of Alberti's lettering on the Rucellai monuments in Florence, and the Tempio Malatestiano in Rimini, by Gray (1986), p. 133; and for a discussion of lettering on the Rucellai sepulchre specifically, see Sperling (1989).

150 'Nolite timere vos: scio enim quod *Jesum* qui *crucifixus* est, *quaeritis. Non est hic: surrexit* enim, sicut dixit, venite, & videre *locum, ubi positus* erat Dominus' (Matthew, 28: 5–6). This translates as 'Fear not ye: for I know that ye seek Jesus, which was crucified. He is not here: for he is risen, as he said. Come, see the place where the Lord lay'. Cf. St Luke, 'Quid *quaeritis* viventem cum mortuis? *Non est hic, sed surrexit*' (Luke, 24: 5–6): 'Why seek ye the living among the dead? He is not here, but is risen'.

151 Peters (1985), pp. 504–5: so it was reported by Father Boniface of Ragusa, who restored the Holy Sepulchre in 1555.

152 Consequently, the sequence of front–side–return–apse–return–side on the sepulchre has a regular number of units (i.e. letters and spaces between words), i.e.: 17–22–1–22–1–22.

153 Written between 1482 and 1492 the *Libellus* was based on Piero's earlier work, the *Trattato d'abaco*. It would appear that Piero wrote the *Libellus* in Italian, that it was translated into humanist Latin, and then retranslated into Italian by Pacioli without reference to his source. For this discussion, see Davis (1977), esp. Appx. I and II. The printed edition of Pacioli (1509) contained an appendix on architecture in three sections (on public, military and private buildings), and was composed for the stonemasons and aspiring architects of his native Borgo Sansepolchro, outside Arezzo. See also Onians (1988), pp. 216–24.

154 Geofroy Tory (1529) believed that Pacioli had stolen this alphabet from Leonardo da Vinci; quoted in Morison (1933), p. 20.

155 Pacioli (1509), pt 1, 8, fol. 29*v*.

156 Morison (1933), p. 21. In fact, Morison demonstrates that in the three alphabets by Felice Feliciano (1463), Damiano Moille (*c.* 1477) and Luca Pacioli each letter is constructed by first applying the geometry of a square. However, the circle does not appear to be used in the construction of the letters, and its only obvious rationale is to ensure that the square is geometrically true. That is, as a compass and straightedge were the graphical tools being employed, the square would have been constructed from the circle.

157 For similar descriptions of the other letters on the frieze, see Sperling (1989) and Tavernor (1994c); see also Mardersteig (1959), p. 297.

158 Gray (1986), pp. 122–50, and illustration 153, p. 127.

159 Petrucci (1993), p. 18.

160 According to Morison (1972), p. 269, the Republican sympathies of the leading political philosophers at that time are thought to have been relevant to the adoption of this style. However, it is not known to what extent Alberti or his contemporaries could distinguish one era of Roman lettering from another, and, in any case, Augustus was not a Republican. See, for example, Gray (1986), p. 136, n. 4. For the alphabets used on other buildings attributed to Alberti, see Petrucci (1994).

161 As Feliciano wrote: 'et questo e quanto per misura io Felice Felic. ha nelle antique caractere ritrovato per molte pietre marmoree cossi nel alma Roma quanto negli altri [siti?]'; quoted in Morison (1933), p. 16.

162 Feliciano (1960). It is likely that Alberti knew or knew of Feliciano. He was certainly a close friend of Andrea Mantegna in Mantua, whose similar fascination with ancient epigraphy is apparent from the inscriptions in his paintings. Feliciano went on to establish a printing press near Verona in 1476 and had considerable influence on the shape of letters to come. See Morison (1933); Mardersteig (1959), p. 303; Gray (1986), p. 140; and Chambers, Martineau and Signorini (1992), pp. 16–18.

163 Quoted in Morison (1933), pp. 21–3; Dürer (1525). On the proportions of the alphabet used for the *Hypnerotomachia* (1499), see Lefaivre (1997), p. 13 and n. 28.

164 Gray (1986), p. 147; see also Cresci (1971).

165 See Preyer (1977), p. 196, n. 1.

166 Hyman (1968), p. 173; Hyman (1975), pp. 105 and 108.

167 Kent (1972), pp. 397 and 400–01.

168 Goldthwaite (1968), p. 264.

169 Brucker (1969), pp. 264–5.

170 Kent (1972), p. 400 and n. 24; p. 401 and notes 31–4.

171 'Gio. di Paolo l'anno 1450 murò il palazzo nella via della Vigna e la loggia: disegno di Leon Battista Alberti': Dezzi Bardeschi (1966), p. 41, n. 54.

172 Vasari (1973), II, pp. 542–3; Engl. trans. from Vasari (1965), p. 211: 'For Cosimo (sic) Rucellai, Alberti designed the palace which was being built in the street called La Vigna and also the loggia which is opposite the palace. In this loggia he turned the arches over the closely spaced columns in the façade and also over the corbels, in order both to have a series of arches on the outside and to follow the same pattern internally. He had to make projections at the inside corners because he had put a space at each corner between the arches. When he came to vault the interior he was unable to use a semicircular barrel vault, which would have looked awkward and mean, and so he resolved to throw small arches across from corner to corner. Here he showed a lack of judgement and design, demonstrating very clearly that theoretical knowledge must be accompanied by experience: no one can develop perfect judgement unless his learning is tempered by practical application'.

173 Mancini (1967), pp. 9, 109–10; as quoted in Kent (1972), p. 401.

174 Ludovico Gonzaga expressed his desire to discuss Alberti's proposals not only for the loggia but for San Sebastiano, San Lorenzo and a statue of Virgil; for San Sebastiano see chapter VIII below.

175 This is the line of reasoning followed by Klotz (1969), pp. 93–103; see also Preyer (1977), p. 192.

176 The lower part of the façade of Santa Maria Novella also combines columns and arches with compressed imposts, though this probably precedes Alberti's intervention there (see p. 103 above). Also, here it is an ornament that has no structural role, being only surface decoration to tie the overall design of the pre-existing family tombs and ornament at the base into his new schema.

177 This argument was first put forward by Preyer (1977), and what follows deviates from her line of reasoning only in detail. Vasari (1973), II, pp. 542–3; (1965), pp. 211–12, was also to confuse the extent of Alberti's role in modifying the tribune of the Santissima Annunziata because of inadequate records about demolition and rebuilding there.

178 Preyer (1977), p. 183, doc. 2a: donation dated 29 April 1456. It would appear that Ugolino's shop and house was on the corner at the junction of via della Vigna and via del Purgatorio; see Preyer (1977), p. 188, and p. 184, doc. 2b. Ugolino was Giovanni's father's second cousin, i.e. a second cousin once removed.

179 Alterations to the existing structure required his permission while he lived, as he retained his home above the shop, and this needed safeguarding.

180 Preyer (1977), p. 184, docs 2b and 3, and her commentary, pp. 187–91.

181 An argument along these lines was first presented by Sanpaolesi (1963), pp. 61–6.

182 Preyer (1977), p. 188.

183 See n. 6 above.

184 Dezzi Bardeschi (1966), p. 19; Preyer (1977), p. 187, doc. 9. Cf. Preyer (1981), p. 163, n. 3, where the description of Bernardo's marriage festivities is thought to have been 'inflated'.

185 Preyer (1977), p. 194, and notes 24–31. Preyer's source

is Frey (1892), p. 47, though she is sceptical about Billi's attribution of the palazzo façade to Rossellino.

186 Cf. Preyer (1977), p. 194, and notes 30–31. Guidotti was employed by Manetti and Giovanni Gaiole to help complete San Lorenzo and Santo Spirito by Brunelleschi: see Gaye (1839), I, p. 168; quoted by Borsi (1977), p. 56.

187 Preyer (1977), p. 193, suggests that its source was derived from the interior details of the crossing at San Lorenzo, which 'has the same square piers with engaged columns starting the arcades, and where the architraves and arches are articulated with thick fascie. Although many differences can be found . . .'.

188 On imitation in Florence at this time, see Goldthwaite (1980), pp. 381–3; and Rykwert (1982), pp. 68–81.

189 Alberti may have made an early design for the villa at Poggio a Caiano; see Passerini (1861), p. 120; and Borsi (1977), p. 49 and n. 20.

190 Preyer (1972), pp. 194–5.

191 Piero's painting is in the Galleria Nazionale delle Marche, Urbino. See Lavin (1972), pp. 34–8, where it is argued that there are detailed similarities between the columns in the painting and those of the Rucellai Chapel.

192 See Preyer (1981), plate 5.

193 On the death of Ugolino's wife Nanna, the house was inherited by Albizzo d'Ugolino di messer Albizzo, Vanni and Niccolo di Paolo di Vanni, and Piero di Cardinale Rucellai. Preyer (1977), p. 188.

194 See the plan drawing by Preyer (1977), p. 186, for alternative suggestions.

VIII   MANTUA AND FLORENCE

1   For a general introduction to the Gonzaga family, see Chambers (1981), pp. xvii–xxiii; and Hollingsworth (1994), pp. 210–23.

2   Jones (1974), p. 124; and Chambers (1981), pp. xvii–xxiii.

3   Jones (1974), p. 124.

4   Jones (1974), p. 129.

5   The religious and commercial importance of the Blood of Christ to the city of Mantua is outlined on p. 143, below.

6   Pius II (1984), I, pp. 414–15.

7   Alberti (1972), p. 36.

8   Pius II (1984), I, pp. 426–9.

9   Pius II (1984), I, pp. 412–13.

10 Pius II (1984), I, pp. 420–21.

11 I am grateful to Neil Leach for this reference and his translation from Pius II (1968), p. 189: 'Et tu Mantua exaltaberis, ita Deo placitum, nec falli numina possunt. Vergilius Mantuanus Aeneam Troianum cecinit. Aeneas Senensis Virgilii patriam ditavit'.

12 For a general discussion of these projects, see Forster (1994), pp. 162–77; and on the renovation of the city, Carpeggiani (1994), pp. 178–85; and Calzona (1994b), esp. pp. 258–60, where it is suggested that work in the

city, and in the vicinity of San Sebastiano, began in 1458, once the pope had decided on Mantua as the venue for the Council.

13 'E [i] modoni de Santo Sebastiano, Sancto Laurentia, la logia, Et V[er]gil[io] sono fatti, credo non vi despiaceranno': Calzona (1994a), p. 142, doc. 3.

14 Forster (1994), p. 172.

15 The idea to erect a statue to Virgil was promoted again around 1499 by Isabella d'Este, and Mantegna's studio produced a design now in the Louvre (Cabinet des Dessins, R. F. 439): Chambers and Martineau (1981), pp. 152–3, cat. no. 92.

16 Amadei (1955), I, p. 119: 'Nota che lano 1460 fo principiato la gexia de San Sebastiano in di prade de Redevallo, la qual gexia la fece chomenzare lo marchexo mes. Lodovigo per uno insonio chel se insonioe una note et fo principiata tanto i freza [fretta] che fo tolto predij e giaronij e chacina che era stato chondute a la porta de la Pradela per livrare [terminare] la rocheta de quela porta'; as transcribed by Vasic Vatovec (1979), pp. 83–4, n. 1. see also Schivenoglia (1857), II, p. 119; and Calzona (1994b), pp. 258–9.

17 Donesmondi (1616), II, p. 178; see also Davari (1975), p. 81.

18 Calzona (1979), p. 218, doc. 39, where it is recorded that in 1488 San Sebastiano had been built as a plague church: 'per devotione al tempo della peste'.

19 The various documents relating to the history of San Sebastiano are transcribed in Calzona (1979), Lamoureux (1979) and Vasic Vatovec (1979). These researchers were working independently from one another, and their conclusions turned out to be quite disparate. For the most up-to-date and detailed account of the building history of San Sebastiano, see Calzona (1994a).

20 The three drawings are attributed to Bastiano alias Aristotile da Sangallo (Lille, Palais des Beaux-Arts, Fonds Wicar, fol. 840), on whom see Millon and Lampugnani (1994), pp. 511–13, with further drawings; Oreste Vannocci Biringucci (Siena, Biblioteca Comunale, s.IV, I, fol. 140), on whom see Lotz (1977), p. 183; and Antonio Labacco (Florence, Gabinetto dei Disegni, Uffizi, 1779A). See Lamoureux (1979), pp. 241–2, for illustrations of each.

21 On the work of Labacco, see Smith (1994b) and Benedetti (1994).

22 Wittkower (1973), p. 51, attributed its design to Pelligrino Ardizzoni who 'completed' the building work after 1499.

23 Schiavi (1932).

24 The church was consecrated in 1529 and restored in 1600. In 1706 the crypt was used as a military storeroom. After 1848 the church became a military storehouse for hay, and the structure deteriorated further. In 1884 the main vault was dismantled for safety reasons; the façade fresco (attributed to the school of Mantegna) was removed, as were the marble panels (cantoria), which acted as balustrades to the three main doors on the façade. A wooden balcony, supported on cast-iron columns, was constructed on entry to the church

25 proper to provide more storage space. See Donesmondi (1616), p. 28; and Gionta (1741), p. 294.

25 The monastery became a school in 1783 and a military prison in 1807; what remains is now a military barracks. See Volta (1807), v, p. 282; and Schiavi (1932), p. 11.

26 See n. 19 above.

27 Wittkower (1973), p. 49. Lamoureux (1979), pp. 54–5, concluded that the portico was only half complete and the vaulting to the central space only a third covered, with no roof protection. See also Burns (1981b), p. 125.

28 Calzona (1979), pp. 74–5, 79 and 122; an interpretation maintained in Calzona (1994a). See also Tavernor (1985), pp. 121–39 and the discussion below, where Calzona's reasoning is followed except for his belief that the crypt was an afterthought that had become an integral part of the project only after three months of construction.

29 Cf. Lamoureux (1979), Appx I, pp. 166–216; and Calzona (1979), pp. 218–49, docs 40–121; for a list of all the relevant documents (author, publication and page references) see also Calzona (1994a), pp. 141–204. Lamoureux and Calzona sometimes date the same document differently, while Vasic Vatovec (1979) offers different transcriptions.

30 'San Bastiano è chavato e fondamenti': Calzona (1994a), p. 143, doc. 6.

31 'sopra a la pelle della tera' (15 May 1460): Calzona (1994a), p. 146, doc. 10.

32 'nella testa dello porticho' (27 May 1460): Calzona (1994a), p. 147, doc. 13.

33 See the letters of 18 August 1460 and 21 May 1461; Calzona (1994a), pp. 148–53, docs 16–23. It is possible that San Sebastiano and the nearby Porta Pusterla shared the resources of just one conveniently placed materials depot.

34 27 December 1462. Calzona (1979), p. 74 and n. 21, dates the letter 27 September 1463; in Calzona (1994a), p. 161, doc. 40, however, it is undated and inserted between letters dated early September and October 1463. In the letter Fancelli refers to the date of 27 December 1463, but Calzona has transcribed the month as September. Professor Giovanni Orlandi (whose transcription of the document is given in n. 43 below) agreed with the conventional reading of 27 December 1463; see also Vasic Vatovec (1979), p. 91, where it is dated 27 December 1463. In fact, this means, after Lamoureux (and Brown, 1972, p. 163 and p. 158, n. 8), that its true date is 27 December 1462, as the Mantuan calendar changed on 25 December.

35 27 August 1463: 'Abiamo atexo a rifar imuri cherano guasta cioe le scorze qualli a bisogniato disfar da tera insu una gran parte e atendo a menar su una parte dela chiexa damezo inanzi questo fo per chomesion di mess. batista'.

36 Mazzoldi (1961), p. 34; Schivenoglia (1857), p. 154; Lamoureux (1979), p. 42 and n. 30. By November 1463 most of the 26,000 inhabitants had fled because of the plague; and only 2890 remained.

37 Morselli and Corti (1982), pp. 55–62.

38 It is possible that the walls of the tribunes were thickened at this time, which caused their depth to be reduced from 12 to 11 braccia. Otherwise, the thickening may have occurred at a much later date, when the vaults to the apses began to sag (see the Alberti Group photogrammetric survey drawing for evidence of this). Presumably this work was done in 1499 when Pelligrinio Ardizzoni was contracted to build the central groin vault (croceria), or in 1488 when the church was dilapidated and in danger of falling into ruin.

39 See Calzona (1979), pp. 73–8 and p. 91, n. 19; and Calzona (1994a), p. 161, doc. 40. In the letter of 27 December 1462, Fancelli reported: 'Abiamo levato tuto el porticho una pontata ella meta desso due, cioe se principiato le volti per lo simile tuta la sinistra parte alintrare del tempio; se principiato le volti quela parte che si truova ne primi termini sie un quinto o meno. Messma batista a gra volonta che si alzi tuto allpavimento. Ami dito piu volte sia buono far provigion di priete.' Thus, the portico had been brought up to the height of one lift of scaffolding (about 1.5 m. from the evidence of the holes in the wall; see the Alberti Group photogrammetric survey drawing).

40 Amadei (1955), pp. 279–80. In 1488 the pope 'concedette molte indulgenze alli fedeli i quali nelli venerdi del mese di marzo andarebbeno a far orazione in detto sotterraneo'.

41 Lamoureux (1979), pp. 32–5; Calzona (1979), p. 116.

42 Borsi suggested they may be the piers to the doors: Borsi (1977), pp. 209–10. The term 'pillastri' is sufficiently imprecise, and they are interpreted as referring to the pilasters on the façade ten years later, on 14 October 1470: cf. Wittkower (1973), p. 49, n. 2; Lamoureux (1979), pp. 44–5; and Tavernor (1985), p. 127. See also Calzona (1979), pp. 83, 121–2, and Calzona (1994a), where it is argued instead that the reference is to the façade pilasters of the original design by Alberti, which had no crypt, and that the subsequent raising of the façade after the first three months of building work had made adjustments necessary.

43 Lamoureux (1979), p. 36. Calzona (1979), pp. 74–5, complicated the issue further by insisting that only one vault was under discussion; see also Calzona (1994a), p. 161, doc. 40. I am grateful to Professor Giovanni Orlandi who helped me to transcribe the relevant document of 27 December 1462, from a photocopy of the original, as follows: 'Illustrissime p. et ex.me d.dne mi singularissime et.r. Perche ieriastanote e piouto due piove asai grandi perlle quali non ho posuto con 50 stuore coprir per modo le volti di san bastiano che quele chessi aprovarono essere ariciate non sino chaduto in parte lariciatura e trabatute dalaqua. Messma Batista ma chon vexo chio facia provigion per coprire di chopi quelo poso far e sollo davixar la V.I.S. per choprire quello che per fino aora innovata bisonera anchora miara vinti di chopi [coppi]. Abiamo levato tuto el portico una pontata ella meta desso due, cioe se principiato le volti per lo simile tuta la sinistra parte alintrare del tempio; se principiato le volti quela parte

che si trouva ne primi termini sie un quinto o meno. Messma batista a gran volonta che si alzi tuto allpavimento. Ami dito piu volta sia buono far provigion di priete. A mio giuditio stimo che 36 miara senavexe sodisfarra a pieno per alzare intorno al pavimento la spexa fata da venere pasato principiando el sabato per fino a tuto anquo venere adi 27 decembre 1463 [1462 by modern reckoning, see n. 34, above] sie questa che in questa ligata monte lire 170 soldi 9 p. 6 albertino mi dice non aver ordine alquno dalla I.S.V. alla qualle sempre mi rachomando Manta. V.F.S. Luca tagliaprieta' (Archivio di Stato di Mantova, AG, F.II.8, busta 2398, lettera n. 606).

Braghirolli (1869), p. 11, interpreted 'per alzare intorno al pavimento' to mean that the pavement/floor was to be raised, believing Fancelli wrote 'el pavimento', i.e. the definite article. Mancini (1967), pp. 393–4, followed Braghirolli's transcription and argued that the portico was to be raised to a height not foreseen originally. Calzona, Lamoureux and Vasic Vatovec correctly transcribed it as a preposition (though they disagreed on its interpretation and the document's date, and there are discrepancies too in spelling). Calzona (1979), pp. 72–8 and doc. 58, suggested this passage referred to an additional heightening of walls just beneath the proposed dome, and the much larger side chapels were the leaking ones. Lamoureux (1979), pp. 39–41 and doc. XIX, and Vasic Vatovec (1979), p. 78 and doc. p. 91, believed that the entire crypt level was now complete, and the crypt vaults were those found to be leaking.

44 There are sets of niches in the small apsidal bays, within the crypt, but there is no record of their intended use. Certainly they are too small for sepulchres, and there is no indication of any kind that relics were deposited in this area. The church inventory made on 13 July 1783 uses the same term (*sotterraneo*) for the space as had been used in 1488: 'Il sotterraneo anzidetto diviso in varie arcate, e volti di coto sostenuto da piloni di mattoni, in altro tempo ha servito ad uso di Chiesa, ma presentemente non e alcun uso, e non vi si trovano che le mense di coto di tre altari, che ivi esistevano. Le finestre sono munite di serrata, e la porta, che introduce in deto soterraneo resta chiuso da spadola di ferro con chiave, e chiusata'; see Calzona (1994a), p. 24.

45 My translation of Labacco's notation reads as follows: 'At Mantua, in the hand of Messer Battista Alberti. The dome is 34 *braccia* wide (that is, from where it ends and begins). The vault over the chapels $56\frac{2}{3}$ *braccia*, and the three apses 8 *braccia* wide, $13\frac{1}{3}$ *braccia* high. The side room[s] in front [i.e. the chapels preceding the apses] 20 *braccia* wide, $33\frac{1}{3}$ *braccia* high. The middle entrance $4\frac{4}{5}$ *braccia*, 8 *braccia* high. The portico is 10 *braccia* wide and $16\frac{2}{3}$ high ... [what then follows is unclear, but mentions a cornice and frieze which is placed above the main door]: cf. Lamoureux (1979), pp. 13–15.

46 This relationship between the design for the ground floor, noted by Labacco, and the existing building, was first described by Lamoureux (1979), pp. 47–9.

47 Additional evidence that the floor was to have been lower than at present is implied by Gianpietro de

Figino's concern, expressed in his letter two months after the foundations were dug, that a height just above ground level (i.e. up to the ground-floor level of the church) should be reached quickly and accurately. For example, a parallel may be drawn with Sant'Andrea where, during the early stages of construction, Ludovico Gonzaga instructed Fancelli to raise the walls to a height of 3 *braccia*, in order 'se vedesse molto bene come dovesse andare' (17 September 1472): 3 *braccia* is equivalent to a height of about 1.4 m., which coincides with the present floor of Sant'Andrea above ground level. This height of 3 *braccia* is also the approximate distance between San Sebastiano's current crypt floor – presumably the original ground level of the site (it would have made no sense to go lower if the ground was waterlogged) – and the datum used by Labacco to describe all the height dimensions. It is likely, therefore, that Figino was concerned to reach the ground floor of the church in the first two months, which would explain why he was already tackling the problem of the stairs 'nello testa dello porticho', and the doors 'allantiqa' (27 May 1460) through which the interior of the church was to be entered.

48 Lamoureux (1979), pp. 32–5; Calzona (1979), p. 116.

49 Calzona (1994a), p. 187 and doc. 107, dated 14 October 1470. Wittkower (1973), p. 49 and n. 2, argued that: '"Minuire" can mean either "reduce in size" or "reduce in numbers", but only the latter makes sense in our context'. This double interpretation has been generally disputed by scholars since Wittkower, and it is recognised that 'reduce in size' is the most likely meaning of 'minuire'. See, for example, Borsi (1977), pp. 209–10; and n. 42, above. My suggestion is that the piers had to be reduced in width so that the arches could be built into them. Ultimately, the result of this intervention was actually to increase the thickness of the piers.

50 Lamoureux (1979), p. 66, relates the impression the crypt had on visitors: 'They have remarked on its large size and "strange magnificence", as well as the great expense that must have been involved in its construction'. The allusion to 'great expense' is almost enough in itself to confirm that the crypt was not part of Alberti's preferred design: one of his fundamental tenets was for economy of structure. Consider his proud boast to Ludovico Gonzaga concerning his Sant'Andrea design, discussed on p. 159 below, that 'it will cost much less' than a design by another architect. Consider also Lamoureux's later comment (1979, p. 161): 'Alberti's is an architecture for effect [...] the heavy piers of the crypt, for example, were hardly needed to support the floor above, but were necessary to provide the effect or quality of a crypt oratory as Alberti conceived it.' Alberti describes spaces for 'oratory' quite differently: cf. his account of the sacerdotal curia, which is considerably taller than the crypt of San Sebastiano (Alberti, 1988, VIII, 9, pp. 282–7). Also, the piers were necessary to support the floor and the many worshippers in the church above, and it is impossible to increase the intervals between the piers without increasing the

size of the vaults, which would mean increasing the height of the crypt.

51   See Lamoureux (1979), illustrations 93–103 for the Tor de' Schiavi, and also 72–3 for Pirro Ligorio's restorations of the tombs of the Calventii and Cercenii.

52   Consequently, the chapels are not now as deep as Labacco indicated they should have been. According to Labacco the chapels on the plan of San Sebastiano he drew were to be 12 *braccia* deep by 20 *braccia* wide (through the addition of 6 + 8 + 6 *braccia*). While the building itself is close to these width dimensions, the chapels are only 11 *braccia* deep, and the corners of the main space appear much thicker than on any of the three sixteenth-century plans; see Volpi Ghirardini (1994b), p. 244, table 3. It is known that on 24 January 1463 Giovanni di Arezzo began repair work to the walls and corners of the structure: 'Alopera de Santo Sebastiano comenzo lunedi a repezar quelli muri e quelli cantoni che si trovano essere guasti'; and on 27 August that year Fancelli reported that 'Abiamo atexo a rifar imuri cherano guasta cioe le scorze qualli a bisogniato disfar da tera insu una gran parte e atendo a menar su una parte dela chiexa damezo inanzi questo fo per chomesion di mess batista'. The 'scorze' are presumably the outer skins of wall which were already built, and which may have been thickened to provide additional stability, especially to the rain-damaged chapel vaults which now show signs of sagging. It is worth noting that in both these letters Alberti is mentioned, so it must be assumed he was fully aware of the repairs and possible changes taking place.

53   Calzona (1979), pp. 73–5; see also his n. 19, where the work of Giovanni Antonio d'Arezzo for the Gonzaga is listed.

54   27 July 1463: 'perche prima procedessimo piu altra a questa nostra fabrica de S. Sebastiano voressemo pur intender bene il parere vostro'. A further extract from this letter is discussed in n. 81 below.

55   13 October 1464: 'per veder con lochio quanto e facto che non credemo vi debia dispiacer'.

56   Alberti was in Mantua between September and October 1465. See Lamoureux (1979), pp. 43–4; Calzona (1979), pp. 81–2; Calzona (1994a), p. 71; and Carra (1961), p. 3. Ludovico suggests sending Luca, 'our engineer', to meet with Alberti.

57   Curiously, the wording resembles the form of Labacco's notation: 'la cornice che va alaporta sopra el cardinale' (see fig. 95). The last progress report for four years is dated 12 December 1466. Subsequent documents relate to the transfer of materials, and on 14 March 1468 it is reported that 'Vollevono esser per Sanctto Sebastiano quella li po mandar a tore'.

58   On the missive from Rome see Calzona (1994a), pp. 74–5.

59   Calzona (1994a), pp. 74–5.

60   20/21 October 1470: 'quelli misure et modi di lavore'. The expression 'modi di lavore' may mean 'working details' or 'templates'.

61   Morselli and Corti (1982), pp. 55–62.

62   At Sant'Andrea, for example, or in preparation for the Nova Domus begun in the summer of 1480; see Vasic Vatovec (1979), p. 83.

63   25 May 1479: 'In questa sera abiamo tirato sù tute due le chornici grandi del porticho di Santo Sebastiano'. It is unclear what Fancelli means by this. The only stone on the façade is around the doors, and the main cornice on the façade is in terracotta; there is a stone cornice inside the portico, at the springing of the internal vault, but this is not particularly large.

64   Alberti (1988), III, 7, p. 71, refers to these protruding bricks as 'claws'.

65   Lamoureux (1979), pp. 55–6. Ardizzoni was contracted by the Lateran canons who received the church into their care on 22 September 1488. The church was then in a poor state of repair. On 12 June 1499 Ardizzoni was instructed to repair and rebuild walls and the *croceria*. For a more detailed and freer description of the same, see Calzona (1979), pp. 50–52; see also Calzona (1994a), p. 86.

66   As illustrated in Calzona (1979), figs 76–82.

67   A circular stair is still to be found behind the portico, which connects the upper-floor level with the room in the portico; a connecting gallery was to be built for the Lateran canons adjacent.

68   Wittkower (1973), p. 53 and plate 17c.

69   I have not been able to find any documentary evidence that this upper room once contained relics of St Sebastian, as proposed by Saalman (1985), an interpretation followed by Jarzombek (1989), p. 181; see also Tavernor (1991b), pp. 311–13.

70   An early photograph, pre-dating Schiavi's restoration, suggests that the 'chapel' wall adjacent to the portico was in fact still open to the upper room, and a balcony had been built within this arm of the cross: see Calzona (1994a), fig. 115. The balcony is also visible in an engraving of San Sebastiano in Seroux d'Agincourt (1823–9): see fig. 113 here.

71   Although they resemble in outline those designed by Fancelli elsewhere in Mantua (on the façade of the Domus Nova, and the pilasters supporting the large vaults of the main side chapels in the interior of the nave of Sant'Andrea), they could perhaps be copies 'after Fancelli' by Ardizzoni.

72   Wittkower (1973), pp. 48–51, does not suggest that Ardizzoni completed the façade, but only its 'supplementary' details. He attributes the staircase on the left, the open arcades of the substructure, and the heavy frame of the classical door to Ardizzoni, finished 'to the best of his poor ability'. Ardizzoni had been supervising street paving in Mantua since 1497. He is thought to be a kinsman, perhaps son, of the engraver Simone Ardizzoni da Reggio whom Mantegna had beaten up in the streets of Mantua for alleged plagiarism some years earlier; see Martineau (1992), pp. 48–51, 58–9.

73   The stone ornament around the central door has been altered, presumably by Schiavi in the 1920s. Inside the porch the details are badly worn, while outside they are much crisper.

74 For reconstructions of the painted render on the façades of San Sebastiano and Sant'Andrea, see Soggia and Zuccoli (1994).

75 The proposal by Paolo Pozzo to transform the convent into a 'Collegio per l'Educazione dei Nobili' in 1783 is published in Calzona (1979), plates 76–82; see esp. plate 76 for the upper-floor plan and subdivision of this space.

76 It is unlikely that Labacco is indicating a thermal window here, because an opening of this shape and size in this position would be obscured by the pediment beneath.

77 'perchè lo ha molto caro e spesso lo legge': Martelli (1965), pp. 191–2; and Morselli and Corti (1982), p. 29.

78 Lorenzo's 'fervour', in the context of a letter dated 11 September 1485, is discussed by Martelli (1965), pp. 191–2.

79 Reumont (1874), p. 418:'A di 1 agosto 1485, prega Luca Fancelli (Mro Luca da Settignano) a Mantova di spedirgli il modello della chiesa di S. Sebastiano di quella città'.

80 Giuliano da Sangallo had used his patron's powerful influence to obtain information in this format for other celebrated buildings. These included detailed drawings of the Palazzo Ducale, Urbino, which he had visited in 1481: Reumont (1883), II, p. 148; see also Goldthwaite (1980), p. 95. The Florentine Baccio Pontelli was asked to send Lorenzo detailed plans of the building including its measurements and decoration.

81 For Alberti's *modello* see his letter of 27 July 1463: Calzona (1979), pp. 223–4, doc. 52. Ludovico thanked Alberti on 28 July 1463 (Calzona, 1994b, p. 158, doc. 33) 'Havemo visto quanto per la vostra ce haveti significato del esser vostro a Firenze e de quello modello haveti visto che ne stato di piacer assai e del scriver vostro ve ringratiamo grandemente'. Baldini (1989) and Calzona (1994b) have argued that a letter from Luca Fancelli to Ludovico Gonzaga mentioning a 'modelo' (first published by Vasic Vatovec, 1979, p. 88) is linked to the design and building of San Sebastiano. It is likely that 'el tempio', which Fancelli mentions later (in a postscript written on the reverse of the letter, as discovered by Calzona, 1994a, pp. 142–3, doc. 5), is a reference to San Sebastiano; he was, however, involved with several other projects for the Gonzaga at this time, in and around Mantua, and this letter may be referring to any of them. Indeed, as the letter does not mention San Sebastiano or Alberti by name, and is undated, to construct an elaborate argument around the possibility that it relates to the model of San Sebastiano is hazardous in the extreme. Nor does the hypothesis of Baldini and Calzona answer the following: if Labacco recorded Alberti's preferred design for San Sebastiano, why, on the discovery of problems with the foundations, did Alberti not simply retain the main proportions of the original design but set them higher, on top of the new crypt? This would have been easy to do if the walls of the church were no higher than the foundations when (as Baldini and Calzona maintain) the problems struck. In my opinion (and as I have set out

in the main text already), the change of design reflects the fact that the church was already as high as the chapel vaults, and it was therefore decided that the crypt was to be *inserted* into the original design recorded by Labacco. Indeed, I contend that the crypt was necessary, as a remedy, in order to keep the area under the church as dry as possible; a contrary view is taken by Calzona (1994b), p. 24, who believes that the crypt has *contributed* to the present damp state of the church. So, while Calzona argues that the undated letter in question should be dated March 1460, more probably it is to be dated around the end of 1462 or early 1463; see also Vasic Vatovec (1979). Consequently, the argument that follows is independent of Calzona's reasoning (1994a and 1994b).

82 Lorenzo was in Mantua in 1483 and, reportedly, on 23 February he walked from the church of San Francesco to Mantegna's house at 16 via Mazzoni; see Kristeller (1901), p. 481, doc. 39; Rosenthal (1962), pp. 327–48, esp. p. 347, n. 20; and Tavernor (1997). On the development of Santa Maria delle Carceri, see Morselli and Corti (1982), p. 15; and especially Davies (1993), p. 3.

83 Morselli and Corti (1982), docs 6 and 7.

84 Though probably not as influential as Wittkower (1973), pp. 20–21, suggested. Lorenzo, or his architect, was probably more directly influenced by Vittorio Ghiberti's Santa Maria della Pietà at Bibbona, near Livorno. The plans of these two pilgrimage churches are almost identical, and as Santa Maria della Pietà was built in Tuscan territory after 1482, and Vittorio was the son of Lorenzo Ghiberti, it was likely to be well known.

85 Labacco had worked on the wooden model of St Peter's for Antonio da Sangallo between 1538 and 1543. The drawing by Oreste Vannocci Biringucci, in the Biblioteca Communale in Siena, is probably a copy of the Aristotile da Sangallo version (attributed by the copyist to Giovanni Battista Alberti): and see nn. 20–21 above.

86 Naredi-Rainer (1977), pp. 134–48; Lamoureux (1979), pp. 14–16. The ratio Lamoureux records is 3:5, which is a major sixth on the Pythagorean musical scale, as Wittkower (1973), pp. 132ff, has noted; it is a ratio for which Palladio later held a predilection. See also Howard and Longair (1982), esp. p. 135, point 2, and Appx table A4, which confirms Wittkower's more tentative observation. Within the context of the perfect numbers of 6 and 10 described by Vitruvius this ratio will be stated as the numbers 6:10 (see pp. 39–41, above); see also Tavernor (1994b); and Volpi Ghirardini (1994b), pp. 219–66.

87 For the most detailed surveys, see Volpi Ghirardini (1994b), pp. 273–7, figs 1–24, and the Alberti Group photogrammetric drawings. Due to past uncertainty about the particular *braccio* employed in the design of this building, attempts have been made to express the numbers Labacco recorded by converting them into Florentine *braccia*: Naredi-Rainer (1977), p. 139. Although there is a close 5:4 ratio between the sizes of the Mantuan and Florentine *braccia*, the significance of the 6:10 ratio (also found at Santa Maria degli

Angeli, described below, n. 110) is lost when the numbers are translated into Florentine *braccia*. Naredi-Rainer believed Alberti used a module of $1\frac{1}{3}$ Florentine *braccia* to design San Sebastiano, which he found also to be the width of the pilasters on the façade. And by clipping fractions, or by rounding numbers up, he believed he had found evidence that Alberti had used a Pythagoreo-Platonic number sequence, where *lambda* is composed of the numbers 2, 4, 8, 16, etc. and 3, 9, 27, 54, etc. But when translated into Florentine *braccia* Labacco's numbers are not all divisible by $1\frac{1}{3}$, and some of them have fractions that are one-fifth of the integer, as $3\frac{4}{5}$, $6\frac{2}{5}$, 8, $9\frac{3}{5}$, $10\frac{2}{3}$, $13\frac{1}{3}$, 16, $26\frac{2}{3}$, $27\frac{1}{5}$, $45\frac{1}{3}$. Joseph Rykwert and I came to a similar conclusion about the Pythagoreo-Platonic sequence in an article written before Naredi-Rainer's thesis became known to us (Rykwert and Tavernor, 1979, pp. 89–90). However, like Naredi-Rainer, we were unaware then that Labacco was listing dimensions in the local Mantuan *braccio*, and that physical correspondences exist between Santa Maria degli Angeli and San Sebastiano, a comparison first made in Tavernor (1985), pp. 42–58.

88 The Sangallo family, by contrast, often modified the building under scrutiny for their own satisfaction. Antonio da Sangallo the Younger completed the upper portion of Alberti's Tempio Malatestiano, ignoring the built details of the façade: Florence, Uffizi, Gabinetto Disegni e Stampi, 1048A; illustrated in Canali (1994b).

89 Reasons for the differences – the lack of a crypt (which was built) and the dome for which he provided dimensions and sketches (unbuilt) – have been suggested already.

90 Letter from Francesco to Ludovico Gonzaga, dated 16/26 March 1473: 'quello edificio sul garbo antiquo non molto dissimile da quello viso fantastico de messer Baptista di Alberti, io per ancho non intendeva se l'haveva a reussire in chiesa o moschea o synagoga'.

91 Mancini (1967), p. 392, suggested that the loggia had been built on top of the former Porta Pusterla, near San Sebastiano, and was not therefore an independent structure at ground level along the lines that Giovanni Rucellai or Pius II built. But see Forster (1994), pp. 169–72.

92 Johnson (1975b), pp. 5–6.

93 Marani (1974), pp. 87–93.

94 Marani (1974), p. 88.

95 Porter (1915–17), I, p. 144, and II, pp. 512–14; Bertinelli-Truzzi (1962); and Calzona (1981).

96 Marani (1974), pp. 88–9.

97 Porter (1915–17), I, p. 144.

98 Krautheimer (1942), p. 32.

99 Marani (1974), p. 88.

100 Krautheimer (1969a), pp. 76–7, 96 and notes 108–9: the rotundas of the Anastasis and Ascension are circular, while the Dome of the Rock is octagonal.

101 Écochard (1977); Wilkinson (1981).

102 Wilson Jones (1989b), esp. catalogue, pp. 140–51.

103 Wilson Jones (1989a); Davies, Hemsoll and Wilson Jones (1987).

104 Vitruvius (1960), III, 11 and 13.

105 On the dimensions of Santo Stefano Rotondo, see Wilson Jones (1989b), p. 146.

106 There was also a profound philosophical foundation to his reasoning. Since antiquity, Pythagoreans had considered the circle to be a symbol of unified perfection and representative of infinity, eternity and deity, being composed of a line without end. Early Christians took the circle to symbolise virtue and, because of the continuity of the line, life after death. Conversely, the square was equated with the physical universe and the material world. These issues are discussed more comprehensively in Heninger (1974).

Attempts at squaring the circle from the Pythagoreans onwards reflect an intellectual desire to reduce infinity to the finite, and of transmuting the divine to the physical realm. Nicholas of Cusa (1401–64), whom Alberti knew, was especially fascinated by the philosophical and geometrical problems that squaring the circle posed. In his *De quadratura circuli*, Nicholas argued that the relationship between the intellect and truth is as distant as a polygon is from a circle: each tends towards the other, but absolute truth, like the purity of the circle, is a perfection that cannot be achieved through the intellect or an infinitely faceted polygon (Eng. trans. from Cusanus, 1954, pp. 11–12): 'The relationship of our intellect to the truth is like that of a polygon to a circle; the resemblance to the circle grows with the multiplicity of the angles of a polygon; but apart from its being reduced to identity with the circle, no multiplication, even if it were infinite, of its angles will make the polygon equal the circle. It is clear, therefore, that all we know of the truth is that the absolute truth, such as it is, is beyond our reach. The truth [. . .] is the most absolute necessity, while in contrast with it, our intellect is [only] possibility'.

107 For their polygonal temples 'the ancients would use six, eight, or even ten angles', and Alberti (1988), VII, 4, p. 196, goes on to describe the construction of the quadrangle, octagon, decagon and dodecagon, using a compass, and starting with the method for drawing the hexagon, a figure in which Nature 'also delights'.

108 The implications of the circle and square for the building types described in *De re aedificatoria* are explored by Morolli (1994), pp. 106–33, and Morolli and Guzzoni (1994); on some ancient sources for San Sebastiano, see Campbell (1984), Lehmann (1988) and Davies (1993).

109 Had it been completed as recorded in a subsequent drawing, the oratory of the Angeli would probably have been similar in appearance to an apse that buttresses the massive dome of Florence Cathedral. For a visual comparison, see Tavernor (1985), p. 336 and fig. 38, p. 343, figs 49 and 50; see also Saalman (1994).

110 A close examination of Santa Maria degli Angeli, and a formal comparison with San Sebastiano, is revealing. It was early in 1434 that Brunelleschi was commissioned to design an 'Oratory of the Scolari at the [monastery of the] Angeli'. (For accounts of the building history, see Bruschi, 1972; Waddy, 1972; Miarelli

Mariani, 1976; Battisti, 1981, pp. 248–58; and Saalman, 1994.) The building funds came from two legacies left by the *condottiere* Filippo Scolari, known, more popularly, as Pippo Spano. It is not known when its plan was set out on site, and work ceased in 1437 when its walls were no higher than about 8 Florentine *braccia* (about 4.8 m.), because the state confiscated and diverted building funds for a war against Lucca. As at San Sebastiano, the unfinished building was later – and expediently – roofed without completing the upper walls or dome Brunelleschi had proposed (it has never functioned as an oratory and is now part of the Faculty of Architecture in Florence).

Twelve fifteenth- and sixteenth-century drawings of the proposed design survive, the earliest and most detailed of which is by Giuliano da Sangallo, drawn to scale some time before 1494; see Battisti (1981), p. 253, and the Codex Barberini in the Vatican Library (Cod. Barb. Lat. 4424). It may have been made some time earlier (a deduction made because the pages of the manuscript were later enlarged). Another detailed drawing, in the Louvre, records that the design is 'di mano di me[ssere] Filippo di s[er] Brunelleschi', recalling the similar statement by Labacco on his drawing of San Sebastiano which was made after 'di mano di mes[s]ere ba[t]tista alberti'. It was once thought to have been drawn by Brunelleschi himself. For an account of Giuliano da Sangallo's drawing, see Miarelli Mariani (1976), p. 64; and Waddy (1972), pp. 36–7, n. 4. The drawing by Giuliano is more detailed than Labacco's, though it lacks vertical dimensions. However, according to Agostino Fortunio's account of the oratory (1579), the plan and section Brunelleschi proposed would appear to have been permeated by the same ratio of 6:10. Fortunio provides the only complete account of the building's dimensions; Eng. trans. in Battisti (1981), p. 253 and n. 14.

According to the *modello* from which he was sketching, Giuliano noted that the sixteen-sided outer polygon had facets 10 [Florentine] *braccia* wide, alternately containing niches 6 *braccia* wide. He also noted that the central octagon of the plan, although articulated by sixteen pilasters, was 31 *braccia* wide to opposing corners, and had a width, face-to-face, of 29 *braccia*. This last statement is inaccurate. An octagon 29 *braccia* wide actually has a diagonal closer to $31\frac{1}{3}$ *braccia* – more precisely, 31.3894 *braccia*. I note this discrepancy since it shows up an irreconcilable aspect of a design which otherwise embodies the 'perfect' numbers described by Vitruvius.

It is possible to reconstruct Brunelleschi's design process from Giuliano's drawing, with some assistance from Alberti's writings, as follows. An octagon, as Alberti (1988), VII, 4, p. 196, describes, can be constructed geometrically using a compass: 'mark out an equilateral, rectangular quadrangle [that is, a square], and draw in the diagonals to each of the right angles; then from each point of intersection [corner] draw an arc, its radius half the diagonal, to cut the sides of the quadrangle on either side; then the line joining these

two cuts made by the arc will become the side of the octagon'.

The plan of Santa Maria degli Angeli is constructed from two polygons derived from squares 29 and 50 *braccia* wide. The smaller square he turned into an octagon with each face 12 *braccia* long, and the larger square a sixteen-sided polygon with each face 10 *braccia* long: perimeter lengths of 96 and 160 *braccia*, respectively. Thus, the perimeter lengths of the inner and outer polygons are as 96 to 160, the same ratio that the niches on the outside of the building (6 *braccia* wide) have to the facets into which they are cut (10 *braccia* wide): that is, the ratio of 6:10 evident in the dimensions of San Sebastiano noted by Labacco.

In fact, what was built of the oratory does not follow these dimensions faithfully. From a published survey of the plan of the building, the central octagon is 30, not 29 *braccia* wide, so that its inner to outer widths are as 30:50 *braccia*, or the ratio 6:10. (From Battisti, 1981, p. 251, fig. 270, the central octagon is 17.5 m., or fractionally under 30 *braccia* wide (29.986 *braccia*); see also Miarelli Mariani, 1976, where the internal faces of the pilasters around the octagon are shown to be 16.2 m., or $27\frac{3}{4}$ *braccia* apart.) Less perfectly, the central octagon has faces 12.43 *braccia* long (not 12) and a longer perimeter length of 99.41 *braccia*, so that the 6:10 ratio (96:160 *braccia*) is lost.

It would appear that Brunelleschi changed his mind about the numbers of the design before (or during the early stages of) construction. He abandoned the perimeter 'lengths' option, where the polygons conform to the 6:10 ratio, in favour of this ratio appearing in the 'widths' of the plan: certainly, he could not achieve this combination of geometry and number in the main fabric of the structure simultaneously. Why Brunelleschi made this last-minute switch in the numbers of the plan went unrecorded. It is possible he miscalculated. For although Brunelleschi was undoubtedly a skilled geometrician, at the scale of a drawing, small errors with a compass may pass unnoticed, and it may only have been as the building was set out on site that a small inaccuracy became a large and blatant incongruence. (And it is true that the three-dimensional complexities of architecture have challenged the most agile of minds, even Alberti's: (1988), IX, 10, p. 317.)

According to Fortunio, the height of the dome was to have been $46\frac{1}{2}$ *braccia*, a dimension that has no obvious relationship in plan which would reflect the ratio of 6:10 evident elsewhere in this design. (Brunelleschi's plan was not built as high as the springing-points of the arches to the niches and internal apses, and there is no way of checking Fortunio's description of the section.) A 29-*braccia* wide octagon would have a height of $48\frac{1}{3}$ *braccia* if this ratio was applied to it, but Fortunio recorded the plan width as 30 *braccia*, which would have made the dome 50 *braccia* high. (I can only suggest that to complete the rotundity of the design the dome was intended to be 50 *braccia* high externally, the same as the exterior width of the building. Alternatively, the height given by Fortunio may be derived from the ornament of the plan: the pilaster faces of the inner octagon are $27\frac{3}{4}$ *braccia*, face-to-face, and $27\frac{3}{4}:46\frac{1}{4} = 6:10$. It is also worth noting that $46\frac{1}{4}$ is a product of 27.75 *braccia* × 1.66r★, which equals 46.25: ★where 1:1.66r is the modern accurate decimal equivalent of 10 ÷ 6.) Interestingly, though, $46\frac{1}{2}$ *braccia* differs from the height Labacco recorded for San Sebastiano by the equivalent of only half a metre. There is also a close correspondence between the plans of these two designs, the difference between the widths of their central spaces being approximately one metre. (According to Labacco the plan and height of the central space of San Sebastiano were to have been 34 and $56\frac{2}{3}$ Mantuan *braccia*, or 15.875 and 26.45 m. (assuming a *braccio* of 466.9 mm: see Volpi Ghirardini, 1994b, pp. 228–34). The equivalent dimensions at Santa Maria degli Angeli according to Fortunio were to be 29 and $46\frac{1}{2}$ Florentine *braccia*, or 16.92 and 27.14 m.)

Although they are not exactly the same size, Santa Maria degli Angeli is articulated in plan by pronounced pilasters which effectively reduce the internal width of the octagon to $27\frac{3}{4}$ *braccia*. It may also be assumed that pilasters would have articulated the central space of San Sebastiano: these would have needed to be shallow, and set into the corners, because, from the dimensions Labacco provides, the dome would have been resting on pendentives. Depending on the precise position of these pilasters at San Sebastiano the distinction between the plan widths may dwindle to nothing, as my reconstruction drawings of the Fortunio and Labacco descriptions would suggest (fig. 116). (At Santa Maria degli Angeli the distance between the pilasters, as built, is $27\frac{3}{4}$ *braccia* or 16.19 m. – just 280 mm greater than the width of San Sebastiano's central space without pilasters. If the pilasters at San Sebastiano were intended to be 140 mm deep, the finished internal width of San Sebastiano would be reduced from 34 to $33\frac{1}{3}$ Mantuan *braccia*.)

111 On the application of number at San Sebastiano, as proposed by Labacco and as built, see Volpi Ghirardini (1994b), pp. 234–66.

112 Krautheimer (1942), pp. 5–8. These geometries were conflated in descriptions of the time. Goro Dati wrote in the earliest guide to Florentine architecture at the beginning of the fifteenth century that the Florentine Baptistery was 'round, with eight faces': Gilbert (1969–70), pp. 41 and 45 for this account in Dati's *Florentine History*.

113 Porter (1915–17), II, pp. 512–14, and n. 3.

114 Amadei (1955) believed that San Lorenzo was rebuilt by the Countess Matilda. Donesmondi (1615–16), Bk 4, p. 225, wrote that 'in the time of the Gentiles it was dedicated to Mars/al tempo de' Gentili questo fosse un tempio a Marte dedicato'. See also Bertinelli and Truzzi (1962); and Calzona (1981).

115 If he believed it to be antique, however, he is unlikely to have considered that it was built for the worship of Mars. As he wrote in his treatise (Alberti, 1988, VII, 3,

p. 194), only those 'who patronise peace, chastity, and the noble arts should have their temples located within the custody of the walls; but those who incite pleasure, strife, and fire – Venus, Mars and Vulcan – should be excluded. Vesta, Jupiter and Minerva, whom Plato called the guardians of the city, they would place in the town centre'.

116 Lang (1954), pp. 290–94.

117 Krautheimer (1942), p. 10. See also Quintavalle (1979), esp. p. 14; and Marani (1974), p. 87. During the Middle Ages several bishops sent surveyors to Jerusalem to record its measurements, and from as far away as Cambridge in England; see Krautheimer (1942), p. 4.

118 Lang (1954), p. 295.

119 Among the most valuable studies concerning the early history of the Annunziata tribune are those by Lang (1954), pp. 228–30; Casalini (1977), pp. 29–63; Brown (1981), pp. 59–145; and Ferrara and Quinterio (1984), pp. 219–26. The research of these scholars has greatly clarified the events surrounding the building of the tribune and the characteristics of the design itself. However, due to the sparsity of clear documentary evidence, many of their conclusions are conjectural and they are frequently at odds. Their views may be summarised as follows.

From the available fifteenth-century survey documents, Susan Lang found sufficient evidence to suggest that two separate designs for the tribune were incorporated in the existing building. She believed that the first design, by Michelozzo, was far more complex in arrangement than the single-vaulted space designed some years later by Alberti. A more comprehensive study of the building history of the tribune by Beverly Brown led her to revert to the more generally held opinion that Alberti's contribution to the project was slight and towards the end of the construction period, and that only one basic design, by Michelozzo, ever existed; see her thesis (1978) and the published extract from it (1981). Padre Eugenio Casalini of the convent of Santissima Annunziata, who has sole access to the original documents on the building of the tribune, supports Lang's reconstruction and hypothesis, and he has been able to expand her general argument. Brown was denied access to these documents and so was unable to frame her arguments as fully as she would have wished (a fact bemoaned by Brown (1981), Appx II, pp. 133–4). An incomplete transcription of the Annunziata building documents is in Tonini (1876; but see n. 121 below), and even after the publication of extracts of the new documents by Casalini, Brown (1981), pp. 133–4, remained firm in her conclusions. Unfortunately, there is no discussion of Brown (1981) in Ferrara and Quinterio (1984: cf. p. 300), who have therefore substantially followed the reasoning of Casalini (1977). Clearly, there is a need to review these arguments.

120 Lang (1954), p. 288.

121 Brown (1981), doc. 13, pp. 116–17, where Brown claims to offer an accurate transcription compared with that by Tonini (1876).

122   These were referred to in the 1455 survey (according to the transcription Lang used) as soon to be demolished: Lang (1954), p. 289 and n. 4, refers to Heydenreich (1930), pp. 268–85; but Brown (1981), p. 81, corrects the transcription and makes it clear that the 'pilastri' were demolished already: cf. Casalini (1977), p. 48; thus, Brown writes that the document does not read 'si fosse chiesto del lavorio fatto' as Lang believed, but 'di sotto di remano del lavorio fatto'.

Brown preferred Heydenreich's reading of the documents and concluded that the 'pilastri' were not columns around a central choir, but the piers around the perimeter of the present tribune which had to be dismantled before being reinforced so that the proposed dome could be adequately supported. There is a variation on this interpretation from Bulman (1971), who suggested that the 'pilastri' were not the perimeter piers but *pietra serena* pilasters that articulated them: their removal facilitated access to the pier foundations, again for the purpose of reinforcement.

In order that 'pilastri' might be interpreted as piers, Brown attempted to define the word by reference to fifteenth-century usage. She concluded that it probably meant 'piers' in the context of the tribune (that is, those piers between the exedrae) and not free-standing columns around a central choir as Lang proposed. However, Brown did concede that a central enclosure – a choir – was built within the *tondo*, but that this was articulated by 'colonne grandi' (which were also mentioned in the documents), not 'pilastri'. Brown (1981), pp. 79–80, suggested that these 'colonne grandi' were ornamental and had no structural function, and were seated on a low wall enclosing the choir; she does not explain how 'colonne grandi' could be construed as small ornamental columns, and the shallow foundations she mentions (p. 79) do not necessarily support her thesis. As part of a wall the 'pilastri/colonne grandi' would exert a uniformly distributed load and not a series of point loads, and would require foundations that are less deep than those required by columns. Casalini's publication of extracts of previously unseen documents lends little support to this interpretation.

An introduction to a survey of 1453, with a more detailed description of the controversial 'pilastri', states clearly that the eight 'pilastri' were square in plan, and were placed around the choir. This text was newly revealed by Casalini (1977), p. 48: 'otto pilastri intorno al coro, grosso l'uno braccia 1, $\frac{1}{2}$ per ogni verso; alti l'uno braccia 12, $\frac{1}{4}$ che montano, quegli otto, braccia 220, $\frac{1}{2}$'. They were each $1\frac{1}{2}$ *braccia* square (0.9 m.), $12\frac{1}{4}$ *braccia* tall (7 m.), and with a combined volume of $220\frac{1}{2}$ *braccia* (128 cubic m.). Casalini (1977), p. 48: 'Somma tutte le braccia degli otto pilastri che sono intorno al coro, e quali s[i h]anno a disfare, montano braccia quadre in tutto 220, $\frac{1}{2}$. per s[oldi] 10 il braccio, il 110 e s[oldi] 5'. That these are the same 'pilastri', meaning piers, as those reported in a survey of 1455, as soon to be demolished, is evident from the precise reference to their combined volume made at that time.

123   Casalini (1977), p. 45. Unfortunately, Casalini does not quote from the original, but paraphrases the document (dated 1449): 'lo scultore o scarpellino Antonio di Pippo Naldini fornisce 4 pilastri lavorati su tre facce, alti l'uno m. 11 e larghi, per ogni faccia, m. 1 sui pilastri vanno i capitelli intagliati, con architrave, fregio, cornice e due archi di pietra lavorati nell'intra e nell'estradosso con quattro intagli'. Brown (1981), Appx II, p. 134, dismissed Casalini's summary, since 'No payments are given for any of these piers nor is there any record of their having been removed in 1455 when Casalini claims that the eight pillars were taken down'. But there would have been no need to demolish them until this passageway was demolished and the new triumphal arch begun, which was not until the dome was finished in 1477.

124   Despite the seemingly unequivocal nature of this evidence, Brown (1981), Appx II, p. 134, considered his reconstruction 'implausible for a number of reasons'. Firstly, she maintained 'it is quite clear that the removal of the eight *pilastri* referred to a portion of the piers between the chapels and not the free-standing columns of the choir' because, as she reconstructed the tribune design, 'the piers, pilasters and columns were three distinct architectural units employed in three distinct places. The piers (*pilastri*) were to support the dome and were adorned by pietra serena pilasters (*colonne*). Under the dome there was a choir surrounded by a wall supporting free-standing columns (*colonne grandi*)': Brown (1981), p. 84. Despite the linking reference to the volume of the eight 'pilastri' in the 1453 and 1455 surveys as '$220\frac{1}{2}$ *braccia*', Brown remained insistent this meant that the outer piers were to be reduced by '$220\frac{1}{2}$ *braccia*', and that they were to be reinforced (following Heydenreich's explanation) to redress an initial miscalculation by Michelozzo of the foundation size required. Furthermore, Brown (pp. 133–4) was critical of Casalini's reconstruction because it seemed doubtful to her that a vaulted ambulatory between a choir and outer exedrae would be feasible considering (an apparent) disparity in height between the $12\frac{1}{2}$ *braccia* 'pilastri' around the choir and the exedrae, or, indeed, whether 'relatively slim pillars' could support a dome and ambulatory vault. As neither Lang nor Casalini have responded to these criticisms I have some observations to make.

As to Brown's criticism that the choir and *tondo* would be incompatible for aesthetic and structural reasons (because $1\frac{1}{2}$ *braccia* square piers would be too slim, and they would be too low), reference need only be made to similar architectural systems employed at San Lorenzo and Santo Spirito in Florence. Their respective naves are flanked by free-standing circular columns linked to the outer walls by vaulted ambulatories. Columns in Brunelleschi's churches have a uniform diameter of $1\frac{1}{2}$ *braccia* – the same width as the square 'pilastri' of the Annunziata – and at Santo Spirito they are linked to semicircular exedrae by a vaulted ambulatory. This arrangement has proven structural stability: see Saalman (1979), pp. 1–5, who writes that 'the column diameters in Brunelleschi's churches, [are] uniformly 0.875 metres [1.5 *braccia*] according to my own check' (p. 2).

Also, while the 'pilastri' of the Annunziata choir were reportedly $12\frac{1}{4}$ *braccia* high when it was decided to dismantle them, this may not have been their intended completed height. San Lorenzo's $1\frac{1}{2}$ *braccia* wide columns are about $15\frac{1}{2}$ *braccia* high, which is about the same height as the vaulted exedrae around the Annunziata tribune. See Stegmann and Geymüller (1924). San Lorenzo's columns are 9.05 m. high including the capitals, while Santo Spirito's are slightly taller. Alternatively, the piers may have been planned with an entablature or superimposed arches above. This would have increased their height such that the inner and outer walls of the ambulatory were compatible.

Nor was the wall around the choir necessarily built low and continuous; see Brown (1981), p. 80 and doc. 13. Brown estimated the height of the wall as $3\frac{1}{6}$ *braccia*, because from the two surveys the wall foundations are 74 *braccia* long (the perimeter length), and the wall $\frac{2}{3}$ *braccia* wide with a volume of $157\frac{1}{4}$ *braccia* (cubic). If the wall was placed centrally on the foundations (as one would expect) its perimeter length would have been reduced by the volume of fabric which made up the 10 'pilastri', and so would be higher than if the wall were continuous and unarticulated. Also, it is likely that this encircling wall was high and pierced, and not low and solid as Brown has assumed, because the 'pilastri' around the choir were square in section, which makes it unlikely that they were free-standing elements. A useful comparison can be made with Alberti's later semicircular apse for San Martino a Ganagalandi, which is articulated by six *pietra serena* pilasters supporting a cornice. Michelozzo may have had an effect like this in mind for the piers around the choir of the Annunziata. In both instances there would have been the same number of piers or pilasters to the semicircle. The walls in between the pilasters of Alberti's San Martino apse were to have been pierced by windows, an arrangement that would have suited the Annunziata choir since the interior would then have been lighter. Spallanzani (1975), pp. 248–9, docs 4 and 9, records that three windows were to have been incorporated into the new apse wall. Consequently the volume of wall stated in the survey would have gone very much further and the structure of the enclosure been much stronger as wall and pilasters combine to create piers which would support a dome above.

125   The survey of 1453 is recorded as follows in Casalini (1977), pp. 45–8:
Scritta di Nencio di Lapo muratore delle misure del lavorio di sopra, facte per Calandra abachista
A nome di Dio al di 9 di giugno 1453.
Nella cappella di dietro a l'altare maggiore e prima le cappelle con la tribuna e pilastri e cornici e tabernacoli e chiave e qualunque altra cosa appartente a dette cappelle e mura, di sotterra murale sopra la ghiaia a mano e ogni braccio di volte in tutto. [. . .] I pilastri della cappella maggiore come stanno [. . .] il muro del

coro d'intorno fuori dai pilastri [. . .] e poi ogni muro fuori del tondo misurato a dritto e con la cordo [. . .] e mattoni soprammattoni [. . .] siano ad onore della Vergine Maria e nulla se ne dia al coro, grosso l'uno braccia $1\frac{1}{2}$ per ogni verso, alti l'uno braccia $12\frac{1}{4}$ che montano quegli otto braccia $220\frac{1}{2}$ . . .

The following extract is after Brown (1981), pp. 116–17, doc. 13 (the parenthesised letters relate to fig. 121, here):
Fondamenti della ghiaia in su.
(A) El fondamento d'un pilastro pelle duo capelle alto br. $2\frac{1}{4}$ largo br. $1\frac{3}{4}$ monta br. $10\frac{1}{2}$ e perche sono 8 pilastri montano br. 84   . . . br. 84
(B) El fondamento sotto el pilastro chon due cholone quadre tra le due chappelle alto br. $2\frac{1}{4}$ largo br. $4\frac{1}{8}$ grosso br. $1\frac{3}{8}$ monta br. $12\frac{3}{4}$ e perche sono 8 pilastri montano br. 102   . . . br. 102
(C) El fondamento d'una capella dove elgiro delle mura gira in sul mezzo br. 19 alto br. $1\frac{1}{3}$ grosso br. $1\frac{11}{12}$ in tutto br. $48\frac{5}{9}$ e perche sono sei chapelle di questa misura montano   . . . br. $291\frac{1}{3}$
(D) El fondamento della capella magiore gira in sul muro br. 21 alto br. $1\frac{1}{3}$ grosso br. $1\frac{11}{12}$ monta br. $53\frac{2}{3}$ . . . br. $53\frac{2}{3}$
(E) El fondamento sotto al muro dove l'ucio che va in sagrestia alto br. $2\frac{1}{4}$ largo br. $2\frac{1}{4}$ grosso br. 2 monta $10\frac{1}{8}$ . . . br. $10\frac{1}{8}$
(F) El fondamento sotto al'uscio della chompagnia de' tedeschi lungo br. $2\frac{1}{4}$ alto br. $2\frac{1}{4}$ grosso br. 2 monta br. $10\frac{1}{8}$ . . . br. $10\frac{1}{8}$
(G) El fondamento delle mura del choro girano intorno in sul mezzo del muro br. 74 alto br. $1\frac{1}{4}$ grosso br. $2\frac{2}{5}$ monta   . . . br. 222
Soma in tutto le br. del fondamento sottera dalla ghiaia in su sono br. quadre per ogni verso br. $242\frac{1}{4}$ . . .
[continued by Brown, p. 116].

The survey of 1453 lists the circumference of the foundations to the central choir as 74 *braccia* (see G above). Because of the difficulty of measuring the circumference of a wall on its inside, I have assumed this refers to the outside of the wall of the central choir. Thus:

$$74\ \textit{braccia}\ = 2\pi R\ \text{[circumference]}$$
$$R\ \text{[radius]} = 74 \div 2\pi$$
$$= 11.772\ \textit{braccia}\ \text{[where}\ \pi = 3\tfrac{1}{7}\text{]}$$

The outer diameter (twice the radius) of the foundations is therefore 23.54 *braccia*.

From the same survey the foundations are recorded as $2\frac{2}{5}$ (or 2.4) *braccia* wide. Assuming that the wall of the choir was placed centrally on its foundations, so the centre line of the foundations would have been 23.54 − 2.4 = 21.14 *braccia*. Sitting on the foundations were eight piers $1\frac{1}{2}$ *braccia* wide. The outer diameter of the piers of the choir was therefore 21.14 + 1.5 = 22.64 *braccia*, the inner diameter 19.64. According to a survey by Roselli (1971), the internal diameter of the tribune is 23.4 m., which translates as 40.09 *braccia* – very close to 40. If we assume that a wall ran inbetween the piers of the choir, and its inner diameter was to be half the outer diameter of the tribune, at 20 *braccia*, then the wall itself would be 0.78 metres, or slightly larger than ¾ *braccio* wide, and the piers would stand proud of the wall by 0.36 *braccio* on either side (assuming it was aligned centrally under the piers), or about 200 mm. According to this reconstruction, the wall around the choir would have had an inner diameter of 20 *braccia*, and 21.56 *braccia* externally.

However, the survey of 1455 (in Brown, 1981, pp. 116–17) describes a wall ⅔ *braccio* thick around the choir. So, either the choir had an internal diameter of 20 *braccia* (half the inner diameter of the tribune, and the surveys miscalculated their quantities) or the width of the choir was only approximately half the width of the tribune. Unfortunately there is not enough information in the survey to establish this either way.

126 On the increase in the width of the outer piers of the Annunziata tribune, see Brown (1981), doc. 22. In 1460 the foundations were thickened to 5 *braccia*, which is also the present thickness of the piers. For the dimensions of the fabric, see Roselli (1971), according to whom the outer facets of one half of the plan have the following metric lengths: 4.45, 4.25, 4.4, 4.15, 4.35, 4.55, 4.3, 4.25, 4.25, 4.7 m. (an average of 4.365 m., or 7.48 *braccio*).

While none of the Quattrocento designs mentioned was completed as designed, the perfection of form and number each architect sought was realised finally in the Bramante's Tempietto at San Pietro in Montorio, Rome, which became a symbol of perfection for leading Italian architects during the next century: it is permeated by the numbers 6 and 10, in multiples of the Roman palm: see Serlio (1996), pp. 131–4, and Palladio (1997), pp. 276–8, on Bramante's Tempietto at Montorio, Rome: and Wilson Jones (1990), who has revealed in its form the all-pervading combination of the numbers and dimensions 6 and 10 Roman *palmi*.

127 Brown (1981), pp. 108–10.

128 Gianfrancesco's instructions were not specific, though it was clear that the 'fabrica' in general should benefit. He also endowed other Italian churches in this will, and in the Holy Land. His contribution to the Annunziata was just one of many that this important Florentine pilgrimage church could hope to receive, especially as papal indulgences were attached to any donations made there; see Brown (1981), p. 63; and Lünig (1725–35), III, col. 1781–1808.

129 Brown (1981), pp. 63–4.

130 Lang (1954), p. 297.

131 Saalman (1980), pp. 208–9.

132 Saalman (1980), pp. 206–12; p. 286, doc. 323.10, and p. 289, doc. 339; Ferrara and Quinterio (1984), p. 24. See also the following for differences of opinion about the importance of this dismissal on Michelozzo's involvement at the Annunziata: Brown (1981), pp. 82–90, who followed an argument by Heydenreich (1930), p. 276, but which was disputed by Lang (1954), p. 297, n. 6. Manetti is recorded as architect of the tribune in 1460 (Brown, 1981, p. 87 and doc. 22), though the date on which his appointment was made is unknown.

133 On Michelozzo see Hyman (1978), Ferrara and Quinterio (1984) and Zervas (1988).

134 The community enjoyed a new self-confidence soon after alterations began, fostered by their religious leader Fra Mariano Salvini who, in 1456, was installed as Bishop of Cortona. But it is unlikely that Salvini's ability and promotion would have encouraged such radical changes: Casalini (1977), pp. 36 and 53.

135 Casalini (1977), pp. 32 and 46; and Brown (1981), p. 62: 'le capelle con la tribuna [. . .] siano ad onore della Vergine Maria'. The full name of the Servites was the 'servi di Santa Maria'.

136 The other thirty-four were planned as martyrial, sepulchral and memorial buildings, or were dedicated to specific helpers against the plague, like San Sebastiano: Sinding-Larsen (1965), pp. 219–20 and n. 1, and Appx I. For the link between the Virgin and roundness, see also Wittkower (1973), p. 31. The association between the Virgin and rotund buildings lasted for a long time. When taken over by Christians, centralised temples were often rededicated to the Virgin: the Pantheon, the first temple in Rome to be Christianised, was converted into a church in 609 when it became Santa Maria Rotonda; and when the Crusaders reconquered Jerusalem in the 12th century, the Dome of the Rock was immediately Christianised by dedicating it to the Virgin (Krinsky, 1970, p. 4). The tomb of Theodoric in Ravenna was turned into the church of Santa Maria Rotonda (Alberti, 1988, p. 370, n. 76). A circular imperial mausoleum attached to the side of the basilica of Old St Peter's in the Vatican was known as either the Temple of Mars or Diana, but was rededicated to Santa Maria delle Febbre (Burroughs, 1982, p. 120 and n. 145). In the sixteenth century, the Pantheon was even compared to the Anastasis in Jerusalem, which is, 'like Santa Maria Rotunda in Rome, open at the centre, but the interior of the Roman [building] has a stone vault, while [that of the Anastasis] is made of huge beams of cedar wood/come quella di S. Maria Rotunda in Rome, aperta nel mezzo, ma quella di Roma, di dentro e fatta di pietre in volta, e questa [Anastasis] a la grossalana di legno cedrino' (Moffitt, 1982, p. 10). The octagonal Dome of the Rock is perhaps more visually arresting than the church of the Holy Sepulchre. It is placed prominently on the platform of the Temple of Jerusalem and surrounded by an open terrace. An erroneous tradition evolved that it had been built by Helena, Constantine's mother, though it was in fact built later, in the seventh century and by Arabs.

137 Trexler (1980), p. 66; and Bergstein (1991).

138 For the dating of the drawing, see Brown (1981), p. 72 and n. 32.

139 The façade of the Tempio Malatestiano is 29.6 m. wide, or the equivalent of 50.7 Florentine *braccia*; the outer diameter of the Annunziata tribune is 50 *braccia*: see p. 75, above, and n. 126.

140 This is generally thought to be Antonio di Ciaccheri Manetti, though there was another Manetti, Antonio di Tuccio, working in Florence at this time: see Brown

141 (1981), p. 88; and pp. 59–61, above for the letter dated November 1454.

141 The ratios of height from floor level to width of the domes of the Old Sacristy and Pazzi Chapel are 1 : 1.66 and 1 : 2 respectively. The domes at the crossings of his churches are higher still. See Battisti (1981).

142 See Roselli (1971), whose drawings are reprinted in Borsi (1977), pp. 191 and 193.

143 On the inadequacies of the set-back position of the tribune see Brunelleschi's comments as transmitted by Giovanni da Gaiole, quoted below, p. 154.

144 According to the drawing of the Annunziata in the Codex Rustici (fig. 120) there were vertical slit-windows in the exedrae. If these existed as indicated they too were probably in-filled at this time. See also the reconstruction by Casalini (1977), p. 47, fig. 9.

145 At the head of the tribune there is now a square chapel capped by a small dome. It was built by Giambologna (1529–1608) as his own tomb, and replaces a semicircular chapel, larger than the others, built by Michelozzo.

146 Evidence for this ornamentation comes from Brown (1981), illustrations 8, 9 and 13, pp. 77–83: the most useful is a late seventeenth-century drawing (fig. 99), thought to be by P. F. Silvani (Archivio di Stato, Florence: Conv. soppr. 119, b. 1273, fol. 27), dated 1675. These show the arches springing directly off the capitals, a detail that would not have been sanctioned by Alberti, though adopted by Brown in her reconstruction (illustration 13, p. 83). The Alberti Group has reconstructed these arches with a full entablature as Alberti recommends in De re aedificatoria.

147 Vasari (1973), II, pp. 540–43.

148 The controversy and its activists are described by Brown (1981), pp. 98–108; for Giovanni da Gaiole, see pp. 103–4.

149 Eng. trans. from Battisti (1981), p. 190.

150 Brown (1981), p. 99, fig. 16, has reconstructed Aldobrandini's plan.

151 Aldobrandini wrote: 'allegando che a Roma sono edifitii in questa forma, dico: quelli da Roma essere stati facti per ornamento di sepulture di quelli imperadori, et per essere ufficiati da 4 o 6 capellani, et non per uno convento simile a questo. Da altre parte sono ornati quale di musaico, et quale daltre cose di grandissimo, et se questa tribuna si facessi tucta biancha sanza altri ornamenti dalle capelle in su, parra una cosa povera et spogliata, sanza che questa chiesa mai piu si potra acconciare'. See Lang (1954), p. 289; and Gaye (1839), I, p. 232.

152 Brown (1981), p. 107.

153 In one of his drawings of Santa Costanza, Giuliano da Sangallo deviated from the building's actual layout by adjusting the position of the outer niches so they align with the intercolumniation of the central ring of columns, and he systematised the sequence of niches by arranging the regular ones opposite each other – cross-wise in plan – with pairs of semicircular niches inbetween. In another drawing he proposed a sequence of niches alternately rectangular and semicircular. On these modifications to Santa Costanza, see Buddensieg (1976), pp. 340–41. The earliest extant measured drawings of Santa Costanza are by Giuliano da Sangallo. These are in the Codex Barberini in the Vatican Library (Cod. Barb. Lat. 4424, fols 33–4). A sepulchre from Santa Costanza which had been displayed in the Piazza San Marco in Rome (close to the Palazzo Venezia) was restored to the chapel at the head of the mausoleum on 30 October 1471; see Lanciani (1902–12), I, pp. 72, 73 and 75. Giuliano referred to it as a 'sepoltura' on his plan of Santa Costanza. The two plans he drew of the mausoleum are accurate and have a scale of units marked alongside in Florentine braccia. The following dimensions, in metres, were arrived at from my own survey of Santa Costanza, Rome [RT], and others by Desgodets (1843) [Des], and Wilson Jones (1989b), p. 145 [Wil]:

	RT	Des	Wil
diameter of central space:	11.30	11.68	11.50
ambulatory width (column to wall surface):	4.08	4.02	4.01
a combined column base width:	1.51	1.55	
Total internal diameter:	**22.48**	**22.82**	**22.28**

Average for the diameter = 22.52 metres

According to Zettler (1943), pp. 76–86, the external diameters of the drum and the base measure c. 14.4 and c. 29.0 m. respectively. The drum, internal and external base diameters of approximately 14.4, 22.5 and 29 m. are equivalent to 24.7, 38.5 and 49.7 Florentine braccia. According to Wilson Jones (1989b), p. 145, they may represent, more properly, 50, 75 and 100 Roman feet. Using this scale, the central space measures 20 braccia wide and the ambulatory 8 braccia with internal and external diameters of 40 and 50 braccia respectively – dimensions which bear comparison with the design by Michelozzo for the Annunziata tribune.

A later drawing by the architect Bernardino della Volpaia illustrates an increased number of paired columns forming the inner ring that is sixteen, not twelve; Francesco di Giorgio was more extreme still and drew eighteen pairs of columns: Buddensieg (1976), p. 341; and Francesco di Giorgio (1967), fol. 88, table 163.

Brunelleschi explored the combination of the numbers 6, 8, 10 and 16 in his polygon for Santa Maria degli Angeli, Alberti the square, cross, and the ratio of 6 : 10 at San Sebastiano, while for Michelozzo the numbers 10 and 20 describe the geometry of the tribune, and it had ten piers around the choir. The same numbers were used by Giuliano da Sangallo for the Greek-cross plan of Santa Maria delle Carceri in Prato. See Morselli and Corti (1982), pp. 38–53; see also the surveys by Stegmann and Geymüller (1924) and Crovato and Dominissini (1968), pp. 52–60. The latter gives the building the following dimensions (in metres and Florentine braccia):

depth of chapels	10 *braccia*	5.827 m. average, or 9.98 *braccia*
height of chapels	30 *braccia*	17.45 m. average, or 29.9 *braccia*
width of crossing	20 *braccia*	11.54 m. average, or 19.77 *braccia*
height of dome	$48\frac{1}{3}$ to $49\frac{1}{3}$ *braccia*★	

★Figures arrived at by Morselli and Corti (1982) and Stegmann and Geymüller (1924), respectively. Morselli found evidence of the Golden Section in vertical ratios of these numbers.

Once Michelozzo's design for the choir was dismantled, the visual impact of these numbers was lost. This is why recent scholars have tended to associate the finished building with the so-called Minerva Medica, rather than Santa Costanza, since both the tribune and Minerva Medica have a central decagonal vaulted space articulated by niches. A comparison first suggested by Willich (1914), p. 85. Minerva Medica was not in fact a temple, as it was assumed during the Renaissance, but a garden nymphaeum.

154 A comparison first suggested by Willich (1914), p. 85. But see Brown (1981), pp. 97–8 and n. 134, who believed that the tribune 'is much closer in appearance to the two imperial rotunda once attached to Old St Peter's or to the mausoleum of St Helena'. However, these are entirely circular and not polygonal in plan. More relevant perhaps is the way one of these, St Petronillae, was attached directly to the end of the transept of Old St Peter's, a conjunction not dissimilar to that being sought by the architects at the Annunziata: or, indeed, perhaps by Alberti at the Tempio Malatestiano. See Lanciani (1990), sheet 13.

155 See Biondo (1953), II. 24, p. 244.

156 See also Campbell (1984), p. 47, where this point is made emphatically.

157 See Buddensieg (1976), pp. 340–41.

158 See the argument in Tavernor (1985), pp. 42–58, and notes, pp. 206–11, an argument advanced considerably in Wilson Jones (1989b and 1990).

159 Braghirolli (1869), p. 271, doc. x; Roselli (1971), p. 33, doc. 45; and Brown (1981), p. 103.

160 Johnson (1975b), Appx II, no. 2, p. 64, and ch. 2, n. 1.

161 Chambers (1977).

162 Johnson (1975b), Appx II, no. 2, p. 64, and ch. 2, n. 1.

163 For Ludovico's letter see Johnson (1975b), Appx II, no. 3, p. 64: 'Havemo etiam visto el disegno de quello tempio ne haveti mandato, el quale prima fatie ne piace ma perche non lo possiamo ben intendere a nostro modo aspectaremo che siamo a Mantova poi parlato che habiamo cum vui dictovi la fantasia nostra et intesa anche la vostra faremo quanto ne parera sia il meglio'.

164 Johnson (1975b), p. 6, and pp. 98–9, n. 25. A record of this event, in May 1401, states that the relics were shown in 'Ecclesia Sancti Andree super podium ipsius ecclesie'.

165 For accounts of the Etruscan temple see Vitruvius (1960), IV, 7, pp. 120–22, and illustration, p. 121; Alberti

(1988), VII, 4, p. 197, concludes his chapter on 'round and quadrangular temples' with a brief description of the 'Templum Etruscum'.

166 A connection between Alberti's Etruscan temple and the Basilica of Maxentius was first suggested in Alberti (1912), pp. 618–20; and see also Alberti (1955), p. 247, n. 144. Krautheimer (1969b) extended this comparison to Sant'Andrea.

167 Krautheimer (1969b), pp. 338–9.

168 At a symposium on Alberti held in Munich, March 1960, Richard Krautheimer and Erich Hubala proposed, quite independently, that the existing Latin-cross plan of Sant'Andrea was a sixteenth-century extension to a smaller nave-only structure by Alberti; see Krautheimer (1969b) and Hubala (1961). Johnson (1975b, p. 19) refuted these claims in his monograph on Sant'Andrea, believing he had found archaeological evidence to suggest otherwise. In a forthright review of Johnson's book, Forster (1977) presented a convincing counter-critique of Johnson's claim.

169 This paraphrased translation follows Chambers (1977). The Italian in the first letter (from Johnson, 1975b, Appx II, no. 7, p. 65) reads as follows: 'Noi voressimo dar principio alla Chiesa di S. Andrea alla qual fabrica abbiamo volto il core si per esser de necesitade, che la viene a terra, si etiam per onor vostro e nostro e do questa cittade e speriamo che in dui anni o tre se gli fara tal principio che sera casone di ingegliardire molto la brigata a spendergli perche sara posto in opera due milioni di prede al creder nostro, advisandone, che secondo uno modello ch'e facto non gli andara la spesa ne il tempo che se credeva, e non tanto a Vui che siete zovene ma ancora Nui compando, qualsia in piacere de Dio [sic]'.

170 Ludovico died in 1478, six years after this letter was written. For the Milan Cathedral comment, see Chambers (1977), p. 11.

171 Pius II built a new church, palace, loggia and piazza in his hometown Corsignano, renamed Pienza, between 1459 and 1462: see Pius II (1984), II, pp. 1745–71; Pius II (1960), pp. 282–92; and Mack (1987).

172 The brick-kiln is mentioned by Johnson (1975b), p. 13.

173 Johnson (1975b), p. 10. The foundation stone of the building was laid by Ludovico on 12 June 1472. Alberti died in early April: Gaye (1893), I, doc. XCIV, and Mancini (1967), p. 495.

174 Johnson (1975b), Appx II, no. 7, p. 65.

175 Sant'Andrea is not mentioned specifically in this letter, dated 27 April 1472: 'Illustrious Prince and Most Honored Lord. I am delighted with the design you have sent me, first because it helps me to understand the work, and secondly, because ambassadors and noblemen often pass by, and we have to pay our respects by showing them some fine work. Now I can show them this wonderful design, the like of which does not exist in my opinion, for which I thank Your Lordship' (Johnson, 1975, Appx II, no. 10, pp. 65–6; see Johnson's doubts about the building being referred to and his concluding comments there).

176 As Alberti's account of the Templum Etruscum is different from Vitruvius' it must be assumed he had already 'designed' this type of building for himself, in order to be able to describe it in *De re aedificatoria*.

177 Calculating the quantity of bricks was also of considerable interest to Filarete: see, for example, Filarete (1965), I, p. 39, on the number of bricks in the walls of Sforzinda. It was a standard problem in manuals of practical arithmetic to make such calculations; see Goldthwaite (1980), p. 150.

178 For a general discussion of the manufacture and application of brick in the fifteenth century, see Goldthwaite (1980), pp. 188–212. In Florence, as elsewhere, brick sizes were strictly controlled and prices fixed by the state. As with other standards, official brick-moulds were made for comparison with those bricks produced at the kilns. The Director of the Archivio di Stato, Mantua, Professor Adele Bellù, referred me to a document in the archive dated 11 January 1732 (AG. Serie I, b. 3237), where an 'ancient' Mantuan brick standard is described as 8 *once* + 2 *punti* × 4 *once* × 2 *once*, or close to 320 × 160 × 80 mm (assuming a Mantuan *braccio* of 46.7 cm). The average brick size at Sant'Andrea is 294 × 140 × 64 mm; see Saalman, Volpi Ghirardini and Law (1992), p. 358. At San Sebastiano they are a similar size, 292 × 144 × 65 mm; see Volpi Ghirardini (1994b), p. 253, n. 96 (and fig. 176 for the standard in bronze used to regulate bricks) and Canali (1994b). Some other examples of sixteenth-century bricks in other states are listed by Goldthwaite (1980), pp. 209–10, n. 67: e.g., Florentine bricks were about 290 × 145 × 50 mm.

179 Goldthwaite (1980), p. 162.

180 Schiavi (1932), p. 31, estimated that there were 200 bricks per cubic metre at San Sebastiano; Volpi Ghirardini (1994b), p. 253, n. 96, estimated 275.

181 See Appendix, pp. 204–6, above.

182 Johnson (1975b), pp. 8–22.

183 See Johnson (1975b), p. 15, and Appx II, no. 45 (for the building campaigns) and no. 48 (for the consecration of the chapels). On 20 May 1480 ten chapels were consecrated; the eleventh was consecrated on 22 August 1481, the twelfth on 14 July 1482. Curiously, Johnson suggested that the eleventh chapel was consecrated at some unknown date, after the twelfth chapel, and dedicated to St Longinus. The entry for August 1481 states that 'unam capellam [...] consecratam sub titolo Sanguinis Christi positam et fundatam'. Johnson argued that this refers to an underground crypt, because that is where the Blood is now stored. But all the other chapels were consecrated sequentially, so why omit the eleventh chapel in favour of a crypt which is not mentioned in these records? The 'third' part of the church vaulting (presumably that over the third group of chapels, nos 9–12) was started in 1494: Johnson, p. 18. The roundel was frescoed in 1488; see Paccagnini (1960), I, p. 52.

184 The drawing is an elevation of the east end of the church made 'in the course of estimating repairs to the temporary wooden screen that closed off the east end of the nave' (Johnson, 1975b, p. 100, n. 32). The full transcription reads: 'la volta d.tezi 6 grossa/la capella antica difora della/chiesa in la fabrica/la paredana d.la testada d.la chiesa/di s.to Andrea ch. sono da refarl-la/alarga braza 41 li ase sivede che livole/n.ro 100 che faremo da baso co./queli vechie eco.li listi p.li comisuri'.

185 Ritscher (1899) first put forward the idea that this chapel was Benedictine and had survived the 1470s demolition work. Johnson (1975b) queried this and proposed instead that the chapel had been built only as a 'temporary' expedient. Baldassare Peruzzi built such a temporary structure to protect the altar and the apostle's tomb during the construction of St Peter's, Rome, during the sixteenth century. No such martyrium existed at Sant'Andrea, however, and none was considered – as far as known documents suggest – until the late sixteenth century when a Gonzaga pantheon was proposed, and when the Blood was moved to the crypt.

186 The chapel Pedemonte drew is unlikely to have been a remnant of the earlier church. The campanile, which had been completed before Alberti's design, and was presumably integral with the Benedictine church, is set at an angle to the present entrance porch, and the nave of the earlier church probably followed the same line.

187 Pedemonte made his drawing in order to describe the timber screen above the chapel. The purpose of the timber is unclear. Perhaps brick-laying had been halted at high level because a decision had been made to extend the church, or maybe it was a makeshift substitute for fenestration. An apostolic visitor to the church five years before Pedemonte's drawing was made observed that windows in the church were unglazed, and some openings covered with dirty cloth: he instructed they be glazed and the old glass, where in position, be cleaned: Johnson (1975b), Appx III, no. 10, pp. 77–9.

188 As reconstructed in Rykwert and Tavernor (1986).

189 Spallanzani (1975).

190 Federico Gonzaga (1500–40) became Marquis in 1519 and Duke in 1530. The second building programme ran between c. 1526 and 1565: Johnson (1975b), pp. 23–7.

191 Negotiations for Giulio's move from Rome to Mantua started in 1521. Baldassare Castiglione was Federico's ambassador as well as a patron of Raphael.

192 Severi (1989).

193 In 1526 two houses close by the church were leased to tenants on the proviso that parts of the houses would be needed once construction on the church began: Johnson (1975b), Appx III, nos. 2 and 35, p. 76; for Johnson's comment on an inscription dated 1550 in the vault of the north transept portico, bearing the name of a mason 'Bernardino Giberto', see p. 23.

194 Johnson (1975b), p. 24, proposed that work finished c. 1565, but little work appears to have been done on the north portico beyond 1550.

195 According to Vasari, Giulio Romano was invited to move back to Rome after the death of Antonio da Sangallo: as stated in Gombrich (1981), p. 82 and n. 19.

196 Campbell (1981), pp. 3–8.

197 There was no tradition of Gonzaga burial in Sant'Andrea until Duke Vincenzo (1562–1612), in his will of 1595, demanded to be buried in Sant'Andrea's crypt. By this time the sacred Blood was already in place 'in cappella inferiori et subterranea' and the will included a redesign of the space. However, Vincenzo was not buried in the crypt, nor were any of his successors. If the Blood had been stored in a chamber below ground in the fifteenth century, as Johnson maintains (see n. 185 above), the western arm of the present crypt, with its curious apsidal end, may be a remnant of this space. Presumably the Blood was moved to the centre of the crossing just before 1595, or at a date when work on the Latin-cross extension was sufficiently advanced. The large mausoleum planned for Vincenzo was to be entered from one arm only (presumably from the west) and directly from the nave by two straight flights of steps; see Signorini (1981), pp. 3–13, and fig. 13. Consequently, the two spiral staircases which lead from the transept to the crypt may well be post-1600, and not earlier as has been suggested by Johnson (1975b), pp. 16–17.

198 Vischer has been associated with Mantua as the engraver and printmaker of some of Mantegna's works around 1515 (though this is a matter of dispute; see Boorsch, 1992, cat. no. 31, p. 187). His drawing is in the Louvre, Paris (Inventaire, 1938, II, no. 333); see also Lotz (1961), pp. 161–74. Vischer's drawing of the façade shows niches above the doors having shell-motif frescoes. This could still be seen around 1945 following the demolition of a fifteenth-century house built adjacent to the façade: see Johnson (1975), plates 1 and 64. In 1830 the façade and interior of the porch were 'restored' and painted white. Its present bleached state is in marked contrast to the colourful façade painted by an unknown artist in the eighteenth century. See Wolters (1986).

199 Johnson argued convincingly that rectangular openings or niches, like those of the west porch, were built internally, between the present oculi of the nave and the doors to the small chapels flanked by the giant pilasters. However, he believes that the oculi were designed by Alberti: Johnson (1975b), pp. 16–18. Quite apart from Alberti's stated disapproval of round windows to Matteo de' Pasti when building the Tempio Malatestiano, their construction suggests otherwise. The brickwork of the lower part of the oculus, which he illustrates in plate 17 (of one in a pier at the crossing), is quite separate from the main structure of the wall opening. Seen from the outside (just visible in his plate 9, within the shadow of the large arched opening in the outer wall, on the right) it has a rectangular shape, and only its top edge is round-headed. The round windows are more likely to be part of Giulio Romano's remodelling of the church.

200 Cf. the broken entablature at San Sebastiano which is usually attributed to Alberti. However, see the discussion of this on p. 140, above.

201 See Johnson (1975b), pl. 9 of the 'north flank of the nave'; see also Tavernor (1985), ch. 3 and Appx 6; and Rykwert and Tavernor (1986).

202 Bazzotti and Belluzzi (1980); Carpeggiani and Tellini Perina (1987), pp. 14 and 16, and compare with pp. 15 and 17, Rykwert and Engel (1994), p. 247.

203 This is a different conclusion from the one I reached with Rykwert, in Rykwert and Tavernor (1986). See Tavernor (1991a), illustrations 48–50 for the relationship of the thermal windows to the interior at the Redentore; and pp. 66–8, for a discussion of Alberti and Palladio's church architecture in relation to the Basilica of Maxentius.

During a restoration of the exterior of Sant'Andrea during the late 1980s, shading of a thermal window outline on the outer side walls of the nave was examined, and the outline has been physically recorded by applying render to the brickwork in the form of a lunette. Could it be that the mortar is a different colour because these 'lunettes' were left open and the structural timber framework supporting the vaults left in place initially, to allow the chapels to be more strongly illuminated while the fresco painting was under way? And that the lunettes had still not been bricked in at the end of the sixteenth century (when Pedemonte made his survey of the east end), so that the bricks and mortar seen there now are newer and lighter than the fifteenth-century originals? Alternatively, the lunettes were rendered in the eighteenth century (which has caused the colour differentiation in the brickwork) in order to harmonize the fifteenth-century exterior with the new dome being built by Filippo Juvarra. There are circular windows on Juvarra's dome too, which further suggests a scheme for modernising and harmonising the various parts of the church at this time. Volpi Ghirardini (1994a) believes the circular windows were part of the original structure; he also argues that large rectangular windows on the external side walls lit the main chapels, and that these were subsequently infilled when buildings were placed against the external side walls of the nave. Such a notion may be acceptable if Alberti had conceived of Sant'Andrea as free-standing, or detached from surrounding buildings. However, the church was built against as soon as it was completed, covering the surface of wall in which Volpi Ghirardini has proposed the low-set rectangular windows.

The windows above the doors and niches were probably meant to provide the only source of natural light in the nave, before the circular panels (tondi) under the main arches were opened up as oculi. Before this, the tondi were probably decorated with paintings, like those once placed on the façade of the church. The painted tondi of the façade and the portico are described by Bertelli (1994); see also Marelli (1994a and 1994b).

204 Evidence of the round-headed rectangular windows in the nave is described by Johnson (1975b), pp. 16–18.

205 For the possible original coloration of the porch, see Soggia and Zuccoli (1994), p. 397, illustrations 9 and 10.

206 Johnson (1975b), p. 19.

207 According to a description of their remains in the early nineteenth century: Johnson (1975b), p. 19, and p. 104, n. 103.

208 The poor state of the mouldings on the façade in the eighteenth century can be seen in the painted view of Sant'Andrea (see fig. 141).

209 Cadioli (1974), p. 61: 'qualche sbaglio nelle misure'.

210 Donesmondi (1616), p. 43.

211 Johnson (1975b), p. 29.

212 See the Alberti Group photogrammetric drawing.

213 The nineteenth-century survey by Ritscher (1899) is also reliable. He records the nave vault height as 27.97 m. or 59.92 *braccia*.

214 This consonance is discussed in relation to architecture by Simson (1956), p. 37.

215 The Temple of Solomon is described in Ezekiel 41 and 1 Kings 6; see also Simson (1956), pp. 37–8. The dimensions of Sant'Andrea are exactly half those of Solomon's Temple, and Alberti was perhaps more concerned to achieve the archetype's precise proportions than its dimensions: see Zorzi's later memorandum on San Francesco della Vigna, Venice, n. 219 below.

216 1 Kings 6: 18: 'And the cedar of the house within was carved with knops and open flowers: all was cedar; there was no stone seen'. Johnson (1975b), p. 20, and Appx VII, remarked that the coffered vaults of Sant'Andrea contain rosettes carved in wood and frescoed with a highly polychromed finish inside the church: except the main vault which is painted in imitation relief.

217 1 Kings 6: 23–35. On Alberti's use of the cherub motif at Rimini and Sant'Andrea, see Onians (1988), pp. 127 and 182.

218 On the influence of the Temple of Solomon on Gothic cathedrals, see Simson (1956); on the proportions of the Sistine Chapel, see Battisti (1957); and on Florence Cathedral, Warren (1973), pp. 92–105; see also the discussion of the Tempio Malatestiano above.

219 Francesco Zorzi, in his memorandum of 1535 for San Francesco della Vigna in Venice, stated: 'When God wished to instruct Moses concerning the form and proportion of the tabernacle which he had built, He gave him as a model the fabric of the world [. . .] it was necessary that the particular place should resemble His universe, not in size, of which He had no need, nor in delight, but in proportion. [. . .] Pondering on this mystery, Solomon the Wise gave the same proportions as those of the Mosaic tabernacle to the famous Temple which he erected'. This translation is from Wittkower (1973), p. 155. For a later appraisal of the same church and a slightly different transcription of Zorzi's text, see Foscari and Tafuri (1983), esp. Appx II. In fact, Zorzi describes the proportions of San Francesco della Vigna as 9:12:27 paces (or 40:60:135 feet: Wittkower, p. 157), or 3:4:9 (not 2:3:6 as at the Temple) where the number 3 figures prominently (the ternary number of Plato, rather than multiples of 10). But as Zorzi writes: 'one can increase the measures and numbers, but they should always remain in the same ratios'.

220 Only partial remains of the Temple of Peace survive: its precinct abuts onto the north-west corner of the Basilica of Maxentius. A misreading of texts referring to the position of the Forum buildings led to the confusion about its identity, and the basilica was described as 'Templum Pacis et Latonae' in medieval documents and as 'Templum Pacis' until correctly identified by Nibby (1819). Rucellai (1960, p. 76) calls the basilica 'Templum Pacis', and relates (after the *Mirabilia*) that the building was ruined on the night Jesus Christ was born; see also Weiss (1969), p. 74.

221 Pliny, *Natural History*, XXXVI, 27.

222 The paintings are now at Hampton Court, London. For a general account, see Martindale (1979) and Martineau (1992), pp. 350–92. It is uncertain who commissioned the paintings, and either Ludovico or Francesco Gonzaga have been identified as patrons. Consequently, it has been proposed that they were begun before 1478, or after 1484: see Hope (1985).

223 By the third quarter of the fifteenth century Rome was in possession of some of the holiest relics in Christendom: Santa Croce held fragments of the Holy Cross; and the Vatican St Peter's tomb, St Andrew's head and six spiral columns from the Temple of Solomon. See Krinsky (1970); see also Campbell (1981), p. 3, who relates that during the Mass commemorating the dedication of the Lateran Basilica, references were made comparing the Lateran to Solomon's Temple. At Santa Croce in Gerusalemme there is an early sixteenth-century inscription in St Helen's chapel asserting that Rome is the truer Jerusalem, a theme explored with reference to the Quattrocento by Westfall (1974).

224 Manetti (1734), as interpreted by Westfall (1974), p. 125. For a similar interpretation, see Ettlinger (1965), p. 79. See also Magnuson (1958).

225 Westfall (1974), pp. 151–4.

226 Krautheimer (1969b). Subsequent generations of architects were also to use the Basilica of Maxentius as an inspirational model for their church designs, not least for the new St Peter's. See Campbell (1981).

227 Burns (1971), p. 281. Furthermore, Focillon (1963), p. 94, remarked that Tuscan churches retained 'those very old and simple volumes which trace their descent from the Early Christian box-basilica'.

228 Manetti (1970), p. 106; Manetti (1976), p. 108.

229 Brunelleschi was critical of an earlier design by someone 'who was better versed in letters than experienced in that kind of building': Vasari (1973), II, pp. 368–9.

230 An observation also made by Burns (1971), p. 281.

231 Johnson (1975b), Appx II, no. 2, p. 64.

232 The following was summarised in Tavernor (1994b); and cf. Hersey (1994).

233 Alberti (1966), pp. 555–7: 'Nonnullis in templis hinc atque hinc vetusto Etruscorum more pro lateribus non tribunal, sed cellae minusculae habendae sunt. Eorum haec fiet ratio. Aream sibi sumpsere, cuius longitudo, in partes divisa sex, una sui parte latitudinem excederet; ex ipsa longitudine partes dabant duas latitudini porticus, quae quidem pro vestibulo templi extabat; reliquum dividebant in partes tris, quae trinis cellarum

latitudinibus darentur. Rursus latitudinem ipsam templi dividebant in partes decem; ex his dabant partes tris cellis in dextram et totidem tres cellis in sinistram positis; mediae vero ambulationi quattuor relinquebant. Ad caput templi unum medianasque ad cellas hinc atque hinc aliud tribunal adigebant. Parietes pro faucibus cellarum efficiebant ex quinta vacui intervalli'.

234 Vitruvius (1960), IV, 7: 'The place where the temple is to be built having been divided on its length in six parts, deduct one and let the rest be given to its width. Then let the length be divided into two equal parts, of which the inner be reserved as space for the *cellae*, and the part next the front left for the arrangement of the columns.

Next let the width be divided into ten parts. Of these, let three on the right and three on the left be given to the smaller *cellae*, or the *alae* if there are to be *alae*, and the other four devoted to the middle of the temple.'

235 Vitruvius (1962), IV, 7, and illustration, p. 121.

236 Krautheimer (1969b), pp. 338–9. See also Alberti (1912), pp. 618–20, and Alberti (1955), p. 247, n. 144, where Alberti's description of an Etruscan temple is considered to be an interpretation of Vitruvius' text mediated by Alberti's own reconstruction of the Templum Pacis cum Basilica of Maxentius.

237 These comments were used by Krautheimer to distinguish the nave of the church from the later Latin-cross extension, which he concluded was not part of Alberti's original conception for this design; see also Rykwert and Tavernor (1986). For Krautheimer's list of differences between the basilica and Sant'Andrea, see Krautheimer (1969b).

238 Dimensions were taken from Minoprio (1932).

239 Ezekiel 4: 5 states that it was built with a long cubit, 'the cubit and an hand breadth'. According to an 'inductive' survey of Herodian masonry by Hastings (1910), III, pp. 898–9, the 'short' cubit of 17.7 inches (450 mm) was most probably used, not the long cubit of about 20.5 inches (527 mm). If Alberti reconstructed the temple for himself, he may well have derived the biblical 'cubit' from the Roman cubit (equivalent to 443 mm), though what would he have made of the 'short' and 'long' cubit? The Mantuan *braccio* is closest in size to the shorter cubit (equivalent to 467 mm).

240 As Alberti wrote to Ludovico: 'I have also learned [. . .] that the chief aim was to have a large space where many people could see the Blood of Christ': Johnson (1975b), pp. 8–10, and Appx II, p. 64, no. 2.

241 In a letter to Alberti quoted above (see p. 159), Ludovico mentioned that he had ideas of his own for Sant'Andrea; see Johnson (1975b), p. 9, and Appx II, p. 64, no. 2.

242 Alberti (1988), p. 402, n. 98. Its design is derived, most probably, from the ancient arches of Constantine and Septimius Severus in Rome.

243 Wittkower (1973), p. 39 on Alberti and p. 89 on Palladio.

244 'Sel ve piasera daro modo de notarlo in proportione': in Johnson (1975b), Appx II, p. 64, no. 2. Similarly, as Alberti commented to his patron on his drawing of a bath building: 'Nam capiet omne genus ornamenti ex dimensionibus': Burns (1979), p. 54, n. 16.

245 For Alberti these chambers were reminiscent perhaps of the numerous cellular spaces around three sides of Solomon's Temple.

246 For the influence of Alberti's Sant'Andrea on the church architecture of Palladio, see Boucher (1994), esp. pp. 192 and 198.

247 To satisfy the large crowds and propriety, there were three separate displays, one of which was reserved for women: Johnson (1975b), Appx I, pp. 62–3, n. 9.

248 Johnson (1975b), Appx II, p. 64, no. 2.

249 Johnson (1975b), pp. 98–9, n. 25; see also Saalman, Volpi Ghirardini and Law (1992).

250 Saalman, Volpi Ghirardini and Law (1992), pp. 357–76.

251 Saalman, Volpi Ghirardini and Law (1992), pp. 357–76: and the team of recent excavators found lime mortar there to be perfectly dry.

252 Johnson (1975b), Appx V, p. 85; Saalman, Volpi Ghirardini and Law (1992), p. 371, n. 21.

253 They are, however, much narrower than the *oculus* of the Pantheon, and have a diameter of 1.54 m. where visible from below (increasing to 1.72 m. at roof level),★ compared with nearly 9 m. at the Pantheon. The nave of Sant'Andrea is much narrower too, being under half the width of the Pantheon. ★I am grateful to Livio Volpi Ghirardini for this information.

254 The coffer effect, on the vault of the nave, had been painted there well before the late eighteenth century when it required retouching (Johnson, 1975b, pp. 41–2), though there is no record of when it was first painted.

255 For a different condusion, see Saalman, Volpi Ghirardini and Law (1992), pp. 371–2 and 375–6.

256 Saalman, Volpi Ghirardini and Law (1992), pp. 372–5.

257 A similar motif appears again in Labacco's sketch of what is assumed to be a side elevation of San Sebastiano, but, from the existing fabric of that church, it is uncertain how this would have been incorporated three-dimensionally.

IX ALBERTI'S DESIGN FOR A BATH BUILDING

1 On the castle of Sigismondo in Rimini, see Arduini, *et al.* (1970), pp. 177–207. See also Battisti (1981), p. 244.

2 On Federico's life and accomplishments, see Clough (1981). See also Hollingsworth (1994), pp. 192–201.

3 Bialostocki (1964), pp. 13–19.

4 For the urban history of Urbino, see Luni (1985), pp. 11–49.

5 The design of the Palazzo Ducale, Urbino, was probably inspired by recent changes at the Vatican palace; see Westfall (1978), pp. 20–45. On the requests for drawings, see Gaye (1839), I, pp. 274–7, doc. CXVII; and Vasic Vatovec (1979), pp. 239–40.

6 Castiglione (1968), p. 5, lines 29–30: 'non ad un palagio ma a dieci (ad un regno) sarebbe stato bastante'. Intriguingly, Sir Thomas Holby echoed Alberti, consciously or otherwise, in the first English translation of

Il cortegiano (1561): 'it appeared not a Palace, but a Citie in forme of a Palace' (Castiglione, 1974, Bk 1, p. 18).

7   Clough (1966), pp. 101–4, and Herstein (1971), pp. 113–28.

8   Bisticci (1970–76), I, pp. 382–3. On Federico's secretary, Francesco Galli, who compared his master to Vitruvius, see Dezzi Bardeschi (1968), p. 7. Luca Pacioli dedicated his *Summa arithmeticae* of 1494 to Federico's son and successor 'the Most Illustrious Prince Guido Baldo, Duke of Urbino', and in the introduction remarked on the relationship between mathematics and architecture, and how Vitruvius 'and the Florentine Leon Battista degli Alberti, in his perfectly proportioned works, developed the application of mathematics to architecture. The same is exemplified in our own day by the new wonder of Italy, the noble, admirable palace of Your Lordship, begun and completed by your father of most happy memory. In this building nature has indeed shown its power and art more than in any other that has yet to be seen. No tongue can express the beauty and harmony of its plan better than the building itself'.

9   Federico da Montefeltro wrote of his friendship with Alberti to Cristoforo Landino, *c.* 1475, when on receipt of a copy of the *Disputationes Camaldulenses*: 'Nihil fuit familiarius neque amantius amicitia qua Baptista et ego eramus coniuncti': cited in Alatri (1949), pp. 102–3. He is first recorded as staying in Urbino in the late summer of 1464: Guidetti (1974), p. 240; Heydenreich (1967), pp. 1–6.

10 Federico studied at the Casa Giocosa in Mantua, founded by Vittorino. The Montefeltro and Gonzaga were to form a lasting alliance when Federico's son Guidobaldo later married Elisabetta, a granddaughter of Ludovico Gonzaga. See Chambers (1981), table, p. xviii, and Cheles (1986), p. 9.

11 Baldi (1824), III, pp. 55–6; see also Mancini (1967), pp. 482–3, n. 1. The suggestion for the gift came from Bernardo Alberti, son of Antonio, Leon Battista Alberti's cousin (erroneously referred to as Alberti's brother in Baldi's original text).

12 Quoted in Mancini (1967), p. 479: 'ogni anno per salute e riposo fuggendo gli autunni romani vo a diporto presso di lui, e mi sembra dalle cene di Sardanapàlo captiare ai conviti d'Alcinoo ed incontrare un ospite socratico'. Landino's Alberti is alluding to the wanderings of Odysseus in Greek legend. Sardanapalus epitomised cultural refinement and luxury to the Greeks, and was ruled over by Assurbanipal, a peaceful and literary prince. Alcinous was King of the Phaeacians in the island of Scheria (usually identified with Corcyra). For his reception and entertainment of Odysseus see *Odyssey*, Bks VI and XII.

13 As translated by Burns (1979), p. 54, n. 15; the original letter of 14 August 1464 is reproduced in Calzona (1994a), p. 171.

14 For a summary of this conjecture, see Zampetti and Battistini (1985), pp. 56–7.

15 For the building history of the Palazzo Ducale, Urbino, see Polichetti (1985) and Cheles (1986).

16 Cheles (1986), pp. 11–14. An English translation of

Laurana's letter of appointment is in Chambers (1970), pp. 164–6.

17 Cheles (1986), p. 12.

18 Francesco di Giorgio (1967), II, p. 340.

19 According to Paolo Cortese, *De cardinalatu* (Casa Cortese, 1510), LXXX–LXXXXIIIv, as cited in Chambers (1992), pp. 22–3, and n. 88. On private bathrooms in later palazzi in Rome, see Frommel (1973).

20 Valtieri (1972), pp. 686–94, supports Vasari's opinion; but Mack (1982), p. 69 and n. 51, rejects this view.

21 Tuccia (1852), pp. 235 and 247; and as described in Burroughs (1990), p. 133; after Manetti (1734), col. 929; and in Chambers (1992), p. 24.

22 Chambers (1992), p. 24.

23 Chambers (1992), pp. 10–11.

24 Chambers (1992), p. 12.

25 Federico was at Petriolo in 1478; see also Chambers (1992), pp. 22–3.

26 Baldi (1590), p. 564; Rotondi (1950–51), I, p. 330 and fig. 286; Fontebuoni (1985), p. 187; and Polichetti (1985), pp. 159–60.

27 For a full description of these rooms, see Polichetti (1985), esp. pp. 155–61.

28 Baldi (1590), pp. 537–8, as quoted by Fontebuoni (1985), p. 190.

29 The enjoyment of fresh air as part of balneotherapy is mentioned in Chambers (1992), p. 27.

30 For a full glossary of these ancient terms, see Yegül (1992), pp. 487–94.

31 Vitruvius VI, 6.2; public bathing spaces are described in V. 10 and private baths in VI. 6.

32 That is, Aulus Aurelius Cornelius Celsus and Galenus Claudius. In *De re aedificatoria* Alberti mentions Celsus four times (alluding to *De medicina*: see esp. II, 14 and 17 of that treatise), and Galen once (alluding to his *De febrium differentiis*): see the index to Alberti (1988). See also Temkin (1973) and Galen (1951).

33 Pliny, *Natural History*, Bk 31, II–XVII, XXXII.

34 This is discussed in Chambers (1992), pp. 6–7.

35 A note on the drawing reads: *Prefurnia & vasa aquaria latebunt hospites; omnia erunt lucidissima expedita & lauta* ('the mouths of the furnaces and the cauldrons of water will be hidden from the guests; everything will be very bright, uncluttered and elegant'). This is the only reference to the bath's intended users. See Burns (1979), p. 48.

36 A point made by Burns (1979), p. 46. In Latin Alberti's note on the bath building plan reads: *Et spectabitur cum summa voluptate.*

37 The drawing is pasted into a volume of sketches, and is in the collection of the Biblioteca Mediceo-Laurenziana, Florence (Cod. Ashb. 1828, App. cc., fols 56v–57r). The other sheets in Oddi's scrap-book include sketches by Francesco di Giorgio as well as drawings by the collector himself, but the plan of the bath building is earlier, and Burns (1979) has deduced from the form of the annotations that the drawing was prepared by Alberti and deposited by him in Urbino. Scaglia (1988), p. 85, doubts the provenance of Urbino and claims that the association with Oddi is faulty. She believes instead that the drawing is in a collection that is 'heavily Sienese',

and suggests several possible Vitruvian authors for it, mainly from the early sixteenth century, and her list of possibles excludes Alberti. Scaglia argues against Burns's attribution to Alberti on the basis of 'a review of his handwriting, style of drawing, and the literary content of his notes'. However, she makes no allowance for the fact that the handwriting is contained mainly in a tight margin, or within the boxed areas of the plan, which would cause it to be 'more compact and upright' (one of her reasons for dismissing it as Alberti's handwriting). There is, of course, no other drawing by Alberti with which to compare its style, but, as Burns argues, there is much to commend the content of the annotations on the drawing as emanating from Alberti – Scaglia even concedes that its author was someone who 'was perhaps familiar with Alberti's treatise'. Scaglia dates the paper on which the drawing is made by a watermark (as does Burns), and as *c*.1450–60, but then goes on to propose that of various early sixteenth century candidates its author may well be the Frenchman Guillaume Philander (1505–56). This would of course mean that the paper was more than sixty years old before it was used. The date of the paper and the design and content of the drawing would suggest to me that Burns' attribution to Alberti is entirely credible, a view which is also tentatively supported by Smith (1994d).

38 Burns (1979), p. 46, who suggests that Alberti's drawing 'had been left by him in Urbino, during one of his regular visits to the city'. It cannot be ruled out that the drawing relates to the design of the papal baths at Viterbo, but its original provenance and Federico da Montefeltro's own bathing habit would suggest that Urbino is more likely.

39 Undertaken by the Soprintendenza per i Beni Ambientali e Architettonici delle Marche: see Polichetti (1985).

40 For a plan diagram conveniently summarising the layout of the Palazzo Ducale, see Rotondi (1950), p. 35.

41 Baldi (1590), ch. XIII, pp. 546–7; see also Rotondi (1950), p. 307, and Westfall (1978), p. 32.

42 Baldi (1590), ch. XIII, pp. 546–7: 'Parti non finite, e non cominciate'.

43 Rotondi (1950), p. 219; Westfall (1978), p. 32.

44 The idea that Alberti may have designed the Palazzo Ducale is suggested most recently in Zampetti and Battistini (1985), pp. 56–7. However, Heydenreich (1967) attributes its design to Federico alone, a notion challenged by Clough (1973), p. 141, who argues that he had neither the time nor the competence to devise such a building.

45 Burns (1979), p. 49, proposed that the design is ordered by a unit of measure having the same width as the piers of the *porticus specularia* on the plan, which are between 8.5 and 9 mm wide. Allowing for conveniently sized door openings, Burns estimated that the piers would have had a width of about one *braccio*, that is (considering the various *braccia* then in use), between 60 and 90 cm. In other words, according to the upper figure, the drawing scales to about 1:100 of life-size (where 9 mm = 90 cm).

46 Burns (1979), p. 49.

47 One of the annotations reads: *Nam capi et omne genus ornamenti ex dimensionibus*. Manetti (1976), p. 100, writes

that Brunelleschi's project for the loggia of the Innocenti 'è dette loro el disegno a punto misurato a braccia piccole'. See Krautheimer and Krautheimer-Hess (1982), pp. 238–9, where it is suggested that Brunelleschi may have used a drawing scaled at 1:60 for his perspective studies of the Florentine Baptistery. From the more numerous drawings that survive from the sixteenth century it is certain that scaled drawings were used. For example, the famous plan of St Peter's (Uffizi, A20) has a grid of lines superimposed on to it, where each square corresponds to 10 *palmi*, a local *canna*; see also Lotz (1982), p. 288.

48 Gaye (1839), I, pp. 274–5.

49 Doursther (1840), p. 417, lists the length of the Urbino *piede* as 0.40957 m. However, from the descriptions of spaces in the palazzo by Baldi (1590), he is using a shorter measure, 0.334 m. long. For example, see Fontebuoni (1985), p. 190; Baldi states that the tennis court measured 65 by 22 and 23 *piedi*, which according to a modern survey is 21.75 by 7.3 and 7.7 m.

50 At a scale of 1:100 the piers on Alberti's drawing are the equivalent of 1.1 m. deep, while those of the Cortile del Pasquino have a similar depth of 1.08 m. Alberti's piers have intervals which scale at 3.3, 3.3 and 3.5 m., while the columns of the main courtyard are 3.2 to 3.25 m. apart, or 7.8 and 7.92 or close to 8 local feet. Tantalisingly, this arcade resembles the dimensions of the side arcades of the Tempio Malatestiano: see fig. 55 above. At its narrowest point Alberti's *ambulatio* measures 4.15 m. wide, and at its widest it is 4.4 m., while the ambulatories of the existing main courtyard are 4.13 m. wide. Similarly, Alberti's *ad penetralia* and vestibule have sides whose lengths range between 4.15 and 4.45 m.

51 That is, as far as can be detected from the early location plan of properties in this area, researched and published by Rotondi (1950–51), illustrations in I, p. 29, and II, p. 406.

52 Burns (1979), p. 47: 'totum hoc edificium thermarum erit estate frigidum p[er] hiemem vero solo radio solis tepescet' and 'Ambulatio que pro vestibulo est hieme habet soles non ventos'. This resembles Alberti's comment (1988, V, 17, pp. 145–51), that 'The ancients preferred their porticoes to face south, because in summer the arc of the sun would be too high for its rays to enter, whereas in winter it would be low enough'. If this prescription is applied to the Urbino siting, the ambulatory is facing the wrong direction, and should be reversed to face south, but there is insufficient information on the drawing to be unequivocal about the intended orientation of this bath building. Burns (1979), p. 47, concluded on the basis of the annotations, and Alberti's comments in *De re aedificatoria* about the orientation of the portico, 'that the *ambulatio* faces south, as does the hot room of the baths (*sudatio*) placed in the warm south-west corner, whereas the *porticus specularia* faces east'. But Alberti emphasises in his annotation of the plan that 'the *ambulatio* which is in front of the vestibule', not the 'whole building', should benefit from the wind and sun. This has curved niches drawn in plan, suggesting some kind of rotund feature above. It was unlikely to have been domical because the ambulatory

is too wide to support a dome, though a groin vault could have been supported here. The niches mark the entrance to the baths, and were perhaps places in which to sit and admire the views. Alternatively, Alberti may have thought of positioning a tower-like lantern at this point – perhaps as a 'tower-of-the-winds' for the summer months, and which would also deflect the sun into the ambulatory in winter.

53 Vitruvius (1960), VI, 4.1.

54 Brunelleschi employed a similar arrangement in the interior of Santo Spirito, Florence, where the main west-east axis of the plan aligns with a column. This was done, presumably, because the altar was the destination on leaving the entrance, while the column (which it obscured) was part of the ambulatory that moves around the perimeter of the church. At the Palazzo Ducale, Urbino, there is an even number of openings down the side of the main courtyard, and its sides are symmetrical about a column. The shorter sides of this courtyard have an uneven number of openings and are symmetrical about an opening, rather than a column or pier. Thus, it has one dominant 'open' axis, running north-south, and a secondary 'closed' axis, running east-west.

55 Fontebuoni and Barbaliscia (1985), p. 194, rooms labelled 21, 27, 28 and 29, at the level marked 'Piano primo seminterrato'.

56 From Polichetti (1985), survey plan no. 2, the *cucina generale* is 96.5 mm long at a scale of 1:200. The *tepidarium* in Alberti's drawing is 214 mm long, according to Burns (1979), p. 47, fig. 2: 96.5 ÷ 214 = 0.451 × 200 = 90.2. Thus, Alberti's drawing scales at 1:90.2, and, more approximately, is closest to the whole number ratio of 1:90.

57 Burns (1979), pp. 47–9.

58 Rotondi (1950), pp. 315–18. The Secret Garden is arranged as a terrace enclosed by buildings on three sides (to the south, north and east) and with a high wall punctuated by windows with views to the west. Begun by Laurana and probably completed by Francesco di Giorgio, the Secret Garden fell into disrepair but was reconstructed by Rotondi from a description by Baldi (1590).

59 Rotondi (1950–51), I, pp. 125 and 330, does not ascribe a particular function to the room now called the main kitchen. He refers to it as 'n. 29' throughout his book.

60 The *tepidarium* is a major organising element in Alberti's bath building plan. In the palace, the main kitchen has two more storeys of rooms of the same size above it – at ground-floor level an anteroom and salon, at first-floor level the ducal salon. Structurally and constructionally these three rooms are integral, the span of their floors and vaults above are large, and it would have been imprudent to subdivide the rooms above the level of the main kitchen – nor have they been. However, there is no surviving evidence that any other of the bathrooms in Alberti's design were built, at least not in the way he drew them. Directly to the east of his *tepidarium*, the area which would have been occupied by the *lavatio* and *sudatio*, is split by a corridor and a service ramp linking the kitchens up to the main courtyard of the palace.

To the west there are more kitchens, a wood store, then the duke's bathrooms. Apart from the *tepidarium* and *ambulatio*, the shapes of the rooms as they now stand do not resemble those indicated by Alberti.

61 Perhaps the kitchens and their stores were originally in the sequence of storerooms immediately south of Alberti's *tepidarium*, which have a terrace in front of them. Here they would have been well ventilated and benefited from natural daylight.

62 Rotondi (1950–51), I, p. 330.

63 For the network of water conduits and the position of major cisterns in this area, see Polichetti (1985), II, drawing 18. The duke's kitchen, south-west of the main kitchen, and adjacent to the south tower, has a cistern 4.5 m. deep under its entire floor area; the original floor is still in place and slopes towards a gulley: Nori (1985), p. 186, room description 21. Assuming that the main kitchen was once intended to be the *tepidarium*, it is possible that the duke's kitchen was the *sudatio* in a modified version of Alberti's bath building plan, with the *lavatio* to its north, and that the baths were entered east of the *tepidarium*, i.e., that his original plan was reversed.

64 A case for Alberti's involvement in the design of Palazzo Ducale has been argued by Morolli (1996).

65 Rotondi (1950–51), I, p. 331 and pp. 453–4, n. 197; Vasari (1973), III, pp. 70–71 and 75: both Vasari and Daniele Barbaro attributed the design of the Palazzo Ducale to Francesco di Giorgio. And see n. 44 above.

X THE ART OF BUILDING IN PRACTICE

1 It has been suggested that Michelozzo reinterpreted the design of the Holy Sepulchre in Jerusalem for his modifications to Santissima Annunziata in Florence and its new circular tribune: Lang (1954); on the Holy Sepulchre as model for the Tempio Malatestiano, see Mitchell (1973) and Verga (1977).

2 This perfection is reflected in the 30 and 50 Florentine *braccia*, the ratio 3:5 – or 'perfect' ratio 6:10 – inner and outer diameters of Santa Maria degli Angeli. It can only be conjectured whether Brunelleschi thought of these dimensions as equivalent to 60 and 100 Roman *pedes*. See Wilson Jones (1989b), where it is suggested that centralised Roman buildings were designed with diameters that were multiples of ten Roman *pedes*.

3 This effect was through the 'eye of the beholder' according to the first English translation of Alberti (1955), IX, 9, p. 204; translated in a less loaded way as 'one's gaze' in Alberti (1988), p. 314; cf. Alberti (1966), p. 851.

4 Smith (1992), esp. ch. 6.

5 This body-building relationship was earlier emphasised by Vitruvius (1960), III, 1.9.

6 Smith (1992), p. 97.

7 This is explained most clearly by Smith (1992), pp. 76–9, and Smith (1994a), pp. 196–215.

8 For the most complete overview of Alberti's urban vision, see Fante (1982) and Choay (1997).

9 For a similar conclusion, but one which was arrived at by a quite different route, see Smith (1992), pp. 96–7.

ALBERTI'S WRITINGS

This list is arranged in chronological order of the various editions of Alberti's writings cited in this book. For full bibliographical details of earlier editions of his work, see Panza (1994), pp. 217–25. Indispensable to a study of Alberti's architectural treatise is H.-K. Lücke, *Index verborum: Leon Battista Alberti, 'De re aedificatoria'*, 4 vols, Munich, 1975–9.

Alberti (1546)
I dieci libri de l'architettura di Leon Battista degli Alberti fiorentino novamente da la latina ne la volgar lingua con molta diligenza tradotti da Pietro Lauro, Venice, 1546.

Alberti (1550)
L'architettura (De re aedificatoria) di Leon Battista Alberti tradotta in lingua fiorentina da Cosimo Bartoli [. . .] con l'aggiunta de designi, Florence, 1550.

Alberti (1568)
Opuscoli morali di Leon Battista Alberti, gentil'huomo fiorentino, ed. C. Bartoli, Venice, 1568.

Alberti (1843)
Opere volgari di L. B. Alberti per la più parte inedite e tratte dagli autografi, ed. A. Bonucci, 5 vols, Florence, 1843, *Vita anonima di Leon Battista Alberti* in vol. 1, XCI–CXVIII; Italian trans. of the Latin in *Rerum italicarum scriptores*, ed. L. A. Muratori, III, cols 295–304.

Alberti (1890)
Opera inedita et pauca separatim impressa, ed. G. Mancini, Florence, 1890.

Alberti (1912)
Alberti's Zehn Bücher über die Baukunst, trans. M. Theuer, Vienna, 1912.

Alberti (1942)
Momus o Del principe, ed. G. Martini, Bologna, 1942.

Alberti (1954)
Opuscoli inediti: 'Musca', 'Vita S. Potiti', ed. C. Grayson, Florence, 1954.

Alberti (1955)
Ten Books on Architecture, trans. J. Leoni (from C. Bartoli's Italian trans. of 1550), London, 1726; edition of 1755, reprinted with notes by J. Rykwert, London, 1955.

Alberti (1960–73)
Opere volgari di Leon Battista Alberti, ed. C. Grayson, 3 vols, Bari, 1960–73.

Alberti (1964)
La prima grammatica della lingua volgare, ed. C. Grayson, Bologna, 1964.

Alberti (1965)
Intercenali inedite, ed. E. Garin, Florence, 1965.

Alberti (1966)
L'architettura, ed. and trans. G. Orlandi, 2 vols, Milan, 1966.

Alberti (1969)
The Family in Renaissance Florence, trans. (from the Italian) R. N. Watkins, Columbia, SC, 1969; for *I libri della famiglia*, see Alberti (1960–73), 1, pp. 3–341.

Alberti (1972)
On Painting and On Sculpture: The Latin Texts of 'De pictura' and 'De statua', ed. and trans. C. Grayson, London, 1972.

Alberti (1974)
Descriptio urbis romae, ed. (with Italian trans.) G. Orlandi, *Convegno internazionale indetto nel V centenario di Leon Battista Alberti (Roma–Mantova–Firenze, 25–29 April 1972), Accademia Nazionale dei Lincei*, 371, Rome, 1974, pp. 112–27.

Alberti (1975)
Rime a versioni poetiche, ed. G. Gorni, Milan, 1975.

Alberti (1976)
De commodis litterarum atque incommodis, ed. L. Goggi Carotti, Florence, 1976.

Alberti (1984)
Apologhi ed elogi, ed. R. Contarino, intro. L. Malerba, Genoa, 1984.

Alberti (1986)
Momo o Del principe, ed. and trans. R. Consolo, Genoa, 1986.

Alberti (1987)
Dinner Pieces, ed. and trans. D. Marsh, Binghamton, NY, 1987.

Alberti (1988)
> *On the Art of Building in Ten Books*, ed. and trans. (from the Latin) J. Rykwert, N. Leach and R. Tavernor, Cambridge, MA, and London, 1988.

Alberti (1989)
> *Apologhi*, ed. M. Ciccuto, Milan, 1989.

Alberti (1991a)
> *On Painting*, trans. C. Grayson [as Alberti (1972)], ed. with intro. M. Kemp, London, 1991.

Alberti (1991b)
> *De equo animante*, ed. (with Italian trans.) A. Videtta, Naples, 1991.

BIBLIOGRAPHY

Dates in brackets denote the year of the edition referred to in the notes, and not necessarily the first edition of that work.

Ackerman (1980)
Ackerman, J. S., 'Observations on Renaissance Church Planning in Venice and Florence, 1470–1570', *Florence and Venice: Comparisons and Relations*, II: *Cinquecento*, ed. S. Bertelli, N. Rubinstein and C. H. Smyth, Florence, 2 vols, 1980, pp. 287–308.

Ackerman (1991)
Ackerman, J. S., *Distance Points: Essays in Theory and Renaissance Art and Architecture*, Cambridge, MA, and London, 1991.

Adimari (1616)
Adimari, R., *Sito riminese*, Brescia, 1616.

Aiken (1980)
Aiken, J. A., 'Leon Battista Alberti's System of Human Proportions', *Journal of the Warburg and Courtauld Institutes*, XLIII, 1980, pp. 68–96.

Alatri (1949)
Alatri, P., *Lettere di stato e d'arte di Federico da Montefeltro*, Rome, 1949.

Alfarano (1914)
Alfarano, T., *De Basilicae Vaticanae antiquissima et nova structura* (1590), ed. M. Cerrati, *Studi e testi*, XXVI, Rome, 1914.

Algarotti (1969)
Algarotti, F., *Dialoghi sopra l'ottica neutoniana*, 1752, in *Illuministi italiani*, ed. E. Bonora, II, Milan and Naples, 1969.

Allason (1819)
Allason, T., *Picturesque Views of the Antiquities of Pola*, 1819.

Amadei (1955)
Amadei, F., *Cronaca universale della Città di Mantova*, 1741; reprinted Mantua, 1955.

Ames-Lewis (1974)
Ames-Lewis, F., 'A Portrait of Leon Battista Alberti by Uccello?', *Burlington Magazine*, CXVI, February 1974, pp. 103–4.

Amiani (1751)
Amiani, P.-M., *Memorie istoriche della città di Fano*, Fano, 1751.

Amico (1953)
Fra Bernardino Amico, *Plans of the Sacred Edifices of the Holy Land*, ed. and trans. T. Bellorini and E. Hoade, *Publications of the Studium Biblicum Franciscanum*, X, Jerusalem, 1953.

Arduini et al. (1970)
Arduini, F., G. S. Menghi, F. Panvini Rosati, P. G. Pasini, P. Sanpaolesi, and A. Vasini, eds, *Città di Rimini: Sigismondo Pandolfo Malatesta e il suo tempo* (Exhib. cat., Rimini), Vicenza, 1970.

Augustine (1955)
Corpus Christianorum, De Civitate Dei, Series Latina, XLVIII, Turnhout, 1955.

Augustine (1972)
The City of God, trans. H. Bettenson, Harmondsworth, 1972.

Bacchiani (1987)
Bacchiani, A., 'Ipotesi per il completamento del progetto albertiano del Tempio Malatestiano', *Romagna arte e storia*, VII, 20, 1987, pp. 17–26.

Badt (1958)
Badt, K., 'Drei plastiche Arbeiten von Leone Battista Alberti', *Mitteilungen des Kunsthistorischen Institutes in Florenz*, VIII, 1958, pp. 78–87.

Baldi (1590)
Baldi, B., 'Descrittione del Palazzo Ducale di Urbino' [of 10 June 1587], in *Versi e prose*, Venice, 1590, pp. 503–90; also in Baldi (1724).

Baldi (1612)
Baldi, B., *De verborum vitruvianorum significatione*, Augusta, 1612.

Baldi (1724)
Baldi, B., *Memorie concernenti la città di Urbino*, ed. F. Bianchini, Rome, 1724; facs. ed., Bologna, 1978.

Baldi (1824)
Baldi, B., *Della vita e de' fatti di Federigo di Montefeltro, duca di Urbino* [F. Zuccardi edn of 1604], 3 vols, Rome, 1824.

Baldini (1989)

Baldini, G., 'L'oscuro linguaggio del tempio di S. Sebastiano in Mantova', *Mitteilungen des Kunsthistorischen Institutes in Florenz*, XXXIII, 1989, pp. 155–204.

Baldini and Casazza (1990)

Baldini, U., and O. Casazza, *La Capella Brancacci*, Milan, 1990.

Baldwin Smith (1956)

Baldwin Smith, E., *Architectural Symbolism of Imperial Rome and the Middle Ages*, Princeton, 1956.

Barbieri (1968)

Barbieri, F., *La Basilica Palladiana*, Corpus Palladianum, II, Vicenza, 1968.

Barfucci (1945)

Barfucci, E., *Lorenzo de' Medici e la società artistica del suo tempo*, Florence, 1945.

Barocchi (1971)

Barocchi, P., ed., *Scritti d'arte del Cinquecento*, Milan, 1971.

Baron (1966)

Baron, H., *The Crisis of the Early Italian Renaissance*, rev. edn, Princeton, 1966.

Bassani, Galdi and Poltronieri (1974)

Bassani, G., A. Galdi, and A. Poltronieri, 'Analisi per il restauro del tempio di San Sebastiano in Mantova', *Il Sant'Andrea di Mantova e Leon Battista Alberti*, Conference report (25–6 April 1972), Mantua, 1974, pp. 243–63.

Battaglini (1794)

Battaglini, F. G., *Della vita e de' fatti di Sigismondo Pandolfo Malatesta*, Rimini, 1794.

Battisti (1957)

Battisti, E., 'Il significato simbolico della Cappella Sistina', *Commentari rivista di critica e storia dell'arte*, VII–VIII, 1957, pp. 96–104.

Battisti (1974)

Battisti, E., 'Il metodo progettuale secondo, il "De re aedificatoria" di Leon Battista Alberti', *Il Sant'Andrea di Mantova e Leon Battista Alberti*, Conference report (25–6 April 1972), Mantua, 1974, pp. 131–74.

Battisti (1981)

Battisti, E., *Brunelleschi, the Complete Work*, London, 1981.

Baxandall (1972)

Baxandall, M., *Painting and Experience in Fifteenth Century Italy*, Oxford, 1972.

Bazzotti and Belluzzi (1980)

Bazzotti, U., and A. Belluzzi, eds, *Architettura e pittura all'Accademia di Mantova (1752–1802)*, Florence, 1980.

Beccadelli (1824)

Beccadelli, A. [Panormita], *Ermaphroditus*, ed. Forberg, Coburg, 1824.

Benedetti (1994)

Benedetti, S., 'Antonio da Sangallo il Giovane', in Millon and Lampugnani (1994), pp. 634–5, cat. no. 346.

Bentivoglio (1975)

Bentivoglio, E., 'Disegni nel "libro" di Giuliano da Sangallo, collegabili a progetti per il S. Giovanni dei Fiorentini a Roma', *Mitteilungen des Kunsthistorischen Institutes in Florenz*, XIX, 1975, pp. 251–60.

Bergstein (1991)

Bergstein, M., 'Marian Politics in Quattrocento Florence: The Renewed Dedication of Santa Maria del Fiore in 1412', *Renaissance Quarterly*, 1991, pp. 673–719.

Bertelli (1994)

Bertelli, C., '"La loggia avanti la Chiesa" a Mantova', in Rykwert and Engel (1994), pp. 242–51.

Berti (1964)

Berti, L., *Masaccio*, Milan, 1964.

Bertinelli and Truzzi (1962)

Bertinelli, L., and A. Truzzi, *La Rotonda di S. Lorenzo in Mantova*, Fraternità Domenica di Mantova, Mantua, 1962.

Bialostocki (1964)

Bialostocki, J., 'The Power of Beauty: A Utopian Idea of Leon Battista Alberti', *Studien zur toskanischen Kunst, Festschrift Ludwig Heydenreich*, ed. W. Lotz and L. L. Möller, Munich, 1964, pp. 13–19.

Billi (1892)

Billi, A., *Il libro di Antonio Billi*, ed. C. Frey, Berlin, 1892.

Biondo (1953)

Biondo, F., 'Roma instaurata', *Codice topografico della città di Roma*, ed. R. Valentini and G. Zucchetti, IV, Rome, 1953, pp. 256–323.

Bisticci (1970–76)

Bisticci, V. da, *Le vite*, ed. A. Greco, 2 vols, Florence, 1970–76.

Bonino (1981)

Bonino, M., 'Maineria riminese e cultura navale nel Quattrocento', *Romagna arte e storia*, II, 1981, pp. 3–10.

Boorsch (1992)

Boorsch, S., 'Master of 1515(?)', in Martineau (1992), cat. no. 31, p. 187.

Borghezio (1934)

Borghezio, G., and M. Vattasso, eds, *Giovanni di M° Pedrino depintore: Cronica del suo tempo*, in *Studi e testi*, LVII, Rome, 1934.

Borsi (1977)
Borsi, F., *Leon Battista Alberti: The Complete Works*, London, 1977; Italian original, Milan, 1973.

Boucher (1994)
Boucher, B., *Andrea Palladio: The Architect in his Time*, New York and London, 1994.

Bovini (1977)
Bovini, G., *Il Mausoleo di Teodorico*, Ravenna, 1977.

Bracciolini (1723)
Bracciolini, Poggio, *Poggii Bracciolini florentini: Historiae de varietate fortunae: Libri quatuor*, ed. D. Georgius, Paris, 1723.

Braghirolli (1869)
Braghirolli, W., 'Leon Battista Alberti a Mantova', *Archivio storico italiano*, IX, 1869, pp. 3–31.

Breydenbach (1961)
Breydenbach, Bernard von, *Peregrinatio in Terram Sanctam, 1486*, in *Die Reise ins Heilige Land*, Wiesbaden, 1961.

Brown (1978)
Brown, B. L., *The Tribuna of SS. Annunziata in Florence*, Unpublished PhD thesis, Northwestern University, Evanston and Chicago, 1978.

Brown (1981)
Brown, B. L., 'The Patronage and Building History of the Tribuna of SS. Annunziata in Florence: A Reappraisal in Light of New Documentation (part I)', *Mitteilungen des Kunsthistorischen in Florenz*, XXV, 1981, pp. 59–146.

Brown (1972)
Brown, C. M., 'Luca Fancelli in Mantua: A Checklist of his 85 Letters to the Gonzaga's', *Mitteilungen des Kunsthistorischen Institutes in Florenz*, XVI, 1972, pp. 153–66.

Bruckner (1969)
Bruckner, G. A., *Renaissance Florence*, New York, 1969.

Bruschi (1961)
Bruschi, A., 'Osservazioni sulla teoria architettonica rinascimentale nella formulazione albertiana', *Quaderni dell'Istituto di storia dell'architettura*, Università di Roma, VI–VIII, 31–48, 1961, pp. 115–30.

Bruschi (1972)
Bruschi, A., 'Considerazioni sulla "maniera natura" del Brunelleschi. Con un'appendice sulla Rotonda degli Angeli', *Palladio*, XXII, 1972, pp. 89–126.

Buddensieg (1976)
Buddensieg, T., 'Criticism of Ancient Architecture in the Sixteenth and Seventeenth Centuries', *Classical Influences on European Culture, A.D. 1500–1700*, ed. R. R. Bolgar, Cambridge, 1976, pp. 335–48.

Bulman (1971)
Bulman, L. B., 'Artistic Patronage of SS. Annunziata', unpublished PhD thesis, University of London, 1971.

Burckhardt (1984)
Burckhardt, J., *The Architecture of the Renaissance in Italy*, trans. J. Palmes, London, 1984, of *Die Baukunst der Renaissance in Italien*, Stuttgart, 1868.

Burns (1971)
Burns, H., 'Quattrocento Architecture and the Antique: Some Problems', *Classical Influences on European Culture, A.D. 500–1500*, ed. R. R. Bolgar, Cambridge, 1971, pp. 269–87.

Burns (1979)
Burns, H., 'A Drawing by L. B. Alberti', *Architectural Design*, XLIX, nos 5–6, 1979, pp. 45–56.

Burns (1981a)
Burns, H., 'The Gonzaga and Renaissance Architecture', in Chambers and Martineau (1981), pp. 27–38.

Burns (1981b)
Burns, H., 'The Church of San Sebastiano, Mantua', in Chambers and Martineau (1981), pp. 125–6.

Burroughs (1982)
Burroughs, C., 'Below the Angel: An Urbanistic Project in the Rome of Pope Nicholas V', *Journal of the Warburg and Courtauld Institutes*, XLV, 1982, pp. 197–207.

Burroughs (1990)
Burroughs, C., *From Signs to Design: Environmental Process and Reform in Early Renaissance Rome*, Cambridge, MA, and London, 1990.

Burroughs (1992)
Burroughs, C., 'The Building's Face and the Herculean Paradigm: Agendas and Agency in Roman Renaissance Architecture', *Res*, XXIII, 1993, pp. 7–30.

Burroughs (1994)
Burroughs, C., 'Alberti e Roma', in Rykwert and Engel (1994), pp. 134–57.

Cadioli (1974)
Cadioli, G., *Descrizione delle pitture, sculture ed architetture che si osservano nella città di Mantova e ne' suoi contorni*, 1763, ed. L. Pescasio, Mantua, 1974.

Calabi and Cornaggia (1927)
Calabi, A., and G. Cornaggia, *Matteo dei Pasti*, Milan, 1927.

Calvesi (1980)
Calvesi, M., *Il sogno di Polifilo prenestino*, Rome, 1980.

Calzona (1979)
Calzona, A., *Mantova Città dell'Alberti. Il San Sebastiano: Tomba, tempio, cosmo*, Parma, 1979.

Calzona (1981)
Calzona, A., *La rotonda e il palatium di Matilde*, Parma, 1981.

Calzona (1994a)

Calzona, A., *Il San Sebastiano di Leon Battista Alberti*, Part I: 'Il San Sebastiano di Leon Battista Alberti', Florence, 1994 (for Part II, see Volpi Ghirardini, 1994b).

Calzona (1994b)

Calzona, A., 'Ludovico Gonzaga, Leon Battista Alberti, Luca Fancelli e il problema della cripta di San Sebastiano', in Rykwert and Engel (1994), pp. 252–75.

Campagnari (1975)

Campagnari, R., 'La Casa del Mantegna', *Civiltà mantovana*, IX, 1975, pp. 44–60.

Campana (1962)

Campana, A., 'Atti, Isotta degli', in *Dizionario biografico degli italiani*, IV, Rome, 1962, pp. 547–56.

Campbell (1981)

Campbell, I., 'The New St Peter's: Basilica or Temple?', *Oxford Art Journal*, IV, no. 1, 1981, pp. 3–8.

Campbell (1984)

Campbell, I., 'Reconstructions of Roman Temples made in Italy between 1450 and 1600', unpublished DPhil thesis, Oxford, 1984.

Canali (1994a)

Canali, F., 'Schizzi di rilievo e di progetto relativi al Tempio Malatestiano di Rimini e ad antichità ravennati', in Rykwert and Engel (1994), cat. no. 115, pp. 511–12.

Canali (1994b)

Canali, F., 'Modello per mattoni, 1554', in Millon and Lampugnani (1994), cat. no. 108, pp. 490–91.

Carpeggiani (1982)

Carpeggiani, P., 'Between Symbol and Myth: The Labyrinth and the Gonzaga', *Daidalos*, III, 1982, pp. 25–37.

Carpeggiani (1994)

Carpeggiani, P., '"Renovatio Urbis": Strategie urbane a Mantova nell'età di Ludovico Gonzaga', in Rykwert and Engel (1994), pp. 178–85.

Carpeggiani and Tellini Perini (1987)

Carpeggiani, P. and Tellini Perini, C., *Sant'Andrea in Mantova, un tempio per la città del Principe*, Mantua, 1987.

Carra (1961)

Carra, G., 'I "pastelli" per Leon Battista Alberti', *Cultura Mantovana*, suppl. no. 8 to *Gazzetta di Mantova*, 15 July 1961, p. 3.

Casalini (1977)

Casalini, E., 'Brunelleschi e Michelozzo all'Annunziata', in *Le due cupole: Conferenze tenute all'Annunziata il 12 e 13 dicembre 1977*, ed. A. Parronchi and E. Casalini, Florence, 1977, pp. 29–63.

Cassazza (1978)

Cassazza, O., 'Il crocifisso ligneo di Filippo Brunelleschi', *Critica d'arte*, XLIII, 1978, pp. 209–12.

Casella and Pozzi (1959)

Casella, M. T., and G. Pozzi, *Francesca Colonna: Biografica e opera*, Padua, 1957.

Castiglione (1968)

Castiglione, B., *Il Cortegiano: La seconda redazione del 'Cortegiano'*, ed. G. Ghinassi, Florence, 1968.

Castiglione (1974)

Castiglione, B., *The Book of the Courtier*, trans. Sir Thomas Holby, 1561, ed. with intro. by J. H. Whitfield, London and New York, 1974.

Ceschi (1948)

Ceschi, C., 'La madre di Leon Battista Alberti', *Bolletino d'arte*, XXXIII, 1948, pp. 191–2.

Chambers (1970)

Chambers, D. S., ed., *Patrons and Artists in the Italian Renaissance*, London, 1970.

Chambers (1977)

Chambers, D. S., 'Sant'Andrea at Mantua and Gonzaga Patronage: 1460–1472', *Journal of the Warburg and Courtauld Institutes*, XL, 1977, pp. 99–127.

Chambers (1981)

Chambers, D. S., 'Mantua and the Gonzaga', in Chambers and Martineau (1981), pp. XVII–XXIII.

Chambers (1992)

Chambers, D. S., 'Spas in the Italian Renaissance', in *Reconsidering the Renaissance: Papers from the 21st Annual Conference*, ed. M. A. Di Cesare, Binghamton, NY, 1992, pp. 3–29.

Chambers and Martineau (1981)

Chambers, D. S., and J. Martineau, eds, *Splendours of the Gonzaga* (Exhib. cat., Victoria and Albert Museum, London), London and Milan, 1981.

Chambers, Martineau and Signorini (1992)

Chambers, D. S., J. Martineau, and R. Signorini, 'Mantegna and the Men of Letters', in Martineau (1992), pp. 8–30.

Chastel (1961)

Chastel, A., *Art et humanisme*, Paris, 1961.

Cheles (1986)

Cheles, L., *The Studiolo of Urbino*, Philadelphia, 1986.

Choay (1979)

Choay, F., 'Alberti and Vitruvius', *Architectural Design*, XLIX, nos 5–6, 1979, pp. 26–35.

Choay (1997)

Choay, F., *The Rule and the Model: On the Theory of Architecture and Urbanism*, Cambridge, MA, and

London, 1997 (trans. of *La Cité du désir et la ville modèle*, Paris, 1979).

Christiansen (1992)

Christiansen, K., 'Andrea Mantegna: Portrait of a Man', in Martineau (1992), cat. no. 102, pp. 337–9.

Christiansen (1994a)

Christiansen, K., 'Rapporti presunti, probabili e (forse anche) effettivi tra Alberti e Mantegna', in Rykwert and Engel (1994), pp. 336–57.

Christiansen (1994b)

Christiansen, K. 'Andrea Mantegna: Ritratto d'uomo', in Rykwert and Engel (1994), cat. no. 136, pp. 533–4.

Clark (1951)

Clark, K., *Piero della Francesca*, London, 1951.

Clementini (1617)

Clementini, *Raccolta istorico della fondazione di Rimino e dell'origine e vite de' Malatesta*, Rimini, 1617.

Clough (1966)

Clough, C. H., 'The Library of the Dukes of Urbino', *Librarium*, IX, 1966, pp. 101–5, 192.

Clough (1973)

Clough, C. H., 'Federigo da Montefeltro's Patronage of the Arts, 1468–1482', *Journal of the Warburg and Courtauld Institutes*, XXXVI, 1973, pp. 129–44.

Clough (1981)

Clough, C. H., *The Duchy of Urbino in the Renaissance*, London, 1981.

Coffin (1979)

Coffin, D., 'Pope Marcellus II and Architecture', *Architectura*, IX, 1979, pp. 11–29.

Cresci (1971)

Cresci, G. F., *A Renaissance Alphabet: Il perfetto scrittore, parte seconda*, Madison, Milwaukee and London, 1971.

Crovato and Dominissini (1968)

Crovato, L., and Dominissini, M., survey of Santa Maria delle Carceri (untitled), *L'architettura*, XIV, 1968, pp. 52–60.

Cusanus (1954)

Cusanus, N. [Nicholas of Cusa], *Of Learned Ignorance*, trans. Fr. Germain Heron, London, 1954.

Dal Poggetto (1992)

Dal Poggetto, P., ed., *Piero e Urbino: Piero e le corti rinascimentali* (Exhib. cat., Palazzo Ducale, Urbino), Venice, 1992.

Damisch (1979)

Damisch, H., 'The Column and the Wall', *Architectural Design*, XLIX, nos 5–6, 1979, pp. 18–25.

Damisch (1994)

Damisch, H., *The Origin of Perspective*, trans. J. Goodman, Cambridge, MA, and London, 1994

Davari (1975)

Davari, S., *Notizie storiche topografiche della città di Mantova nei secoli XIII-XIV*, 1897; reprinted Mantua, 1975.

Davidsohn (1956–68)

Davidsohn, R., *Storia di Firenze*, 8 vols, Florence, 1956–1968.

Davies (1992)

Davies, P., 'The Tempio Malatestiano "in gli anni 1453"', unpublished essay, 1992.

Davies (1993)

Davies, P., 'The Madonna delle Carceri in Prato and Italian Renaissance Pilgrimage Architecture', *Architectural History*, XXXVI, 1993, pp. 1–18.

Davies, Hemsoll and Wilson Jones (1987)

Davies, P., D. Hemsoll, and M. Wilson Jones, 'The Pantheon, Triumph of Rome or Triumph of Compromise?', *Art History*, X, 1987, pp. 131–51.

Davies and Hemsoll (1997)

Hemsoll, D., and P. Davies, 'Alberti, Leon Battista', *The Dictionary of Art*, ed. J. Turner, London, 1997, I, pp. 555–69.

Davis (1977)

Davis, M. D., *Piero della Francesca's Mathematical Treatises*, Ravenna, 1977.

De Angelis d'Ossat, G.: see, Ossat, d', below.

Delorme (1648)

Delorme, P., *L'architecture*, Rouen, 1648.

Desgodets (1843)

Desgodets, A., *Monumenti aggiunti al opera sugli edifizi antichi di Roma*, with drawings by L. Canina, 2 vols, Rome, 1843.

Dezzi Bardeschi (1963)

Dezzi Bardesch, M., 'Nuove ricerche sul Santo Sepolcro nella Cappella Rucellai a Firenze', *Marmo*, II, 1963, pp. 135–61.

Dezzi Bardeschi (1966)

Dezzi Bardeschi, M., 'Il complesso monumentale di San Pancrazio a Firenze ed il suo restauro (nuovi documenti)', *Quaderni dell'Istituto di storia dell'architettura*, XIII, 73–8, 1966, pp. 1–66.

Dezzi Bardeschi (1968)

Dezzi Bardeschi, M., 'Gli architetti Dalmati e il ricorso all'antico nel rinascimento italiano', *Bollettino degli ingegneri*, II, 1968.

Dezzi Bardeschi (1970)

Dezzi Bardeschi, M., *La facciata di Santa Maria Novella a Firenze*, Pisa, 1970.

Dezzi Bardeschi (1974)

Dezzi Bardeschi, M., 'Sole in leone. Leon Battista Alberti: Astrologia, cosmologia e tradizione ermetica nella facciata di Santa Maria Novella', *Psicon*, I, 1974, pp. 33–67.

Donesmondi (1616)
Donesmondi, I., *Dell'istoria ecclesiastica di Mantova*, Mantua, 1616.

Doursther (1976)
Doursther, H., *Dictionnaire universel des Poids et Misure anciens et modernes*, Brussels, 1840; reprinted Amsterdam, 1976.

Dürer (1525)
Dürer, Albrecht, *Unterweysung*, Nuremberg, 1525.

Eck (1994)
Eck, C. van, *Organicism in Nineteenth-century Architecture: An Enquiry into its Theoretical and Philosophical Background*, Amsterdam, 1994.

Écochard (1977)
Écochard, M., 'Filiation de monuments grecs, byzantins et islamiques', *Bibliothèque d'études islamiques*, XI, Paris, 1977, pp. 1–54.

Edgerton (1966)
Edgerton, S. Y., Jr, 'Alberti's Perspective: A New Discovery and a New Evaluation', *Art Bulletin*, XLVIII, 1966, pp. 367–78.

Edgerton (1973)
Edgerton, S. Y., Jr, 'Brunelleschi's First Perspective Picture', *Arte lombarda*, XVIII, 1973, pp. 172–95.

Edgerton (1991)
Edgerton, S. Y., Jr, *The Heritage of Giotto's Geometry, Art and Science on the Eve of the Scientific Revolution*, Ithaca, NY, and London, 1991.

Eiko Wakayama (1971)
Eiko Wakayama, M. L., '"Novità" di Masolino a Castiglione Olona', *Arte lombarda*, XVI, 1971, pp. 1–16.

Eisler (1974)
Eisler, C., 'A Portrait of L. B. Alberti', *Burlington Magazine*, CXVI, September 1974, pp. 529–30.

Ettlinger (1965)
Ettlinger, L. D., *The Sistine Chapel before Michelangelo*, Oxford, 1965.

Ettlinger (1990)
Ettlinger, H. S., 'The Sepulchre on the Facade: A Re-evaluation of Sigismondo Malatesta's Rebuilding of San Francesco in Rimini', *Journal of the Warburg and Courtauld Institutes*, LIII, 1990, pp. 133–143.

Fallows (1987)
Fallows, D., *Dufay*, London and Melbourne, 1982, rev. edn, 1987.

Fante (1982)
Fante, L. Del, *La città di Leon Battista Alberti*, Florence, 1982.

Feliciano (1960)
Feliciano, Felice, *Alphabetum romanum*, facs. ed. G. Mardersteig, Verona, 1960.

Fernie (1978)
Fernie, E., 'Historical Metrology and Architectural History', *Art History*, I, 1978, pp. 383–99.

Ferrara and Quinterio (1984)
Ferrara, M., and F. Quinterio, *Michelozzo di Bartolomeo*, Florence, 1984.

Feuer-Tóth (1978)
Feuer-Tóth, R., 'The "Apertonium Ornamenta" of Alberti and the Architecture of Brunelleschi', *Acta historiae artium hungarium*, XXIV, 1–4, 1978, pp. 147–52.

Filarete (1965)
Filarete's Treatise on Architecture, c.1461–4, trans. with intro. and notes by J. R. Spencer, New Haven, 1965.

Filarete (1972)
Filarete, Antonio Averlino, *Trattato di architettura*, ed. A. M. Finoli and L. Grassi, Milan, 1972.

Flemming (1916)
Flemming, W., *Die Begründung der modernen Aestetik und Kunstwissenschaft durch L. B. Alberti*, Berlin and Leipzig, 1916.

Foçillon (1963)
Foçillon, H., *Romanesque Art*, vol. 1 of *The Art of the West in the Middle Ages*, Oxford, 1963.

Fondelli (1992)
Fondelli, M., 'La restituzione della pavimentazione della Flagellazione di Cristo di Piero della Francesca', in Dal Poggetto (1992), pp. 502–3.

Fontebuoni (1985)
Fontebuoni, L., 'Destinazioni d'uso dal sec. XV al XX', in Polichetti (1985), pp. 185–203.

Fontebuoni and Barbaliscia (1985)
Fontebuoni, L., and G. Barbaliscia, 'Piante con individuazione delle destinazioni d'uso del secolo XV', in Polichetti (1985), pp. 194–5.

Forster (1977)
Forster, K. W., 'Review of E. J. Johnson – "Sant'Andrea in Mantua", and the "Atti del Convegno" Mantua', *Journal of the Society of Architectural Historians*, XXXVI, 1977, pp. 123–5.

Forster (1994)
Forster, K. W., 'Templum, Laubia, Figura: L'architettura di Alberti per una nuova Mantova', in Rykwert and Engel (1994), pp. 162–77.

Fortunio (1579)
Fortunio, A., *Historiarum Camaldulensium pars posterior*, Venice, 1579.

Foscari and Tafuri (1983)
Foscari, A., and M. Tafuri, *L'armonia e i conflitti: La chiesa di San Francesca della Vigna nella Venezia*, Turin, 1983.

Francesco di Giorgio (1967)
Francesco di Giorgio Martini, *Trattati di architettura, ingegneria e arte militare*, c. 1482, Milan, ed. L. Maltese Degrassi and C. Maltese, 1967.

Fraser-Jenkins (1970)
Fraser-Jenkins, A. D., 'Cosimo de' Medici's Patronage of Architecture and the Theory of Magnificence', *Journal of the Warburg and Courtauld Institutes*, XXXIII, 1970, pp. 162–70.

Fresne (1651)
Fresne, R. du, *Trattato della Pittura di Lionardo da Vinci [. . .] con la Vita dell'istesso autore scritta da Raffaello du Fresne. Ci sono giunti I tre libri della Pittura, ed il trattato della Statua di Leon Battista Alberti, con la Vita del medesimo*, Paris, 1651.

Frommel (1973)
Frommel, C. L., *Der römische Palastbau der Hochrenaissance*, I, Tubingen, 1973.

Frommel (1983)
Frommel, C. L., 'Francesco del Borgo: Architekt Pius II und Pauls II', *Romisches Jahrbuch für Kunstgeschichte*, XX, 1983, pp. 107–53.

Fubini and Menci Gallorini (1972)
Fubini, R., and A. Menci Gallorini, 'L'autobiografico di L. B. Alberti: Studio e edizione', *Rinascimento*, XII, 1972, pp. 21–78.

Gadol (1969)
Gadol, J., *Leon Battista Alberti: Universal Man of the Early Renaissance*, Chicago and London, 1969.

Galen (1951)
Claudius Galenus, *Galen's Hygiene*, trans. R. Green, Springfield, IL, 1951.

Gaye (1839)
Gaye, G., *Carteggio inedito d'artisti dei secoli XIV, XV, XVI, 1326–1500*, Florence, 1839.

Geihlow (1915)
Geihlow, K., 'Die Hieroglyphenkunde des Humanismus in der Allegorie der Renaissance', *Jahrbuch der Kunsthistorischen Sammlungen in Wien*, XXXII, 1915.

Gilbert (1969–70)
Gilbert, . . . , 'The Earliest Guide to Florentine Archirecture', *Mitteilungen des Kunsthistorischen Institutes in Florenz*, XIV, 1969–70, pp. 33–46.

Gill (1959)
Gill, J., *The Council of Florence*, Cambridge, 1959.

Ginzburg (1982)
Ginzburg, C., *Indagini su Piero*, Turin, 1982.

Giorgio (1742)
Giorgio, D., *Vita Nicolai V pontificis maximi*, Rome, 1742.

Gionta (1741)
Gionta, S., *Fioretto delle croniche di Mantova*, Verona, 1570; reprinted 1741.

Giuliano da Sangallo (1910)
Il libro di Giuliano da Sangallo, ed. C. Hülsen, 2 vols, Leipzig, 1910.

Goldthwaite (1968)
Goldthwaite, R. A., *Private Wealth in Renaissance Florence: A Study of Four Families*, Princeton, NJ, 1968.

Goldthwaite (1972)
Goldthwaite, R. A., 'Schools and Teachers of Commercial Arithmetic in Renaissance Florence', *Journal of European Economic History*, I, 1972, pp. 418–33.

Goldthwaite (1980)
Goldthwiate, R. A. *The Building of Renaissance Florence*, Baltimore and London, 1980.

Gombrich (1967)
Gombrich, E. H., 'From the Revival of Letters to the Reform of the Arts: Niccolò Niccoli and Filippo Brunelleschi', in *Essays in the History of Art Presented to Rudolf Wittkower*, ed. D. Fraser, H. Hibbard and M. Lewine, London, 1967, pp. 71–82.

Gombrich (1981)
Gombrich, E. H., '"That rare Italian Master . . .", Giulio Romano, Court Architect, Painter and Impresario', in Chambers and Martineau (1981), pp. 77–85.

Gorni (1972)
Gorni, G., 'Storia del certame coronario', *Rinascimento*, XII, 1972, pp. 135–82.

Grandjean and Famin (1837)
Grandjean de Montigny, A., and A. Famin, *Architecture toscane*, Paris, 1837.

Gray (1986)
Gray, N. A., *History of Lettering: Creative Experiment and Letter Identity*, London, 1986.

Grayson (1954)
Grayson, C., 'A Portrait of Leon Battista Alberti', *Burlington Magazine*, XCVI, 1954, pp. 177–8.

Grayson (1956)
Grayson, C., 'Alberti and the Vernacular Eclogue in the Quattrocento', *Italian Studies*, XI, 1956, pp. 16–29.

Grayson (1957)
Grayson, C., *Alberti and the Tempio Malatestiano: An Autograph Letter from Leon Battista Alberti to Matteo de' Pasti*, New York, 1957.

Grayson (1960a)

Grayson, C., 'Alberti, Leon Battista', in *Dizionario biografico degli italiani*, I, Rome, 1960, p. 707ff.

Grayson (1960b)

Grayson, C., 'The Composition of L. B. Alberti's "Decem libri de re aedificatoria"', *Münchner Jahrbuch der bildenden Kunst*, XI, 1960, pp. 152–61.

Grayson (1960c)

Grayson, C., 'A Renaissance Controversy: Latin or Italian?', *An Inaugural Lecture Delivered before the University of Oxford on 6 November, 1959*, Oxford, 1960.

Green (1990)

Green, L., 'Galvano Fiamma, Azzone Visconti and the Revival of the Classical Theory of Magnificence', *Journal of the Warburg and Courtauld Institutes*, LIII, 1990, pp. 98–113.

Greenhalgh (1989)

Greenhalgh, M., *The Survival of Roman Antiquities in the Middle Ages*, London, 1989.

Grigioni (1910)

Grigioni, C., 'Giorgio da Sebenico e la costruzione del Tempio Malatestiano in Rimini', *Rassegna Bibliografica dell'Arte Italiana*, XIII, 1910, pp. 89–91.

Guidetti (1974)

Guidetti, G., 'Leon Battista Alberti direttore della fabbrica de San Sebastiano', in *Il Sant'Andrea di Mantova e Leon Battista Alberti*, Mantua, 1974, pp. 237–41.

Günther (1981–2)

Günther, H., 'Die Rekonstruktion des antiken römischen Fussmasses in der Renaissance', *Sitzungsberichte: Kunstgeschichtliche Gesellschaft zu Berlin*, XXX, 1981–2, pp. 8–12.

Günther (1988)

Günther, H., *Das Studium der antiken Architektur in den Zeichnungen der Hochrenaissance*, Tübingen, 1988.

Hammond (1981)

Hammond, J. H., *The Camera Obscura: A Chronicle*, Bristol, 1981.

Hastings (1910)

Hastings, J., ed. *Dictionary of the Bible*, 3 vols, London, 1910.

Hatfield (1970)

Hatfield, R., 'The Compagnia de' Magi', *Journal of the Warburg and Courtauld Institutes*, XXXIII, 1970, pp. 107–61.

Heninger (1974)

Heninger, S. K., Jr, *Touches of Sweet Harmony: Pythagorean Cosmology and Renaissance Poetics*, San Marino, CA, 1974.

Hersey (1976)

Hersey, G. L., *Pythgorean Palaces, Magic and Architecture in the Italian Renaissance*, Ithaca, NY, 1976.

Hersey (1994)

Hersey, G. L., 'Alberti e il tempio etrusco, postille a Richard Krautheimer', in Rykwert and Engel (1994), pp. 216–23.

Herstein (1971)

Herstein, S. R., 'The Library of Federico da Montefeltro, Duke of Urbino', *Private Library*, IV, 1971, pp. 113–28.

Heydenreich (1930)

Heydenreich, L. H., 'Der Tribuna der S. S. Annunziata in Florenz', *Mitteilungen des Kunsthistorischen Institutes in Florenz*, III, 1930, pp. 268–85.

Heydenreich (1937)

Heydenreich, L. H., 'Pius II als Bauherr von Pienza', *Zeitschrift für Kunstgeschichte*, VI, 1937, pp. 105–46.

Heydenreich (1967)

Heydenreich, L. H., 'Federico da Montefeltro as a Building Patron: Some Remarks on the Ducal Palace of Urbino', *Studies in Renaissance and Baroque Art presented to Anthony Blunt on his 60th Birthday*, London and New York, 1967, pp. 1–6.

Heydenreich and Lotz (1974)

Heydenreich, L. H., and Lotz, W., *Architecture in Italy, 1400–1600*, Harmondsworth, 1974.

Hill (1978)

Hill, G., *Medals of the Renaissance*, rev. and enlarged G. Pollard, London, 1978.

Hollingsworth (1984)

Hollingsworth, M., 'The Architect in Sixteenth-century Florence', *Art History*, VII, 1984, pp. 385–410.

Hollingsworth (1994)

Hollingsworth, M., *Patronage in Renaissance Italy: From 1400 to the Early Sixteenth Century*, London, 1994.

Holmes (1992)

Holmes, G., *The Florentine Enlightenment*, Oxford, 1969; rev. 1992.

Hope (1985)

Hope, C., 'The Chronology of Mantegna's Triumphs', in *Renaissance Studies in Honor of Craig Hugh Smyth: II, Art, Architecture*, ed. A. Morrogh, F. Superbi Gioffredi, P. Morselli and E. Borsook, Florence, 1985, pp. 297–316.

Hope (1992)

Hope, C., 'The Early History of the Tempio Malatestiano', *Journal of the Warburg and Courtauld Institutes*, LV, 1992, pp. 51–154, and plates 7–23.

Howard and Longair (1982)

Howard, D., and M. Longair, 'Harmonic Proportion and Palladio's Quattro Libri', *Journal of the Society of Architectural Historians of Great Britain*, XLI, no. 2, 1982, pp. 116–43.

Hubala (1961)
>   Hubala, E., 'L. B. Albertis Langhaus von Sant Andrea in Mantua', in *Festschrift für Kurt Badt*, Berlin, 1961, pp. 83–120.

Hülsen (1910)
>   Hülsen, C., *Il Libro di Giuliano da Sangallo*, 2 vols, Leipzig, 1910.

Hyman (1968)
>   Hyman, I., 'Notes and Speculations on San Lorenzo, the Palazzo Medici and a Ledger from the Church of San Lorenzo', unpublished PhD thesis, New York University, 1968.

Hyman (1977)
>   Hyman, I., *Fifteenth Century Florentine Studies: The Palazzo Medici and a Ledger from the Church of San Lorenzo*, New York and London, 1977.

Hyman (1978)
>   Hyman, I., 'Towards Rescuing the Lost Reputation of Antonio di Manetto Ciaccheri', in *Essays Presented to M. P. Gilmore*, II, ed. S. Bertelli and G. Ramakus, Florence, 1978, pp. 261–80.

Isidore of Seville (1911)
>   *Isidori Hispalensis Episcopi Etymologiarum sive originum libri XX*, ed. W. M. Lindsay, Oxford, 1911.

Jarzombek (1989)
>   Jarzombek, M., *On Leon Battista: His Literary and Aesthetic Theories*, Cambridge, MA, and London, 1989.

Johnson (1975a)
>   Johnson, E. J., 'A Portrait of L. B. Alberti in the Camera degli Sposi?', *Arte lombarda*, XLII–XLIII, 1975, pp. 67–9.

Johnson (1975b)
>   Johnson, E. J., *S. Andrea in Mantua: The Building History*, Philadelphia, 1975.

Jones (1974)
>   Jones, P. J., *The Malatesta of Rimini and the Papal States: A Political History*, Cambridge, 1974.

Kahn (1980)
>   Kahn, D., 'Notes and Correspondence on the Origin of Polyalphabetic Substitution', *Isis*, LXXI, 1980, pp. 122–7.

Karvouni (1994)
>   Karvouni, M., 'Il ruolo della matematica nel "De re aedificatoria" dell'Alberti', in Rykwert and Engel (1994), pp. 282–91.

Kelley (1979)
>   Kelley, D. R., 'Civil Science in the Renaissance: Jurisprudence Italian Style', *Historical Journal*, XXII, no. 4, 1979, pp. 777–94.

Kemp (1990)
>   Kemp, M., *The Science of Art: Optical Themes in Western Art from Brunelleschi to Seurat*, New Haven and London, 1990.

Kent (1972)
>   Kent, F. W., 'The Rucellai Family and its Loggia', *Journal of the Warburg and Courtauld Institutes*, XXXV, 1972, pp. 397–401.

Kent (1974)
>   Kent, F. W., 'The Letters Genuine and Spurious of Giovanni Rucellai', *Journal of the Warburg and Courtauld Institutes*, XXXVII, 1974, pp. 342–9.

Kent (1977)
>   Kent, F. W., *Household and Lineage in Renaissance Florence: The Family Life of the Capponi, Ginori and Rucellai*, Princeton, NJ, 1977.

Kent (1981)
>   Kent, F. W., 'The Making of a Renaissance Patron of the Arts', *Giovanni ed il suo Zibaldone*, II: *'A Florentine Patrician and his Palace'*, London, 1981, pp. 9–95.

Kidson (1990)
>   Kidson, P., 'A Metrological Investigation', *Journal of the Warburg and Courtauld Institutes*, LIII, 1990, pp. 71–97.

Kimball (1927–8)
>   Kimball, S. Fiske, 'Luciano Laurana and the High Renaissance', *Art Bulletin*, X, 1927–8, pp. 124–51.

Kircher (1671)
>   Kircher, A., *Ars magna lucis et umbrae*, 2nd edn, Amsterdam, 1671.

Klotz (1969)
>   Klotz, H., 'L. B. Albertis "De re aedificatoria" in Theorie und Praxis', *Zeitschrift für Kunstgeschichte*, XXXII, 1969, pp. 93–103.

Krautheimer (1942/1969)
>   Krautheimer, R., 'Introduction to an "Iconography of Mediaeval Architecture"', *Journal of the Warburg and Courtauld Institutes*, V, 1942, pp. 1–33; reprinted with postscript in *Studies in Early Christian, Medieval, and Renaissance Art*, New York and London, 1969, pp. 115–50.

Krautheimer (1969a)
>   Krautheimer, R., 'Santo Stefano Rotondo and the Rotunda of the Holy Sepulchre', in *Studies in Early Christian, Medieval, and Renaissance Art*, New York and London, 1969, pp. 69–106.

Krautheimer (1969b)
>   Krautheimer, R., 'Alberti's "Templum Etruscum"', in *Studies in Early Christian, Medieval, and Renaissance Art*, New York and London, 1969, pp. 333–44.

Krautheimer (1969c)
>   Krautheimer, R., 'Alberti and Vitruvius', in *Studies in Early Christian, Medieval, and Renaissance Art*, New York and London, 1969, pp. 323–32.

Krautheimer (1969d)

Krautheimer, R., 'The Tragic and Comic Scene of the Renaissance: The Baltimore and Urbino Panels', in *Studies in Early Christian, Medieval, and Renaissance Art*, New York and London, 1969, pp. 345–59.

Krautheimer (1980)

Krautheimer, R., *Rome: Profile of a City, 312–1308*, Princeton, NJ, 1980.

Krautheimer (1985)

Krautheimer, R. *St Peter's and Medieval Rome*, Rome, 1985.

Krautheimer (1994)

Krautheimer, R., 'La tavole di Urbino, Berlino e Baltimora riesaminate', in Millon and Lampugnani (1994), pp. 233–57.

Krautheimer and Krautheimer-Hess (1982)

Krautheimer, R., and T. Krautheimer-Hess, *Lorenzo Ghiberti*, Princeton, rev. edn, 1982.

Kretzulesco-Quaranta (1986)

Kretzulesco-Quaranta, E., *Les Jardins du songe: 'Poliphile' et la mystique de la Renaissance*, Paris, 1986.

Krinsky (1970)

Krinsky, C. H., 'Representations of the Temple of Jerusalem before 1500', *Journal of the Warburg and Courtauld Institutes*, XXXIII, 1970, pp. 1–19.

Kristeller (1902)

Kristeller, P., *Andrea Mantegna*, London, 1901; German edn, Berlin and Leipzig, 1902.

Kuhn (1990)

Kuhn, J. R., 'Measured Appearances: Documentation and Design in Early Perspective Drawing', *Journal of the Warburg and Courtauld Institutes*, LIII, 1990, pp. 114–32.

Lamoureux (1979)

Lamoureux, R., *Alberti's Church of San Sebastiano in Mantua*, New York and London, 1979.

Lanciani (1902–12)

Lanciani, R., *Storia degli scavi di Roma*, 4 vols, Rome, 1902–12.

Lanciani (1990)

Lanciani, R., *Forma Urbis Romae*, Rome, 1990.

Landino (1481)

Landino, C., *Chomento di Christoforo Landino fiorentino sopra la Comedia di Dante Aligheria poeta fiorentino*, Florence, 1481.

Landino (1952)

Landino, C., *Disputationes Camaldulenses*, 1474, in *La letteratura italiana, storia e testi*, Milan and Naples, XIII, 1952, pp. 715ff.

Lang (1954)

Lang, S., 'The Programme of the SS. Annunziata in Florence', *Journal of the Warburg and Courtauld Institutes*, XVII, 1954, pp. 288–300.

Lang (1965)

Lang, S., '*De Lineamentis*, Alberti's Use of a Technical Term', *Journal of the Warburg and Courtauld Institutes*, XXVIII, 1965, pp. 331–5.

Lavin (1972)

Lavin, M. A., *Piero della Francesca: The Flagellation*, London, 1972.

Lefaivre (1997)

Lefaivre, L., *Leon Battista Alberti's Hypnerotomachia Poliphili: Re-cognizing the Architectural Body in the Early Italian Renaissance*, Cambridge, MA, and London, 1997.

Lehmann (1936)

Lehmann, H., 'Une vue de la place Ognissanti a Florence', *Gazette des beaux-arts*, LXXVIII, 1936, pp. 244–7.

Lehmann (1988)

Lehmann, P. W., 'Alberti and Antiquity: Additional Observations', *Art Bulletin*, LXX, 1988, pp. 388–400.

Levi D'Ancona (1977)

Levi D'Ancona, M., 'An Image not made by Chance: the Vienna St Sebastian by Mantegna', in *Studies in Late Medieval and Renaissance Painting in Honor of M. Meiss*, ed. I. Lavin and J. Plommer, New York, 1977, pp. 98–114.

Lewis (1994)

Lewis, D., 'Leon Battista Alberti', in *The Currency of Fame: Portrait Medals of the Renaissance*, ed. S. K. Scher (Exhib. cat., Frick Collection, New York, and National Gallery of Art, Washington, DC), New York, 1994, pp. 41–3.

Longhi (1942)

Longhi, R., *Piero della Francesca*, Rome, 1942.

Lorenz (1976)

Lorenz, H., 'Zur Architektur L. B. Albertis: Die Kirchenfassaden', *Weiner Jahrbuch für Kunstgeschichte*, XXIX, 1976, pp. 65–100.

Lotz (1961)

Lotz, W., 'Zu Hermann Vischers d. J. Aufnahmen italienischer Bauten', *Miscellanea Bibliotecae Herzianae*, Munich, 1961, pp. 167–74.

Lotz (1977)

Lotz, W., *Studies in Italian Renaissance Architecture*, Cambridge, MA, and London, 1977.

Lotz (1982)

Lotz, W., 'Sull'unità di misura nei disegni di architettura del Cinquecento', *Bollettino del Centro internazionale di studi di architettura – Andrea Palladio*, XXI, ed. R. Cevese, 1979 (published 1982), pp. 223–32, figs 113–32.

Lowry (1976)
Lowry, M., *The World of Aldus Manutius*, Ithaca, NY, 1976.

Lücke (1994)
Lücke, H.-K., 'Alberti, Vitruvio e Cicerone', in Rykwert and Engel (1994), pp. 70–95.

Luni (1985)
Luni, M., 'Urvinum Mataurense (Urbino): Dall'insediamento romano alla città medioevale', in Polichetti (1985), pp. 11–49.

Lünig (1725–35)
Lünig, J. C., *Codex Italiae Diplomaticus*, Frankfurt, 1725–35, III, cols 1781–1808.

Lyttleton and Sear (1977)
Lyttleton, M., and F. Sear, 'A Roman Villa near Anguillera Sabazia', *Papers of the British School at Rome*, XLV, 1977, pp. 227–51.

McAndrew (1980)
McAndrew, J., *Venetian Architecture of the Early Renaissance*, Cambridge, MA, and London, 1980.

Macdougall (1979)
Macdougall, E. B., 'Review of C. W. Westfall, *In This Most Perfect Paradise*', *Art Bulletin*, LXI, 1979, pp. 311–12.

Mack (1974)
Mack, C. R., 'The Rucellai Palace: Some New Proposals', *Art Bulletin*, LVI, 1974, pp. 517–29.

Mack (1982a)
Mack, C. R., 'Rossellino, Bernardo', in *Macmillan Encyclopedia of Architects*, ed. A. K. Placzek, III, New York and London, 1982, pp. 611–12.

Mack (1982b)
Mack, C. R., 'Bernardo Rossellino, L. B. Alberti, and the Rome of Pope Nicholas V', *Southeastern College Art Conference Review*, X, 1982, pp. 60–69.

Mack (1987)
Mack, C. R., *Pienza: The Creation of a Renaissance City*, Ithaca, NY, and London, 1987.

Magda (1988)
Magda, S., 'Architecture and the Law in Early Renaissance Urban Life: Leon Battista Alberti's "De re aedificatoria"', unpublished PhD thesis, University of California, Berkeley, 1988.

Magnuson (1958)
Magnuson, T., *Studies in Roman Quattrocento Architecture*, Rome, 1958.

Mancini (1967)
Mancini, G., *Vita di Leon Battista Alberti*, 2nd rev. edn with illustrations, Rome, 1967.

Manetti (1970)
Manetti, A. di Tuccio, *The Life of Brunelleschi*, trans. C. Enggass, University Park and London, 1970.

Manetti (1976)
Manetti, A. di Tuccio, *Vita di Filippo Brunelleschi*, ed. D. de Robertis and G. Tanturli, Milan, 1976.

Manetti (1734)
Manetti, G., 'Vita Nicolai V', *Rerum italicarum scriptores*, III, pt 2, ed. L. Muratori, Milan, 1734.

Marani (1974)
Marani, E., 'Tre chiese di Sant'Andrea nella storia dello svolgimento urbanistico Mantovano', in *Il Sant'Andrea di Mantova e Leon Battista Alberti*, Conference report (25–6 April 1972), Mantua, 1974.

Mardersteig (1959)
Mardersteig, G., 'Leon Battista Alberti e la rinascita del carratere lapidario romano nel '400', *Italia medioevale e umanistica*, II, 1959, pp. 286–303.

Marelli (1994a)
Marelli, I., 'Pietro Ogliani', in Rykwert and Engel (1994), pp. 499–501.

Marelli (1994b)
Marelli, I., 'Antonio Allegri', in Rykwert and Engel (1994), pp. 522–3.

Marolda (1988)
Marolda, P., *Crisi e conflitto in Leon Battista Alberti*, Rome, 1988.

Marsh (1985)
Marsh, D., 'Petrarch and Alberti', in *Renaissance Studies in Honor of Craig Hugh Smyth*, II: *Art, Architecture*, ed. A. Morrogh, F. Superbi Gioffredi, P. Morselli and E. Borsook, Florence, 1985, pp. 363–75.

Martelli (1965)
Martelli, M., *Studi Laurenziani*, Florence, 1965.

Martindale (1979)
Martindale, A., *The Triumphs of Caesar by Andrea Mantegna*, London, 1979.

Martineau (1992)
Martineau, J., et al., eds, *Andrea Mantegna* (Exhib. cat., Royal Academy of Arts, London, and Metropolitan Museum of Art, New York), London, 1992.

Martini (1976)
Martini, A., *Manuale di metrologia*, Turin, 1883; reprinted Rome, 1976.

Martini, Francesco di Giorgio: see Francesco di Giorgio above.

Massèra (1924)
Massèra, A. F., ed., *Cronache Malatestiane dei secoli XIV e XV*, in *Rerum italicarum scriptores*, XV, 2, rev. edn, Bologna, 1924.

Massèra (1928)
     Massèra, A. F., 'Il sequestro di un corriere diplomati-
     co malatestiano nel 1454', *La Romagna*, I, 1928, pp.
     125–47.

Mazzocco (1975)
     Mazzocco, A., 'Petrarca, Poggio, and Biondo:
     Humanism's Foremost Interpreters of Roman
     Ruins', *Francis Petrarch, Six Centuries Later: a
     Symposium*, ed. A. Scaglione, Chapel Hill, NC, 1975,
     pp. 354–63.

Mazzoldi (1961)
     Mazzoldi, L., *Mantova: La storia*, Mantua, 1961.

Miarelli Mariani (1976)
     Miarelli Mariani, G., 'Il Tempio Fiorentino degli
     Scolari: Ipotesi e notizie sopra una irrealizzata
     immagine Brunelleschiana', *Palladio*, XXIII–XXV, 1976,
     pp. 45–74.

Millon and Lampugnani (1994)
     Millon, H., and V. M. Lampugnani, *Rinascimento da
     Brunelleschi a Michelangelo: La representazione dell'ar-
     chitettura* (Exhib. cat., Palazzo Grassi, Venice), Milan
     and London, 1994.

Minoprio (1932)
     Minoprio, A., 'A Restoration of the Basilica of
     Constantine, Rome', *Papers of the British School at
     Rome*, XII, 1932, pp. 1–25.

Mirabilia (1953)
     Mirabilia: Codice topografico della città di Roma, ed. R.
     Valentini and G. Zucchetti, III, Rome, 1953, pp.
     17–65.

Mitchell (1951)
     Mitchell, C., 'The Imagery of the Tempio
     Malatestiano', *Studi romagnoli*, II, 1951, pp. 77–90.

Mitchell (1973)
     Mitchell, C., 'An Early Christian Model for the
     Tempio Malatestiano', *Intuition und Kunstwissenschaft:
     Festschrift für Hans Swarzenski*, ed. P. Bloch, Berlin,
     1973, pp. 427–43.

Mitchell (1978)
     Mitchell, C., 'Il Tempio Malatestiano', *Studi
     Malatestiani*, ed. P. J. Jones *et al.*, Rome, 1978.

Moffitt (1982)
     Moffitt, J. F., 'Anastasis-Templum: "Subject or Non-
     subject" in an Architectural Representation by Jacopo
     Bellini?', *Paragone*, XXXIII, no. 391, 1982, pp. 3–24,
     plates 1–6b.

Morscheck (1986)
     Morscheck, C. R., Jr, 'The Profession of Architect in
     Milan before Bramante', *Arte lombarda*, LXXVIII, 1986,
     pp. 94–100.

Morison (1933)
     Morison, S., *Fra Luca de Pacioli of Borgo S. Sepolcro*,
     New York, 1933.

Morison (1972)
     Morison, S., *Politics and Script*, Oxford, 1972.

Morolli (1992)
     Morolli, G., 'Nel cuore del palazzo, la città ideale', in
     Dal Poggetto (1992), pp. 215–30.

Morolli (1994)
     Morolli, G., 'I "templa" albertiani: Dal Trattato alle
     fabbriche', in Rykwert and Engel (1994), pp. 106–
     33.

Morolli (1996)
     Morolli, G., 'Federico da Montefeltro e Salomone:
     Alberti Piero e l'ordine architettonico dei principi-
     costruttori ritrovato', *Città e corte nell'Italia di Piero
     della Francesca*, ed. C. Cieri Via, Venice, 1996, pp.
     319–46.

Morolli, Acidini Luchinat and Marchetti (1992)
     Morolli, G., C. Acidini Luchinat and L. Marchetti,
     eds, *L'architettura di Lorenzo il Magnifico* (Exhib. cat.,
     Ospedale degli Innocenti, Florence), Milan, 1992.

Morolli and Guzzon (1994)
     Morolli, G., and M. Guzzon, *Leon Battista Alberti: I
     nomi e le figure*, Florence, 1994.

Morselli and Corti (1982)
     Morselli, P., and G. Corti, *La chiesa di Santa Maria delle
     Carceri in Prato*, Florence, 1982.

Mühlmann (1981)
     Mühlmann, H., *Aesthetische Theorie der Renaissance:
     Leon Battista Alberti*, Bonn, 1981.

Nardi (1813)
     Nardi, L., *Descrizione antiquario-architettonica con rami
     dell'Arco di Augusto, Ponte di Tiberio e Tempio
     Malatestiano di Rimino*, Rimini, 1813.

Naredi-Rainer (1977)
     Naredi-Rainer, P von., 'Musikalische Proportionen,
     Zahlenästhetik und Zahlensymbolik im architek-
     tonischen Werk L. B. Albertis', *Jahrbuch des
     Kunsthistorischen Institutes der Universität Gräz*, XII,
     1977, pp. 81–213.

Naredi-Rainer (1994)
     Naredi-Rainer, P von., 'La bellezza numerabile:
     L'estetica architettonica di Leon Battista Alberti', in
     Rykwert and Engel (1994), pp. 292–9.

Nelli (1733)
     Nelli, G. B., *Descrizione e studi dell'insigne fabbrica di S.
     Maria del Fiore*, Florence, 1733.

Nibby (1819)
     Nibby, A., *Del Tempio della Pace e della Basilica di
     Constantino*, Rome, 1819.

Nori (1985)
     Nori, G., 'Situazione patrimoniale del bene', in
     Polichetti (1985), pp. 183–203.

Onians (1971)
Onians, J., 'Alberti and *ΦΙΛΑΡΕΤΗ*: A Study in their Sources', *Journal of the Warburg and Courtauld Institutes*, XXXIV, 1971, pp. 96–114.

Onians (1982)
Onians, J., 'Brunelleschi: Humanist or Nationalist?', *Art History*, V, 1982, pp. 259–72.

Onians (1988)
Onians, J., *Bearers of Meaning: The Classical Orders in Antiquity, the Middle Ages, and the Renaissance*, Cambridge, 1988.

Onians (1989)
Onians, J., 'A Critique of Renaissance Historiography: Wittkower's Reconstruction of San Sebastiano in Mantua', *AA Files*, XVII, 1989, pp. 9–14.

Onofrio (1978)
Onofrio, C. d', *Castel S Angelo e Borgo tra Roma e Papato*, Rome, 1978.

Orlandi (1974a)
Orlandi, G., 'Testo latino della "Descriptio Urbis Romae" e traduzione italiana di G. Orlandi', in *Convegno internazionale indetto nel V Centenario di Leon Battista Alberti (Roma-Mantova-Firenze, 25–29 April 1972), Accademia Nazionale dei Lincei*, 371, 1974, pp. 112–27.

Orlandi (1974b)
Orlandi, G., 'Nota sul Testo', in *Convegno internazionale indetto nel V Centenario di Leon Battista Alberti (Roma-Mantova-Firenze, 25–29 April 1972), Accademia Nazionale dei Lincei*, 371, 1974, pp. 129–37.

Orlandi (1955)
Orlandi, S., *'Necrologio' di Santa Maria Novella*, Florence, 1955.

Ossat, d' (1958)
Ossat, G. De Angelis d', 'Enunciati Euclidei e "Divina Proporzione" nell'architettura del primo rinascimento', *Il mondo antico nel rinascimento: Atti del V Convegno internazionale di studi sul rinascimento, 1956*, Florence, 1958, pp. 253–64.

Paccagnini (1960)
Paccagnini, G., *Mantova: Le arti*, I, Mantua, 1960.

Pächt (1951)
Pächt, O., 'Giovanni de Fano's Illustrations for Basinio's *Epos Hesperis*', *Studi romagnoli*, II, 1951, pp. 91–111.

Pacioli (1509)
Pacioli, Luca, *De divina proportione*, Venice, 1509.

Pagnotti (1891)
Pagnotti, F., 'La vita di Niccolò V scritta da Giannozzo Manetti: Studio preparatorio alla nuova edizione critica', *Archivio della Società romana di storia patria*, XIV, 1891, pp. 411–36.

Palladio (1570)
Palladio, A., *I quattro libri dell'architettura*, Venice, 1570.

Palladio (1997)
Palladio, A., *The Four Books on Architecture*, trans. of Palladio (1570) by R. Tavernor and R. Schofield, Cambridge, MA, and London, 1997.

Palmieri (1748)
Palmieri, M., 'De temporibus suis', in *Rerum italicarum scriptores . . . ex Florentinarum bibliothecarum codicibus* (series L. Muratori), ed. J. Tartinius, I, Florence, 1748, cols 239–78.

Panza (1994)
Panza, P., *Leon Battista Alberti: Filosofia e teoria dell'arte*, Milan, 1994.

Parronchi (1964)
Parronchi, A., *Studi su la 'dolce' prospettiva*, Milan, 1964.

Parronchi (1972)
Parronchi, A., 'Otto piccoli documenti per la biografia dell'Alberti', *Rinascimento*, ser. 2, XII, 1972, pp. 229–35.

Partner (1972)
Partner, P., *The Lands of St Peter*, Oxford, 1972.

Pasini (1974)
Pasini, P. G., 'Cinquanta anni di studi sul Tempio Malatestiano', appendix to Ricci (1974), pp. I–XXXII.

Passerini (1861)
Passerini, L., *Genealogia e storia della Famiglia Rucellai*, Florence, 1861.

Pastore and Rosen (1984)
Pastore, N., and E. Rosen, 'Alberti and the Camera Obscura', *Physis*, fasc. 2, Florence, 1984, pp. 259–69.

Pavan (1975)
Pavan, G., 'Leon Battista Alberti a Rimini: Considerazioni e aggiunte', *Studi romagnoli*, XXVI, 1975, pp. 381–93.

Penninck (1986)
Penninck, J., *De Jeruzalemkerk te Brugge*, Bruges, 1986.

Perosa (1981)
Perosa, A., 'Lo zibaldone di Giovanni Rucellai', in *Giovanni ed il suo zibaldone*, II: *'A Florentine Patrician and his Palace'*, ed. A. Perosa, London, 1981, pp. 99–154.

Peters (1985)
Peters, F. E., *Jerusalem: The Holy City in the Eyes of Chroniclers, Visitors, Pilgrims, and Prophets from the Days of Abraham to the Beginnings of Modern Times*, Princeton, NJ, 1985.

Petrie (1877)
Petrie, W. M. Flinders, *Inductive Metrology or the Recovery of Ancient Measures from the Monuments*, London, 1877.

Petrini (1981a)

Petrini, G., *La capella del S. Sepolcro: Catalogo della mostra sul restauro*, Florence, 1981.

Petrini (1981b)

Petrini, G., 'Ricerche sui sistemi proporzionali del Tempio Malatestiano', *Romagna arte e storia*, II, 1981, pp. 35–50.

Petrucci (1993)

Petrucci, A., *Public Lettering: Script, Power and Culture*, trans. L. Lappin, Chicago and London, 1993; after *La scrittura: Ideologia e rappresantazione*, Turin, 1980 and 1986.

Petrucci (1994)

Petrucci, A., 'L'Alberti e le scritture', in Rykwert and Engel (1994), pp. 276–81.

Pieper (1994)

Pieper, J., 'Un ritratto di Leon Battista Alberti architetto: Osservazioni su due capitelli emblematici nel duomo di Pienza', in Rykwert and Engel (1994), pp. 54–63.

Pius II (1960)

Pope Pius II [Aeneas Sylvius Piccolomini], *Memoirs of a Renaissance Pope: The Commentaries of Pius II*, trans. F. A. Gragg, London, 1960.

Pius II (1968)

'Aeneae Silvii Piccolomini Senensis: Opera inedita', in *Reale Accademia dei Lincei*, ed. J. Cugnoni, Rome, 1883; reprinted 1968.

Pius II (1984)

Pope Pius II, *I commentarii*, ed. L. Totaro, 2 vols, Milan, 1984.

Polichetti (1985)

Polichetti, M. L., ed., *Il Palazzo di Federico da Montefeltro: Restauri e ricerche* (Exhib. cat., Palazzo Ducale, Urbino), 2 vols, Urbino, 1985.

Pope-Hennessy (1972)

Pope-Hennessy, J., *The Portrait in the Renaissance*, London and New York, 1966, 2nd edn, 1972.

Porta (1558)

Porta, G. B. della, *Magiae naturalis*, 2 vols, 1558.

Porta (1957)

Porta, G. B. della, *Natural Magick*, London, 1658; reprinted New York, 1957.

Porter (1915–17)

Porter, A. K., *Lombard Architecture*, 4 vols, New Haven, 1915–17.

Prager and Scaglia (1972)

Prager, F. D., and G. Scaglia, *Mariano Taccola*, Cambridge, MA, and London, 1972.

Preyer (1976)

Preyer, B., 'Giovanni Rucellai and the Rucellai Palace', unpublished PhD thesis, Harvard University, 1976.

Preyer (1977)

Preyer, B., 'The Rucellai Loggia', *Mitteilungen des Kunsthistorischen Institutes in Florenz*, XXI, 1977, pp. 183–97.

Preyer (1981)

Preyer, B., 'The Rucellai Palace', in *Giovanni ed il suo zibaldone*, II: *'A Florentine Patrician and his Palace'*, ed. A. Perosa, London, 1981, pp. 156–225.

Quintavalle (1979)

Quintavalle, A. C., 'Alberti Urbanista a Mantova', introduction to Calzona (1979), pp. 11–18.

Ragghianti (1965)

Ragghianti, C. L., 'Il Tempio Malatestiano, 2', *Critica d'arte*, XII, 74, 1965, pp. 27–39.

Ragghianti (1977)

Ragghianti, C. L., *Filippo Brunelleschi: Un uomo, un universo*, Florence, 1977.

Ramírez (1981)

Ramírez, J. A., *Cinco lecciones sobre arquitectura y utopia*, Malaga, 1981.

Ravaioli (1950)

Ravaioli, G., 'La facciata romanica del S. Francesco di Rimini sotto i marmi albertiana', *Studi romagnoli*, I, 1950, pp. 291–5.

Ravaioli (1951)

Ravaioli, G., 'Il Malatestiano: Studi, proposte e realizzazioni', *Studi romagnoli*, II, 1951, pp. 121–36.

Reber (1889)

Reber, F. von, *Sitzungsberichte der philosophisch-philologischen . . . Classe der k. b. Akademie der Wissenschaften zu München*, Munich, 1889.

Reumont (1874)

Reumont, A. von, Summary of his *Lorenzo de' Medici il Magnifico*, in *Archivio storico italiano*, XIX, 1874, pp. 409–22.

Reumont (1883)

Reumont, A. von, *Lorenzo de' Medici il Magnifico*, 2 vols, Leipzig, 1874, 2nd edn, 1883.

Ricci (1913)

Ricci, C., *Ravenna*, Bergamo, 1913.

Ricci (1974)

Ricci, C., *Il Tempio Malatestiano*, Milan and Rome, 1924; reprinted, with an appendix by P. G. Pasini, Rimini, 1974.

Richa (1755)

Richa, G., *Notizie istoriche delle chiese fiorentine*, 5 vols, Florence, 1755.

Ritscher (1899)

Ritscher, E., 'Die Kirche S. Andrea in Mantua', *Zeitschrift für Bauwesen*, XLIX, 1899, pp. 1–20, 181–200.

Roselli (1971)

Roselli, P., *Coro e cupola della SS. Annunziata a Firenze*, Pisa, 1971.

Rosenthal (1962)
Rosenthal, E., 'The House of Andrea Mantegna in Mantua', *Gazette des Beaux-Arts*, LX, 1962, pp. 327–48.

Rossi (1572)
Rossi, G., *Historiae Ravennates*, 1572.

Rotondi (1950–51)
Rotondi, P., *Il Palazzo Ducale di Urbino*, 2 vols, Urbino, 1950–51.

Rotondi (1969)
Rotondi, P., *The Ducal Palace of Urbino: Its Architecture and Decoration*, London, 1969.

Rowe (1976)
Rowe, C., *The Mathematics of the Ideal Villa and other Essays*, Cambridge, MA, 1976.

Rubinstein (1967)
Rubinstein, N., 'Vasari's Painting of the "Foundation of Florence" in the Palazzo Vecchio', in *Essays in the History of Architecture Presented to Rudolf Wittkower*, ed. D. Fraser, H. Hibbard and M. J. Lewine, London, 1967, pp. 64–73.

Rubinstein (1981)
Rubinstein, N., 'Introduction' to Perosa (1981), pp. 3–5.

Rucellai (1953)
Rucellai, B., 'De urbe Roma, *c*.1496', in *Codice topografico della città di Roma*, ed. R. Valentini and G. Zucchetti, IV, Rome, 1953.

Rucellai (1960)
Giovanni Rucellai ed il suo zibaldone, I: *Il zibaldone quaresimale*, ed. A. Perosa, London, 1960.

Rüther-Weiss (1991)
Rüther-Weiss, V., 'Studien zur L. B. Albertis Architektursystem: Venustas-Dignitas-Pulchritudo-Ornamentum', unpublished PhD thesis, University of Bonn, 1991.

Rykwert (1982)
Rykwert, J., 'On the Oral Transmission of Architectural Theory', *Res*, III, Spring 1982, pp. 68–81.

Rykwert (1994)
Rykwert, J., 'Leon Battista Alberti a Ferrara', in Rykwert and Engel (1994), pp. 158–161.

Rykwert (1996)
Rykwert, J., *The Dancing Column: On Order in Archirecture*, Cambridge, MA, and London, 1996.

Rykwert and Engel (1994)
Rykwert, J., and A. Engel, *Leon Battista Alberti* (Exhib. cat., Palazzo Te, Mantua), Milan, 1994.

Rykwert and Tavernor (1979)
Rykwert, J., and R. Tavernor, 'Church of S. Sebastiano in Mantua: A Tentative Restoration', *Architectural Design*, XLIX, nos 5–6, 1979, pp. 86–95.

Rykwert and Tavernor (1986)
Rykwert, J., and R. Tavernor, 'Sant'Andrea, Mantua', *Architects' Journal*, CLXXXIII, no. 21, 21 May 1986, pp. 36–57.

Saalman (1966)
Saalman, H., 'Tommaso Spinelli, Michelozzo and Rossellino', *Journal of the Society of Architectural Historians*, XXV, no. 3, 1966, pp. 151–64.

Saalman (1979)
Saalman, H., 'Designing the Pazzi Chapel: The Problem of Metrical Analysis', *Architectura*, IX, no. 1, 1979, pp. 1–5.

Saalman (1980)
Saalman, H., *Filippo Brunelleschi: The Cupola of Santa Maria del Fiore*, London, 1980.

Saalman (1985)
Saalman, H., 'Alberti's San Sebastiano in Mantua', in *Renaissance Studies in Honor of Craig Hugh Smyth*, II: *Art, Architecture*, ed. A. Morrogh, F. Superbi Gioffredi, P. Morselli and E. Borsook, Florence, 1985, pp. 645–50.

Saalman (1988)
Saalman, H., 'Palazzo Rucellai', *Journal of the Society of Architectural Historians*, XLVII, no. 1, 1988, pp. 82–90.

Saalman (1994)
Saalman, H., *Brunelleschi: The Buildings*, London, 1994.

Saalman (1996)
Saalman H., 'Alberti's Letter to Matteo de' Pasti Revisited', *Architectural Studies in Memory of Richard Krautheimer*, ed. C. L. Striker, Mainz, 1996, pp. 147–50.

Saalman, Volpi Ghirardini and Law (1992)
Saalman, H., L. Volpi Ghirardini, and A. Law, 'Recent Excavations under the "Ombrellone" of Sant'Andrea in Mantua: Preliminary Report', *Journal of the Society of Architectural Historians*, LI, no. 4, 1992, pp. 357–76.

Salmi (1951)
Salmi, M., 'Il Tempio Malatestiano', *Studi romagnoli*, II, 1951, pp. 151–67.

Sanpaolesi (1949)
Sanpaolesi, P., 'Le prospettive architettoniche di Urbino e di Filadelfia', *Bollettino d'arte*, ser. 4, XXXIV, 1949, pp. 322–77.

Sanpaolesi (1963)
Sanpaolesi, P., 'Precisazioni sul Palazzo Rucellai', *Palladio*, XIII, 1963, pp. 61–6.

Sanpaolesi (1965)
Sanpaolesi, P., 'Il tracciamento modulare e armonico del S. Andrea di Mantova', *Arte pensiero e cultura a Mantova nel primo rinascimento in rapporto con la Toscana e con il Veneto, Atti del VI Convegno internazionale di studi sul rinascimento, 1961*, Florence, 1965, pp. 95–101.

Sanpaolesi (1981)
Sanpaolesi, P., 'L'architettura del Palazzo Rucellai', in Perosa (1981), pp. 229–37.

Santinello (1962)
Santinello, G., *Leon Battista Alberti: Una visione estetica del mondo e della vita*, Florence, 1962.

Scamozzi (1615)
Scamozzi, V., *L'idea della architettura universale*, Venice, 1615.

Scaglia (1988)
Scaglia, G., 'A Vitruvianist's "Thermae" plan and Vitruvianists in Roma and Siena', *Arte Lombarda*, LXXXIV/LXXXV, 1988, pp. 85–101.

Scaglia (1994)
Scaglia, G., 'Alberti e la meccanica della tecnologica descritta nel "De re aedificatoria" e nei "Ludi matematici"', in Rykwert and Engel (1994), pp. 316–29.

Scapecchi (1986)
Scapecchi, P., 'Victoris imago: Problemi relativi al tempio malatestiano', *Arte cristiana*, LXXVI, 1986, pp. 155–64.

Schedel (1493)
Schedel, H., *Liber Chronicarum*, Nuremberg, 1493.

Schiavi (1932)
Schiavi, A., *Il restauro della chiesa di San Sebastiano di L. B. Alberti in Mantova*, Mantua, 1932.

Schivenoglia (1857)
'Cronaca di Mantova di A. Schivenoglia dal MCCC-CXLV al MCCCCLXXXIV', ed. C. d'Arco, in *Raccolta di cronisti e storici lombardi inediti*, ed. G. Muller, Milan, 1857, pp. 16–26.

Schlosser (1896)
Schlosser, J. von, *Quellenbuch zur Kunstgeschichte des Abendländischen Mittelalter*, Vienna, 1896.

Schneider (1990)
Schneider, L., 'Leon Battista Alberti: Some Biographical Implications of the Winged Eye', *Art Bulletin*, LXXII, 1990, pp. 261–70.

Scoto (1665)
Scoto, F., *Itinerario overo Nuova descrittione de viaggi principali d'Italia*, Venice, 1665.

Seitz (1893)
Seitz, F., *San Francesco in Rimini*, Berlin, 1893.

Serlio (1584)
Serlio, S., *Tutte l'opere d'architettura et prospettiva*, Venice, 1584.

Serlio (1996)
Serlio, S., *On Architecture*, trans. of Serlio (1584), Books I–V, by V. Hart and P. Hicks, New Haven and London, 1996.

Seroux d'Agincourt (1823–9)
Seroux d'Agincourt, J. B. L. G., *Histoire de l'art par les monumens depuis sa décadence au IVe siècle jusqu'à son renouvellement au XVIe*, 8 vols, Paris, 1823–9.

Seroux d'Agincourt (1847)
Seroux d'Agincourt, J. B. L. G., *History of Art by its Monuments from the Decline in the IVth century until its Renewal in the XVIth*, 3 vols, London, 1847.

Severi (1989)
Severi, R., 'What's in a Name: La fortuna di Giulio Romano nel periodo shakesperiano', in *Giulio Romano (Atti del Convegno internazionale)*, Mantua, 1989, pp. 403–16.

Signorini (1981)
Signorini, R., 'Gonzaga Tombs and Catafalques', in Chambers and Martineau (1981), pp. 3–13.

Simson (1962)
Simson, O. G. von, *The Gothic Cathedral*, London, 1956, rev. edn, 1962.

Sinding-Larsen (1965)
Sinding-Larsen, S., 'Some Functional and Iconographical Aspects of the Centralised Church in the Italian Renaissance', *Acta ad archaeologiam et artium historium pertinentia: Institutum Romanum Norvegiae*, II, 1965, pp. 203–52 and plates I–XII.

Smith (1992)
Smith, C., *Architecture in the Culture of Early Humanism: Ethics, Aesthetics, and Eloquence 1440–1470*, New York and Oxford, 1992.

Smith (1994a)
Smith, C., 'Leon Battista Alberti e l'ornamento: Rivestimenti parietali e pavimentazioni', in Rykwert and Engel (1994), pp. 196–215.

Smith (1994b)
Smith, C. 'Antonio Labacco', in Millon and Lampugnani (1994), cat. no. 45, pp. 456–7.

Smith (1994c)
Smith, C., 'Scatola a imitazione dal Santo Sepolcro dell'Alberti nella Cappella Rucellai, Chiesa di San Pancrazio, Firenze', in Millon and Lampugnani (1994), cat. no. 44, p. 456.

Smith (1994d)
Smith, C., 'Attribuito a Leon Battista Alberti. Pianta di un complesso termale', in Millon and Lampugnani (1994), cat. no. 48, p. 458.

Smith (1994e)
Smith, C., 'Francesco Colonna: Hypnerotomachia Poliphili', in Millon and Lampugnani (1994), cat. no. 53, p. 461.

Smith and Karpinski (1911)
Smith, D. E., and L. C. Karpinski, *The Hindu-Arabic Numerals*, Boston and London, 1911.

Soergel (1960)

Soergel, G., 'Die Proportionslehere Albertis un ihere Anwendung an der Fassade von S. Francesco in Rimini', *Kunstchronik*, XIII, 1960, pp. 348–51.

Soggia and Zuccoli (1994)

Soggia, R., and Zuccoli, N., 'Finiture di facciata nei costrutti albertiani: San Sebastiano e Sant'Andrea a Mantova', in Rykwert and Engel (1994), pp. 392–401.

Soranzo (1926)

Soranzo, G., *Un atto pio della diva Isotta*, Bologna, 1926 (offprint from *Atti e memorie della R. Deputazione di storia patria per le Romagne*, ser. IV, xv).

Spallanzani (1975)

Spallanzani, M., 'L'abside dell'Alberti a San Martino a Gangalandi: Nota di storia economica', *Mitteilungen des Kunsthistorischen Institutes in Florenz*, XIX, 1975, pp. 241–50.

Sperling (1989)

Sperling, C. M., 'Leon Battista Alberti's Inscriptions on the Holy Sepulchre in the Cappella Rucellai, San Pancrazio, Florence', *Journal of the Warburg and Courtauld Institutes*, LII, 1989, pp. 221–8; illustrations, pp. 42–4.

Sprague de Camp (1960)

Sprague de Camp, L., *Ancient Engineers*, Cambridge, MA, and London, 1960.

Stegmann and Geymüller (1924)

Stegmann, C. von, and H. von Geymüller, *The Architecture of the Renaissance in Tuscany*, 2 vols, New York, 1924.

Steinberg (1994)

Steinberg, L., 'Leon Battista Alberti e Andrea Mantegna', in Rykwert and Engel (1994), pp. 330–35.

Stinger (1978)

Stinger, C. L., 'Ambrogio Traversari and the "Tempio degli Scolari" at S. Maria degli Angeli in Florence', in *Essays presented to M. P. Gilmore*, ed. S. Bertelli and G. Ramakus, Florence, 1978, pp. 271–86.

Stinger (1985)

Stinger, C. L., *The Renaissance in Rome*, Bloomington, 1985.

Syson (1994)

Syson, L., 'Alberti e la ritrattistica', in Rykwert and Engel (1994), pp. 46–53.

Tafuri (1987)

Tafuri, M., '"Cives esse non licere": The Rome of Nicholas V and Leon Battista Alberti: Elements towards a Historical Revision', *Harvard Historical Review*, VI, 1987, pp. 61–75.

Tavernor (1985)

Tavernor, R., '"Concinnitas" in the Architectural Theory and Practice of Leon Battista Alberti', unpublished PhD thesis, University of Cambridge, 1985.

Tavernor (1991a)

Tavernor, R., *Palladio and Palladianism*, London, 1991.

Tavernor (1991b)

Tavernor, R., Review of Jarzombek (1989), in *Journal of the Society of Architectural Historians (USA)*, September 1991, pp. 311–13.

Tavernor (1994a)

Tavernor, R., 'La ritrattistica e l'interesse dell'Alberti per il futuro', in Rykwert and Engel (1994), pp. 64–9.

Tavernor (1994b)

Tavernor, R., 'Concinnitas, o la formulazione della bellezza', in Rykwert and Engel (1994), pp. 300–15.

Tavernor (1994c)

Tavernor, R., 'I caratteri albertiani dell'iscrizione del sepolcro Rucellai a Firenze', in Rykwert and Engel (1994), pp. 402–7.

Tavernor (1995)

Tavernor, R., 'Architectural History and Computing', *Architectural Research Quarterly*, I, autumn 1995, pp. 56–61.

Tavernor (1996)

Tavernor, R., 'Casting New Light on "The Flagellation" by Piero della Francesca', *Computers and the History of Art*, VI, nos 1–2, 1996, pp. 13–19.

Tavernor (1997)

Tavernor, R., 'The Natural House of God and Man: Alberti and Mantegna in Mantua', in *La corte di Mantova nell'età di Andrea Mantegna: 1450–1550*, ed. C. Mozzarelli, R. Oresko and L. Ventura, Rome, 1997, pp. 225–34.

Temkin (1973)

Temkin, O., *Galenism: Rise and Decline of a Medical Philosophy*, Ithaca, NY, and London, 1973.

Teubner (1978)

Teubner, H., 'Das Langhaus der SS. Annunziata in Florenz', *Mitteilungen des Kunsthistorischen Institutes in Florenz*, XXII, 1978, pp. 27–60.

Thiem (1964)

Thiem, C., and G., *Toskanische Fassaden-Dekoration in Sgraffito und Fresko, 14–17 Jahrhundert*, Munich, 1964.

Thomson (1993)

Thomson, D., *Renaissance Architecture: Critics, Patrons, Luxury*, Manchester, 1993.

Tiraboschi (1772–82)

Tiraboschi, G., *Storia della letteratura italiana*, 4 vols, Modena, 1772–95.

Tomei (1977)

Tomei, P., *L'architettura a Roma nel Quattrocento*, Rome, 1977, facs. of 1942 edn.

Tommaso (1972)
Tommaso, A. di, 'Nature and the Aesthetic Social Theory of Leon Battista Alberti', *Medievalia et humanistica*, new ser., 3, 1972, pp. 31–49.

Tonini (1876)
Tonini, P., *Il santuario della Santissima Annunziata di Firenze*, Florence, 1876.

Tory (1529)
Tory, G., *Champ Fleury*, Paris, 1529.

Tosi (1927)
Tosi, A., 'Alcune note sul Tempio Malatestiano', *La romagna*, XVI, 1927, pp. 214–35.

Traversari (1759)
Ambrosii Traversarii, *Generalis Camaldulensium, epistolae et orationes*, ed. L. Mehus, 1759.

Trenti (1991)
Trenti, L., 'Roma entro Firenze: Una lettera del Poliziano e un probabile ritratto dell'Alberti', in *Roma nel rinascimento*, 1991, pp. 62–73.

Trexler (1980)
Trexler, R. C., *Public Life in Renaissance Florence*, New York and London, 1980.

Tuccia (1852)
Tuccia, N. della, *Cronaca de' principali fatti d'Italia 1417–1468*, ed. F. Orioli, Rome, 1852.

Ullman and Stadter (1972)
Ullman, B. L., and P. A. Stadter, *The Public Library of the Renaissance: Niccolò Niccoli, Cosimo de' Medici and the Library of San Marco*, Padua, 1972.

Uzielli (1899)
Uzielli, G., *Le misure lineari mediovale e l'effigie di Cristo*, Florence, 1899.

Vagnetti (1973)
Vagnetti, L., 'Concinnitas: Riflessioni sul significato di un termine Albertiano', *Studi e documenti di architettura*, II, 1973, pp. 139–61.

Vagnetti (1974)
Vagnetti, L., 'Lo studio di Roma negli scritti Albertiani', *Convegno internazionale indetto nel V centenario di Leon Battista Alberti (Roma-Mantova-Firenze, 25–29 April 1972)*, Accademia Nazionale dei Lincei, 371, 1974, pp. 73–110.

Valtieri (1972)
Valtieri, S., 'Rinascimento a Viterbo: Bernardo Rossellino', *L'architettura: Cronache e storia*, XVII, 1972, pp. 686–94.

Varese (1985)
Varese, R., 'Un altro ritratto di Leon Battista Alberti', *Mitteilungen des Kunsthistorischen Institutes in Florenz*, XXIX, 1985, pp. 181–89.

Vasari (1965)
Vasari, G., *The Lives of the Artists*, trans. G. Bull, Harmondsworth, 1965.

Vasari (1973)
Vasari, G., *Le vite de' più eccellenti pittori, scultori ed architettori (nelle redazioni del 1550 e 1568)*, ed. G. Milanesi, Florence, 1906; rev. edn, 7 vols, Florence, 1973 (for Alberti and Brunelleschi, see vol. II).

Vasic Vatovec (1979)
Vasic Vatovec, C., *Luca Fancelli, Architetto: Epistolario Gonzaghesco*, Florence, 1979.

Verga (1977)
Verga, C., 'Un altro Malatestiano', *Ricerca 2*, Crema, 1977.

Vickers (1989)
Vickers, B., *In Defence of Rhetoric*, Oxford, 1989.

Vignati (1959)
Vignati, B., 'Alcune osservazioni sul "De rebus memorabilibus basilicae sancti Petri"', *Studi su Mafeo Vegio*, ed. S. Corvi, Lodi, 1959, pp. 58–69.

Vitruvius (1521)
Marcus Vitruvius Pollio, *Di Lucio Vitruvio Pollione De architectura libri decem traducti de latino in vulgare affigurati*, trans. C. Cesariano, Como, 1521.

Vitruvius (1960)
Marcus Vitruvius Pollio, *The Ten Books on Architecture*, trans. M. H. Morgan, New York, 1960.

Vitruvius (1962)
Marcus Vitruvius Pollio, *On Architecture* (from Harleian MS. 2767), ed. and trans. F. Granger, 2 vols, London, 1931–4, reprinted 1962.

Vitruvius (1987)
Marcus Vitruvius Pollio, *I dieci libri dell'architettura, tradotti e commentati da Daniele Barbaro*, 1567, facs. ed. M. Tafuri and M. Moresi, Milan, 1987.

Volpi Ghirardini (1994a)
Volpi Ghirardini, L., 'Sulle tracce dell'Alberti nel Sant'Andrea a Mantova: L'avvio di un'analisi archeologica e iconometrica', in Rykwert and Engel (1994), pp. 224–41.

Volpi Ghirardini (1994b)
Volpi Ghirardini, L., *Il San Sebastiano di Leon Battista Alberti*, Part II: 'L'iconometria del San Sebastiano', Florence, 1994 (for Part I, see Calzona, 1994a).

Volpi Ghirardini (1994c)
Volpi Ghirardini, L., *La 'porta dei sette cieli': Numeri e geometrie del portico principale di Sant'Andrea in Mantova*, Mantua, 1994.

Volta (1807)
Volta, L., *Compendio cronologico-critico della storia di Mantova dalla sua fondazione sino ai nostri tempi*, Mantua, 1807.

Waddy (1972)
Waddy, P., 'Brunelleschi's Designs for S. Maria degli Angeli in Florence', *Marsyas*, XV, 1972, pp. 36–45.

Warren (1973)
Warren, C. W., 'Brunelleschi's Dome and Dufay's Motet', *Musical Quarterly*, LIX, 1973, pp. 92–105.

Waterhouse (1901)
Waterhouse, J., 'Notes on the Early History of the Camera Obscura', *Photographic Journal*, new ser., XXV, 1901, pp. 270–90.

Watkins (1957)
Watkins, R., 'The Authorship of the Vita Anonima of Leon Battista Alberti', *Studies in the Renaissance*, IV, 1957, pp. 101–2.

Watkins (1960)
Watkins, R., 'L. B. Alberti's Emblem, the Winged Eye, and his Name, Leo', *Mitteilungen des Kunsthistorischen Institutes in Florenz*, IX, 1960, pp. 256–8.

Weinberger (1941–2)
Weinberger, M., 'The First Façade of the Cathedral of Florence', *Journal of the Warburg and Courtauld Institutes*, IV–V, 1941–2, pp. 67–79.

Weiss (1958)
Weiss, R., *Un umanista veneziano: Papa Paolo II*, Venice and Rome, 1958.

Weiss (1969)
Weiss, R., *The Renaissance Discovery of Classical Antiquity*, Oxford, 1969.

Westfall (1969)
Westfall, C. W., 'Society, Beauty and the Humanist Architect in Alberti's *De re aedificatoria*', *Studies in the Renaissance*, XVI, 1969, pp. 61–79.

Westfall (1974)
Westfall, C. W., *In this Most Perfect Paradise: Alberti, Nicholas V, and the Invention of Conscious Urban Planning in Rome, 1447–55*, University Park and London, 1974.

Westfall (1978)
Westfall, C. W., 'Chivalric Declaration: The Palazzo Ducale in Urbino as a Political Statement', in *Art and Architecture in the Service of Politics*, ed. H. A. Millon and L. Nochlin, Cambridge, MA, 1978.

Whitfield (1988)
Whitfield, J. H., '*Momus* and the Language of Irony', *The Language of Literature in Renaissance Italy*, ed. P. Hainsworth, Oxford, 1988, pp. 31–43.

Whitfield (1993)
Whitfield, J. H., 'Portraits of Alberti: A Not Inconsiderable Harvest', *Apollo*, July 1993, pp. 25–8.

Wilkinson (1981)
Wilkinson, J., 'Architectural Procedures in Byzantine Palestine', *Levant*, XIII, 1981, pp. 156–72.

Willich (1914)
Willich, H., *Die Baukunst der Renaissance in Italien*, Berlin, 1914.

Wilson Jones (1989a)
Wilson Jones, M., 'Designing the Roman Corinthian Order', *Journal of Roman Archaeology*, II, 1989, pp. 35–69.

Wilson Jones (1989b)
Wilson Jones, M., 'Principles of Design in Roman Architecture: The Setting out of Centralised Buildings', *Papers of the British School at Rome*, LVII, 1989, pp. 106–51.

Wilson Jones (1990)
Wilson Jones, 'The Tempietto and the Roots of Coincidence', *Architectural History*, XXXIII, 1990, pp. 1–25.

Wind (1980)
Wind, E., *Pagan Mysteries in the Renaissance*, Oxford, 1980.

Wittkower (1973)
Wittkower, R., *Architectural Principles in the Age of Humanism*, rev. edn, London, 1973.

Wittkower and Carter (1953)
Wittkower, R., and B. A. R. Carter, 'The Perspective of Piero della Francesca's "Flagellation"', *Journal of the Warburg and Courtauld Institutes*, XVI, 1953, pp. 292–302.

Wolters (1986)
Wolters, W., 'Die ursprüngliche Gestalt der Fassade von S. Andrea in Mantua', *Mitteilungen des Kunsthistorischen Institutes in Florenz*, XXX, 1986, pp. 424–32.

Woodall (1996)
Woodall, J., 'Samuel van Hoogstraten's Perspective Box', *Art History*, XIX, 1996, pp. 208–46.

Yegül (1992)
Yegül, F., *Baths and Bathing in Classical Antiquity*, Cambridge, MA, and London, 1992.

Yriarte (1882)
Yriarte, C., *Un condottière du XVe siècle, Rimini: Etudes sur les lettres et les arts à la cour des Malatesta*, Paris, 1882.

Zabughin (1909–12)
Zabughin, V., *Giulio Pomponio Leto*, 2 vols, Rome, 1909–12.

Zampetti and Battistini (1985)
Zampetti, P., and R. Battistini, 'Federico da Montefeltro e il Palazzo Ducale', in Polichetti (1985), pp. 51–66.

Zanobini Leoni (1978)

Zanobini Leoni, T., 'La Flagellazione di Urbino di Piero dei Franceschi', *Sound Sonda*, III–IV, 31 May 1978.

Zervas (1979)

Zervas, D. F., 'The Florentine Braccio da Panna', *Architectura*, IX, no. 1, 1979, pp. 6–11.

Zervas (1988)

Zervas, D. F., '"Quos volent et eo modo quo volent": Piero de' Medici and the *Operai* of SS. Annunziata, 1445–55', *Florence and Italy: Renaissance Studies in Honour of Nicolai Rubinstein*, ed. P. Denley and C. Elam, London, 1988, pp. 465–79.

Zettler (1943)

Zettler, M., 'Zur Rekonstruction von S. Costanza', *Mitteilungen des deutschen Archäologischen Instituts, Römische Abteilung*, LVIII, 1943, pp. 76–86.

Zippel (1890)

Zippel, G., *Niccolò Niccoli*, Florence, 1890.

INDEX